William Jones

**The Broad, Broad Ocean and Some of Its Inhabitants**

William Jones

**The Broad, Broad Ocean and Some of Its Inhabitants**

ISBN/EAN: 9783337317249

Printed in Europe, USA, Canada, Australia, Japan

Cover: Foto ©ninafisch / pixelio.de

More available books at **www.hansebooks.com**

THE

# BROAD, BROAD OCEAN

AND

## SOME OF ITS INHABITANTS.

By WILLIAM JONES, F.S.A.,
AUTHOR OF THE "TREASURES OF THE EARTH," ETC.

> " Thy universal works are full of Thee,
> The least, the greatest—each and all divine!
> While Nature, eloquent of Deity,
> Holds everywhere her mild triumphant sign,
> Through which Thine everlasting glories shine!
> The changing seasons and the march of time,
> The trees, the flowers, the fields, the rivers, Thine!
> Heaven, earth, and sea, in one harmonious chime,
> Hymn forth the Holy God—the Beautiful—Sublime!"
> MÜLLER.

*SPECIAL EDITION.*

WITH ILLUSTRATIONS.

NEW YORK:
R. WORTHINGTON, 750, BROADWAY.

TO MY YOUNGEST SON,

CUTHBERT,

THIS BOOK IS AFFECTIONATELY INSCRIBED.

# PREFACE.

 HAVE endeavoured, in the following pages, to impress upon the youthful mind some of the grand and wonderful objects of creative excellence in the "Broad, Broad Ocean." The subject is exhaustless. I have been able only to treat upon a few of its most salient and interesting features, such as the young—always ardent and impressionable—would be most likely to appreciate.

A portion of this volume was written at a very sequestered coast of North Devon—Croyde Bay, a few miles from Barnstaple, where I had ample opportunities of witnessing a glorious expanse of ocean in all its features: calm and serene as Wordsworth describes it—

> "The gentleness of Heaven is on the sea.
> Listen! The Mighty Being is awake,
> And doth with His eternal motion make
> A sound like thunder, everlastingly;"

or in tempestuous gales, when we see

> "The ambitious ocean swell, and rage, and foam,
> To be exalted with the threatening clouds."

My youngsters were lively amateur fishers, captors of prawns and shrimps, and occasional takers of small strange fish, the birth and parentage of which became a marine study to us in the evening. I find that occasional visits to the sea-side open the young inquiring mind, and prepare it for the reception of more serious and thoughtful studies of the ocean—

> "The paragon of elemental powers,
> Mystery of waters, never-slumbering sea!
> Impassioned orator with lips sublime,
> Whose waves are arguments which prove a God."

I trust that the present work will be received with the same favour as its "companion" volume, the "Treasures of the Earth," which, although but recently published, has had the honour of a second edition.

BROADGATE,
    BARNSTABLE.

# CONTENTS.

### CHAPTER I.
#### THE WORLD OF WATERS.

Vastness and sublimity of the creation — The ocean a theme for poetry — The ocean essential to the existence of man and vegetation — Marine productions — Wonder and mystery in regard to the ocean — What is water? — Saltness of the ocean — Currents — The Gulf-Stream — Its effects on climate — Scylla and Charybdis — Tides — Wind-waves — Crossing of waves — Depth of the ocean — Colour — Milky Seas — Divisions of the ocean — Atlantic, Pacific, Indian, Arctic, and Antarctic Oceans — The Atlantic — Origin of the name — Its extent — Submarine cable — Divisions of the Atlantic — Mediterranean Sea — the central ocean of the ancients — Gulf of Mexico — Caribbean Sea — Pacific Ocean — Its discovery by Balboa — Magellan — His discoveries — Derivation of the name "Pacific" — Boundaries of the Pacific — Islands — Voyages of Captain Cook — Beauty of scenery in the South Sea Islands — Indian Ocean — Boundaries — Earliest voyages on the ocean . . . . . . . . . . . . 1—19

### CHAPTER II.
#### THE FROZEN OCEAN.

Instances of extreme cold in the Arctic regions — M'Clure and Parry — Dr. Kane — Esquimaux — Ice dwellings — Attempts to discover a shorter passage to India across the Northern seas — Fate of Sir Hugh

Willoughby—Arctic voyagers—Sir John Franklin—His sad end—Relics of the expedition discovered—Sir Robert M'Clure and the North-West Passage—Release from his perilous position—Meaning of the term "Arctic"—Reason of the cold in the Polar regions—Dangers from floating ice—Fearful incident in the frozen seas—Perils encountered by Arctic voyagers . . . . . . . 20—30

## CHAPTER III.
### ICEBERGS.

Icebergs among the wonders of the ocean world—Grand and imposing—Mimicking every style of architecture—Differ in colour—Strange and sudden formations—Many of great height—Origin—Greenland—Glaciers—Their immense length—Birth-places of icebergs—Moved by powerful currents—Dangers from icebergs on their floating voyages—Terror excited by them among the early navigators—Awful sublimity of the floating ice mountains—Hair-breadth escape of Captain Duncan—Supposed loss of the "President," and other vessels, from collisions with icebergs—Danger of mooring vessels to icebergs—Incident to two sailors—A "picnic" on an iceberg—Rash conduct of some French officers—Formation and destruction of ice, a bountiful provision of Nature—Danger from ice-fields and floes—Wonderful escape of Captain Scoresby—Miles of drifting ice—The "Resolute" exploring-ship—Extraordinary escape of Captain Knight and his crew—Packed ice . . . . . . . . . 31—43

## CHAPTER IV.
### SEALS.

Arctic summer—Presents many interesting features—Description of an Arctic sunrise—Melting of the ice—Excessive heat for a short time—Effect of the dry air upon the skin—Preparations for the seal fishery by the Esquimaux—Industry of the natives—Value of seals' flesh and skins—Use of the blubber—Expertness in capturing seals—Skin-covered boats—Dexterity in their management—A herd of seals—Curious tricks for entrapping them—The chase of the seal sometimes dangerous—Destruction of skin-covered boats by seals—Different species of seals—The sea-calf—Encounters with bears—Subject to violent fits of anger—Irritation of the muscular parts after death—

Bearded or great seals—Their enormous size—Seals' "weddings"—
Harp seal—Derivation of the word "seal"—General description of
seals—Wonderful adaptation to their wants—Their fondness for music
—The famous "talking" seal—Some species easily tamed—Anecdotes
of Cuvier—Seals of the Southern seas distinct from the Northern—
Sea-elephant—Its enormous size—Anecdote of a tame young one—
Sea-leopard—Monk seal—Otaries, a species of seal—Sea-lion—Sea-
bear . . . . . . . . . . . 44—56

## CHAPTER V.
### THE MONARCHS OF THE OCEAN.

Peculiarities in whales—Distinct from fishes and land animals,
though partaking the characters of both—Description of the whale—
Wonderful strength in the tail—"Lob-tailing"—Enormous size of the
head—Food of whales—Smallness of the throat—Whalebone—Tongue
of the whale—The skin—Blubber—A provision against cold—Quantity
and value of the oil of a Greenland whale—Ears, eyes, and fins of
the whale—Flesh eaten raw by the Esquimaux—Esquimaux method
of attacking the whale—Various uses to which the whale is applied
—Southern or Cape whale—Northern rorqual—Its immense speed
and activity—Smaller rorqual—Rorqual of the Southern seas—
Cachalot or Sperm whale—Spermaceti and ambergris—Description of
the sperm whale—Capacious throat—Food—Schools and schoolmasters
—surprising feats of the whale—The white whale—Its beautiful colour
—Captured by nets in Greenland—The deductor whales—The most
sociable of their kind—Herd in flocks—capture of ninety-eight near
the island of Lewis—Wanton butchery of whales—Other enemies than
man to the whale—The saw-fish—Combat between a whale, saw-fishes,
and fox-sharks—The whale and the grampus—Sword-fish—tremendous
power in its bony snout—Attachment of whales to their young. 57—69

## CHAPTER VI.
### THE WHALE FISHERIES.

Falling off in the whale fisheries—Peterhead and Hull the principal
ports of the fishery—Old customs and usages at Hull—Early history
of the whale fishery—The Biscayans—Hakluyt—Description of ships

employed in the whale fishery—Amusing ceremonies formerly observed among the whale fishers—Hard work in the Polar seas—Mode of fishing—The harpoon—Struggles of the whale—Disappointment of a Dutch whaler—Dead whales—Cutting up the whales—Settlements for the whale fishery—Whale fishery in the Southern seas—New Zealanders expert in capturing the whale—Productions of the whale fishery at the International Exhibition of 1863 . . . . . . 70—78

## CHAPTER VII.
### PERILS OF THE WHALE FISHERY.

Dangers attending the whale fishery—Incident to the "Essex" in the Pacific Ocean—Ship destroyed by collision with a whale—A whale's victory—Story of a Dutch harpooner—Anecdote of Scoresby—Destruction of a whaling-boat—New Zealand Tom—Incident in the Pacific to the whaling-vessel "Independence"—Paying out the rope—Serious consequences of inattention—Incident to the whaling-vessel "Aimwell"—Dangers of whaling vessels in the Arctic seas from ice—Loss of the "Princess Charlotte"—Wonderful instance of preservation of the whale-ship "Trafalgar"—Calamities of a whaling squadron—Escape of Captain Scoresby—Operation of flensing . . 79—88

## CHAPTER VIII.
### THE PIRATE OF THE OCEAN.

Fossil sharks—Enormous tooth—Means of acquiring a knowledge of the size of an antediluvian shark—The white shark—Its extreme voracity—Great tenacity of life—Habit of bounding out of the sea—Slaves given to sharks—Punishing a shark—Mode of taking sharks in the South Sea Islands—Captain Basil Hall's account of the capture of a shark—Flesh eaten by the natives of Guinea—Worship of the shark by some African tribes—Strange superstitions respecting the shark of the South Sea islanders—Rapacity of the shark—Hooks for taking sharks in the South Seas—The large blue shark—Fearful encounter with sharks by the South Sea islanders—Fearful incident to the crew of the "Magpie"—Hammer-headed shark—Smooth shark—Dog-fish—Spinous shark—Angel-fish—Greenland shark—Barking shark—Taken for the sea-serpent—Pilot-fish—Companion to the shark—Pet sharks—Sharks the scavengers of the ocean . . . 89—105

## CHAPTER IX.

### SEA-HORSES, NARWAHLS, AND POLAR BEARS.

The morse, walrus, or sea-horse—Description—Immense slaughter of them—For what purposes—Ferocity when attacked—Affection of the mother for its young—Battles between the walrus and the Polar bear—Sword-fish attacks the walrus—Sea-unicorn described—Herd in flocks—Playfulness—Greenland bear—Its mode of attacking prey—Appearance described—Fondness for its offspring—Anecdote of Scoresby—Sagacity of a mother bear—Nelson's adventure with a Polar bear—A bear in the tower . . . . . . 106—118

## CHAPTER X.

### MINUTE ANIMAL LIFE IN THE OCEAN.

Vastness of organic life in the ocean—Food to the larger marine animals—Abundance in the Northern seas—Sea-nettles—Colour of the ocean influenced by them—Application of the microscope—Scoresby's calculation of the number of animalculæ—Animals in a drop of water—Ideas thus afforded of the immensity of creation—Sea-weeds, animated worlds—Aquatic forests of the Southern Hemisphere—Minute creation governed by the same laws as larger—Jelly-fish—Medusæ—Abound in the South Atlantic—Curious shapes—Stevens's description of the jellyfish—Annelides, or sea-worms—Sea-mouse—Its beautiful colours—Curious arms of marine worms—Nereids—Their changing light—White rag worm—Its pearly lustre—Sea-leech—Leaping worms—"Jumping Johnnies"—Butterflies of the deep—Existence of animal life at great depths—Temperature determines the abundance—Sea-soundings—Throwing the lead—American sounding apparatus of Lieutenant Brook—Description of the apparatus . . . . . 119—131

## CHAPTER XI.

### THE ROCK-BUILDERS OF THE OCEAN.

Remarkable beauty of coral—Form and colour in the ocean—Formerly supposed to be marine plants—Discovered to be the work of minute animals—Placed by Linnæus at the head of the zoophytes—Coral workers described—The polyp an extraordinary creature—Mode in which the coral habitations are made—Coral examined under the microscope—Islands and continents constructed by the polyps—Immense extent of coral reefs—Surface of the globe changed by the operations of the coral workers . . . . . . 132—137

## CHAPTER XII.

### PERILS OF THE CORAL REEFS.

Coral reefs dangerous to navigation—Shipwreck of the "Cabalve" on a coral reef . . . . . . . . . 138—142

## CHAPTER XIII.

### INSTINCT OF THE ROCK-BUILDERS—CORAL FISHERIES.

Wonderful instinct of the coral workers in building—Highest part of the coral walls on the windward side—Resistance to powerful waves—Remarkable arrangements of some species—Common red coral—Where obtained—Coral fisheries in the Mediterranean—Coral highly prized in India—Black coral—Its scarcity—Fabrication of false coral—Coral formerly supposed to possess singular properties—Ovid's account of the origin of red coral—Coral beads worn as charms . . 143—146

## CHAPTER XIV.

### PEARLS.

Pearls rare and beautiful objects of creation—Perilous employment of the pearl-divers—Condemned criminals formerly employed—Ceylon renowned for large pearls—Characteristics of the pearl-divers—Dread of sharks—Shark-charmers—Confidence of the divers in their powers—Pearl fishing in the Gulf of Manaar—Off the Bahrem Islands—Method pursued by the Cingalese divers—Treatment of the pearl-oysters—Pearl fishery in ancient times—Extent of the pearl fishery in Ceylon—System pursued at the Pearl Islands—Oriental pearls—Their beautiful colours and richness—Preparation of them for the market—Operation of drilling a delicate one—How pearls are formed in the oyster—Amusing account given by Pliny—Story of the king of the pearl-oysters—Suppositions respecting pearls—Curious methods of the Chinese to procure pearls—The pearl-oyster not the only mollusc which produces pearls—Transparent oyster-shells used in China and elsewhere as a substitute for glass—Pearls found on the British coasts—Motive of

Julius Cæsar for invading Britain—The ancients extravagantly fond of pearls—Cleopatra swallowing a pearl dissolved—Powdered pearls used as medicine—Pearls esteemed according to size—Names applied to each kind—Largest pearl on record—Runjeet Sing and his string of pearls . . . . . . . . . . 147—154

## CHAPTER XV.
### THE VEGETATION OF THE OCEAN.

A sea covered with weeds—An object of terror during the voyages of Columbus—The Gulf-weed—A refuge for innumerable marine animals—Enormous expanse of the Atlantic Ocean covered with vegetation—Tropical grapes—Difference in the character of sea-weeds and land-plants—Sea-weeds brought from a great depth—Submarine forests —Meadows of lovely hues—Contrast between gigantic and minute sea-weeds—The nereocystus—Tree sea-weed—Sea-weeds in the Arctic seas—Floating by means of air-vessels—Great length of some species —Sea-weed cables—Enormous thickness—Sea-weeds of smaller growth —Water-flannel—Bladder-weed—Sea-silk—Whip-lash—Net-weed— Feathery callithamnion—Fern-leaf—Fan-weed—Peacock's-tail—Its glorious tints—Sea-thongs—Varieties of form and substance in sea-weeds—Marine plants vie with land-flowers—Colours exceedingly beautiful—Richness of ocean vegetation—influence of sea-weeds on the currents—Sea-weeds as food—The Chinese great consumers— Ceylon moss—Carrageen moss—Tangles—Dulse—Cattle fond of it— Laver—Importance of sea-weeds as manure—The Channel Islands— Numerous applications of sea-weeds—Kelp—Discovery of glass by accidentally burning sea-weeds—Iodine from the ashes of sea-weeds— Sea-weeds used for packing—Ulva marina—Gum obtained from sea-weeds by the Chinese . . . . . . . . 155—163

## CHAPTER XVI.
### SPONGES.

Ancient use of the sponge, for helmets, &c.—One of the most valuable spoils taken from the ocean—Long undecided whether sponges belong to the animal or vegetable kingdom—Ranked as "zoophytes," or animal-plants—Aristotle's definition of the sponge—Discoveries of Mr. Ellis—Result of Dr. Grant's experiments on the sponge—Manner in which, and where, sponges are obtained—Finest qualities come from the Ottoman Archipelago—Sponge fishery at the island of Calymnos—Depth at which sponges are found—Mode of proceeding by the sponge-diver—The sponge in its natural state—Different from what we are accustomed to see—Microscopic examination of the exterior skin of the sponge—Framework of the sponge—Growth and increase of the sponge . . . . . . . . . . 164—168

## CHAPTER XVII.
### SHELLS.

Wonderful shaping out and moulding of shells—Structure of shells adapted to the requirements of their inhabitants—Apparatus of bivalves, or two-shelled animals—The hinge—power over the valves—The adductor muscle—Conchology—Derivation of the term—Shells formerly regarded as toys—Looked upon afterwards as treasures—A science of the greatest importance—Especially to geologists—Shells of Southern Europe—Tarento rich in shells—Greater portion of the shell animals carnivorous—Shells of tropical America—Western coasts of Africa—Harp-shell—The cockle—The cowry—A substitute for coin in the East—Beautiful and rare shells found on the Australian coasts—Deep-sea shells—Eagerly sought after by collectors—Grains of chalk microscopic shells—Lowest parts of the earth consist of shell remains—Sea-banks and coasts covered with broken shells—Abundance of the shell Carinthium telescopium in Calcutta—Employed in road-making—Shells possess a more or less distinct organic structure—Testacea—Univalves—Bivalves—Multivalves—Helix or snail genus—Paletta or limpet—Turbo—Clam or bear's-paw—Curious shells: the murex or purple shell—Highly valued by the ancients for its dye—Volute or mitre-shell—Strombus—Use and value of shells—Formation of shells—Sea-shells perform an important part in the economy of Nature—Sea-shells and sea-insects conservators of the ocean—Use of shells multifarious—Mother-of-pearl shells used in the decoration of churches and houses—Shell-trumpets or horns—Trumpet-shell—Employment of shells for sacred uses in Ceylon—Shell-fish as an article of food—Scallops—Worn in former times by pilgrims—Giant clams—Porcelain-shells—Poached-eggs and weaver's-shuttle shells—Fusus or spindle-shells—Roaring buckie—Wordsworth's lines on the voices of shells—Wentletrap-shells—Trough-shells—Haliotes used for adorning *papier maché* ornaments — Ear-shells — Fountain-shells — Razor-shells — Top-shells — Pheasant-shells — Rock-limpets . . . . 169—180

## CHAPTER XVIII.
### SUBMARINE SCENERY.

Glory of submarine scenery in the tropics—Wonderful transparency of the water—The Bahamas—China seas—Wonders of the submarine depths—Deepest colours of fishes and marine vegetation in the tropical seas—The Indian and Caribbean Seas remarkable—Splendid colours of tropical fishes — The Balistes or cross-bow fishes—Description—Imperial chœtodon—Its singular splendour—Beauty of fishes no criterion for excellence of food—Marine gems—Ruby-coloured etelis—Indian Ocean rich in submarine scenery—Schleiden's vivid description—Beautiful fish—Illuminated submarine gardens—The moon-fish—Loveliness in the transparent waters of the warm seas — Abundance and beauty of the marine fauna — Wonders of coral scenery in the ocean depths of the tropics — The asterias or star-fishes — Caput medusæ, or basket-fish — Description of madrepores, millipores, and nullipores—Anemones the loveliest ornaments of sea-gardens — Their brilliant colours—Representing the land-flowers of the same name—Submarine rock-basins at Barbadoes — Beauty of the anemones confined to their ocean habitats—The mesembryanthemum a gem of the aquarium—The crassicornis, actinia, or animal-flowers—Sea-anemones a hungry class — Power of reproducing lost limbs — Singular transparency of the waters of the Red Sea — Forests of pale pink and red coral distinctly seen in its depths—Sea-slug and sea-cucumber—Their splendid colours—Gorgonias—Serpula—Ringed animals like worms—Their splendid colours — Sertularia — Very beautiful — Waters of the North Sea remarkable for transparency—Beautiful submarine scenery of the Norway Seas . . . . . . . . 181—193

## CHAPTER XIX.
### THE FLOATING NAVIGATORS OF THE OCEAN.

The nautilus, the ocean Mab and fairy of the sea—Very little known, until a recent period, about the nautilus—The fish described by Professor Owen—Real method of its propulsion—The paper-nautilus—its supposed sails—The glaucus a real rower on the ocean—The nautilus a wonderful builder—Intelligence displayed by the nautilus — Pearly-nautilus — The gem of the deep — Shells manufactured into various shapes by the Chinese—Snail-slime fishes—Inhabitants of the Arctic seas — Shells of the nautilus abound in the coral seas — Argonaut — Differs from the true nautilus—Sea-bladder, or Portuguese man-of-war —Description—Wondrous beauty of its colours—Have the appearance of prismatic shells—Colours fade when the zoophytes are taken from the ocean — Their stinging properties — Incident to a sailor on incautiously handling one of them — Origin of the term "sea-nettle"—Fossil nautili—Specimens in the British Museum—Ammonites—The primitive navigator of the ancient seas—The most beautiful of all our fossils — Derivation of the name — Petrified snakes — Strength and beauty of the ammonite—Different in the construction of the shell to the nautilus—The nautilus still rides on the ocean waves—The ammonite extinct — The floating pteropoda — Ianthina, or ocean snails — The cephalopoda—Cuttle-fish—Description—One of the pests of the fisherman—Their ink-bags—Useful application of the cuttle-fish—Power of reproducing limbs—Prodigious size of some species—Fearful apparatus of arms—Highly prized as food by the ancients—Still relished in some countries—a queen of one of the Pacific Islands regaling on a cuttle-fish — Mode of fishing with the cuttle-fish described by Columbus—Contrivances of the South Sea islanders for taking the cuttle-fish—The cuttle-fish belongs to a period before the Flood   194—207

## CHAPTER XX.
### PHENOMENA OF THE OCEAN—ATMOSPHERIC INFLUENCES.

The mirage an optical deception in the atmosphere—Singular appearance in the Polar seas—Various fantastic forms assumed—Aurora borealis — Varied appearances — Origin of the phenomenon — Superstitions of the Indians respecting the aurora — Other meteors in the Northern Ocean arising from refraction—Fall of icy particles—Their remarkable beauty—Parhelia, or mock suns — Singular phenomenon observed in the Arctic seas—Splendour of an Arctic sunset—Ice-blink —Tide-rip—Luminosity of the ocean—Whence originated—Its singular beauty—Phosphorescent particles—Water-spouts—Described—Common in the Mediterranean—Their danger—Water-spouts in the Pacific —Their fearful grandeur—Natives of the South Sea Islands terrified at their appearance—Tornadoes—Typhoons—Trade-winds—Alarm of

the crew of Columbus—Advantage of the trade-winds—Monsoons—
Exercise an important and beneficial office in nature—Origin difficult
to explain—Vivid lightning accompanying monsoons—Hurricanes or
cyclones—More destructive than earthquakes—Hurricane at Barbadoes
in 1780—Noise of the wind in hurricanes—The "bore"—Tremendous
force and rapidity—Volcanic action at the bottom of seas—Remarkable
submarine volcanic tract—Earthquakes and volcanic eruptions at
different periods—Islands rising from the sea—Santorin—Earthquakes—Red
fogs or shower-dust . . . . . 208—230

## CHAPTER XXI.
### SUPERSTITIONS CONNECTED WITH THE OCEAN.

Seamen naturally superstitious—Strange notions in ancient times—
Trifling incidents regarded as prodigies—Omens and good luck—
Belief in saintly interpositions in the middle ages—Superstitions of
sailors in Sardinia—Conspicuous sea-saints—St. Nicholas—Phantom
ship—Originated by the Dutch—Terror excited by water-spouts—
Superstitious practices for averting them—Lightning considered ominous—St.
Elmo—Power of raising tempests at sea by witchcraft—Incident
to James VI. of Scotland—The Evil One supposed to influence
the winds and waves—Procuring favourable breezes by turning stones
—Wind-pillars—Particular seasons held in superstitious regard by
seamen—Custom of the sailors at Folkestone—Belief of the Finn
seamen—Double sight—Blessing the waters of the Neva by the
Russians—Espousal of the sea formerly by the Doge of Venice—The
Greek patriarch at Constantinople throwing a cross into the sea—
Superstitious customs of the fishermen on the coasts of the Baltic—
Customs at Hartlepool—Prejudices regarding certain days of the week
—Apparitions—Amusing incident—Superstitious influence of bells—
Calming the sea at Malta—Bells of Bottreaux in Cornwall—Rats
leaving a ship—Omens for good or evil—Birds and marine animals—
"The Ancient Mariner"—Barnacles—Carrying dead bodies in ships—
Anecdote of Lord Nelson—Turning the boats for good luck. 231—247

## CHAPTER XXII.
### MONSTERS OF THE DEEP—SEA-DRAGONS.

Gigantic reptiles inhabiting the ocean before the Deluge—Interesting

*b—2*

fossil remains in the British Museum—Derivation of "fossil"—These reptiles fearful scourges in the ocean—First discovery of the icthyosaurus—Limestone rocks at Lyme Regis—Mary Anning—Dragons in story-books—Description of the icthyosaurus—Head like a crocodile—Numerous immense teeth—Enormous eyes—Body like that of a fish—Buckland's remarks on the remains of food found in the fossil—The plesiosaurus—Somewhat allied to the icthyosaurus—The fossil also discovered at Lyme Regis—Peculiarities of this huge monster—Head of a lizard—Teeth of a crocodile—Neck of enormous length—Body rounded like that of a marine turtle—Conybeare's description of its habits—The teleosaurus—The great pirate of the ocean—Armed to the teeth—Its enormous jaws—Able to swallow animals as large as an ox—The mœsasaurus—Discovered at Maestricht—Thought to be a crocodile—Character of the fossil skeleton exposed by Cuvier . . 248—252

## CHAPTER XXIII.
### MARINE PRODIGIES.

Sea-divinities of the ancients—Prodigies described by Rondelet in the sixteenth century—"Monk" and "bishop" fishes—How manufactured—To excite the superstitious veneration of the people—Aldrovandus—His curious notions respecting fishes—The kraken, a wonderful sea-monster—The back a mile and a half in circumference—Able to pull men-of-war to the bottom of the ocean—Floating islands—Identity of the cuttle-fish with the kraken—Great sea-monster seen by Captain Neill—Appeared like a vessel lying on her beam-ends—Snout fifty feet long—Pliny's vast animal—The great sea-serpent—Described by Pontoppidan as six hundred feet in length—Appearing like hogsheads floating in a line—Sea-serpents seen on the Norwegian coasts at various times—Marvellous stories told by the Americans—Sea-serpent seen by the crew of the "Dædalus"—Drawings made of this monster—Account forwarded to the Admiralty—Doubts expressed by Professor Owen on the existence of a great sea-serpent—Many marine prodigies may be yet unknown to us—Sea-monster seen in 1857 by the crew of the "Castilian"—Account given by Captain Harrington—Upwards of two hundred feet long—The supposed sea-serpents probably a large species of seals—Fishes of the Ribbon family may give rise to what are called sea-serpents—The "serpent in the sea" a very general superstition in ancient times—The Scandinavian prose "Edda"—"How Odin went to

fish for the Midgard sea-serpent"—Elastic imaginations of the old Northern writers—Olaus Magnus—His account of sea-prodigies—Fish of horrible forms—Eyes appear like burning lamps—Whirlpool described as a stupendous fish—Mermaids and mermen—Belief prevalent through remotest ages—Creature half man and half fish found represented among the excavations at Khorsabad—Figures on coins—Peruvians had semi-fish gods—The Tritons and Sirens—Stories told of mermaids and mermen—Icelandic description of a mermaid—Monster shows itself before heavy storms—Merman found on the coast of Denmark—Appearance like that of an old man—Stuffed mermaids—Barnum's famous exhibition—Stories about mermaids and mermen probably originate in the appearance of seals, walruses, &c.—The manatee—The dugong—The stellerus—Strange creatures in the ocean near Ceylon—Exhibition of prodigies in the reign of Elizabeth—A mermaid shown in London in 1822—A hoax—Lines on the subject
253—267

## CHAPTER XXIV.
### MODES OF FISHING IN VARIOUS COUNTRIES.

Use of nets dates from the earliest times—Frequent mention of them in the Holy Scriptures—Represented in the *bas-reliefs* of Assyria, Greece, and Rome—The Egyptians fond of fishing—Greeks and Romans used nets—Trawling at sea a favourite pursuit—Papyrus nets—Nets used by the Saxons—St. Wilfred taught the use of nets—Great improvements of late in the manufacture of nets—Variety of nets used by fishermen—The seine—The trawl—The drift—Description of them—Fishery "exhibitions" at Arcachon and Boulogne—Fishing by the electric light—Animals employed for getting fish—Birds trained for the purpose by the Chinese—Their wonderful sagacity—Fishing with geese by the Earls of Menteith—Various modes of the Chinese for getting fish—Shooting fishes with bows and arrows—South Sea islanders expert fishermen—Singular mode of taking the needle-fish—Spears frequently used—Shell and bone hooks—Taking large fish by means of a "mast"—Description—Many fish taken by torchlight—Indian method of taking the candle-fish—Its valuable products—White porpoise fishing in the St. Lawrence—Flesh of the porpoise much esteemed formerly in our own country—Fishing for the sea-pike in the Ionian Islands—The tunny fishery—Mode of taking this fish in the

Mediterranean—Sturgeon fishery in Russia—" Caviare" made from the roe of the sturgeon—Conger-eel fishery in Cornwall—Great sea-conger described—Sand-eel fishery in the Channel Islands—Mackerel fishery—Nets employed for this purpose—Mackerel described—Yarmouth—Herring fishery—Derivation of the name—Mode of fishing—Description of boats employed at Yarmouth—Salting of the herrings—Bloaters—Pilchard fishery at St. Ive's Bay, Cornwall—Nets employed for this purpose—Sentinels placed on hills to announce the arrival of the shoals—Pilchard "curing"—Sprats and whitebait, how taken—The sardine—Abounds in the Mediterranean—Cod fishery on the banks of Newfoundland—Value attached to every part of this fish—Cod abundant on the coasts of Iceland—Iceland fisheries described—Modern cod smacks—Method of fishing in England—The dog-fish, a pest to fishermen—Haddocks taken by trawl-nets and lines—Coal-fish, a relative of the cod—Method of capturing it—Other members of the cod family—The ling—The hake—Stock-fish—Turbots—The Romans particularly fond of them—Captured by beam-trawling—Annual consumption of soles in London—Turtles—Mode of taking them—Value of the shells—Singular practice of taking turtles by "fisher-fishes" among the Chinese—Crabs—Mode of taking them—Hermit crab—King crab—Pill-maker—Prawns—Shrimps—Mussels—Cultivation of them by the French—Mussel farms near Rochelle—Story of Captain Walton—Mussels described—Oyster-farming—Extensively carried on in France and England—Oysters described—Scallops—Clams—Enemies of the oyster—Lobsters—Caught in traps, nets, and pots—The lobster a standing romance of the sea—Enormous supply of lobsters and crabs to the London markets—Description of lobsters and crabs—Catching fish by violent noises—Bombardment of fishes with stones in Denmark—A similar practice in Wales . . . . . . 268—309

## CHAPTER XXV.
### ODDS AND ENDS ABOUT FISHES.

Strange and varied characters of fishes—Universality of fish diet—The money of commerce in some countries—Mythological honours rendered to fishes in ancient times—Fish perpetuated on coins, &c.—Form of fishes—The most varied creatures in the world—All adapted to the modes of obtaining food—The tail the great organ of motion—The fins serve to balance the body—Differences of fins—Paley on the action of the fins—Air or swimming-bladder—Isinglass—Bodies of fishes—Circulation of blood peculiar—Respiration—Smell—Baits made attractive by scents—Mode of preparing bait in America—Nostrils of fishes—Taste—Touch—Scales—Eyes—Fishes require great power of vision in the deep—Teeth—Present more varieties in fishes than in other animals—Hearing—Singular stories of fishes attracted by musical sounds—Brain—Attachment of some fishes to their young—Eggs—Northern seas most prolific in fishes—Uses of fish—For agricultural purposes—Ornaments made from fish-scales—Mock pearls—Various uses of the entrails of fishes by the natives of north-west America—Oil of the dog-fish—Skin used to refine liquors, &c.—Curative properties of certain fish—Strange belief of our ancestors—Electrical fish—The torpedo—Violent shocks—Felt by fishermen when drawing their nets—Torpenididæ divided into several genera—Two species occasionally found on our coasts—The marmorata—The nobiliana—These and other species plentiful in the Mediterranean—Electric apparatus described by Cuvier—Power of stinging in some fishes—The sting-ray—Inflicts severe wounds—Formidable weapon of offence—Enormous fins—Bright eyes—The great and little weever—Troublesome to encounter—Description—Stinging powers of the physalis—The acanthuri—Dangerous stings—Remarkable for beauty of form and varied colours—Fishes, with few exceptions, carnivorous—The sea a vast slaughter-house—Sucking-fishes—The sea-owl snail—Lumpsucker—Its beautiful colours—The far-famed remora—Use of the sucker—The remora a subject of imaginative terror to the ancients—Power attributed to it of stopping a vessel—Pliny's remarks—Adhesive powers of the fish extraordinary—Remora of the Mediterranean described—The sea-lamprey— Its powerful sucker — Historical renown of the lamprey — A favourite dish of the Romans—Lampreys fed on human flesh—Death of Henry I. from a surfeit of lampreys—Another use to which the sucker is applied—Present of lamprey pies to sovereigns—The gurnard group of fishes—Peculiarities—Derivation of the name—Many of the species remarkable for beauty of colours—Rose, red, and grey gurnards most common species on our coasts—New Zealand gurnard remarkably beautiful—The sea-scorpion—Its formidable tail-sting—Sticklebacks—Name derived from their spiny backs—Pugnacious propensities—Beauty of their changing colours—The sea-adder—Its rapacity—Anecdote respecting the fighting habits of the sticklebacks—Nest-builders —Sea-gudgeons also nest-builders—The flying gurnard—Great size of its pectoral fins—Flying leaps out of the water—Inhabits the warm seas—Emits phosphoric light—Flying fishes—One species visits our coasts—Musical fish—Curious statements respecting them—Give a peculiar sound called "drumming"—The famous maigre of the Mediterranean—Singular sounds heard by the crew of an American vessel in the China seas—Incident related by Humboldt—The pogonia, sometimes called the "drum-fish"—Incident related by Sir Emerson Tennant at Ceylon—Sounds from under water heard at other places—Queer fish—The devil-fish—Lieutenant Lamont's account of one taken at Jamaica—Its enormous size and strength—Devil-fish taken in Delaware Bay—Monstrous skates—Surprising stories related of them—The fishing-frog, or angler—A most repulsive animal—Description—Its boldness and voracity—Said to pass some time on shore—Curious story of Rondelet—Derivation of the name "angler"—Mode of attracting its prey—Singular provision of Nature for attaining this object—Something more about sword and saw-fishes—Incident related by Captain Wilson—Capture of an immense saw-fish—Its prodigious strength—An East Indiaman attacked by a sword-fish—Fragment of the vessel with the sword embedded in the wood, preserved in the British Museum—The "Dreadnought" attacked by a sword-fish in 1868—Curious action at law in consequence of damages—Evidence of Professor Owen . . . . . . . . . 310—336

## CHAPTER XXVI.
### BEAUTIFUL FISHES.

Dolphin—Belongs to an extensive family—The Atlantic species—Splendid colouring and varying tints—Falconer's description—Other fish change colour—Cat-fish—Sucking-fish—Sea-peacock—Blue-fish—The true dolphin—Described—Regarded as a sacred fish by the ancients—The Dauphin of France named from this fish—Pursue the flying-fish—Incident related by Captain Basil Hall—The dolphin preyed upon in turn by the fox-shark and the grampus—Some species of sea-breams remarkable for their beauty—The Spanish—The gilt-heads—The mackerel family—The common mackerel a beautiful fish—The John Dory—Derivation of the name—Called St. Peter's fish—Legend attached to it—The boar-fish—The opah or king-fish—Splendour of its colours—Marine members of the Perch family—The red mullet—Highly esteemed by the Romans—Purchased at enormous prices—

Kept in aquariums—The basse or sea-perch—The armed emplessus—
The two-banded diploprion—The Mediterranean apogon—The lettered
seranus—Derivation of the name—The spined seranus—The beautiful
plectropoma—Its singular beauty—The one-spotted mesoprion—The
golden-tailed mesoprion — Scaly-finned family of fishes — Numerous
species—Their remarkable richness of colouring—The chœtodon—The
archer—So named from its peculiar habit—A favourite with the Chinese
—Wonderful dexterity of the fish in procuring its prey—The Toxotus
jaculata, another member of the archery family—Riband-shaped fish
family—Includes the most singular and extraordinary fishes in creation
—Description—The riband-fish—Lath or deal-fish—Wonderful beauty
of these fishes—The onion-fish—Banner-fish—Scabbard-fish—The
Goby family—The gemmous dragonet—So named from brilliance of
its colours — Described—The ocellated blenny, or butterfly-fish—
Wrasses, or old wives of the sea—Some very attractive species—The
rainbow—Parrot-fish The scarus—Its ruminating powers—The goldsinny—The wrasse — Rock-fish—The ballan wrasse—Pike-mouthed
fishes—Trumpet-fish, or sea-snipe—The hippocampus, or sea-horse—
Origin of its name—The chimæra, or rabbit-fish — Called in Norway
the gold and silver fish—Also the sea-rat and king-fish—Eyes brilliantly lustrous—Repulsive form—Somewhat allied to sea-monsters—
Beauty of colours intended for the admiration of man . 337—350

## CHAPTER XXVII.
### TREASURES RECOVERED FROM THE OCEAN.

Immense amount of treasures buried in the ocean — Shakspere's
allusion to submarine spoils—Sir Charles Lyell on ocean treasures—
Attempts made to recover submerged vessels—William Phipps, the
founder of the Normanby family—His adventures—Recovery of lost
treasures—The origin of the diving-bell traditionally ascribed to him—
His wonderful perseverance and courage—Recovery of sunken wealth
—Appointed Sheriff of New England in America—Governor of Massachusetts—His death—Companies formed in England for the recovery
of ocean treasures—Use of diving-bell—Operations on the submerged
wreck of the "Royal George"—Much ingenuity employed—Incident
to the "Royal George"—Death of Admiral Kempenfeldt—Nine hundred
of the crew lost—The "Royal George" the subject of many submarine
operations — Divers succeed in bringing up guns — Condition of the

"Royal George" when examined—Pasley's method of destroying the remains of the vessel in 1839—Recovery of many valuables—Sufficient to pay the expenses of the operation—Improvements made on the diving-bell by Halley, Spalding, Farey, Smeaton, and others—Description of the diving-bell—Singular case of John Day, who perished in 1774 from an almost incredulous stupidity—Many operations now carried on for the recovery of lost ocean treasures—The British ship "Lutine"—Foundered off the Dutch coast—Great loss of life—One survivor only—Reward offered for the recovery of the lost treasures—American Submarine Company—The search for sunken riches—Recovery of an immense sum of money—Treasure-ships sunk in the Bay of Vigo during the war of the Spanish Succession—Recovery of some of the treasures by means of the diving-bell . . . 351—362

## CHAPTER XXVIII.
### SEA-BIRDS.

Number and variety of marine birds—Roosting-places—Interesting spectacle at Saldanha Bay—The Gull family—General description—Beauty and lightness of the wings—Some gulls expert in breaking the shells of mollusca—Tyranny of the burgomaster gull—Tricks played by seamen on gulls—The skuas—Power of their bills—Anecdote of a sailor and a skua—Its pugnacity—Encounter between the skua and the eagle—The petrels—Among the most interesting of marine birds—The stormy petrel—Terns, or sea-swallows—The roseate tern—Breeding-places on the Farne Islands—The albatross—A very powerful bird—A great fish-eater—Instances of their gluttony—The divers—Expert in fishing—Description of them—The guillemots—Immense numbers at the breeding stations—The great auk—The puffin, or sea-parrot—The penguins—Darwin's description of the "jackass" penguin—The cormorant—One of the greatest destroyers of fish—Trained to fish by some nations—Ferocity of the cormorant when angry—The pelican—Peculiar pouch for storing fish—Singular method in fishing—The gannet—Its fishing exploits—Assemble at breeding-times in myriads on the Bass Rock—The hooper, or wild swan—Fishing-birds of the eagle kind—The great sea-eagles—War waged against them in the Hebrides—The osprey—Encounter with the white-headed eagle—Fishing habits of the osprey—Wonderful adaptations by Nature for this purpose—The phaeton, or tropic birds—The frigate-bird—Its tyrannical treatment of the booby . . . . . 363—388

## CHAPTER XXIX.

### THE SENTINELS OF THE SEAS.

The lighthouse an object of the greatest interest—Absence of sea-lights a calamity—Earliest allusion to lighthouses—Beacons—Homer's description of the flash of a beacon-light—Navigation made its first efforts in the Mediterranean Sea—Voyages of the Egyptians and Phœnicians—Lighthouses or sacred towers of antiquity—Used as naval schools—The buildings described—The fire-tower of the early ages—Watch-towers—Mode of lighting them—Sounding of conch-shells—The Pharos, the oldest lighthouse on record—Island of Pharos—Description of the lighthouse—The colossal statue of Apollo, at Rhodes, a lighthouse—Erected three hundred years before Christ—Description—The Lamp of Diogenes—Beacons or watch-fires in our own country—Lighthouse erected by the Romans at Boulogne—Roman lighthouse at Dover—Description—Mandate of Henry III. for the maintenance of coast-lights—Permanent regulations for lighthouses in the reign of Elizabeth—The Corduan lighthouse the noblest of its kind—Lighthouses in the time of Charles I.—The North Foreland lighthouse—Charter of the Trinity Board—Control of the "sentinels of the seas"—Smeaton and the Eddystone lighthouse—Winstanley's efforts—Destruction of his erection—Rudyard's lighthouse—Destroyed by fire—Erection of the present lighthouse—Description—Sad incident to a lighthouse-keeper—Bell-Rock tower in Scotland—Difficulties of its erection—Perils of Stephenson and the workmen—Lighthouse struck by a tremendous sea in 1812—Lighthouse on the Skerryvore Rocks—Other stone lighthouses—Iron constructions—Height of lighthouses—Bells as a warning to mariners—Guns—Horns—Tamed sea-birds employed as signals—Gongs—Steam trumpet—Whistles—Illumination of lighthouses—Wood and coal—Light of a coal fire kept up by bellows at the North Foreland in 1732—The last coal light extinguished in 1822—Tallow candles—Oil—Lamps with cotton wicks—Argand lamps—Fresnel's invention of the annular or built lens—Gas—Attended by uncertainty—Convenient as harbour lights—The Drummond light—The electric light—Something about the *animated* "sentinels of the seas"—Life in a lighthouse—Previous occupations of lighthouse-keepers—Reasons for seeking such an employment—Several keepers have been born in the service—Long service—The keepers, in general, comfortably lodged—Employ their time in various pursuits—A butler turning his cleaning talents to advantage as a lighthouse-keeper—Severe hardships and perils sometimes—Violence of the waves—The Casket lighthouse much exposed to storms — Privations and ailments of some keepers—Black flags hoisted on the Longship lighthouse — A distress signal—Bishop's Rock lighthouse at Scilly—Dangerous approach to it —Struck by a water-spout in 1860 — The Double Stanners lighthouse swept away in a storm—Grace Darling—Her heroism—Floating lights —Birds caught at lighthouses—A young seal caught by a keeper—Lantern of Calais lighthouse smashed by a swan—Concluding lines.

389—412

# THE BROAD, BROAD OCEAN.

## CHAPTER I.

### THE WORLD OF WATERS.

"Thou glorious mirror, where th' Almighty's form
Glasses itself in tempests, in all time,
Calm or convuls'd, in breeze, or gale, or storm,
Icing the pole, or in the torrid clime,
Dark-heaving; boundless, endless, and sublime,
Th' image of eternity, the throne
Of th' Invisible; even from out thy slime
The monsters of the deep are made; each zone
Obeys thee: thou goest forth, dread, fathomless, and alone."

BYRON.

"IN the beginning," the sacred historian informs us, "God created the heavens and the earth: and the earth was without form and void, and darkness was upon the face of the deep (or abyss), AND THE SPIRIT OF GOD MOVED UPON THE FACE OF THE WATERS."

How wondrously solemn and grand, my dear young friends, are these inspired and holy words! What human imagination can fully realize their sublimity? In a few plain but soul-stirring sentences the great mystery of creative power is unfolded, and the mind gets bewildered in the contemplation of such vastness, beauty, and beneficence. We may exclaim with the royal psalmist, "Thou, even Thou, art Lord alone; Thou hast made heaven, the heaven of heavens, with all their host; the earth, and all things that are therein; the seas, and all that are therein; and Thou preservest them all."

"On the second day, or generation, uprose progressively the fine fluids or waters (as they are poetically and beautifully denominated) of the firmament, and filled the blue ethereal void with a vital atmosphere. The third day, or generation, the waters more properly so called, or the grosser or more compacter fluids of the general mass, were gathered together into the vast bed of the ocean, and dry land began to make its appearance."

It is with this ocean, which constitutes nearly three-fourths of the entire surface of the whole globe, that I wish, my young friends, in the following pages, to make you better acquainted; and not only to amuse, but to *instruct* you upon the many wonderful objects it contains. I can only do this in a very imperfect degree, but you may supply my deficiences later, when you read the open book of Nature with thoughtful minds eager for knowledge.

No subject, surely, could be more delightful than the study of the "world of waters" and its strange inhabitants, and there is none upon which the mind of man has been more absorbed in inquiry and research.

Besides the magnificent language of Scripture in reference to the ocean, poets of all times and countries have expatiated on the ever-varying phenomena it presents. The very beautiful lines of Campbell ought never to be forgotten:

> " Earth has not a plain
> So boundless or so beautiful as thine;
> The eagle's vision cannot take it in;
> The lightning's glance, too weak to sweep its space,
> Sinks half-way o'er it, like a wearied bird;
> It is the mirror of the stars, where all
> Their hosts within the concave firmament,
> Gay marching to the music of the spheres,
> Can see themselves at once."

There are other equally lofty and noble thoughts on the same subject embodied in verse by other writers. But, besides the sublimity and grandeur of the ocean, there are other matters of paramount interest to consider. The ocean is essential to the existence of man and of all vegetation; "it is the great moderator and equalizer of terrestrial climates," purifying the atmosphere that we breathe, and sending off a perpetual supply of vapours, which condense into clouds, and are the sources of moisture and fertility to the soil. We must also think of the facilities afforded for an intercourse with distant nations. Humboldt remarks: "Contact with the ocean has unquestionably exercised a beneficial influence on the cultivation of the intellect and formation of the character of many nations, on the multiplication of those bonds which should unite the whole human race, on the first knowledge of the true form of the earth, and on the pursuit of astronomy, and of all the mathematical and physical sciences. This beneficial influence, enjoyed by the dwellers on the Mediterranean and on the shores of South-western Asia, was long limited to them; but since the sixteenth century it has spread far and wide, extending to nations living even in the interior of continents. Since Columbus was 'sent to unbar the gates of ocean' (as the unknown voice said to him in a dream, on his sick-bed near the river Belem), man has boldly adventured into intellectual as well as geographical regions before unknown to him."

Besides these incalculable benefits, I must not omit to mention the innumerable marine productions which contribute, in so many ways, to the nourishment, comfort, and pleasure of the human race. How truly wonderful and mysterious are the operations of the Omnipotent Being in regard to the ocean! "If the existing waters were increased only one-fourth of their present area, they would drown the earth, with the exception of some high mountains. If the volume of the ocean were augmented only by one-eighth, considerable portions of the present continents would be submerged, and the seasons would be changed all over the globe. Evaporation would be so much extended, that rains would fall continually, destroy the harvests fruits, and flowers, and overturn the whole economy of nature."

There is, perhaps, nothing more beautiful in our whole system than the process by which the fields are irrigated from the skies, the rivers are fed from the mountains, and the ocean restrained within bounds which it never can exceed so long as that process continues on the present scale. The vapour raised from the sea by the sun floats wherever it is lighter than the atmosphere; condensed, it falls upon the earth in water. And what is *water?* Chemists tell us that it is composed of equal quantities of two important gases—oxygen and hydrogen—these being, probably, the two most abundant and essential substances in nature, as regards ourselves and our earth.

> "For mark how oxygen with azote gas
> Plays round the globe in one aërial mass;
> Or fused with hydrogen in ceaseless flow,
> Form the wide waves which foam and roll below."

These, when combined, become converted into vapour, many gallons of them in this state forming one small drop of fluid water. "It is the simplest of combinations, and the compound most resembling a simple element; the most universal solvent at all temperatures; the most widely distributed substance in nature; the most powerful agent; the most perfect representation of perpetual motion, penetrating everything, passing everywhere, always present, in sight or out of sight, and everywhere producing a marked effect. When it is remembered that a very large proportion of the weight of every living being, animal or vegetable, consists of water, and that for life to continue at all, an incessant supply of fresh fluid is required, the necessity of water will be fully understood."

The *Saltness* which distinguishes the waters of the ocean is explained by the circumstance that chloride of sodium (common salt) and other dissolvable salts, which form essential ingredients of the earth, are being constantly washed out of the soil and rocks by rain and springs, and carried down by the rivers; and as the evaporation which feeds the rivers carries none of the dissolved matter back to the land, the tendency is to accumulate in the sea. We know that beds of rock-salt, of enormous thickness, form part of the crust of the globe; and we may infer that immense banks of salt exist in the bed of the deep. The uniformity of this saltness is preserved by the constant movement of the waters, caused by the regular and perpetual action of the winds. Maury illustrates this in a very impressive manner. "If," he remarks, "all the salts of the sea were precipitated, and spread equally over the northern half of this continent (America), it would cover the ground one mile deep! What force could move such a mass of matter on dry land? Yet, the machinery of the ocean, of which it forms a part, is so wisely, marvellously, and wonderfully compensated, that the most gentle breeze that plays on its bosom—the tiniest insect that secretes solid matter for its sea-shell—is capable of putting it instantly in motion. Still, when solid and placed in a heap, all the mechanical contrivances of mankind, aided by the tremendous forces of all the steam and water power of the world, could not move so much as an inch in centuries of time this matter, which the sunbeam, the zephyr, and the infusorial insect keep in perpetual motion and activity."

*Currents*, which exercise so great an influence on the circulation of the waters, and in producing remarkable changes in the form of coasts, are described as constant, periodical, and variable; the two latter classes being determined chiefly by the winds and tides. The first motion of the ocean waves is derived either from the attraction of the sun or moon, or from the winds which blow over the surface of the waters; the second arises from the sun, which directly through its heat, and indirectly by scorching dry winds, produces evaporation, to a great extent, of the parts most exposed to its influence; and by its similar action on the atmosphere, causes a transference of this vapour to remote latitudes, where it descends as rain, and by destroying the equilibrium of the ocean, gives rise to currents. The principal currents of the ocean are four, two warm, and two cold; these originate, the former among the islands of the Archipelago and in the Gulf of Mexico, &c., the latter in the Arctic and Southern Oceans.

The most important and best known of ocean currents, the *Gulf-Stream*—" the river in the ocean," one of the most marvellous things in this world of waters—derives its name from the Gulf of Mexico. The general direction of this stream is in the arc of a great circle, towards our own shores, by which it is divided; one branch, passing to the west and north, reaches the coast of Norway, and can be perceived on the southern borders of Iceland and Spitzbergen. The waters are of a deep indigo blue, "and are so distinctly marked, that their line of junction with the common sea-water may be traced by the eye. Often one-half of a vessel may be perceived floating in Gulf-Stream water, while the other half is in the common water of the sea. So sharp is the line, and such is the want of affinity between those waters, and such, too, the reluctance, so to speak, on the part of those of the Gulf-Stream to mingle with the common water of the sea." The existence of the Gulf-Stream can also be readily ascertained by means of a thermometer, the temperature being so elevated. It is this warmth which tempers and softens the climate of our own country and of all Western Europe. "It is," says Professor Johnston, "the influence of the Gulf-Stream upon climate that makes Ireland the Emerald Island of the sea, and clothes the shores of England with evergreen robes; while in the same latitude, on the other side of the Atlantic, the shores of Labrador are fast bound in fetters of ice. How wonderful is this beneficent operation of Providence, when we think that this warm stream felt on our own shores, which are thus bathed with water heated under a tropical sun, comes from a distance of four thousand miles! Nor is its influence thus circumscribed. In mid-winter, off the inclement coasts of America, between Cape Hatteras and Newfoundland, ships when beaten back from their harbours by fierce north-westers, loaded down with ice, and in danger of founding, turn their prows to the east, and seek relief and comfort in the Gulf-Stream. In high northern latitudes, "after having run three thousand miles towards the north, it still preserves even in winter the heat of summer. With this temperature, it spreads itself out for thousands of square leagues over the cold waters around, and covers the ocean with a mantle of warmth that serves so much to mitigate in Europe the rigours of winter."

With a breadth of about fifty miles in its narrowest portions, the Gulf-Stream has a velocity, at times, of five miles an hour, pouring on like an immense torrent. The great cause of ocean currents and of the Gulf-Stream is supposed to be the winds perpetually blowing from east to west over the tropical seas, and evaporation. The currents of the Red Sea and the Mediterranean may be accounted for by the latter. More water passes into vapour than is supplied by all the great rivers of Europe and Africa emptying into the latter sea.

The effect of currents was perceived long before anything was known of their direction and velocity, and Columbus was strengthened in his belief that land might be reached across the Atlantic westward, by substances which had drifted from that quarter. After the commencement of his great undertaking, when, day after day, nothing had been seen but a shoreless horizon, and hope had nearly expired in his own breast, while his crew were on the verge of open rebellion, the effect of the oceanic currents restored his confidence and allayed their clamours. A branch of thorn, with berries on it, appeared; a reed was picked up, and a staff artificially carved — intimations that an inhabited land lay before the adventurers, which was at length revealed to their gaze, and terminated for ever the mystery which had rested upon the western flood.

The currents of the ocean materially affect its navigation. While an intimate knowledge of them is necessary, in order to avoid the danger of mistaking the true position of a vessel, its progress to port may be facilitated by falling in with a local stream, or steering clear of it, according as its direction is favourable or adverse. Currents pursuing an inverse course sometimes meet and conflict; and when this occurs in narrow channels, it renders their passage troublesome and dangerous. When two currents thus meeting together are of equal force, they often cause eddies or whirlpools, such as the famous Maelström off the coast of Norway. Its influence is felt for more than nine miles, and its power is such that vessels drawn into it have been destroyed. Charybdis, in the Straits of Messina, with its companion, Scylla, have been described by ancient writers as monsters. Virgil says:

> "Here Scylla bellows from her dire abodes,
> Tremendous pest! abhorred by man and gods!
> Hideous her voice, and with less terror roar
> The whelps of lions in the midnight hour."

Homer writes of Charybdis:

> "Beneath, Charybdis holds her boisterous reign,
> 'Midst roaring whirlpools, and absorbs the main.
> Thrice in her gulfs the boiling seas subside,
> Thrice in dire thunder she refunds the tide."

A *Tide* is a wave of the whole ocean, which is elevated to a certain height, and then sinks after the manner of a common wave. The interval between the two positions forms the tide. The principal cause is the attraction of the sun and moon, the latter being the more potent agent. The sea rises or flows, as it is called, by degrees, about six hours; it remains stationary about a quarter of an hour; and then retires or "ebbs" during another six hours, to flow again after a brief repose. Thus every day, or the period elapsing between successive returns of the moon to the meridian of a place—which is twenty-four hours fifty minutes and a half— the sea ebbs and flows twice, much less, indeed, towards the poles than within the tropics, where the waters lie under the direct influence of the lunar attraction. It is in the southern hemisphere that the tidal wave originates, and from thence moves northward, influenced in its direction by the motion of the earth. Almost excluded from the Northern Pacific by the barrier islands and coral reefs which stretch across from Australia nearly to South America, the effect of the tides, excepting on the west coast of that continent, is little felt in that ocean. In the Indian Ocean, compressed between Africa on the north and Australia and Sumatra on the east, it bursts in full strength on the shores of Hindostan. In the narrow channel of the Atlantic the tidal wave progresses northward with great rapidity, and on the shores both of Europe and America, producing, as in Southern India, the "Bore," which I have described in the chapter on the "Phenomena of the Ocean."

The highest floods and the lowest ebbs occur at the period of new and full moon near the equinoxes, in March and September when the moon is nearest the earth.

Winds have also a powerful influence over the tidal currents, especially in narrow seas, keeping them back when blowing from an opposite quarter, and quickening their flow when pursuing the same direction; but the motion of the water in the tide-wave is totally unlike that in an ordinary surface-wave, such as the wind produces; and it differs, also, in affecting the whole depth of the ocean equally from the bottom to the surface, while the wind-waves, even in the most violent storms, agitate it to a very trifling depth. In the deep water of the ocean the tidal wave does not exceed twelve feet in height.

The ancients knew that the time of high water, and also the height of the tide, were in some way connected with the age of the moon. It was the illustrious Sir Isaac Newton who made the first attempt to explain the phenomena of the tides, on the principle of the influence of gravitation, the grand agent in the movement of the universe.

What are called *wind-waves* are small at their first origin, commencing with a mere ripple, or, as the sailors term it, a "cat's-paw." But each wave, as it advances, acquires increased height by the continued pressure of the wind. Thus it is that the larger waves are not developed in narrow seas, or where the wind blows off the land; they require breadth of water and continued pressure for their formation. The greatest waves known are those of the Cape of Good Hope, under the influence of a north-west gale (the storm-wind of that region), which drifts the swell round the Cape, after traversing obliquely the vast area of the South Atlantic. In such gales, the waves attain a height of above forty feet, so that two ships in the trough of the sea, with such a wave between them, lose sight of one another from their decks. Off Cape Horn, also, the waves reach upwards of thirty feet in height. In our own seas they rarely exceed eight or nine feet.

The crossing of waves, instead of dividing the water into parallel ridges, causes the pitching and rolling so distressing to passengers and trying to vessels. When more than two series of waves cross one another, they give rise to the term "chopping" seas.

The tremendous power of waves, when breaking against rocks or any other obstacle, is fearful. They are known to dash up one hundred and fifty feet from the sea level against the Eddystone Lighthouse, and descend like a cataract on its summit.

With regard to the *depth* of the ocean, it is only very recently that "deep-sea soundings," on the principle of Brooke's apparatus, which I have explained in the chapter on "Minute Animal Life in the Ocean," have been made with any accurate results generally, but even at the present time our knowledge is confined chiefly to the North Atlantic, the greatest depth of which, as far as it has (according to Maury's opinion) been satisfactorily ascertained, is twenty-five thousand feet; though there are, in all probability, considerably greater depths in the region between the United States, the Bermudas, and Newfoundland. Soundings by Lieutenant Brooke gave a depth of more than three miles in the Pacific. It is generally believed that the Arctic is the shallowest of the oceans.

Judging from what has been lately discovered concerning the North Atlantic, it would seem as if the land surface under water were the counterpart, as regards eminences and hollows, chasms, valleys, &c., of the land surface above. "From the top of Chimborazo, to the bottom of the Atlantic, in the deepest part yet reached," says Maury, " the distance in a vertical line is nine miles. Could the waters of the Atlantic be drawn off so as to expose to view the great sea-gash (the basin of the Atlantic) which separates continents, and extends from the Arctic to the Antarctic, it would present a scene the most rugged, grand, and imposing. The very ribs of the solid earth, with the foundations of the sea, would be brought to light, and we should have presented to us, in one view, in the empty 'cradle of the ocean,' a thousand fearful wrecks, with that dreadful array of dead men's skulls, great anchors, heaps of pearls and inestimable stones, which, in the dreamer's eye, lie scattered at the bottom of the sea, making it hideous with sights of ugly Death."

Whatever relates to the *colour* of the ocean is a matter on which many and various opinions have been expressed. Very curious is the statement of Martyn, one of our early voyagers, in his "Spitzbergen and Greenland" (1671), attributing these changes in the sea to the colour of the skies: "If," he says, "the sky be clear, the sea looks as blewe as saphire; if it is covered somewhat with clouds, the sea is as greene as an emeralde; if there be a foggy sunshine, it looketh yellow; if it be quite darke, like unto the colour of indigo; in stormy and cloudy weather, like blacke sope, or exactly like unto the colour of blacke leade."

In the chapter on "Minute Animal Life in the Ocean," I have mentioned Scoresby's remarks on the Greenland Sea, which varies in colour from ultramarine blue to olive green; differences which he found, on examining the water, were due to the presence of innumerable minute animals. The red, brown, and white patches of the Pacific and Indian Oceans are attributed to the presence of swarms of animalculæ, and the colours of the Red and Yellow Seas to matters of vegetable origin. "On both sides of the island of Ceylon," remarks Sir Emerson Tennant, "during the south-west monsoon, a broad expanse of the sea assumes a red tinge, considerably brighter than brick-dust, and this is confined to a space so distinct, that a line seems to separate it from the green water which flows on either side. On examining some of this water with a microscope, it proved to be filled with animalculæ, probably similar to those which have been noticed near the shores of South America, and whose abundance has imparted a name to the Vermilion Sea off the coast of California."

Captain Kingman passed through a tract of water twenty-three miles in breadth, and of unknown length, so full of minute (and some not very minute) phosphorescent animal organisms, as to present the aspect at night of a boundless plain covered with snow. Some of the animals were "serpents" six inches in length, of a transparent jelly-like nature. This appearance is noticed by Dr. Collingwood as a "milky sea," the whole surface composed of a white fluid like milk. The contrast of the ocean, thus coloured, with the dark sky is very striking.

Having briefly glanced at some of the most important features of the world of waters, I will now direct your attention to its principal divisions; and these are five: the Atlantic, Pacific, Indian, Arctic, and Antarctic Oceans. Although no portion of the great ocean is completely detached from the rest, the intervening continents and islands mark it off into divisions in this manner. What may be called the *Northern Basin* contains the Arctic Ocean surrounding the North Pole, and is bounded by the northern extremities of Asia, Europe, and America, and the Arctic circle. The *Western Basin* extends from the Arctic circle on the north to a line drawn from the extremity of Africa, to that of America on the south, and forms the bed of the Atlantic Ocean. The *Southeastern Basin* includes the Pacific Ocean between America and Asia, extending in breadth nearly half round the globe, or about eleven thousand miles, and in length about eight thousand miles, from Behring's Straits on the north, to where it meets the Southern Ocean. Its limit on the south is the Antarctic continent. This vast bed of waters comprises also the Indian Ocean.

Each of these vast ocean tracts is divided into lesser compartments or seas.

The ATLANTIC (supposed to be thus termed from a fabulous island called "Atlantis," which was said by the ancients to be situated in the Atlantic Ocean) includes the Mediterranean, Black Sea, Baltic, Baffin's Bay, Gulf of St. Lawrence, Gulf of Mexico, and the Caribbean Sea. Its extreme breadth is about five thousand miles, and its narrowest part about sixteen hundred miles. Owing to the numerous seas and inlets connected with this vast ocean, the extent of its shores is immense—above fifty thousand miles,—several thousands more than that of the shores of the Pacific and Indian Oceans together. Small in breadth and comparatively narrow as it is, the Atlantic, from its position in relation to civilized countries, and as the most frequented highway of communication for commerce, is regarded as the most important ocean, and is consequently much better known than the Pacific.

The submarine cable that now links the Old and the New Worlds together—one of the most wonderful events in the annals of mechanical engineering—is another bond of peace and good-will between two great nations. As was observed in a New York journal when the cable was first floated out into the Atlantic by the British line-of-battle ship "Agamemnon" and the American frigate "Niagara,"—"What a satire this work will be upon any warlike armaments! How it will put great guns, and cutlasses, and boarding-pikes to shame! Gallant Jack Tars of the old time will soon see that their vocation will henceforth be gone. What would Nelson and Collingwood have said of meeting a foreign first-rate in mid-ocean *to lay a cable* at the bottom of the ocean?"

The Atlantic is naturally divided into three—North, South, and Intertropical. It stands in open connection with the North and South Polar Seas; in the former the ice reaches the land on each side during the whole of every winter, and, indeed, for the greater part of every year. In the chapter on the "Frozen Regions" you will find some particulars on this subject.

The *Mediterranean Sea* (so named from its being almost entirely enclosed by the continents of Europe, Asia, and Africa) is connected with the Atlantic Ocean by the Straits of Gibraltar. It is one of the greatest inland seas in the world, and its shores were the successive seats of the government of the earth for thousands of years, "its waves washing the coasts of Palestine and Egypt, of Greece and Italy. It was the 'central ocean' of the ancients, on which all the early discoveries and hardships of navigation were experienced."

The *Gulf of Mexico* and the *Caribbean Sea* form altogether a basin double the size of the Mediterranean.

The sister ocean of the Atlantic now claims our notice. It was on the 29th of September, 1513—three hundred and fifty-seven years ago—that the discovery of the PACIFIC, the largest of the oceans, as I have remarked, was effected by Vasco Nuñez de Balboa, a brave and enterprizing Spaniard, Governor of the Spanish Colony of Santa Maria, in the Isthmus of Darien. If you have read the adventures of the great Columbus, you will remember that the principal object of his research was a more direct communication to the East Indies—the reputed country of fabulous wealth; and this led him to the borders of the New World. In that immense and unexplored region his followers pursued their discoveries, and the result was the finding of the great "South Sea" (so called because vessels sailing from Europe can only enter it after a long southerly course) by the persevering Balboa. In his march across the isthmus (which, if you consult your map, you will find separates the Atlantic from the Pacific) he had the first intimation that such an ocean existed. In one of his incursions against the native inhabitants in his neighbourhood, he procured a large quantity of gold. While he was dividing the treasures among his followers, much disputing took place in the presence of a young chief, who, disdaining broils for what seemed so mean an object, struck the scales with his hand, and scattered the gold on the ground, exclaiming, "Why should you quarrel for such a trifle? If this gold is indeed so precious in your eyes that you forsake your homes for it, invade the peaceful lands of strangers, and expose yourselves to such sufferings and perils, I will tell you of a province where you may gratify your wishes to the utmost. Behold those lofty mountains!" he said, pointing to the south; "beyond these lies a mighty sea, which may be seen from their summit. It is navigated by people who have vessels not much less than yours, and furnished like them with sails and oars. All the streams which flow down the southern side of these mountains into that sea abound in gold; and the kings who reign upon its borders eat and drink out of golden vessels. Gold is as plentiful and common among these people of the south, as iron is among you Spaniards."

From the moment in which he heard this intelligence, the mind of Balboa became occupied with this one object, and he steadfastly devoted all his thoughts and actions to the discovery of the southern sea indicated by this chief. It was not until the 1st of September, 1513, that he set forth, however, accompanied by no more than one hundred and ninety soldiers. After incredible toil in marching through hostile tribes, he at length approached the base of the last ridge he had to climb, and rested there for the night. On the 26th, with the first glimmering of light, he commenced the ascent, and by ten o'clock had reached the brow of the mountain, from the summit of which he was assured he would see the promised ocean. Here he caused his followers to halt, and mounted alone to the bare hill-top, when a bewildering and entrancing sight met his eyes. Below him extended forests, green fields, and winding rivers, and, beyond, he beheld the SOUTH SEA, illuminated by the morning sun. At this glorious sight Balboa fell on his knees, and extending his arms towards the ocean, weeping for joy, returned thanks to Heaven for being the first European who had been permitted to behold these long-sought waters. He then made signs to his companions to ascend, and when they had obtained a view of the magnificent scene, a priest who was among them began to chant the *Te Deum*, all the rest kneeling and joining in the solemn strain. After this Balboa caused a tall tree to be felled and formed into a cross, which was erected on the spot whence he first beheld the Southern Ocean. He then descended to the shore, and on the 29th of the same month reached a large bay, named by him San Miguel. Unfurling a banner on which was painted a figure of the Virgin with the arms of Castille at her feet, he marched, with his drawn sword in his hand and his shield on his shoulder, knee-deep into the rushing tide, and in a loud voice took possession of the sea and of all the shores it washed. He concluded the ceremony by cutting with his dagger a cross on a tree that grew in the water and his followers, dispersing themselves in the forest, expressed their devotion by carving similar marks with their weapons.

Tidings of this great discovery were immediately sent to Spain, and received with delight and triumph. But, instead of being rewarded, Balboa was superseded in his command, and publicly executed by his successor in 1517.

It was seven years after the discovery of the Pacific Ocean, that Fernando de Magellan (or Magalhaens), a famous Portuguese voyager, was dispatched by the Court of Spain (by whom the offer of his services had been accepted), to examine the exact position of the Molucca Islands. He sailed the 20th of September, 1519, with five ships and two hundred and thirty-six men, from San Lucar, and proceeding to the mouth of La Plata and along the shores of Patagonia (the most southerly country of South America), discovered the Straits—about three hundred miles in length—that bear his name, and passing through them, first launched the ships of Europe into the Southern Sea.

The Pacific derived its name from the smooth surface its waters presented to its earliest discoverers; though this is scarcely applicable, for it is subject to very fearful storms at times. Boldly pursuing his way across the untraversed surface of this immense ocean, Magellan discovered the Ladrone Islands and the Philippines, in 1521, more than twelve hundred in number, and the greater part of which still belong to the Spanish Government.

The distinguished honour belongs to the adventurous Magellan, of his ship the "Victory" having made the first voyage ever accomplished round the world; but the brave commander of the expedition lost his life, without reaching his original destination, having been killed in a quarrel with one of the chiefs of the Philippine Islands.

If you will turn to a map of the world, you will see that the Pacific Ocean lies between America on the east, and Asia and Australia on the west. It does not, like the Atlantic and Indian Oceans, send off branches which penetrate deeply into the adjacent continents; but extensive peninsulas project from the continents which border on it, and these, together with some adjacent rows of islands, stretching far into the sea, separate considerable portions of it from the main body of the ocean. This is less the case on the American than on the Asiatic side. Only two peninsulas project from the former, that of California (which divides the Gulf of California), and the peninsula of Alashka, with the Aleutian Islands, which divide the Kamtchatka Sea from the Pacific. The peninsula of Kamtchatka, which projects from the continent of Asia, divides the Kamtchatka Sea from the Sea of Okhotsk, which latter is separated from the open expanse of the Pacific by the Kurile Islands. The Yellow Sea, which is farther south, is less distinctly separated from the Pacific than the seas farther north; still the boundary-line between both seas is marked by a series of islands, which extend from the most southern extremity of the island of Kinsui to the northern extremity of Formosa. This

# EARLY VOYAGES OF DISCOVERY.

remarkable formation continues still farther south, and the Chinese Sea, which extends from this island (Formosa), on the northern tropic to the equator, although it properly belongs to the Indian Ocean, must be considered as the last link in this chain of sea-basins. On the north the Chinese Sea is separated from the Pacific by a single row of islands, and farther south, by a double and triple row. Thus we find that, although the continent of Asia forms the western boundary of the Pacific north of the equator, no part of it is immediately washed by that ocean, and its shores can only be reached by passing through one of these subordinate sea-basins.

The islands near the Asian coast of the Pacific form one great division, called the Indian Archipelago. Another division, under the name of Australia (or Southern Lands), consists of New Holland (which, although ranked as an island, is considered by some geographers as entitled to be regarded as a continent, on account of its extent), New Zealand, the New Hebrides, and adjacent islands. The remaining islands east of the Philippines and New Zealand are classed together, forming the Polynesian Islands of the English and the Oceanica of the French.

Most of the early voyages of discovery in the Pacific Ocean attracted unusual attention; those made in the sixteenth and seventeenth centuries, from the facilities they were expected to afford in the ultimate discovery of the long-sought southern continent, or the rich booty they afforded the daring adventurers, who often captured the Spanish vessels loaded with money and precious stones.

At the close of the eighteenth century the voyages of the illustrious Captain Cook excited universal interest. They were instrumental in a great degree in diverting public attention from the splendid and stupendous discoveries in the New World, and directing it to the clustering islands spread over the Pacific Ocean, exhibiting them in all the loveliness of their natural scenery, the interesting simplicity and novel manners of their inhabitants.

Down to the time of Cook it was generally believed that a great continent existed around the Southern Pole, and which is represented in ancient maps as "unknown southern lands."

The second voyage of Cook was expressly designed to solve this problem, and after penetrating into high southern latitudes without finding anything but a few islands, the supposed continent was given up, and land was imagined to exist only slightly depressed beneath the surface of the ocean. The result of the third voyage of Cook, commenced in 1776, with the view of discovering the North-west Passage, resulted in the death of this brave sailor, one of England's greatest navigators, 14th of February, 1779, by the hand of savages on the island of Hawaii. After Cook came our famous Anson; the French navigators, the Bougainvilles, La Perouse, and D'Entrecasteaux; the Englishmen, Carteret, Vancouver, &c.

The islands of the Pacific are historically interesting, especially as regards the period of our early intercourse with them. They have advanced our commerce and afforded means for the progress of science. The islands are both low and elevated. The former are of very small extent, and are founded on coral reefs, which encircle a small space of sea. It was supposed that they derived their origin entirely from marine animals; but it has been since ascertained that these animals cannot exist in a depth of more than about ten fathoms, and as the islands rise with great steepness from a sea usually more than three hundred fathoms deep, the question of the origin of the islands has engaged still more the attention of naturalists. The volcanic islands—those raised by the action of fire—are of moderate extent, and generally rise to a great elevation in their centre. Some of them are encircled by coral reefs.

Every writer on the South Sea Islands has been lavish in praise of their scenery, and if you read the descriptions of them in "Cook's Voyages," you will be able to judge of their correctness.

With a few remarks on the Indian Ocean I will close this present chapter, which, although some of you, my young readers, may regard as a *lesson* in geography, is a necessary preliminary in matters highly interesting and of the deepest importance, and to which the following chapters more or less relate. With a map of the world placed before you, it will be an easy and pleasant *task* to trace the different localities and boundaries to which I have referred. You will perceive that the Indian Ocean is bounded on the south by a line drawn from the Cape of Good Hope to the most southern extremity of Tasmania or Van Diemen's Land. Its other limits, reckoning from the last-mentioned point, are, Van Diemen's Land, Australia, the Indian Archipelago, Farther India, Hindostan, Persia, Arabia, and Africa. Gradually narrowing from south to north, the Indian Ocean forks at Cape Cormorin into the Bay of Bengal on the east, and the Arabian Sea on the west, the latter again branching off into two arms, the Persian Gulf and the Red Sea; which reach respectively the mouth of the Euphrates, and the neighbourhood of the Mediterranean. These details exclude the waters of the Archipelago, as belonging rather to the Pacific Ocean.

The Indian Ocean possesses a remarkable interest, inasmuch as the earliest voyage on record, beyond the land-locked Mediterranean, was taken on its waters, for the navy of Solomon went farther than the Straits of Bab-el-Mandeb, by which the Red Sea is connected with the Gulf of Aden and the Indian Ocean. In this respect it virtually maintained its superiority during two thousand years, navigation being facilitated by the periodical *monsoons* (explained in the chapter on the "Phenomena of the Ocean") of the northern part of the Indian Ocean, blowing, as they do, alternately from the south-west and the north-east.

## CHAPTER II.

### THE FROZEN OCEAN.

> "Miserable they
> Who, fast entangled in the gathering ice,
> Take their last leave of the descending sun;
> While, full of death and fierce with tenfold frost,
> The long, long night, encumbent o'er their heads,
> Falls horrible."
> 
> THOMSON.

THOSE of us, my young friends, who pass our days in a sun-favoured and temperate portion of the earth, with every comfort we could desire around us, the green face of nature only covered at brief wintry intervals with a mantle of snow, and a wide-spread fertility attesting the bounty of an indulgent Providence, cannot realize the dark and repelling picture of the frozen North described in the lines I have quoted, and applied by the poet to the disastrous fate of the earliest adventurers who endeavoured to pierce the gloom of the Arctic seas.

We can only fancy, with a shudder, a winter of nine months reigning over the boundless regions of ice; and we might wonder how human nature is able to support such an intensity of cold with its attendant privations, did we not know that the inhabitants of this bleak climate, accustomed to hardships which we could not endure, pursue an existence which *we* might consider miserable, but which *they*, active, self-reliant, and with but few wants to satisfy, except the cravings of hunger, are contented with, and would not, probably, exchange for what we might consider a happier lot.

You may remember the lines of Goldsmith:

> "But where to find the happiest spot below—
> Who can direct when all pretend to know?
> The shuddering tenant of the frigid zone
> Boldly proclaims that happiest spot his own,
> Extols the treasures of his stormy seas,
> And his long nights of revelry and ease."

**It is** astonishing what amount of cold can be endured by the human frame. Dr. Kane, one of the latest of Arctic navigators, records, 7th of February, 1851, a frost three degrees below the freezing-point of mercury! Only a few degrees above this, the crew of the ship engaged in the expedition performed a farce called "The Mysteries and Miseries of New York." One of the sailors had to enact the part of a damsel with bare arms, and when a cold flat-iron, which was employed in the play, touched his skin, the sensation was like that of burning with a hot iron. On the 22nd of the same month (Washington's birthday) there was another theatrical performance. "The ship's thermometer *outside* was at —46°; inside, the audience and actors, by aid of lungs, lamps, and hangings, got as high as —30°, *only* sixty-two degrees below the freezing-point, perhaps the lowest atmospheric record of a theatrical representation. It was a strange thing altogether. The condensation was so excessive, that we could barely see the performers: they walked in a cloud of vapour. Any extra vehemence of delivery was accompanied by volumes of smoke. Their hands steamed. When an excited Thespian took off his coat, it smoked like a dish of potatoes."

As another instance of extreme cold in these fearful regions, I may mention to you how, under a temperature of 15° below zero, Captain M'Clure, one of the most adventurous of our Arctic explorers, spent the night of the 13th of October, 1851, on the ice, amid prowling bears, and that without food or ammunition, his only guide being a pocket compass, which, however, the darkness, aided by mist and drift, rendered useless. He, nevertheless, wiled away the time by sleeping three hours on "a famous bed of soft dry snow" (just imagine our own feelings in changing a warm blanket for a coverlet of ice!), and by wandering ten miles by the crow's flight over a surface so rugged with ice and snow as to endanger his limbs. It was at the close of a walking expedition of nine days, on a very short allowance of food and water, he accomplished his desire of reaching the winter quarters of the expedition, so as to ensure a warm meal ready for his men when they arrived at their destination.

Sir Edward Parry mentions his experience of Arctic rigours thus: "Our bodies appeared to adapt themselves so readily to the climate, that the scale of our feelings, if I may so express it, was soon reduced to a lower standard than ordinary, so that after being some days in a temperature of —15° or —20°, it felt quite mild and comfortable when the thermometer rose to zero—that is, when it was 32° below the freezing-point!" One of Dr. Kane's crew put an icicle at —28° into his mouth to crack it; one fragment stuck to his tongue, and two to his lips, each taking off a bit of skin, *burning* it off, if this term might be used in an inverse sense. The same writer observes, "that at —25° the beard, eyebrows, eyelashes, &c., acquire a delicate, white, and perfectly enveloping cover of venerable hoar-frost. The moustache and under-lip form pendulous beads of dangling ice. Put out your tongue, and it instantly freezes to this icy crusting, and a rapid effort and some hand-aid will be required to liberate it. Your chin has a trick of freezing to your upper jaw by the biting aid of your beard. My eyes have often been so glued as to show that even a wink may be unsafe."

One day Dr. Kane walked himself into "a comfortable perspiration" with the thermometer *seventy* degrees below freezing-point! A breeze sprang up, and instantly the sensation of cold was intense. His beard, coated before with icicles, seemed to bristle with increased stiffness, and an unfortunate hole in the back of his mitten "stung like a burning coal." On the next day, while walking, his beard and moustache became one solid mass of ice. "I inadvertently put out my tongue, and it instantly froze fast to my lip. This being nothing new, costing only a smart pull, and a bleeding afterwards, I put up my mittened hands to 'blow hot,' and thaw the unruly member from its imprisonment. Instead of succeeding, my mitten was itself a mass of ice in a moment: it fastened on the upper side of my tongue, and flattened it out like a batter-cake between the two disks of a hot griddle. It required all my care with the bare hands to release it, and then not without laceration."

Such is a relation of the rigours experienced by Arctic navigators in the frozen regions; and although, as I before remarked, the inhabitants of this dreary country are accustomed to the climate, they are frequently exposed to the most severe privations. The Esquimaux, on the approach of winter, cut the hard ice into tall square blocks, with which they construct their dwellings. They pass their nights covered with bear and seal-skins, near a stove or lamp, every portion of the hut being closed against the piercing cold. Their provisions are often frozen so hard as to require to be cut with a hatchet. The whole of the inside of the hut sometimes becomes lined with a thick crust of ice; and, if a window is opened for a moment, the moisture of the confined air is immediately precipitated in the form of a shower of snow.

Without interest and adventure to stimulate the energies and excite the curiosity of mankind, these gloomy regions might not, probably, have been penetrated by the brave seamen who have imperilled their lives amidst those icy waters or on the inhospitable coasts, and "whose explorations have developed and tasked more heroism and skill than, perhaps, the exploration and discovery of all the rest of the world since the age of Columbus." But for these Arctic voyagers, let me repeat, we should have been ignorant of the strange and wonderful countries of the North, and their inhabitants. These voyages originated in an attempt to discover a shorter passage to India across the Northern seas. In 1553 an expedition of three vessels for this purpose left England. The results to two of these ships were most disastrous, the crews, seventy in number, and the commander of the expedition, Sir

Hugh Willoughby, being frozen to death. Since this period, upwards of a hundred expeditions have been made in search of the North-west Passage, that is, a navigable channel from the Atlantic to the Pacific Ocean, round the northern margin of America. Among the heroic leaders of these expeditions are the conspicuous names, of which you cannot be ignorant, of Parry, John and James Ross, Back, Franklin, Beecher, Austin, Kellett, Osborne, Collinson, M'Clure, Rae, Simpson, M'Clintock, and other famous men.

So great was the anxiety of our Government to trace the North-west Passage, that in 1745 Parliament offered a reward of £20,000 to whoever should discover it, but in 1828 this offer was withdrawn, as the problem was still unsolved.

The fate of the unfortunate Sir John Franklin, one of the bravest and boldest of the Arctic explorers, must be well known to you: how, in 1845, when nearly sixty years of age, he started on his last and fatal voyage to the frozen regions, with the ships "Erebus" and "Terror." The vessels were seen three months afterwards, but for eleven years their fate remained a mystery, although twenty expeditions were sent, at the cost of a million sterling, to discover traces of the missing crews. In 1857 the "Fox," commanded by the gallant M'Clintock, was fitted out, at the expense of Lady Franklin, on the same mission; and in 1859 the sad end of Franklin and his associates was ascertained. The "Erebus" and "Terror" had been beset by ice and abandoned in 1848; the commander himself died the year previously (11th of June), and was thus spared the agony of witnessing and sharing the sufferings of his crews, all of whom had, it is presumed, perished on those fearful shores. Many sad and interesting relics of the Franklin expedition were recovered and brought home. The discoverers obtained their information in a remarkable manner: lying amongst some stones, which had evidently fallen off from the top of a pillar, was a small tin case, deposited on this spot by the crews of the abandoned vessels, and containing the record of the long-lost expedition.

The sorrowful end of these brave men has been commemorated in some sweet verses by a Devonshire poet, Mr. W. R. Neale:

"What though for them no marble shrine,
　　Carved by the sculptor's hand, be found,
　Or, chisell'd by his art divine,
　　A tomb on consecrated ground!

Nor wrapt in winding-sheet nor shroud,
　　Unblest, their whitening bones decay,
While rude winds sing their requiem loud,
　　By headland bleak and ice-bound bay?

Theirs the imperishable name
　　That as a meteor gleams afar,
An immortality of fame
　　Beyond the beam of Polar star!

And Duty, when on danger's track
　　She bids the brave her call pursue,
Dauntless and firm, not turning back
　　Though Death be there,—resolv'd and true,
One glorious end, one aim in view,
Shall point to FRANKLIN and his crew!"

It was in one of the attempts in search of Franklin and his companions that the discovery of the North-west Passage was effected in 1850, by the successful though perilous exertions of Captain (now Sir Robert) M'Clure, who had shared in the Arctic expedition of Captain Back in 1836, and in the voyage of Sir James Ross in 1848. Captains M'Clure and Collinson were sent out in the "Investigator" and the "Enterprise." The course of the latter vessel was chiefly in open waters, close to the American shores; but M'Clure steered in a more northern route, and encountered fearful perils from the ice in those storm-bound regions. During four years he underwent trials and exposures which would have daunted many a navigator, however accustomed to these dangers. His vessel, several times beset by ice, was at length so firmly "locked in," that M'Clure, seeing no hope of release, decided upon sending thirty of his crew to make their way homewards; some by way of North America, up the Mackenzie River, and the others by Cape Spencer, Beechey Island; while he himself, with the remainder of the officers and crew, would stay by the ship, spend a *fourth* winter in those dreary regions, and then, if not relieved, endeavour to retreat upon Lancaster Sound. Such was the arrangement, when an incident occurred that thrilled their hearts with joy. The captain and his first lieutenant were walking near the ship conversing, when they perceived a figure rapidly approaching them from the rough ice at the entrance of the bay. When about a hundred yards from them, he shouted and gesticulated, but without enabling them to guess who he might be. At length he approached, and to their astonishment thus announced himself: "I am Lieutenant Pym, late of the 'Herald,' and now in the 'Resolute.' Captain Kellett is in her at Denby Island." Lieutenant Pym had come from Melville Island, in consequence of one of Captain Kellett's parties having discovered an inscription left by M'Clure on Parry's famous sandstone rock in Winter Harbour.

The ship was abandoned, and the commander and his crew, released from a very perilous position, returned to England. This was in 1854. Although he was obliged to leave his ship blocked in mountains of ice, and had to walk and sledge over hundreds of miles of ice to reach other ships which had entered the frozen regions in the opposite direction, still, he had *water under him* all the way, and was thus the first commander of a vessel who really solved the problem of the famous North-west Passage. For this discovery he was rewarded by the Government with £10,000 and the honour of knighthood.

You may know that the term "Arctic" means properly, "lying near the constellation of the Bear" (in Greek *arctos*), and hence, "northern." If you examine a map of the world, you will see that the Arctic and Antarctic Circles are the boundaries which separate the frigid and temperate zones, as they are called. The seas which surround the North and South Poles are named the Arctic Ocean and the Antarctic Ocean or South Polar Sea. At the poles themselves there is only one day of six months, during which the sun never sets, and one night of six months, when the sun never rises. At the Arctic Circle the greatest length of continuous light is twenty-four hours, at the summer solstice or Midsummer's Day;

whilst, at the same time, at the Antarctic Circle, the sun is twenty-four hours below the horizon, and the reverse at the opposite seasons of the year.

The coldness of the Polar regions arises from the sun's rays striking the earth obliquely, as, at the equator, the heat is produced by the sun's rays falling upon the earth vertically. In the Arctic Ocean—that part of the universal sea which surrounds the North Pole—lie the most fearful dangers which can beset the seaman on his perilous course, arising from floating ice, the ship being frozen in, the fogs, the blinding snow, the darkness, the storms, and the tides and currents, comparatively unknown, which he has to encounter.

I will relate to you a thrilling incident that occurred in the frozen seas many years ago, and is described in the "Westminster Review." It is one of the most fearful histories that have been recorded.

"One serene evening in the middle of August, 1775, Captain Warrens, the master of a Greenland whale-ship, found himself becalmed among an immense number of icebergs, in about 77° of north latitude. On one side and within a mile of his vessel these were of an immense height and closely wedged together, and a succession of snow-covered peaks appeared behind each other as far as the eye could reach, showing that the ocean was completely blocked up in that quarter, and that it had probably been so for a long period of time. Captain Warrens did not feel altogether satisfied with his situation; but, there being no wind, he could not move one way or the other, and he therefore kept a strict watch, knowing that he would be safe as long as the icebergs continued in their respective places. About midnight the wind rose to a gale, accompanied by thick showers of snow, while a succession of thundering, grinding, and crashing noises gave fearful evidence that the ice was in motion. The vessel received violent shocks every moment, for the haziness of the atmosphere prevented those on board from discovering in what direction the open water lay, or if there was actually any at all on either side of them. The night was spent in tacking as often as any case of danger happened to present itself, and in the morning the storm abated, and Captain Warrens found, to his great joy, that his ship had not sustained any serious injury. He remarked with surprise that the accumulated icebergs, which had the preceding evening formed an impenetrable barrier, had been separated and disengaged by the wind, and that in one place a canal of open sea wound its course among them as far as the eye could discern.

"It was two miles beyond the entrance of this canal that a ship made its appearance about noon. The sun shone brightly at the time, and a gentle breeze blew from the north. At first some intervening icebergs prevented Captain Warrens from distinctly seeing anything but her masts, but he was struck by the strange manner in which her sails were disposed, and with the dismantled aspect of her yards and rigging. She continued to go before the wind for a few furlongs, and then grounding upon the low icebergs, remained motionless. Captain Warrens' curiosity was so much excited that he immediately leaped into his boat, with several seamen, and rowed towards her.

"On approaching, he observed that her hull was considerably weather-beaten, and not a soul appeared on the deck, which was covered with snow to a considerable depth. He hailed her crew several times, but no answer was returned. Previous to stepping on board, an open port-hole near the main-chains caught his eye, and on looking in he perceived a man reclining back in a chair, with writing materials before him, but the feebleness of the light made everything indistinct. The party went upon deck, and having uncovered the hatchway, which they found closed, they descended below.

"They first came to the cabin which Captain Warrens had viewed through the port-hole. A tremor seized him as he entered it. Its inmate retained his former position, and seemed to be insensible to the presence of the strangers. He was found to be a corpse, and a green damp mould had covered his cheeks and forehead, and veiled his eye-balls. He had a pen in his hand, and a log-book lay before him, the last sentence in whose unfinished page ran thus :—'November 11th, 1762. We have now been enclosed in the ice seventeen days. The fire went out yesterday, and our master has been trying ever since to kindle it again, but without success. His wife died this morning. There is no relief.'

"Captain Warrens and his men hurried from the spot without uttering a word. On entering the principal cabin, the first object that attracted their attention was the dead body of a female, reclining on a bed in an attitude of deep interest and attention. Her countenance retained the freshness of life, and a contraction of the limbs alone showed that her form was inanimate. Seated on the floor was the corpse of an apparently young man, holding a steel in one hand and a flint in the other, as if in the act of striking fire upon some tinder which lay beside him. In the forepart of the vessel several sailors were found lying dead in their berths, and the body of a boy was crouched at the bottom of the gangway stairs.

"Neither provisions nor fuel could be discovered anywhere; but Captain Warrens was prevented, by the superstitious prejudices of his seamen, from examining the vessel as minutely as he wished to have done. He therefore carried away the log-book already mentioned, and, returning to his own ship, immediately steered to the southward, deeply impressed with the awful example which he had just witnessed of the danger of navigating the Polar seas in high northern latitudes. On returning to England he made various inquiries respecting vessels that had disappeared in an unknown way; and by comparing these results with the information which was afforded by the written documents in his possession, he ascertained the name and history of the imprisoned ship and of her unfortunate master, and found that she had been frozen in thirteen years previous to the time of his discovering her imprisoned in the ice."

I could relate other instances, and I am sorry to add, *many* such, of fearful calamities that have occurred in the ice regions; but I have no inclination to dwell upon such sad topics further than is necessary to show you the perils encountered by our brave navigators in those dreary quarters.

The poet Thomson, in his "Seasons," has drawn a graphic picture of the accumulated horrors of an Arctic winter:

" Ill fares the bark, with trembling wretches charged,
That, toss'd amid the floating fragments, moors
Beneath the shelter of an icy isle,
While night o'erwhelms the sea, and horror looks
More horrible.  Can human force endure
The assembled mischiefs that besiege them round?
Heart-gnawing hunger, fainting weariness,
The roar of wind and waves, the crush of ice,
Now ceasing, now renew'd with louder rage,
And in dire echoes bellowing round the main."

## CHAPTER III.

### ICEBERGS.

> "These are
> The palaces of Nature, whose vast walls
> Have pinnacled in clouds their snowy scalps,
> And throned eternity in icy halls
> Of cold sublimity."
>
> BYRON.

AMONG the most imposing and grand of the many wonders of the ocean world, are the fixed and floating icebergs, the "palaces of nature," which assume extraordinary and fantastic shapes, and more than realize the most sublime conceptions of the imagination. "Well, indeed," observes Snow in his "Journal of the Arctic Seas," "may the mind become awe-struck and the heart almost cease to beat as the lips exclaim, 'Wonderful Thou art in all Thy works! Heaven and earth are full of the majesty of Thy glory!' on beholding these mighty and surpassing works of the great Creator. East and west, and north and south, the Arctic regions present a picture of grandeur and magnificence nowhere to be equalled—great beyond conception—impossible to be truly pourtrayed."

These icebergs are described by Arctic navigators as mimicking every style of architecture on earth; cathedrals with pillars, arches, portals and towering pinnacles, overhanging cliffs, the ruins of a marble city, palaces, pyramids, and obelisks; castles with towers, walls, bastions, fortifications, and bridges; a fleet of colossal men-of-war under full sail; trees, animals, and human beings: one is described as an enormous balloon lying on its side in a collapsed state. A number of icebergs seen at the distance of a few miles presented the appearance of a mountainous country, deceiving the eyes of experienced mariners.

These icebergs differ somewhat in colour according to age, solidity, or the atmosphere. A very general appearance is that of cliffs of chalk, or of white-grey marble. A few have a bluish or emerald-green tint. The sun's rays, reflected from them, give a glistening appearance to their surface, like that of silver. In the night they are readily distinguished in the distance by their natural effulgence, and, in foggy weather, by a peculiar blackness of the atmosphere.

The Rev. Mr. Noble thus describes the strange and sudden transformations and the changing tints of icebergs. "One resembled, at first, a cluster of Chinese buildings, then a Gothic cathedral of the early style. It was curious to see how all that mimicry of a grand religious pile was soon to change to another like the Coliseum, its vast interior now a delicate blue, and then a greenish white. It was only necessary to run on half a mile to find this icy theatre split asunder. An age of ruin seemed to have passed over it, leaving only to the view inner cliffs, one a glistening white, and the other blue, soft and airy as the July heavens." Another berg shone like polished silver, dripping with dews, the water streaming down in all directions in little rills and falls, glistening in the light like molten glass. Veins of gem-like transparency, blue as sapphire, crossed the mass.

"Solomon in all his glory," observes Dr. Hayes, in his "Open Polar Sea," "was not clothed like the flowers of the field. Would you behold an iceberg apparelled with a glory that eclipses all floral beauty, and makes you think not only of the clouds of heaven at sunrise and sunset, but of heaven itself, you must come to it at sunrise and sunset. Lofty ridges of the shape of flames have the tint of flames; out of the purity of the lily bloom the pink and the rose. I will not say cloth of gold drapes, but water of gold *washes*—water of green, orange, scarlet, crimson and purple wash—the crags and steeps; strange metallic tints gleam in the shaggy caverns, copper, bronze and gold: endless grace of form and outline."

These icebergs—so beautiful in summer, so grand and awful under a wintry aspect—project above the surface of the sea like high hills composed of rugged and steep rock. Navigators have frequently stated that they have seen them rising from four to five hundred feet above the water, and extending more than a mile in length. During the first voyage of Captain John Ross, Lieutenant Parry measured an iceberg, which was aground in Baffin's Bay, in sixty-one fathoms of water. It was 4,169 yards long, 3,689 broad, and fifty-one feet elevated above the sea. Its weight was calculated to be equal to 1,292,397,673 tons! Captain Graah, a Danish navigator, examined an iceberg on the eastern coast of Greenland, and estimated its circuit, at its base, at four thousand feet. In height it was one hundred and twenty feet above the sea-level. He calculated that its contents amounted to upwards of nine millions of cubic feet. Dr. Hayes estimated the cubical contents of one at about twenty-seven millions of feet.

You doubtless wish to know the origin of these stupendous floating bergs, whence they come, how they are formed, and their ultimate destination. It has been ascertained, beyond all doubt, that they originate in the land, being nothing more than fragments of glaciers—a name given to immense masses of ice, or appendages to snow mountains. By far the larger number of these are formed on the coasts of Greenland. The mountains are always covered with snow; the valleys between them are filled with ice, derived from the higher portions of the mountains, and are thus converted into enormous glaciers. If the extent of all the shores of Greenland, in which the glaciers advance to the very sea, were put together, it is probable they would constitute a coast-line exceeding six hundred miles in length. These are the birth-places of the icebergs. The average height or depth of the ice at its free edge, or seaward in these valleys, is about twelve or fifteen hundred feet. As the glaciers advance farther into the sea, the rise and fall of the tide undermine the base, and enormous masses become detached and fall into the sea with a crash like thunder. The icebergs thus formed—vast moving mountains or islands—are drifted along, some finding their way to the Northern Atlantic—a distance of more than two thousand two hundred miles from the place of their departure—brought down by a powerful current which appears to originate under the immense masses of ice which surround the Arctic Pole.

> "Winter's flotilla by their captain led
> (Who boasts with them to make his prowess known,
> And plant his foot beyond the Arctic zone):
> Islands of ice so wedged and grappled lie,
> One moving continent appals the eye,
> And to the ear renews those notes of doom
> That brought portentous warnings through the gloom:
> For loud and louder, with explosive shocks,
> Sudden convulsions split the frost-bound rocks,
> And launch huge mountains on the frothing ooze,
> As pirate barks on summer seas to cruise."

Fearfully appalling are the dangers arising from these icebergs on their floating voyages, and we cannot wonder at the terror excited by their appearance among the early navigators among these ice-bound seas. In the expedition of Captain James Hall, under Danish auspices, for exploring Greenland, in 1605, we learn that the sailors were in sight of the south point of that country, and, to avoid the ice which encompassed the shore, they stood to the westward, and fell in with "mighty islands of ice, being very high, like huge mountains of ice, making a hideous and wonderful noise," and on one of them was observed "a huge rockstone of the weight of three hundred pounds or thereabouts." Finding nothing but ice and fog from the 1st to the 10th of June, the "Lion's" people hailed the admiral, "calling very fearfully, and desiring the pilot to alter his course, and return homeward."

The alarm spread to the admiral's ship, and they had determined to put about had not Cunningham (the captain) protested he would stand by the admiral "as long as his bloode was warme, for the good of the Kinge's majestie." This pacified the seamen for a moment, but the next floating island of ice renewed the terrors of those on board the "Lion," who, having fired a piece of ordnance, stood away to the southward.

All later voyagers in the Arctic Seas describe the sublimity of these moving mountains and islands of ice, and the fearful perils encountered among them. A thrilling instance of hairbreadth escape is related by Captain Duncan in his "Voyage to Davis Straits in 1826:" "It was awful to behold the immense icebergs, working their way to the north-east from us, and not one drop of water to be seen; they were working themselves right through the middle of the ice. The dreadful apprehensions that assailed us yesterday, by the near approach of the iceberg, were this day awfully realized. About three p.m. the iceberg came in contact with our floe, and in less than one minute it broke the ice we were frozen in quite close to the shore; the floe (similar to field-ice, but smaller, as its extent can be seen), was shivered to pieces for several miles, causing an explosion like an earthquake, or one hundred pieces of cannon fired at the same moment. The iceberg, with awful but majestic grandeur (in height and dimensions resembling a vast mountain), came almost up to our stern, and every one expected it would have run over the ship. The intermediate space between the berg and the vessel was filled with heavy masses of ice, which, though they had been previously broken by the immense weight of the iceberg, were again formed into a solid body by its pressure. The iceberg was drifting at the rate of about four knots and, by its force on the mass of ice, was pushing the ship before it, and, as it seemed, to inevitable destruction. A gracious Providence ruled this otherwise: the iceberg, that so lately threatened destruction, was driven completely out of sight to the north-east."

It has been supposed that the unfortunate steamship the "President," which left England for New York in 1841, was crushed to pieces between icebergs. In the year that this magnificent vessel was lost, the Atlantic Ocean was more thickly beset with icebergs, and at an earlier season, than commonly occurs. This is ascertained from a report of the "Great Western" steamer, which was published at New York. This vessel left England about the middle of April in the same year, and encountered an ice-field, which extended far more than a hundred miles, and along the southern edge of which she proceeded. This edge was lined by a broad border of loose ice, consisting of numerous floes and icebergs, and a considerable quantity of floating ice. To make way between these masses, the steamer was compelled frequently to change her course, for fear of coming in contact with them. The number of icebergs which were in sight of the vessel amounted to three hundred, and the largest was three-fourths of a mile long, and about a hundred feet high. A similar calamity to that which is supposed to have befallen the "President" is said to have well-nigh occurred to the brig "Anne" of Poole, which, in a voyage from Newfoundland to England, was so completely beset by ice that no means of escape were visible. The ice in its whole extent rose above fourteen feet above the surface of the water. It drifted towards the south-east, and bore the ship along with it for twenty-nine successive days. An opening most providentially occurred, by which the vessel became disengaged.

The "President," in 1841, the "City of Glasgow," in 1854, the "Pacific," in 1856, and recently in the present year, the "City of Boston," have disappeared, from, it is supposed, their contact with icebergs.

Captain Ross draws a vivid picture of what a vessel is exposed to in sailing amidst these moving hills. He reminds his readers that ice is like stone, as solid as if it were granite, and he bids them "imagine these mountains hurled through a narrow strait at a rapid rate, meeting with the noise of thunder, breaking from each other's precipices huge fragments, or rending each other asunder, until, losing their former equilibrium, they fall over headlong, lifting the sea around in breakers, and whirling it in eddies. There is not a moment in which it can be conjectured what will happen in the next; there is not one which may not be the last."

It is generally found that a strong current runs along the sides of an iceberg, and a vessel approaching too near is violently forced against the mass, and dashed to pieces.

Another source of danger arises from mooring vessels to icebergs, which is frequently done for shelter in strong adverse winds, or when the vessel is rendered unmanageable by the accumulation of drift-ice around; but there is this danger: the icebergs are very nicely poised; if a large piece of ice breaks off from one side, the whole mass is suddenly and rapidly turned over, by which vessels have often been wrecked or destroyed, while boats have been upset, even at a considerable distance, by the vast waves produced by the sudden change of position of an iceberg.

Scoresby relates the incident of two sailors who were attempting to fix an anchor to an iceberg. They began to hew a hole in the ice, but scarcely had the first blow been struck, when suddenly the immense mass split from top to bottom, and fell asunder, the two halves falling in contrary directions, with a prodigious crash. Fortunately the men escaped.

Sometimes vessels moor to icebergs when in want of water, and obtain it from the deep pools which, in the summer season, are found on the depressed surface of some bergs, or from the streams running down their sides; but if, meanwhile, the iceberg should fall to pieces, which is likely at any moment during the summer season to be the case, the vessel is liable to be buried under its icy mooring. The precarious character of these huge mountains of ice will be understood from an anecdote related by Dr. Hayes, the Arctic navigator: "A few years ago, while a French man-of-war was lying at anchor in Temple Bay, Labrador, the younger officers resolved on amusing themselves upon an iceberg a mile or more distant in the straits. They made sumptuous preparations for a picnic upon the very top of it, the mysteries of which they were curious to see. All warnings of the fishermen in the ears of the smartly-dressed gentlemen who 'had seen the world,' were useless. It was a bright summer morning, and the jolly-boat with a showy flag went off to the iceberg. By twelve o'clock the colours were flying from the icy turrets, and the wild young midshipmen were shouting from its walls. For two hours or so they hacked and clambered the crystal palace, frolicked and feasted, drank toasts to the King and the ladies, and laughed at the thought of peril where all seemed so fixed and solid. As if in amazement of such rashness, the grim Alp of the sea made neither sound nor motion. A profound stillness reigned on its shining pinnacles and in the blue shadows of its caves. When the youngsters, like thoughtless children, had played themselves weary, they went down to their boat. As if the time and distance were measured, they were scarcely out of harm's way when the mighty iceberg collapsed and broke up into myriad fragments, which filled the surrounding waters. This was, no doubt, the first and last day of amusement on an iceberg by the daring young seamen."

Icebergs are not affected by the swell of the sea, which breaks up the largest fields of ice in the space of a few hours; they rise and fall with a tremendous noise, though their size and form remain the same. But, when acted upon by the sun or a temperate atmosphere, they become hollow and fragile. Few icebergs are destroyed in the Northern seas; a large number get as far as the great bank of Newfoundland, which is occasionally crowded with them.

The formation and destruction of ice within the Arctic Circle is a beautiful provision of Nature for adjusting the inequality of temperature. Had only dry land been thus exposed to the sun, it would, in summer, have been actually scorched by its beams, yet severely pinched during the darkness of the winter by the most intense and penetrating cold. None of the animal or vegetable tribes could have supported such extremes. But in the actual arrangement the surplus heat of summer is spent in melting away the ice. As long as ice remains to thaw or water to freeze, the temperature of the atmosphere can never vary beyond certain limits.

The navigation among ice-fields and floes is beset with even greater danger than with icebergs. The fields frequently have a whirling movement, produced by the different force with which the current acts on the various sides of such a large body of ice. By this movement their outer borders acquire a velocity of several miles an hour. A field thus in motion, coming in contact with one at rest, or which is moving in a contrary direction, produces a terrific shock. The weaker field is crushed with an awful noise;

pieces of huge size and immense weight are frequently piled on the top to a height of thirty feet or upwards. "Except earthquakes and volcanoes," observes Dr. Hayes, "there is not in nature an exhibition of force comparable with that of the ice-fields. They close together with the pressure of millions of moving tons, and the crash, and noise, and confusion are truly terrific. Of course no ship could escape destruction thus caught. Numbers of whalers have been lost in this way, and others have been overrun by the ice and buried in the ocean."

Captain Scoresby relates a wonderful escape of his vessel amidst an ice-field, under these fearful circumstances: "Passing," he says, "between two fields of ice newly formed, about a foot in thickness, they were observed to approach each other rapidly, and before our ship could pass the strait they met with a velocity of three or four miles an hour. The one overlaid the other, and presently covered many acres of surface. The ship proving an obstacle to the course of the ice, it squeezed up on both sides, shaking her in a dreadful manner, and producing a loud, grinding or lengthened, acute, tremulous noise, according as the degree of pressure was diminished or increased, until it had risen as high as the deck. After about two hours the motion ceased, and soon afterwards the two sheets of ice receded from each other nearly as rapidly as they had before advanced. The ship in this case did not receive any injury, *but had the ice been only half a foot thicker*, she might have been wrecked."

Another remarkable instance of preservation is given by the same writer. During a gale attended by a heavy fall of snow, he had moored his ship to a floe. "About six p.m. the snow became so thick that we could scarcely see a hundred yards distinctly, and the wind was, if possible, more furious. The small icebergs now appeared setting towards the ship; but as they were not of a magnitude sufficient to endanger us without auxiliary pressure, we quietly awaited their approach. The first, which was about thirty-six feet above the level of the sea, struck the ship on the starboard quarter and turned her broadside to the wind; it then slipped clear without occasioning us any damage whatever. The second iceberg approached us with more alarming rapidity, but as we had not the power of getting clear of it, we were obliged to receive the shock upon whatever part of the ship it might chance to fall. It came in contact with the rudder, and slightly bruised one of its timbers; then grazing the ship's quarter and broadside, it passed forward to the bows, and being fortunately kept from close contact aloft by a tongue projecting from its base, it cleared all our boats. At this juncture, when the ship was so much involved with icebergs as to render casting off impossible, had the state of the weather permitted it, two floes came in sight from different quarters. One of them appeared to be rapidly closing upon us from the west, and the other from the south, which, with the floe that we were moored to occupying the eastern quarter, almost completely locked us in. To secure ourselves as far as possible against the crush which now appeared certain, we fastened by a hawser a large heavy piece of ice ahead of the ship, where the floes threatened the first contact, with the view of subjecting the interposed mass to the pressure, and with the hope of being then defended from partaking of it. The first shock of the floes was sustained by this mass with full effect, and for some time afterwards all things seemed quiet and safe. Suddenly, however, the pressure was renewed, in consequence, it was supposed, of some new stoppage to the drift of the floes, with tenfold violence. Our barrier was squeezed deeply into the floe, and prodigious blocks of ice were broken off and raised up by the pressure. While we contemplated their mighty effect with great anxiety, the berg which shortly before had passed the ship began a revolving and retrograde motion so quick as to overtake us before we could get the ropes off to slack astern, and suddenly nipped the ship on the larboard beam and bow against the floe by which we rode. The force was irresistible; it thrust the ship completely upon a broad tongue (or shelf under water) of the floe, until she was fairly grounded, and continued to squeeze her rapidly up the inclined plane formed by the tongue until the ice came in contact beneath the keel. This was the work of a few moments, and in ten minutes all was again at rest. When the pressure ceased we found that the ship had risen six or eight feet forward, and about two feet abaft. The floe on the starboard side was about a mile in diameter, and forty feet in thickness, having a regular wall-side of solid ice five feet in height above the sea; on the tongue of this the ship was grounded. The iceberg on the larboard side was about twenty feet high, and was in contact with the railing of the bows. It was connected with a body of floes to the westward, several leagues in breadth. The only clear space was directly astern, where a small interstice and vein of water was produced by the intervention of the bergs. Any human exertion for our extrication from such a situation was now in vain, the ship being firmly cradled upon the tongue of ice which sustained her weight. Every instant we were apprehensive of total destruction, but the extraordinary position of the ice beneath her was the means of her preservation. The force exerted upon the ship to place her in such a situation must evidently have been very violent. Two or three sharp cracks were heard at the time the ship was lifted, and a piece of plank, which proved to be part of the false keel, was torn off and floated up, but no other serious injury was yet discovered. Our situation, however, was at this time as dangerous and painful as possible. Every moment threatened us with shipwreck, while the raging of the storm, the heavy, bewildering fall of sleet and snow, and the circumstance of every man on board being wet to the skin, rendered the prospect of our having to take refuge on the ice most distressing. We remained in this state of anxiety and apprehension about two hours. On the one hand we feared the calamity of shipwreck, on the other, in case of her preservation, we looked forward to immense difficulties before the ship, so firmly grounded, could be got afloat. While I walked the deck under a variety of conflicting feelings, I was suddenly aroused by another squeeze of the ice, indicated by the cracking of the ship and the motion of the berg, which seemed to mark the moment of destruction. But this renewed pressure, by a singular and striking Providence, was the means of our preservation. The nip took the ship about the bows, where it was received on a part rendered prodigiously strong by its arched form and the thickness of the interior fortifications. It acted like the propulsion of a round body squeezed between the fingers, driving the ship astern, and projecting her clear of all the ice fairly afloat with a velocity equal to that of her first launching."

This is one of the most extraordinary instances on record of preservation from almost certain destruction. I have given the narrative entire, in order that you may understand the many dangers that beset the hardy navigator among these moving ice-mountains and ice-fields of the storm-bound North.

The fields of ice that float in the Polar Seas are often twenty or thirty miles in diameter, and some hundreds of feet in thickness. It is calculated that upwards of twenty thousand square miles of drifting ice come down every year along the coast of Greenland into the Atlantic, moving on during the winter at the rate of about five or six miles a day. The "Resolute" exploring-ship, which was abandoned in Melville's Straits, on account of its being enclosed firmly in a vast field of ice, was afterwards found in Baffin's Bay, having been carried a thousand miles from its former position by the drift of an ice-field, three hundred thousand square miles in extent and seven feet thick. This will give an idea of the quantity of ice which is carried out of the Polar regions, independent of the icebergs, and drifted into warmer climates. One of the most appalling instances of encounters with the ice is related by the Rev. Mr. Noble: "Captain Knight, the commander of a fine brig, with a costly outfit for a sealing voyage, lost his vessel near Cape Bonavista in 1862. Immersed in the densest fog, and driven by the gale, he was running down a narrow lane or opening in the ice, when the shout of 'Breakers ahead!' and the crash of the bows upon a reef came in the same moment. Instantly overboard they sprang, forty men of them, and saw their beautiful vessel almost immediately buried in the ocean. There they stood on the heaving field of ice, gazing in mournful silence upon the great black billows as they rolled on, one after another, bursting in thunder on the sunken cliffs, a tremendous display of surf where the brig had disappeared. To the west were the precipitous shores of Cape Bonavista, lashed by the surge, and the dizzy roost of wild sea-birds. For this, the nearest land, in single file, with Captain Knight at their head, they commenced, at sunset, their dreadful and almost hopeless march. All night, without refreshment or rest, they went stumbling and plunging on their perilous way, now and then sinking into the slush between the ice-cakes, and having to be drawn out by their companions. But for their leader and a few bold spirits, the party would have sunk down and perished. At daybreak they were still on the rolling ice-fields, beclouded with fog, and with nothing in prospect but the terrible cape, and its solitary chance of escape. Thirsty, famished, and worn down, they toiled on all the morning and the afternoon, more and more slowly, bewildered and lost in the dreadful cloud, travelling along parallel with the coast, and passing the cape without knowing it at the time. But for some remarkable interposition of Divine Providence, the approaching sunset would have been their last; only the most determined would have continued the march into the next night; the worn-out and helpless ones would drop down singly, or gather into little groups on the cold ice and die. They had shouted until they were hoarse, and looked into the endless grey cloud until they lost heart, when, wonderful to relate! just before sunset they came to a vessel. A few steps to the right or the left, and they would have missed it, and inevitably perished."

The "packed ice," which results from the fracture and piling up of the field-ice, accumulates in immense quantities. Sir J. C. Ross, in the daring voyage of the "Erebus" and "Terror," had to force his way through a thousand miles of such obstructions, reminding us of the lines in the "Ancient Mariner:"

> "And now there came both mist and snow,
>   And it grew wondrous cold;
> And ice, mast-high, came floating by,
>   As green as emerald.
>
> "And through the drifts the snowy cliffs
>   Did send a dismal sheen:
> Nor shapes of men nor beasts we ken—
>   The ice was all between.
>
> "The ice was here, the ice was there,
>   The ice was all around;
> It cracked and growled, and roared and howled,
>   Like noises in a swound!"

## CHAPTER IV.

### SEALS.

"Man bends the ocean monsters to his sway
No terrors daunt him on his arduous way;
Through frozen waters, or in sunlit waves,
He seeks the SEAL, unnumber'd hardships braves
To gain a prize so rich in useful store."

IN the second chapter I described the severities of the Arctic *winter:* fearfully grand, even under such a repelling aspect, are the ice-bound regions; impressing the mind with awe of that Omnipotent Being "whose foot-stool is the earth," and "who measureth out the waters in the hollow of His hand."

I will now draw your attention to the Arctic *summer*, which, although of very brief duration, presents many interesting features.

"O'er the pure expanse
The sun like lightning throws its earliest glance.
Yet must imagination half supply
The doubtful streak dividing sea and sky,
Not clearly known, 'till in sublimer day
From icy cliffs refracted splendours play;
And clouds of sea-fowl high in ether sweep,
Or fall like stars in sunshine on the deep."

The transformation of a gloomy scene, upon which the sleep of death seems to have rested for the greater portion of the year, into bright, warm, though short-lived sunshine, is a change that can only be fully realized by those who have experienced its cheering effects.  Commander Inglefield, in his "Summer Search for Sir John Franklin" in 1852, thus describes an Arctic sunrise: "I kept the morning watch, and was well repaid by the sight of as glorious a sunrise as ever gladdened the face of nature: the yellow tints of the golden orb shedding their refulgence on the rude and grotesque masses of ice scattered here and there; and the land, just tipped on its snow-capped heights by his beams, seemed to hail the warmth which would soon send the melting torrents down its steep glaciers, or hurl its frozen masses on the deep, there to be slowly carried to the wild Atlantic.  To no one whose mind is not wholly engrossed by the world and its busy matters, can a sunrise fail to lead his thoughts heavenward."

By degrees, as the sun reappears above the horizon, the further progress of the frost is stayed.  In May, as the luminary acquires elevation, the melting process begins, and vast fragments of ice, detached from the cliffs, fall on the shore with a crash like thunder. The ocean is unbound, and before the end of June the shoals of ice are commonly scattered and dispersed, and a dense mist or fog covers the surface of the sea.

In the course of July the superficial water is brought to an equilibrium of temperature with the air, and the sun now shines forth with a bright and dazzling radiance.  For a short time before the close of summer, such excessive heat prevails in the bays and sheltered spots, that pitch and tar are sometimes melted, and run down the ships' side.  The air on land often becomes oppressively sultry.  The excessive heat, being conjoined with moisture, engenders clouds of mosquitoes, often obliging the natives to take refuge in their huts, where they smoke them out.

The extreme dryness of the air in winter, contrariwise, is remarkable, communicating an electric effect on the skin.  One cold night Sir John Richardson, the Arctic voyager, rose from his bed, and having lighted a lantern, was going out to observe the thermometer with no other clothing than his flannel night-dress, when, on approaching his hand to the iron latch of the door, an electric spark was elicited.

At the approach of the Arctic summer, all is bustle and activity among the natives. The materials for the summer huts are got ready, and the whole household, consisting of five or six families, move downwards to the fishing-place, which is generally an island with a low beach, in a southern aspect, for the convenience of launching their boats or drawing the seals which have been taken ashore. They are not confined to any particular spot in the summer, unless abundance of seals are seen; but they generally shift to some other station, which, in the course of former seasons, they may have observed as more suitable.

The Esquimaux have their regular divisions of work. The men are the carpenters; the women are the tailors, shoemakers, and cooks, helping their husbands or fathers occasionally in their fishing. It is heavy work for these poor females, but Providence has endowed them with a strength of constitution and powers of endurance far greater than women in more genial climates possess. They have to haul the seals that have been taken by the men, ashore, and convey them to the huts. They also flay and cut up the spoil. Seals' flesh forms their chief food, and they employ various methods for preserving it for future use. The most common plan is to cut it into thin strips, and dry them over a line in the interior of the huts. The seal-skins, which the Esquimaux have a mode of rendering waterproof, form the chief articles of dress; when tanned, they make excellent shoes.

I may mention here that the Romans believed a seal's skin was a preservative against lightning, and they made tents of it to shelter themselves during thunder-storms. The Emperor Augustus is said by Suetonius never to have travelled without one of these skins, having a great dread of lightning.

The blubber of the seal is most carefully preserved by the Esquimaux, being useful in many ways to their domestic comfort, and more precious to them by far than wine is to others. The oil is the luxury of their meals, and is of a superior quality to that of the common whale; their bread is nothing more than the dried muscular parts of seals or birds. Whatever we may think of the Esquimaux' partiality for seal-flesh, it is well to remember that our ancestors considered it a delicacy. The seal and the porpoise are mentioned in the bill of fare of a feast given at the enthronization of George Neville, Archbishop of York, in 1465. Sir J. C. Ross describes the meat as tender, but it certainly has a look and smell which would not be agreeable to any but very hungry persons.

The Esquimaux are exceedingly expert in their mode of capturing the seal. This is done either individually or in company, or in winter on the ice. Their *kayaks*, or skin boats, are very curious: they are about six yards in length, pointed at the head, and shaped like a weaver's shuttle; they are, at the same time, scarcely a foot and a half wide over the middle, and not more than a foot deep. They are built of a slender skeleton of wood, consisting of a keel and long side-laths, with cross-ribs like hoops, but not quite round. The whole is covered with seal-skin. In the middle of this covering is a round aperture, supported with a strong rim of wood or bone; the Esquimaux slip into this cavity, their feet resting on a board covered with skin. The lance, harpoon, and tackle are arranged before the boatman. He uses his oar or paddle with wonderful dexterity, striking the water on either side alternately, by which means he can proceed at the rate of twenty leagues or more in a day. In this frail bark, which only those accustomed to such can manage, the Greenlander fears no storm or the roughest breakers, so long as he retains his oar, which enables him to sit upright; and if overturned, while the head is downward in the water with one stroke he can recover himself.

> " Train'd with inimitable skill to float,
> Each balanced in his bubble of a boat,
> With dexterous paddle steering through the spray,
> With pois'd harpoon to strike his plunging prey,
> As though the skiff, the seaman, oar, and dart
> Were one compacted body, and one heart,
> With instinct, motion, pulse, empowered to ride—
> A human nautilus upon the tide."

As the natives are ever on the watch, as soon as they discover a herd of seals—driven usually by stormy weather into some creek or inlet—they endeavour to cut off their retreat, and frighten them under water by shouting, clapping, and throwing stones. As, however, the seals must speedily come to the surface of the water to breathe, they are surrounded and killed with long or short lances.

There are various modes of capturing seals on the ice. As the animals make holes in it for breathing, the Esquimaux seat themselves on stools, watching their appearance at the apertures, and rarely fail to harpoon them, enlarging the holes to withdraw and kill them. Sometimes, on seeing a seal lying on the ice near a hole, the Greenlander slides along on his stomach towards it, wagging his head, and making a sound like a seal, thus deceiving the poor animal into a belief that it is one of its companions. But the seal is usually wary—that is, the older ones—and takes every opportunity of escaping from its pursuers. When one is seen at sea, a signal is passed to the different boats engaged in the chase, and the animal is surrounded; a careful watch is kept for the moment of its reappearing, and on this taking place, one of the boats having advanced near enough, a dart is hurled with unerring aim. The seal, terrified and wounded, dives in the greatest hurry; but a float being attached to the dart, it is soon forced up again and dispatched. The wounds of the seal are then carefully staunched, to save as much of the blood as possible, and the body is distended by blowing into the cellular part, in order to render the animal buoyant, or, otherwise, it would sink to the bottom as soon as dead.

The chase of the seal, however, is not free from danger, even to the expert fishermen of the Arctic shores. Should the animal be not too exhausted when pursued, it sometimes turns on its adversary, seizes his frail skin boat, and with its sharp teeth pierces a hole, when the *kayak* sinks with its unfortunate owner. Many risks also occur from the lines to which the floats are attached getting foul of the paddle or the arms or neck of the fisherman, when the seal dives suddenly on being wounded. The males are very pugnacious, and have terrible fights among themselves.

Seal-hunting, or fishing, as it is often called, is the great occupation of the Greenlanders, and is also extensively pursued by various nations in other northern parts of the world.

You will, no doubt, wish to know something more about an animal so useful and valuable in many respects, and particularly to the hardy dwellers in the ice regions. A great many species of seals are met with on the western coast of Greenland; but the most highly-prized by the natives is what sailors call the *Sea-Calf* —so named from a supposed resemblance of the voice to that of a calf—or *Phoca vitulina*. These animals live in families, the old male being attended by his progeny for several generations. They are chiefly seen in flocks, amounting sometimes to hundreds. The teeth are very sharp, and the bite is severe. The habits of the seal are filthy, and singularly mischievous. A perpetual tyrant over weaker animals, it is also an object of constant pursuit with others. The white bear—with whom the seal is as great a dainty as the turtle is to an alderman—is constantly on the watch to surprise it when sleeping on the ice; but the cautious animal usually selects a single piece of ice for its nap, from which it may gain a full view of all around, and the proximity of the water may afford a ready means of escape. They are also said to have a great dread of the toothed whales. If a grampus perceives a seal of any species basking on floating ice, it does its best to upset the ice, or beat the seal off with its fins, when the animal becomes an easy prey.

Seals are easily stunned by a blow on the forehead, but from this state they often recover, and are desperate in their revenge. The sea-calf, in particular, is subject to violent fits of anger. After it has been hoisted on board a ship from the boat in which it had been carried, apparently dead from the blows it had received, it has been known to recover unexpectedly, and seizing with its teeth the nearest object within reach, tear away such a portion as it could grasp. Even after death this irritation manifests itself, as the muscular parts of the animal—though stripped of its outer integuments or coverings — still retain the principle of vitality, starting and quivering long after the dismemberment of the body has taken place.

When seals are observed making their escape into the water before a boat reaches the ice, the sailors give a loud, prolonged shout, which, causing them to stop in amazement at a sound so uncommon, sometimes delays their retreat until arrested by the fatal blows of their pursuers.

In the higher latitudes, the *Bearded* or *Great Seals* are mostly found. These are usually of an enormous size, sometimes ten or twelve feet in length, and of proportionate magnitude of body. This seal migrates in families, the elder ones leading the van, while the young follow confusedly behind, playing, tumbling, and frisking along in the highest enjoyment, and frequently in the extravagance of their fun flinging themselves quite out of the water. The sailors call these antics "seals' weddings."

Though the bearded seal does not yield much oil, yet its fat is esteemed delicious by the northerners. The *Harp Seal*, so named from a large black crescent-shaped mark on each side of the back, belongs also to the ice regions, though sometimes seen on the British coast. It attains the length of eight, and even nine feet.

The seal, a name derived from the Anglo-Saxon *seol*, belongs to the Mammalia, or animals that suckle their young, and constitute the family *Phocidæ*. All the animals of this class are mainly aquatic, but also frequently resort to land, or ice-islands, where they remain for days, and even months, suckling their young, or basking in the sun during the brief summer. The *Fur Seal* seems to possess remarkable powers of agility on land, often escaping when pursued by men running fast. They cannot walk, but shuffle along, especially over the ice, very quickly. On land the hind feet are never employed, nor the fore feet unnecessarily, but in moving forward it bends the hinder part of the spine underneath it, thus making a kind of arch, and then fixing the latter end, it suddenly straightens out the whole body in front, and in a repetition of this movement consists the peculiar kind of "jerking" leap for which these animals are remarkable. When the seal ascends an ice-island or rock, the ease with which it accomplishes its purpose is wonderful. It then makes especial use of its fore paws, and those which have claws are implanted into them like so many grappling-irons, and having thus secured a fixed point, they raise their monstrous bodies with the greatest rapidity. The general shape of a seal resembles in its trunk that of a fish and a common quadruped; the head is like that of a dog; the arms, which are destitute of collar-bones, are so hid beneath the skin of the body that only the wrists and hands appear, and they are then so short that they can scarcely be advanced forwards at all. But what they lose in extent they gain in power. They are admirably adapted for swimming, and serve also for seizing or holding. The fingers have an intervening membrane, but they can be separated so as to diminish or increase the surface of the paws. In all the species the fingers can be distinguished through the paw, and in most the nails appear at the termination; but in one group of seals there is this difference, that the membrane or web extends beyond the nails, not joined, but hanging down in the water like broad leathern strips, which the sailors call "flippers." The face is provided with strong whiskers placed on each side of the mouth and at the corner of the eye, communicating with nerves of considerable size, and the slightest impression produces sensation.

The ground colour of the hair or skin of the common seal, when the animal is alive and dry, is a pale whitish-grey, with a very slight tinge of yellow. When just out of the water and wet, the colour is ash; after death, and as seen in museums, the ground colour is pale yellowish-grey, the oil having penetrated the skin and rendered the hair of a more yellow hue. The fur of seals is very smooth, and abundantly lubricated with an oily secretion. There is generally an inner coating of rich fur, through which grow long hairs, forming an outer covering. Another adaptation to aquatic life and a cold climate is the layer of fat under the skin, from which the oil is obtained, and serving, as in the case of the whale, not only for support when food is scarce, but protection from the cold, besides rendering the whole body lighter. The respiration of the seal differs considerably from what has been observed in most animals: the nostrils are habitually closed, instead of being uniformly opened. Buffon examined a tame seal, and remarked that the period between its several inspirations was very long: the creature opened its nostrils to make a strong expiration, which was immediately followed by an inspiration; after which it closed them, often allowing two minutes to intervene without taking another breath. This power of suspension for a considerable time is of great use, enabling the seals to pursue their prey under water. Seals are often subjected to enormous pressure under water, which must be resisted, at the respective apertures of the body, by an appropriate mechanism. A similar provision is made for the eyes, as well as the nostrils, in more ways, perhaps, than one. At the inner angle of the eye (which is very large and round) there is a third eyelid, which can be drawn over the whole eye. The ears as well as the eyes can be closed at will, so as to resist pressure.

How very wonderful is the provision thus afforded to the seal, as, in fact, to all created objects, and how the contemplation of such subjects should raise our hearts to the Omnipotent God!

"To know and feel His care for all that lives."

Captain Scoresby, who had numerous opportunities of observing the habits of the seal, states that the animal hears well under water, and that music, and particularly a person whistling, draws it to the surface, and induces it to stretch out the neck to its utmost extent, so as to prove a snare, by bringing them within reach of the shooter. Many similar observations of this curious faculty in seals have been related by different writers. One remarks: "In walking along the shore, a few notes of my flute would bring half a score of seals within thirty or forty yards of me; and there they would swim about, with their heads above water, like so many black dogs, evidently delighted with the sounds. For half an hour, or indeed for any length of time I chose, I could fix them to the spot; and when I moved along the water edge, they would follow me with eagerness."

The food of the seal appears to be chiefly fish, although it does not reject other animal food, and it is said to derive part of its nourishment from marine vegetables. It has been found that seals have a remarkable habit of swallowing large stones, for which no probable reason has been yet assigned. The keeper of the celebrated "talking seal" in the Zoological Gardens is reported to have given his pet fifty pounds' weight of fish in a day, but this is by no means a limit of appetite, for double the quantity would no doubt have found a ready reception. This will give you an idea of the vast consumption of fish in its native element. A good-sized Spitzbergen seal in good condition is about ten feet in length and six feet in circumference, weighing about six hundred pounds or upwards. The skin and fat amount to about one-half the total weight. The blubber yields about one-half of its own weight in oil.

It has been supposed that seals can be easily tamed, but such cases are exceptional. Some of the common species, however, have shown great attachment to their owners, and exhibited considerable powers of intelligence. Cuvier relates an anecdote of a seal that performed very cleverly what it was ordered to do, and would raise itself on its hind legs, take a staff in its paws, and act the sentinel. At the word of command it would lie down on its right side or left, and tumble head over heels. It would give either of its paws when desired, and was equally ready at a *kiss*. Another was kept by Cuvier for a considerable time and became very tame. When teased it resisted, and when much irritated barked very feebly. It was particularly attached to the old woman who had charge of it, and recognized her at a considerable distance, keeping its eyes upon her as long as she was in sight, and running to her as soon as she approached its enclosure. If free when food was brought, it ran and urgently solicited it by the motion of its head, and still more by the expression of its countenance.

Of another species of seal called the "*Marbled*," and found on the coast of France, which was kept for several weeks in the Jardin des Plantes at Paris, M. F. Cuvier says: "I have never known any wild animal which was more easily tamed, or attached itself more strongly. When it first came it endeavoured to escape when I wished to touch it, but in a very few days all its apprehensions vanished; it had discovered my intentions, and rather desired my caresses than feared them. It was in the same enclosure with two small dogs, which amused themselves by frequently mounting on its back, with barking, and even biting it; and although these sports and the vivacity of the attending movements were little in harmony with its own actions and habits, yet it appreciated their motive, and seemed pleased with them. It never offered any other retaliation than slight blows with its paws, the object of which was to encourage rather than repress the liberties taken. If the puppies escaped from the enclosure, the seal endeavoured to follow them, notwithstanding the difficulty it experienced in creeping along the ground covered with stones and rubbish. When the weather was cold, the three animals huddled closely and kindly together, that they might contribute to their mutual warmth." The creature did not exhibit any alarm at the presence of man or animals, and did not get out of the way unless when threatened to be trod upon. Though very voracious, it did not show any opposition or anger when robbed of its food. "Often," adds M. Cuvier, "have I tried him when pressed with hunger, and he never opposed my will; and I have seen the dogs, to whom he was much attached, amuse themselves when he was feeding, by snatching the fish from his mouth, without his exhibiting any rage. On the other hand, when their mess was supplied to the seals (for he had a companion), as they were lying in the same trough, a battle was the usual result, and blows with their paws followed, and as usually happens, the more feeble and timid gave way to the stronger."

> "The great Creator condescends to write,
> In beams of inextinguishable light,
> His names of Wisdom, Goodness, Power, and Love,
> On all that blooms below or shines above;
> To catch the wandering notice of mankind,
> And teach the world, if not perversely blind,
> His gracious attributes."

The seals of the Southern seas are quite distinct from those of the Northern. The most remarkable of these animals is the *Sea-Elephant*, or *Proboscis Seal*, named thus partly on account of the very peculiar appearance of its short trunk, and also from its being much the largest of its kind, doubling the dimensions of its terrestrial namesake, reaching the enormous length of twenty-five and thirty feet, and being also of a proportionate thickness. Its colour is sometimes greyish, or bluish-grey, and more rarely blackish-brown. There is an absence of everything like external ears; it has great whiskers of strong coarse hairs, very long, and twisted somewhat like a screw, with other similar hairs over each eye, supplying the place of eyebrows; the eyes are very large and prominent; strong and powerful swimming-paws, having at their margins five small black nails; a very short tail, which is almost hid between two flat horizontal fins: these form the distinguishing peculiarities of this strange animal. When the sea-elephant is in a state of repose, its nostrils, shrunk and hanging down, serve only to make the face appear larger; but whenever he rouses himself, when he respires violently, or when about to attack or defend himself, the proboscis becomes lengthened in the form of a tube to the length of about a foot, and then not only is the countenance changed, but the character of the voice is modified in a not less striking manner. Though furnished with large and powerful tusks, the sea-elephant is mild and inoffensive in his habits; but when assailed is a formidable adversary. In Anson's "Voyages" it is related that one of the sailors having killed a young one, and skinned it in the presence of its mother, she came behind him, and seizing his head in her mouth, so injured his skull, that he died in a day or two afterwards. This is not, however, their usual habit, as I have remarked. A young one, petted by an English seaman, became so attached to his master from kind treatment for a few months, that it would come at his call, allow him to mount upon its back and put his hands into its mouth.

The cry of the female and the young is said to be like the lowing of an ox; but the hoarse, gurgling, singular voice of the male—strengthened by the proboscis—is heard from a great distance, and is wild and frightful. They are found in the Atlantic and Southern Oceans. The great object for which this animal is hunted is for the oil, which is remarkably pure in quality; the skin is used extensively for carriage and horse harness, on account of its thickness and strength.

The *Sea-Leopard* is a rare species of seal, in length about nine feet ten inches, which has been found in South Shetland. The *Monk Seal* frequents the southern shores of Europe.

The *Otaries* are a species of seal thus named because their heads are furnished with external ears, of which the others are deprived, and from whom they also differ in other particulars. These include the *Sea-Lion* of the Northern seas, about fifteen feet in length, and found chiefly on rocky coasts and islet rocks, on the ledges of which it climbs, and its roaring is sometimes useful as warning sailors of danger. The old males have a fierce aspect, but it is only when driven to extremities that they fight furiously. The *Sea-Bear*, or *Ursine Seal*, is an inhabitant of the Northern Pacific, and attains a length of about eight feet. The hinder limbs of this animal being better developed, it can stand and walk almost like a land quadruped. It swims with great swiftness, and is fierce and courageous. The skin is much prized for clothing in the regions where it abounds.

## CHAPTER V.

### *THE MONARCH OF THE OCEAN.*

> "Come, coil in the warp, see the hatchets be sharp,
>   And make ready the irons and lance;
> Each man ship his oar, and leave nothing on shore
>   That is needful the voyage to advance.
>     See the buoy be made tight,
>     And the drag fitted right,
>   See that nothing be wanting anon.
>     Never doubt, but look out
>     Round about—there's a spout!
>   Come away, boys! let's launch if we can!"
>         *Old Ballad on the Greenland Fishery.*

F all the industrial pursuits which engage the venturous seaman on the wide ocean, those connected with the capture of the WHALE,—

"the mightiest that swims the ocean stream,"

and, I may add, in point of dimensions the monarch also of creation,— are the most exciting and perilous; requiring the greatest endurance, hardihood, and courage, and at the same time yielding, under favourable circumstances, a substantial return for the dangers encountered. Large navies are annually sent on these expeditions by various nations, and thousands of sailors get accustomed to the fearful severity of the Polar regions, where the principal whale fishery is carried on, though many lives are lost and ships are destroyed in these enterprises.

Before relating to you some of the exciting adventures which occur in the pursuit and capture of the unfortunate whales, I will give you a few particulars about the animals themselves.

There are many peculiarities to be observed in these huge monarchs of the ocean. They comprise a class of animated creatures distinct from both fishes and land animals, though partaking of the characters of both. They are classed in the order of warm-blooded Mammalia, or creatures that suckle their young; that is to say, they breathe as the land Mammalia, and yet are as completely aquatic as true fish, which are cold-blooded. Fish never breathe, and if removed from the water into the air, they immediately die; but whales, if deprived of air, and confined under the water, would be literally drowned. They usually come to the surface to breathe at intervals of eight or ten minutes, but they are capable of remaining under water nearly an hour. The whale has no gills, but a heart with two ventricles or cells, and very elastic lungs in a great bony chest, into which the air is freely admitted, not through the mouth; for, although the animal is of such prodigious dimensions (some species attaining upwards of one hundred feet in length, and a weight of nearly as many tons), yet the throat is so small that it could not dispose of a morsel which is swallowed by an ox. Through what are popularly called "blowers" or *spiracles*, huge nostrils which open on the summit of the head, from eight to twelve inches long, but of small breadth, the whale can send a column of moist vapour forty to fifty feet high; and when this breathing, or blowing, is performed under the surface of the ocean, a vast quantity of water is also thrown into the air, and the noise made in this operation can, it is said, be heard at the distance of between two and three miles.

Another peculiarity about these wonderful creatures—which, I should tell you, belong to the class *Cetacea* (from the Greek word *ketos*, a whale), and which comprises not only all the varieties of the whale tribe, but likewise the grampus, the porpoise, the dolphin, the dugong, and some others of comparatively very small size— is the tail, which is not vertical as in most fishes, but level, by which they are able to reach the surface of the water with greater facility for the purposes of respiration; and such is the strength of this tail that even the largest whales are able, with its assistance, to force themselves entirely out of the water; and you may easily understand this tremendous force when I tell you that in the large whales the surface of the tail comprises from eighty to one hundred square feet. In length it is only from five to six feet, but in width it measures from eighteen to twenty-six feet.

Providence has given this immense power to serve as a defence as well as a means of propulsion to the huge animal, for the tail is nearly the sole instrument of its protection. With one stroke of it the whale will send a large boat with its crew into the air, and shatter the wood into a thousand pieces. The tail enables the animal to rise in the water by striking a few slight blows with it downwards, when the head is naturally carried in an opposite direction, and when the whale wishes to sink, a few similar strokes with the tail upwards at once serve to bury the head beneath the surface.

Sometimes the animal takes a perpendicular position in the water, with the head downwards, and rearing the tail on high, beats the waves with fearful violence. On these occasions the sea foams for a wide space around, and the lashing is heard at a great distance, like the roar of a tempest. This performance is called by the sailors "lob-tailing."

The head is of enormous size, being about one-third of the entire bulk of the whale, and the lips, nearly twenty feet long in some species, show a cavity large enough to hold a ship's jolly-boat and crew; but, as I observed before, the throat is very narrow. It is stated to be no more than an inch and a half in diameter even in a large whale, so that only very small animals can pass through it. The basis of the head consists of the crown-bone, from each side of which descend the immense jaw-bones, from sixteen to twenty feet in length, extending along the mouth in a curved line until they meet and form a kind of crescent.

In the Arctic seas whales find an abundance of food in the shape of animalculæ, several species of marine worms, jelly-fish, crabs, and especially shrimps, which abound in those regions. Sir

John Parry relates that joints of meat hung by his crew over the sides of the ship were in a few days picked to the bone by shrimps.

Some species of whales are entirely destitute of teeth, but Nature has provided them with an apparatus of whalebone, for the purpose of straining out of the water the small animals which form their nourishment. There are several hundreds of these plates on each side of the mouth, the whole quantity in that of a large whale sometimes weighing nearly two tons.

The tongue of the whale is a soft thick mass, not extending beyond the back of the mouth. It was formerly considered a great delicacy of the table, and a right of royalty. The sword-fish, an implacable enemy of the whale, has a similar relish for the tongue, and, it is said, leaves the rest of the carcase untouched. The skin of the whale is naked and smooth, with the exception of a few bristles about the jaws, and is covered with an oily fluid, which renders it very slippery; beneath this is a thick layer, from eight to twenty inches, of a fatty substance, called *blubber*, the most valuable part of the animal, and which yields on boiling nearly its own bulk of thick coarse glutinous oil. It is by this wrapper that Providence enables the whale, a warm-blooded animal, as I told you, to defy the utmost extremity of cold, and to retain a sufficient proportion of heat even under the icy Polar seas. It also serves to make the specific gravity of the body much lighter than it otherwise would be, so as to resist the pressure of the water at the great depths to which the whale descends. Yet it is this warm covering, so essential to the animal itself, that has excited the cupidity and deadly pursuit of man, causing him to brave the most appalling dangers, trusting to the resources of art in the instruments of destruction where brute force alone could never prevail.

To give an idea of the quantity and value of the oil obtained from a Greenland whale of sixty feet in length, it has been stated that the weight of the animal, being seventy tons, would be nearly that of three hundred fat oxen. Of this vast mass the oil of a rich whale comprises about thirty tons, which renders it a valuable capture.

The whale has no external ear, but, when the skin is removed, a small opening is perceived for the admission of sound. This sense may seem imperfect, yet the animal, by a quick perception of all movements made on the water, discovers danger at a great distance. The eyes appear small for such a huge animal, being about the size of those of an ox; but the sense of seeing is very acute. Behind them are the fins; these are about nine feet long and four or five feet broad, and are enclosed by very elastic membranes, also provided with bones, similar in form and number to those of the human hand.

The whale does not attain his full growth under twenty-five years, and is said to reach a very great age. The flesh is red, firm, and coarse, and is eaten raw by the Esquimaux, who also drink the oil with much enjoyment. Captain Hall, however, who lived some years among this people, declares the meat "to be tougher than any bull beef in Christendom."

I think we should scarcely like to try *our* appetites upon such food, but in the bleak Polar regions, where the means for satisfying hunger are very scanty, the capture of a whale by the natives is an occasion for great rejoicing.

Captain M'Clure mentions the Esquimaux method of attacking the whale:

"An *omaiak*, or woman's boat, is *manned* by ladies, having as harpooner a chosen man of the tribe, and a shoal of small fry in the form of *kayaks*, or single men canoes, are in attendance. The harpooner singles out a whale and drives his weapon into its flesh. To the harpoon an inflated seal-skin is attached by means of a walrus-hide thong. The wounded fish is then incessantly harassed by the men in the *kayaks* with harpoons, a number of which, when attached to a whale, baffle its efforts to escape and wear out its strength, until, in the course of a day, the whale dies from sheer exhaustion and loss of blood.

"The harpooner, after a successful day's sport, is a very great personage, and is invariably decorated with the Esquimaux order of the blue ribbon, that is, he has a blue line drawn down his face over the bridge of his nose."

The whale not only serves for food to the hardy Greenlanders, but is also valuable in many other ways: some membranes of the stomach are used for the upper articles of clothing; the bones are converted into harpoons and spears for striking the seals or darting at sea-birds, and are also employed in the erection of their tents, and some tribes use them in the formation of their boats.

My preceding remarks have applied to the whale tribe generally, but with a more direct allusion to the "Greenland" or "right" whale, as it is called, from its producing the greatest amount of oil. This animal inhabits the seas of the Northern parts of the world, and abounds chiefly in the Arctic regions. The "Southern," or "Cape" whale is a distinct species, the head being smaller in proportion than its Northern relative, and its colour an uniform black. It attains the length of from fifty to sixty feet.

The *Northern Rorqual*, which exists in great numbers in the Northern seas, is the largest of the whale tribe, the mightiest giant among giants, attaining the vast length of from one hundred to one hundred and ten feet, with a bodily circumference of from thirty to forty feet. The amazing speed and activity of this immense animal renders it a dangerous object to attack; besides, the small quantity of oil it affords does not repay the fisherman for his risk. This whale has no teeth. When struck by a harpoon, it has been known to run off four hundred and eighty fathoms (two thousand eight hundred and eighty feet) of rope in a *minute*. Martyns, an old Arctic navigator, mentions an instance of a "razor-back," as the great rorqual is called by seamen, dragging a large boat with its crew amongst loose ice, where they all perished.

The *Smaller Rorqual*, measuring from fifteen to twenty-five feet, frequents the rocky bays of Greenland, and is considered a tender morsel by the natives. There is also a "Rorqual" of the Southern seas, an animal of great power and a fast swimmer, very difficult to capture. The most valuable whale in the Southern seas is one of which you have no doubt often read, the "*Cachalot*" (so named from *cachose*, a tooth, in the Basque language—having teeth in the lower jaw only) or "*Sperm*" whale, which supplies the spermaceti and ambergris of commerce. This immense animal, which grows to the length of from seventy to eighty feet, is found in almost every part of the warm latitudes. It has some curious peculiarities: the head has in front a very thick blunt extremity called the snout or nose, and constitutes one-third of the whole length of the animal: at its junction with the body the animal has what the whalers call a "bunch of the neck," a large protuberance on the back, immediately behind which is the thickest part of the body, which from this part gradually tapers off to the tail; and where this commences there is another large prominence called the "hump," after which the body contracts so much as to become finally not thicker than the body of a man. An immense cavity in the head contains cells filled with oil, which is fluid when the animal is alive, and after its death takes a concrete form known as spermaceti. The size of this cavity may be judged from what is said, that in a large whale it sometimes contains a ton, or more than ten barrels of spermaceti. As a contrast to the contracted gullet of the Greenland whale, the throat of the sperm whale is capacious enough to give passage to the body of a man. The food of this huge monster consists principally of a species of polypus called "squid" by the sailors, and it is supposed that they are attracted by the shining white of the inner part of the whale's mouth. The sperm whale is generally seen in herds, or "schools" as they are called, consisting of several hundreds. With each herd of females, large males or "schoolmasters" are always associated, who are extremely jealous of intruders, and fight fiercely to maintain their rights. The large whale is generally incautious, and if alone is attacked without much difficulty, and is easily killed, as he frequently after receiving the first plunge of the harpoon appears hardly to feel it, but continues lying like a log of wood before he attempts to escape. Large whales, however, are sometimes very cunning and courageous, and commit fearful havoc with their tails and jaws. When alarmed they are said to perform many unusual actions: one of these consists in moving the tail slowly from side to side on the surface of the water, as if feeling for any object that may be near. It also rolls over and over on the surface, especially when harpooned, and in this way will coil an amazing length of line around it. One of its most surprising feats is leaping out of the water. Darwin in his "Journal of Researches," remarks that off Tierra del Fuego he saw several spermaceti whales performing this stupendous leap, and as they fell into the water sideways the sound reverberated like distant thunder.

The *White Whale* is described as a very beautiful animal, frequenting chiefly the Arctic seas, varying in length from ten to twenty feet. It is usually of a cream colour, though Scoresby remarks having seen some of a yellowish colour, approaching to orange. In the dreary monotony of the icy regions, a lively herd of these animals, by their gambols and the exhibition of their smooth, slippery white bodies, affords a pleasing relief. The shape of this whale is highly symmetrical, resembling a double cone, one end of which is considerably shorter than the other: the tail is very powerful, and being bent under the body in swimming, is worked with such force as to impel the animal forward with the velocity of an arrow. The food of this whale is said to be cod, haddock, flounders, and smaller fish of this description. They are not at all shy, but often follow ships and tumble about amidst the boats in herds of thirty and forty. Fortunately for them, this fearlessness of danger does not often expose them to the deadly harpoon, their comparative little value being their preservative from the whale-fishers. They do not, however, experience the same immunity from the natives of the Greenland coast, where they arrive in great numbers at the close of the year in stormy weather. They are then chiefly captured by nets, which are extended across the narrow sounds between the islands, and when thus entangled they are killed with lances.

Another whale, called the *Deductor*, resembles somewhat the white whale, and appears to be the most sociable of all the Cetacean tribe, herding together in innumerable flocks. This leads, however, to a prodigious slaughter of these poor animals when (although frequenting chiefly the Northern Ocean) they wander away from their usual haunts, and get driven on shore by the fishermen, the main body of the drove following the leading whales as a flock of sheep.

In the "Caledonian Mercury" there is an account of the capture of ninety-eight of these whales, in 1832, in the island of Lewis:

"An immense shoal of whales was, early in the morning, chased to the mouth of the harbour of Stornoway by two fishing-boats, which had met them in the offing. This circumstance was immediately seen from the shore, and a host of boats, about thirty or forty in number, set off to join the others in pursuit, and engage in combat with these giants of the deep. The chase soon became one of bustle and anxiety on the part both of man and whale. The boats were arranged by their crews in the form of a crescent, in the fold of which the whales were collected, and where they had to encounter tremendous showers of stones, splashings of oars, frequent gashings with harpoons and spears, whilst the din created by the shoutings of the boats' crews and the multitude on shore was in itself sufficient to stupefy and stun the bottle-nosed foe into a surrender. On more than one occasion, however, the floating phalanx was broken, and it required the greatest activity and tact before the breach could be repaired and the fugitives regained. The shore was neared by degrees, the boats advancing and retreating by turns, till at length they succeeded in driving the captive monsters on the beach opposite the town and within a few yards of it. The movements of the whales were now violent, but, except when one became unmanageable and enraged when harpooned, or his tail fixed in a noose, they were not dangerous to approach. One young sailor, however, received a stroke from the tail of one of the largest of them, which promised to be fatal. In a few hours the whales were captured, the shore was strewed with the dead carcases, whilst the sea presented a troubled and bloody appearance, giving evident proof that it was with no small effort that they were subdued and made the property of man."

This exciting scene reminds us of the lines by Waller, in his poem "The Battle of the Summer Isles:"

"They man the boats, and all the young men arm
With whatsoever may the monsters harm:
Spikes, halberts, spits, and darts that wound so far—
The tools of peace the implements of war!

## FIGHT BETWEEN A WHALE AND A GRAMPUS.

> Now was the time for vigorous lads to show
> What love or honour could invite them to;
> A goodly theatre! where rocks around
> With rev'rend age and lovely lasses crowned.'

The deductor whale has a very prominent head, short and round, with something like a pad over its mouth, which gives it a peculiar appearance. In length it is from sixteen to twenty-four feet, and in circumference ten or eleven feet. Almost the whole body is black, smooth, and shining like oiled silk. When the mouth is shut, the teeth lock into each other like those of a rat-trap. They are generally very fat, and yield a large quantity of good pale oil.

It is impossible not to feel an emotion of pity for the whale— timid and inoffensive, with all its immense power for mischief, apparently unconscious of it until roused by danger—subjected to such cruel treatment by the cupidity of man: the deadly harpoons inflict tremendous wounds, and the blood, rushing in torrents from its sides, crimsons the sea for a wide space around. In the two following chapters I shall allude more particularly to this subject.

The whale has, however, other enemies to contend with besides man. Commodore Wilkes, in "The United States Exploring Expedition," gives an animated account of a sea-fight between a whale and a grampus, or "killer," as this fish is called by the Americans.

"At a distance from the ship a whale was seen floundering in a most extraordinary manner, lashing the smooth sea into a perfect foam, and endeavouring apparently to extricate himself from some annoyance. As he approached the ship, the struggle continuing and becoming more violent, it was perceived that a fish, apparently about twenty feet long, held him by the jaw, his contortions, spouting, and throes all betokening the agony of the huge monster. The whale now threw himself at full length from the water, with open mouth, his pursuer still hanging to the jaw, the blood issuing from the wound and dyeing the sea to a distance around; but all his flounderings were of no avail, his pertinacious enemy still maintaining his hold and evidently getting the advantage of him. Much alarm seemed to be felt by the other whales around. These 'killers,' as they are called, are of a brownish colour on the back, and white on the belly, with a white dorsal fin. They attack a whale in the same manner as dogs bait a bull, and worry him to death. They are armed with strong sharp teeth, and generally seize the whale by the lower jaw. It is said that the only part of the huge monster that they eat is the tongue. The whalers give marvellous accounts of the immense strength of these 'killers.' They have been known to drag a whale from several boats which were towing it to the ship."

The saw-fish is also a most formidable assailant of the whale. The upper jaw of this fish is prolonged into a projecting flattened snout, the greatest length of which is about six feet, forming a saw, armed at each edge with about twenty large bony spines or teeth. Mr. Yarrel mentions a combat that occurred on the west coast of Scotland, between a whale and some saw-fishes, aided by an auxiliary force of "thrashers" (fox sharks). The sea was dyed in blood from the stabs inflicted by the saw-fishes under the water, while the thrashers, watching their opportunity, struck at the unwieldy monster as often as it rose to breathe.

The sword-fish is also said to attack the whale, furnished, also, with a powerful weapon for defensive or aggressive war, in the shape of a bony snout about four or five feet long, not serrated like the saw-fish, but of a much stronger consistency—in fact, the hardest material known.

Beset by powerful enemies, the whale must have a troublous existence; and if one thing can enlist our sympathies for these animals more than another, it is the well-known attachment they have to each other, and particularly for their young. It is said that when a female whale is wounded, her companions will remain around her until the last moment, or when they are themselves wounded. The whalers strike the young cubs, or "suckers," as they are called, not for their value, for these would hardly produce a barrel of oil, but the men know that the mother will start forth in their defence. She joins her cub at the surface whenever it has occasion to rise for respiration, encourages it to swim off, and seldom deserts it while life remains. She is then dangerous to approach, but affords frequent opportunities of attack. She loses all regard for her own safety in anxiety for the preservation of her young, dashes through the midst of her enemies, and even voluntarily remains with her offspring after various attacks on herself.

"In 1811," says Scoresby, "one of my harpooners struck a sucker with the hope of leading to the capture of the mother. Presently she arose close to the 'fast boat,' and seizing the young one, dragged about six hundred feet of line out of the boat with remarkable force and velocity. Again she rose to the surface—darted furiously to and fro, frequently stopped short, or suddenly changed her direction, and gave every possible intimation of extreme agony. For a length of time she continued thus to act, though pursued closely by the boats, and, inspired with courage and resolution by her concern for her young, seemed regardless of the dangers around her. At length one of the boats approached so near that a harpoon was hove at her: it hit, but did not attach itself. A second harpoon was struck, but this also failed to penetrate; so that, in a few minutes, three more harpoons were fastened, and in the course of an hour afterwards she was killed."

Alas, for the poor whale! how sad it is to think of its torture and destruction while showing a degree of affectionate regard for its offspring which would do honour to human beings!

The poet Waller, in his "Battle of the Summer Isles," draws an affecting picture of these traits in the whale. Two of these animals, an old and young one, are embayed in the shallows.

> "The bigger whale like some high carrack lay,
> Which wanted sea-room with her foes to play;
> This sees the cub, and does himself oppose,
> Betwixt his cumber'd mother and her foes;
> With desperate courage he receives her wounds,
> And men and boats his active tail confounds;
> Their forces join'd, the seas with billows fill,
> And make a tempest though the winds be still.
> Now would the men with half their hoped-for prey
> Be well content, and wish this cub away:
> Their wish they have; he (to direct his dam
> Unto the gap through which they thither came)
> Before her swims, and quits the hostile lake,
> A prisoner there, but for his mother's sake:

She, by the rocks compell'd to stay behind,
Is by the vastness of her bulk confined.
They shout for joy! and now on her alone
Their fury falls, and all their darts are thrown;
Their fixéd javelins in her sides she wears,
And on her back a grove of pikes appears;
Roaring, she tears the air with such a noise
As well resembled the conspiring voice
Of routed armies when the field is won,
To reach the ears of her escaping son.
He, though a league removed from the foe,
Hastes to her aid.—
The men amazed, blushed to observe the seed
Of monsters human piety exceed!
Their courage droops, and hopeless now they wish
For composition with th' unconquer'd fish;
Not daring to approach their wounded foe,
Whom her courageous son protected so.
The rising tide ere long their efforts aid,
And to the deep a passage for them made;
And thus they parted with exchange of harms,
Much blood the monsters lost, and they their arms."

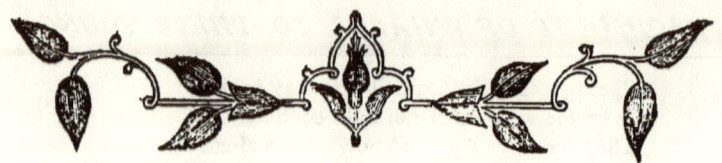

## CHAPTER VI.

### THE WHALE FISHERIES.

"Why stay we at home, now the season is come?
Jolly lads, let us liquor our throats:
Our interests we wrong if we tarry too long;
Then, all hands! let us fit out our boats.
    Let each man prepare
    Of the tackling his share,—
By neglect a good voyage may be lost.
    Come, I say, let's away,—
    Make no stay or delay,
For the winter brings whales on the coast!"
        *Old Ballad on the Greenland Fishery.*

THE preparation for "a cruise among the whales" is very exciting; not so much as it used to be, because the supply of oil from other sources, the general use of gas, and other circumstances, have diminished the necessity which formerly prevailed for a means of illumination. Still there is a considerable demand for the valuable products of the whale—the oil, the whalebone, the spermaceti, and the ambergris, which constitute essential articles of commerce.

The Arctic regions have for several centuries been the chief haunts of the whale fishery. There has been, however, of late years a great decrease in the number of whales, and the fishery as a speculation has become more precarious, for you can readily understand how, owing to the dangers which beset the Polar seas in these pursuits, and to which I shall call your attention in the next chapter, many vessels are destroyed and valuable lives lost.

Within a period of twenty years, no less than twenty whale-ships were wrecked or crushed by the ice, and the sufferings of the crews were fearful.

Peterhead, in Aberdeenshire, and Hull are now the principal British ports for the whalers, but only a few vessels, comparatively speaking, are engaged in the fishery. Hull has been for generations one of the head-quarters of the Greenland whalers, and it is there that many old customs and usages existed in connection with the fishery. The author of the "Home Tour in the Manufacturing Districts," while noticing the arrival of one of these vessels at Hull, says:

"The interest evinced by all descriptions of persons is very remarkable, for it may be said that the moral and physical affections of half the inhabitants are more or less excited—some in the hope or reality of profit, direct or indirect, and others by a host of domestic joys and anxieties. A custom prevails among the seamen of these vessels, when traversing the Polar seas, to fix, on the first day of May, a garland aloft, suspended midway on a rope leading from the maintop gallant-mast-head to the foretop mast-head; a garland, not indeed bedecked with flowers, but ornamented with knots of ribbon, love-tokens of the lads for their lasses; each containing, as it were, a little tender history, sanctified in the heart's treasury, and with the details of which they were alone acquainted. This garland remains suspended, 'blow high, blow low,' in spite of sleet and hail, till the ship reaches once more her port. No sooner does she arrive at the docks than, according to long-established custom, it becomes an object of supreme emulation among the boys of the town, seamen's sons, to compete for the aforesaid symbol, to which end, animated by the gaze of their friends on shore and a spirit of rivalry among themselves, they vie with each other in a perilous race up the rigging. The contest was at this moment about to take place, the garland being suspended aloft, in the position described, and containing within its centre the model of a ship, cut from the heart of an English oak, the type of honest affection."

The whale fishery was carried on successfully during the twelfth, thirteenth, and fourteenth centuries by the Biscayans. The whales taken by them in the Bay of Biscay appear to have been of a smaller species than those since found in more northern latitudes. This fishery has long ceased, owing, probably, to the great destruction of these animals. It is to the voyagers who, near the end of the sixteenth century, attempted to find a passage through the Northern Ocean to India, that we owe the discovery which led to the establishment of the whale fishery in the seas of Greenland and Spitzbergen. The English and the Dutch were the first to embark in this adventure; but the French, the Danes, the Hamburgers, and others, were not slow to follow the example. At first the whales were so numerous that the fishing was comparatively easy; in the progress of time, however, the whales became fewer, and when found, more difficult to take. It therefore became necessary to pursue them farther into the open sea. The English began seriously to engage in the whale fishery during the reign of Elizabeth. Hakluyt, under the year 1575, reports "the request of a rich merchant, to a friend of his, to be advised and directed in the course of killing a whale," with the answer "that there ought to be a ship of two hundred burthens, with proper utensils and instruments, and that all the necessary hands were to be obtained from Biscay," the people of which, as I have told you, were the earliest whale fishers in Europe.

The ships employed in the Northern fishery are constructed expressly for that object, and strengthened so as to encounter exposure in the ice regions. They are generally of from three to four hundred tons, each having a crew of about fifty men—experienced, hardy sailors—accustomed to the dangers of these particular expeditions. Six or seven light swift boats are requisite for each vessel; and another requirement is what is called a "crow's-nest," a kind of watch-tower, placed on the main-topmast to shelter the man on duty, whose office it is to keep a steady look-out with a telescope, for the spout of a whale in the distance, or the approach of drifting ice.

In the cold and dreary regions into which the whale-ship penetrates, it is not, or rather *was* not (for old customs, as I remarked, are passing away) so cheerless as one would suppose. An amusing ceremony, similar to that of "shaving" all nautical tyros on crossing the "line," prevailed amongst the seamen engaged in the whale fishery at Greenland on the First of May. It is thus described in "Hone's Table Book:"

The unfortunates, upon whom the initiation of the mysteries of the Arctic circle were to be performed, were kept from between-decks, and all intruders were excluded, whilst the principal performers got ready the necessary apparatus and dresses. The "barber" was the boatswain, the "barber's mate" was the cooper; and on a piece of tarpauling fastened to the entrance of the fore-hatchway was the following inscription:

"*Neptune's Easy Shaving Shop, kept by John Johnson.*"

The performers then appeared as follows: First, the fiddler, playing as well as he could on an old fiddle, "See the Conquering Hero comes!" Next four men, two abreast, disguised with matting and rags, so as completely to prevent them from being recognized, each armed with a boat-hook. Then came Neptune himself, also disguised, mounted upon the carriage of the largest gun in the ship, and followed by the barber, barber's mate, swab-bearer, shaving-box carrier, and as many of the ship's company as chose to join them, dressed in such a grotesque manner as to baffle all description. Arrived on the quarter-deck, they were met by the captain, when his briny majesty immediately dismounted, and the following dialogue ensued:

"Are you the captain of the ship?"
"I am."
"What is the name of your ship?"
"The 'Neptune,' of London."
"Where is she bound to?"
"Greenland."
"What is your name?"
"Matthew Ainsley."
"You are engaged in the whale fishery?"
"I am."

"Well, I hope I shall drink your honour's health, and I wish you a prosperous fishery."

Here the captain presented the first libation of three quarts of rum. Neptune, filling a glass with evident satisfaction, unmixed with sea-water, exclaimed,

"Here's health to you, captain, and success to our cause! Have you got any fresh-water sailors on board? for, if you have, I must christen them so as to make them useful to our King and country."

"We have eight of them on board, at your service," replied the captain; "I therefore wish you good morning!"

The procession then returned in the same manner as it came, the candidates for nautical distinction following in the rear. After descending the fore-hatchway, they collected between-decks, when all the offerings to Neptune were given to the deputy (the cook), consisting of whisky, tobacco, &c. The barber then stood ready with his box of lather, and the landsmen were brought before Neptune, when the following dialogue took place with each, only with the alteration of the man's name:

"What is your name?"
"Gilbert Nicholson."
"Where do you come from?"
"Shetland."
"Have you ever been to sea before?"
"No."
"Where are you going to?"
"Greenland."

At each of these answers, the brush (dipped in the lather, consisting of soap-suds, oil, tar, paint, &c.) was thrust into the respondent's mouth and over his face; then the barber's man scraped his face with a razor made of a piece of iron hoop well notched. He was then wiped with a *damask* towel (a boat-rug dipped in filthy water), and this ended the ceremony.

On reaching the Polar seas, the real hard work commences, the men being on watch night and day, and the boats kept ready for instant use whenever a whale is seen. On receiving an indication to that effect from the man in the "crow's-nest," a boat is launched, having a harpooner, a man to steer, one to look after the ropes, together with three or four rowers, and provided with an immense quantity of rope ready for use. The boat is steered rapidly and silently towards the whale, and on arriving within a few yards of it, the harpooner hurls his weapon so that it may enter under one of the monster's fins—a vulnerable part. The harpoon, in its most simple form, is a spear of about five feet in length, with a much-flattened point, having sharp-cutting edges, and two large flattened barbs. These are attached to a long line at the opposite end of the barbed joint. The gun-harpoon is a short bar of iron with the barbed spear at the end, and a ring with a chain for the attachment of the line. This is fired from a small swivel cannon attached to the whaler's boat; but the difficulty in whale fishing is to secure the capture of the animal, who sinks to a great depth on being struck, alternately rising to breathe, and sinking, so that the only chance of success is to tire it out. This is a critical moment for the crew in the boat, who are exposed to the most violent blows of the whale's head or fins, and still more of its tail, the tremendous power of which I have mentioned to you. The moment that the wounded whale disappears, a flag is displayed in the boat, at sight of which those who are on watch in the ship give the alarm by stamping on the deck, and those of the crew who are sleeping below, hastily throwing on a few clothes, launch the boats, and proceed to the assistance of their companions.

The greatest care is necessary by the boatman who has charge of the rope, in letting out and guiding the line to which the harpoon is attached. Should it be entangled for a moment, the whale would draw the boat beneath the waves. The time a wounded whale remains under the water is generally half an hour, but some stay much longer. The boats take up a position near which it is likely to rise, when each harpooner strikes his weapon into the animal, and long and sharp lances are thrust into its side, until, exhausted with the loss of blood, the whale gives signs of approaching death by discharging blood from the blow-holes or nostrils, sometimes drenching the ice, boats, and men with it.

As the huge animal plunges along in agony, its course is marked by a broad line of oil on the sea, issuing from its wounds.

The final capture is generally preceded by an awful and convulsive struggle; the tail lashes the water with fury, and the circles formed on the surface of the violently agitated waves extend to a great distance. When dying, the whale turns over on its side or back, a circumstance announced from the boats by loud cries and striking the flags. No time is lost: the tail is pierced and fastened with ropes to the boats, which drag the carcase to the ships with boisterous cheers.

A curious instance is related of a Dutch whaling crew, who had as they thought secured their capture to the ship's side, after towing it in triumph from the scene of conflict, missing their prize. The crew were giving vent to their delight, and the security seemed complete, for they were sailing a long distance from the ice-banks. They were having a good dinner to strengthen themselves before proceeding to the nauseous task of cutting up the animal. The feast was prolonged, but at length the men selected for the operation went on deck, with an air of importance and full confidence. What was their astonishment to find that the whale was no longer alongside! It seems that the ship, driven before the wind, had dragged at the animal, the cord had broken, and the rich prize, which had cost so much peril and fatigue, had sunk to the bottom of the sea!

A dead whale, if left in the water, soon putrefies: it swells to an enormous size, until at least a third of the carcase appears above the surface of the water, and sometimes the body bursts by the force of the air generated within.

After the whale has been secured to the ship's side, the next operation is what is called "flensing," or securing the blubber and whalebone, which occupies about four hours, and is, as you may well imagine, anything but an agreeable occupation. The harpooners, having spikes on their feet to prevent their falling from the slippery surface, begin with a kind of spade and huge knives to make long parallel cuts from end to end, which are divided by cross-cuts into pieces of about half a ton. These are hoisted on deck, and after being reduced into smaller pieces, are put into casks and stowed away in the hold. When the flensing is proceeding and reaches the lips, which contain much oil. the whalebone is exposed and detached by means of bone handspikes and bone knives, and is hoisted upon deck in one mass, where it is split and stowed away. The two jaw-bones, from the quantity of oil they contain, are taken on deck, after which the huge carcase is abandoned to the birds and sharks, which are always waiting for their share, and speedily devour it. In Ambrose Parey's works, representing the manner of cutting up a whale, a woodcut displays a drummer and fifer standing upon it and playing; drum-beating and bell-ringing being the signals given to the inhabitants of Aquitaine of the capture of a whale.

In the early period of the Northern whale fishery, the animals being numerous and easier of capture, settlements were formed on the ice-coasts for boiling the blubber and extracting the oil, which was sent home in casks; but when the whales diminished, and the fishermen were obliged to seek them in the open sea, the capture became more difficult and dangerous, the settlements were abandoned, and the blubber was, for economy's sake, sent home to be boiled. In the different parts to which whale-ships are bound, there are establishments for extracting the oil; those at Hull are on the outskirts of the town. The blubber when conveyed to the boiling-house is emptied from the casks into large vats, where it undergoes certain processes for extracting the oil.

The whale fishery in the Southern seas does not present the same amount of dangers which beset the whalers of the ice regions, and differs in some particulars, being specially for the capture of the sperm whale, which I described to you in the last chapter. The principal occupiers of this fishery are the Americans; still, there is a scarcity of whales even here. Melville, the author of "Omoo," mentions the remarkable expertness of the natives of New Zealand as harpooners in the Southern whale fishery. One morning, he relates, a whale was seen in the Pacific, the boat was pulled up to it, and a New Zealander, balancing himself on the gunwale, darted his harpoon at the animal and missed. After several hours' chase under a tropical sun the whale was approached a second time, and the harpooner aimed twice, but missed again. Then the bitterest disappointment arose among the tired boat's crew, and their taunts maddened the New Zealander, who, on the boat being pulled up again near the whale, bounded on the animal's back, and for one dizzy second was seen there; the next all was foam and fury, and both were out of sight. The men in the boat pushed off, flinging line over as fast as they could, while ahead nothing was seen but a red whirlpool of blood and brine. Presently a dark object swam out, the line began to strengthen, and the boat sped like an arrow through the water. But where was the New Zealander? His brown hand was on the boat's gunwale, and he was hauled aboard in the very midst of the mad bubble that burst under the boat. He had struck the whale in a vital part, and more than regained his former reputation for skill.

How wonderful are human power and energy in grappling with the monarchs of the ocean!

"Leviathan—
Hugest of living creatures, on the deep
Stretch'd like a promontory, sleeps or swims,
And seems a moving land, and at his gills
Draws in, and at his trunk spouts out the sea."

In the Tasmanian Courts at the International Exhibition of 1863 were many interesting productions of the whale fishery, which has become so important a portion of the industry of that colony. There are more than twenty whaling vessels attached to the port of Hobart Town, and these employ a fleet of nearly one hundred and fifty boats.

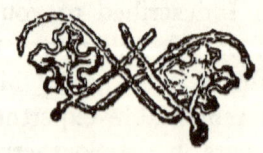

## CHAPTER VII.

### *PERILS OF THE WHALE FISHERY.*

" Laugh at fear!
Plunge in deep the barbéd spear;
Strike the lance in swift career;
Give him line! give him line!
Down he goes in the foaming brine!"

IT was well remarked by an old whaling captain that "if the Almighty had gifted the whale with a knowledge of his strength, few indeed would be caught." It is truly so, and there are occasions when the whale, inoffensive in its general habits, displays an amount of power and hostility which forms one of the grandest and most exciting spectacles that could be witnessed. In fact, the dangers which the whalers incur in their hazardous occupation are frequently most imminent.

As an instance of the spirit of mischief which sometimes animates the ocean monarch, I will relate what happened to an American whale-ship, the "Essex," Captain Pollard, in the Pacific Ocean. A number of sperm whales being signalled by the look-out, three boats were manned and sent in pursuit. The mate's boat was struck by one of them, and he was obliged to return to the ship to repair the damage. While he was thus engaged, a sperm whale, thought to be about eighty-five feet long, broke water about twenty yards from the ship on the weather-bow. He was going at the rate of about three knots an hour, and the ship at nearly the same rate, when he struck the bows of the vessel just forward of her chains. At the shock produced by the collision of two such mighty masses of matter in motion, the ship shook like a leaf. The whale passed under the ship, grazing her keel, and then appeared at about the distance of a ship's length, lashing the sea with fins and tail, as if suffering intense agony. He was evidently hurt by the collision, and greatly enraged. In a few minutes he seemed to recover himself, and started with great speed directly across the vessel's course to windward. Meanwhile the hands on board discovered the ship to be gradually settling down at the bows, and the pumps were instantly rigged. While working at them, one of the men cried out, "God have mercy! he comes again!"

The whale had turned about one hundred yards from the ship, and was making for her with double his former speed, his pathway white with foam. Rushing head on, he struck her again at the bow, and the tremendous blow stove her in. The whale dived under again and disappeared, and the ship went down in ten minutes from the first collision.

The crew took to their boats as the vessel was sinking, and after fearful hardships and sufferings, the survivors of this catastrophe reached the low island called Ducies. It was a mere sandbank, nearly barren, and they could only obtain water and some wild-fowl. On this uninhabited island, dreary as it was, three of the men chose to remain, rather than experience again the uncertainties of the sea. The poor fellows were never afterwards heard of. The three boats, with the remainder of the crew, put off for the island of Juan Fernandez, two thousand miles distant. The mate's boat was taken up by the "Indian," of London, ninety-three days from the time of the catastrophe, with only three survivors. The captain's boat was fallen in with by the "Dauphin," but with only two men living. Thus, out of a crew of twenty, only five remained to tell the story of the whale's victory.

If the huge monster, in the exercise of his enormous strength, can shatter a large sailing vessel in such a way as to cause its destruction, you may readily imagine what fearful perils are encountered by the hardy crews of the whaling-boats. A singular story is related of a Dutch harpooner, James Vienkes. A wounded whale had disappeared by diving, and the seaman was preparing to deal it a second stab, when the animal, on returning to the surface, struck its head against the boat and dashed it to atoms. Vienkes was hurled into the air, and fell on the monster's back, but contrived to bury his harpoon, which he had not let go, into it, and by means of this and the line he still held in his hand, he secured himself from slipping off. He called the other fishermen to his assistance, but their efforts to approach the whale were in vain. The captain of the ship, seeing no other way of saving Vienkes' life, called out to him to cut the rope; but the harpooner was unable to do this, as his knife was in his trouser's pocket, and he could not let go his hold for an instant. The whale was meanwhile advancing along the surface of the water at a swift rate, and it was fortunate for its rider that it did not dive. The sailors were beginning to despair of their comrade's life, when the harpoon by which he was supporting himself came out of the animal's body. Vienkes profited by the circumstance to cast himslf into the sea, and struggling against the waves, regained the boats which had been unable to succour him. He was picked up at the moment his strength was exhausted, and his companions, furious at the disaster, pursued the whale, and at length killed it.

Scoresby relates: "Being myself in the first boat which approached a whale, I struck my harpoon at arm's length, by which we fortunately evaded a blow which appeared to be aimed at the boat. Another boat then advanced, and another harpoon was struck, but not with the same result, for the stroke was immediately returned by a tremendous blow from the fish's tail. The boat was sunk by the shock, and at the same time whirled round with such velocity that the boat-steerer was precipitated into the water on the side next to the fish, and carried down to a considerable depth by its tail. After a minute or so he arose to the surface, and was taken up along with his companions into another boat."

"In one of my earliest voyages," observes the same writer, "I remarked a circumstance which excited my highest astonishment. One of the harpooners struck a whale: it dived, and all the assisting boats had collected round the fast boat before it rose to the surface. The first boat that approached it advanced incautiously. It rose with unexpected violence beneath the boat, and projected it and all the crew to the height of some yards into the air. It fell on its side, and cast all the men into the water; one was somewhat injured, but the rest escaped."

In the year 1804, the ship "Adonis," being in company with several others, struck a large whale, off the coast of New Zealand, which became furious, and destroyed nine boats belonging to the different vessels, and then escaped. It was captured afterwards, however. Many harpoons of various vessels were found in its body.

This whale was extensively known to the fishermen under the name of "New Zealand Tom."

Sometimes, as I before mentioned, the rope to which the harpoon is attached gets carried off, at a prodigious rate, by a whale in its efforts to escape, and the boat is carried far out to sea, and exposed to fearful perils. The annals of the whale fishery have many thrilling stories of wonderful escapes in such instances. A very remarkable instance occurred in connection with the American ship "Independence," Captain Belair. While cruising in the Pacific Ocean, a whale was seen, and two boats were sent to capture it. The harpoon was fixed, and the boats were soon out of sight of the ship. An hour or two passed away, when suddenly another whale rose in the water, only a few yards from the vessel. The temptation to effect its capture was too strong for the captain, who ordered the remaining boat to be lowered, and leaving but one man and two boys to take care of the ship, sprang into the boat with the rest of the crew. The harpoon was plunged into this whale also, and they were carried with the speed of the wind about fifteen miles from the ship. Then the whale plunged perpendicularly into the depths of the ocean. It was not long before they saw him, fathoms deep in the crystal waters, rushing up with open jaws to destroy the boat. By skilfully evading the attack, they escaped twice; but the third time, as the monster rose, he struck the boat in the centre of the keel, threw it some fifteen feet in the air, scattering the fragments and the crew over the waves, and then plunging into

BOAT STRUCK BY A WHALE.—P. 82.

the deep, disappeared. The captain and the men were now in the water, clinging to the pieces of the demolished boat. They were many miles from the ship, and could not be seen from the deck. The other boats were gone they knew not where. The hours passed slowly away, as they were drifting along at the mercy of the waves, until six o'clock in the evening.

The sun had now disappeared behind the distant waves, and a dreary night was settling down over the ocean. Just then they saw in the distance one of the absent boats returning to the ship. It was, however, far off, apparently beyond the reach of their loudest cries, and their hopes again fell. The boat at length drew nearer, and they redoubled their shouts; and at length they were heard, taken from the water, and carried almost lifeless to the ship.

The utmost care is requisite in "paying out" the rope when the whale is harpooned, so that no impediment occurs. The safety of the boat's crew depends upon the watchfulness of the man entrusted with this important duty. Scoresby, one of the most distinguished whalers that have ever been known on these perilous enterprises, records an instance which had a fatal consequence:

"As soon as the boats came within hail (sent in pursuit of the whales), my anxiety induced me to call out and inquire what had happened. 'We have lost Carr!' This awful intelligence, for which we were altogether unprepared, shocked me exceedingly, and it was some time before I was able to inquire into the particulars of the accident which had deprived us of one of our shipmates. As far as could be collected from the confused accounts of the crew of the boat of which he went out in charge, the circumstances were as follow: The two boats that had long been absent on the outset, separated from their companions, and, allured by the chase of a whale and the fineness of the weather, they proceeded until they were far out of sight of the ship. The whale they pursued led them into a vast shoal of the species. They were, indeed, so numerous that their 'blowing' was incessant, and there could not have been less than one hundred. Fearful of alarming them without striking any, the crews in the boats remained for some time motionless, watching a favourable opportunity for commencing the attack. A whale at length arose so near the boat of which William Carr was harpooner, that he ventured to pull towards it, though it was meeting him, and afforded but an indifferent chance of success. He, however, fatally for himself, succeeded in harpooning it: the boat and fish, passing each other with great rapidity after the stroke, the line was jerked out of its place, and instead of 'running over' the stern, was thrown over the gunwale. Its pressure in this unfavourable position so careened the boat, that the side sank below the water, and it began to fill. In this emergency the harpooner, who was a fine active fellow, seized the bight of the line, and attempted to relieve the boat by restoring it to its place; but, by some singular circumstance which could not be accounted for, a turn of the line flew over his arm, in an instant dragged him overboard, and plunged him under water to rise no more! So sudden was the accident, that only one man, who had his eye upon him at the time, was aware of what had happened; so that when the boat righted—which it immediately did—though half full of water, they all at once, on looking round at an exclamation from the man who had seen him launched overboard, inquired, 'What had got Carr?' It is scarcely possible to imagine a death more awfully sudden and unexpected."

Some boats of the whale-ship "Aimwell" being in pursuit of these monarchs of the ocean, harpooned one. When struck, the animal only dived for a moment, and then rose again beneath the boat, struck it in the most vicious manner with its tail and fins, broke and upset it, and then disappeared. The crew, seven in number, got on the bottom of the boat; but the unequal action of the lines, which remained entangled with the boat, rolled it over occasionally, and thus plunged the men repeatedly beneath the water. Four of them recovered themselves, and clung to the boat; but the other three were drowned before assistance could arrive.

In the Arctic seas the whalers are exposed to many dangers from the ice. About the year 1856, Captain Deuchars, a most experienced navigator, in command of a fine strong vessel, the

"Princess Charlotte," lost it in Melville Bay. It was a fine morning, and all on board were anticipating a very successful voyage; the steward had just reported breakfast ready, when the captain, seeing the floes of ice closing together ahead of the ship, remained on deck to see her pass safely between them; but they closed too quickly—the vessel was almost through when the points of ice caught her sides abreast of the mizzen-mast, and passing through, held the wreck up for a few minutes, barely allowing time enough for the crew to escape and save their boats. Poor Captain Deuchars thus lost his breakfast and his ship within *ten minutes*.

A wonderful case of deliverance from apparently certain destruction among the ice is recorded of the "Trafalgar," an Arctic whaleship. The account is given by Mr. Gibson, surgeon of the ship:

"Blowing a fresh gale, with rain, the floe to which the vessel was made fast set down under the lee ice, so as to render our situation perilous. Towards midnight we became unexpectedly entangled among heavy pieces of ice and floes, when the ship received some severe blows on her beams. Finding it impossible to get out, we lay to, and in half an hour the ship was close beset. Though I retired to bed when the ship was enclosed, I expected every minute to be called to quit it. Soon after, a large piece of ice pressing on the vessel opposite my bed-cabin, broke two or three of the timbers with a dismal noise. Thinking all was over, I sprang out of bed, and found to my great consternation that the ship was under an enormous pressure from numerous large masses of ice surrounding her on all sides, without an opening of water sufficient for a boat within two miles; and no other ship was in sight, although the weather was clear. Most of the crew were providing for shipwreck, and many of the people were supplicating Divine mercy for deliverance. Four days' allowance were cooked with all speed, other provisions were taken on deck, and everything of importance placed in readiness to be thrown on the ice. At noon, the man on the mast-head saw a ship, on which we instantly made signals of distress. At this time a dead silence prevailed throughout the ship, the crew looking on one another in awful suspense. At one time the pressure was so strong that the panels of the captain's stateroom were forced out of their framing. About half an hour after this the ship was suddenly thrown upon her larboard side, on which all hands sprang upon deck. I shall never forget the confusion of the poor men, nor their wild looks when they gained the deck—for half of them were below at the time of the shock, and from the smallness of the hatch only one could get up at a time. Some leaped upon the ship's side and were going upon the ice, when the captain cried out to them to behave like men, and to stick to the ship so long as she remained above water. We all stood on that part of the vessel nearest the ice, with our bags of clothing on our shoulders. For fifteen minutes we had patiently waited our doom, when, by the interposition of Divine Providence, the wind changed, the ice began to set off from the ship, and in fifteen minutes more she recovered her upright position. The water now rapidly spread among the surrounding ice, and finally the vessel was warped out and floated safely on the waves."

A fearful series of calamities befell a small squadron of **six** very fine whaling vessels in 1830, during a storm in Baffin's Bay. Masses of ice were driven upon them, by which they were completely beset. The ships were ranged under the shelter of a large floe, having water barely sufficient to float them. Here they formed a line, one behind the other, standing close, stern to stern, and being at the same time so pressed against the ice, that in some places a boat-hook could with difficulty be inserted in the space. The sky darkened, the gale increased, the floes began to overlap each other, and closed upon the ships in an alarming manner. The sailors then attempted to saw out a sort of dock, where they hoped to be relieved from this severe pressure; but soon a huge floe was driven upon them with irresistible violence. The "Eliza Swan," of Montrose, received the first shock, and was saved only by the ice raising her up. It next struck the "St. Andrew," of Aberdeen, amidship, breaking about twenty of her timbers, and staving a number of casks; but it then, fortunately, moved along her side, and went off by the stern. It now reached successively the "Baffin," of Leith; the "Achilles," of Dundee; the "Ville de Dieppe," a French ship; and the "Rattler," of Leith, and dashed against them with such tremendous fury, that these four noble vessels, which had braved for years the tempests of the Polar seas, were in a quarter of an hour shattered into fragments. The scene was awful: the grinding noise of the ice tearing open their sides, and the masts breaking off and falling in every direction, were added to the cries of two hundred sailors, leaping upon the frozen surface with only such portions of their clothes as they could snatch in a single instant. The "Rattler" is said to have become the most complete wreck ever known. She was literally turned inside out, and her stem and stern carried to the distance of a gun-shot from each other; and the "Achilles" had her sides pressed together, her stern thrust out, and her decks and beams broken into innumerable fragments.

Scoresby, in his journal, mentions a narrow escape which he had while pursuing a wounded whale through the ice, equipped with a pair of ice-shoes (consisting simply of pieces of deal, six feet long, attached by the middle to the foot), his own invention for walking over loose ice.

"I followed the whale on its second appearance, carrying with me a harpoon, and dragging a large quantity of line after me, until I fastened the harpoon by sticking it through the ice. Then returning for a lance, I again attacked the whale, following it as it retreated, and in a short time killed it. On one occasion, when I was waiting for its return to the surface, it happened to rise directly under my feet, so as to break the ice all around me, and lifted me up on its crown. As I must have inevitably followed it in its descent, had I retained my position, I slipped my feet out of the ice-shoes, and, at all risks, ran off to one side. Fortunately, the ice at that spot consisted of two or three folds, and supported my weight until I recovered my shoes."

A Dutch harpooner happened to get too near a monstrous whale, which struck him such a violent blow with its tail that the poor fellow was some time before he could regain his breath. The men of another boat harassed the animal in their turn, and at length the boat was upset. All saved themselves with difficulty by swimming, and hiding their heads under the water as long as they could. The cold was intense, and they were picked up all trembling; their hair was frozen, and they had a cap of ice on their heads. The greatest danger in such a case is sleep, which is the twin brother of death. They were obliged to be watched, and kept awake in spite of themselves. After some time they were allowed to sleep for an hour, and were then aroused with considerable difficulty. Without these precautions, men who have been long exposed to cold would not wake again.

The perils incurred in the pursuit of the whale do not always end with its capture. The operation of "flensing" or cutting up the animal, to which I alluded in the last chapter, is sometimes attended with danger. In a heavy sea, the men occupied in this disagreeable duty are liable to be washed over, or to be thrown into the monster's mouth at the risk of being suffocated. Occasionally they have their ropes broken, and are wounded by each other's knives. Scoresby mentions an instance of a man who, after the flensing was completed, happened to have his foot attached by a hook to the carcase, when it was inadvertently let go. He caught hold of the gunwale of the boat; but the whole immense mass was now suspended by his body, occasioning the most excruciating torture, and even exposing him to the risk of being torn asunder, when his companions contrived to hook afresh the carcase with a grapnel, and brought it back to the surface.

Such are some of the perils which have been related by the hardy travellers of the ocean whose years have been spent in continued struggles, not only with the element,

"Boundless, endless, and sublime,
The image of eternity,—"

but with the huge monarch of the waters, whose reign has been disputed by a greater power in creation, who "sees all things for his use,"

"Thou little knowest
What he can brave, who, born and nurst
In Danger's paths, has dared her worst!"

## CHAPTER VIII.

*THE PIRATE OF THE OCEAN.*

" Blood and rapine, death and slaughter
Crown thee, tyrant of the water;
Scourge of all that dwells in ocean;
Thrilling men with deep emotion,
Even the boldest, those whom battle
Blanches not with murderous rattle;
But whom, superstition-nursed,
Regard thee as a fiend accursed,
An omen of impending peril,
Of shadows dark with doubt and evil."

IMAGINE, my young readers, a SHARK seventy feet long, with a tooth four inches and a half in the enamel, or the part visible above the socket, jaws with the bow above thirteen feet, and a mouth capable of gaping more than twenty-six feet around! This was one of the species of *fossil* sharks, an antediluvian animal, which has been discovered in the limestone rocks, the teeth and the vertebræ (small bones or joints composing the spine or back-bone) enabling the geologist to determine the species to which the animal belongs.

A tooth, the size of that I have mentioned, was shown to the distinguished French naturalist, Lacépède, and, in order to discover the proportions of the animal to which it belonged, he measured first the teeth, and next the stuffed specimens of all the sharks preserved in the Museum of Natural History in Paris, and he found in every instance that the relative proportions they bore to each other was as one to two hundred, and he was thus enabled to ascertain the prodigious size and capacity of this formidable antediluvian animal.

Although the sharks of our own time are not of the same monstrous proportions, they are, from their immense strength and voracity, the objects of dread to those who behold them in their native element.

> "The type of horror and remorseless hate,
> Of villany the worst."

The *White Shark* in particular, one of the largest of the tribe, and frequently weighing as much as a thousand pounds, sometimes measuring from twenty-five to thirty feet in length, abounding in warm latitudes, and attacking everything in his reach, deserves the title given to him of "the pirate of the ocean." When I tell you that a lady's work-box has been found in the stomach of one of these sharks, and the papers of a ship that had been thrown overboard; that the baskets, shavings, cordage, ducks, hens, and buffalo-hides, &c., which had been thrown into the sea one morning from Captain Hall's ship, the "Alceste," were found in the body of a captured monster shortly afterwards; that in another was discovered a tin canister, which, on being opened, was found to be nearly filled with old coins, you will have some idea of his indiscriminate appetite. He will devour even those of his own species. An anecdote is related of a Laplander capturing a shark, and fastening it to his canoe: he soon missed it, however, without an idea of how it had happened. A short time afterwards he took another shark of much larger size, in which, when opened, he found the shark he had lost. An officer states (we read in the "United Service Journal") that when some midshipmen had caught a shark, they pulled him up in their boat, cut open his stomach, and then sent him back into the water. His body was instantly attacked by the sharks nearest to him, and was torn in pieces. The experiment was repeated with the same result.

The tenacity of life in the shark family is something extraord nary. The fish has been known to be active for many hours in the sea after its head has been taken off. Instances have been known of a shark having taken a bait in the depth of the sea, after its liver had been cut out for the purpose of extracting oil, and also when the whole of the entrails had been removed.

But a far worse character attaches itself to the shark, which is, his preference for human flesh: of all other food, it is this which he most prizes, and numbers of persons fall victims to his voracity in the seas he frequents. It is terrible to think of such a fate, for the huge monster is not only capable of snapping off a limb in a moment, or biting a person in two, but has been known to swallow a man alive. It is also stated on good authority that a shark was taken off the island of St. Margaret, which weighed fifteen hundred pounds, and the stomach was found to contain the whole body of a horse, which had probably been thrown overboard from some ship.

In the "Illustrated London News" (14th of April, 1860), the following horrible tragedy is related: "As the ship 'Karnak' was leaving the port of Nassau, a pilot fell overboard from her boat, in which he was being towed. The ship was stopped, and the boat instantly left for his rescue, while two life-buoys were thrown from the ship. The boat got close enough to give him the end of an oar, which he took, and cried, 'For God's sake save me!' The men were about to haul him into the boat, when he was carried down by a large shark which came up at the moment, taking the oar with him.

A few days after the fatal accident, a shark was captured in Nassau harbour, and on being opened, the pilot's right hand and wrist, with a portion of his shirt (by which the hand was identified), a goat's head, with horns nine inches long, and a turtle's head were found in his stomach."

The French name this fearful animal the *Réquin*, or Requiem (the rest or stillness of death), in allusion to the deadly character of his habits: to add to the horror of his appearance, a phosphoric light is emitted from his huge body when near the surface of the water. To get at human flesh, the shark has been known to bound several feet out of the sea, and seize the unwary sailor occupied in the rigging of the vessel when in full sail, and to leap into fishing-boats, and grapple with the men at their oars. You have, no doubt, read of the cruelties inflicted during the Slave Trade on the unhappy negroes who were forced from their country on board ship, and subjected to the most shameful treatment. It was frequently the practice of the captains and crews of these vessels to suspend a dead negro from the bowsprit, in order to watch the efforts of the shark to reach him, and this was accomplished at a height of several feet above the level of the sea.

> "Increasing still the terrors of the storms,
> His jaws horrific, armed with threefold fate,
> Here dwells the direful shark. Lured by the scent
> Of steaming crowds, of rank disease, and death,
> Behold! he, rushing, cuts the briny flood,
> Swift as a gale can bear the ship along;
> And from the partners of that cruel trade
> Which spoils unhappy Guinea of her sons,
> Demands his share of prey—demands themselves.
> The stormy fates descend;—one death involves
> Tyrants and slaves, when straight their mangled limbs
> Crushing at once, he dyes the purple seas
> With gore, and riots in the vengeful meal."

No wonder that every man's hand should be raised against this ferocious monster; and although of such fearful strength and audacity, he is sometimes overcome. The natives on the African coast show great courage and dexterity in attacking him. The mouth of the shark being placed in the lower part of the head, he is obliged, in order to seize his prey, to turn round in the water, and the negroes, taking advantage of this, thrust a knife into his stomach, the part where he is most vulnerable, for the skin on the upper portion of the body is so hard and rough that it forms a kind of armour, defending him from the bites of any animals he may encounter in the deep. This skin is even made use of by joiners for polishing hard-grained wood, and it is also employed for other purposes where hardness and strength are required.

An amusing instance of punishing a shark for his greediness was related in the "Edinburgh Observer," some years ago. The author of the article says:

"Looking over the bulwarks of the schooner, I saw one of these watchful monsters winding lazily backwards and forwards like a long meteor; sometimes rising until his nose disturbed the surface, and a gushing sound like a deep breath rose through the breakers; at others resting motionless on the water, as if listening to our voices and thirsting for our blood. As we were watching the motions of this monster, Bruce, a lively little negro and my cook, suggested the possibility of destroying it. This was, briefly, to heat a firebrick in the stove, wrap it up hastily in some old greasy cloth as a sort of disguise, and then to heave it overboard. This was the work of a few minutes, and the effect was triumphant. The monster followed after the hissing prey; we saw it dart at the brick like a flash of lightning, and gorge it *instanter*. The shark rose to the surface almost immediately, and his uneasy motions soon betrayed the success of the manœuvre. His agonies became terrible: the waters appeared as if disturbed by a violent squall, and the spray was driven over the taffrail where we stood, while the gleaming body of the fish repeatedly burst through the dark waves, as if writhing with fierce and terrible convulsions. Sometimes, also, we thought we heard a shrill, bellowing cry, as if indicative of anguish and rage, rising through the gurgling waters. His fury was, however, soon exhausted; in a short time the sounds broke away into distance, and the agitation of the sea subsided. The shark had given himself up to the tides, as unable to struggle against the approach of death, and they were carrying his body unresistingly to the beach."

In the South Sea Islands sharks are caught by means of a log of wood, set afloat with a strong rope attached to it, having a noose at the head. The fish, with his natural impetuosity, gets his head entangled, and floundering about in attempts to escape, becomes tired out, and is then easily dispatched.

Captain Basil Hall gives, in his "Voyages and Travels," an interesting account of the capture of one of these huge monsters. He says:

"The sharp, curved dorsal (the back) fin of an enormous shark was seen rising about six inches above the water, and cutting the glazed surface of the sea by as fine a line as if a sickle had been drawn along it. 'Messenger, run to the cook for a piece of pork,' cried the captain, taking the command with as much glee as if an enemy's cruiser had been in sight. 'Where's your hook, quartermaster?' 'Here, sir, here!' cried the fellow, feeling the point, and declaring it was as sharp as any lady's needle; and at the next instant piercing with it a huge junk of pork, weighing four or five pounds. The hook, which is as large as a little finger, has a curvature about as large as a man's hand when half closed, and is six or eight inches in length, while a formidable line, furnished with three or four feet of chain attached to the end of the mizzen-topsail-halyard, is now cast into the ship's wake.

"Sometimes the very instant the bait is cast over the stern, the shark flies at it with such eagerness that he actually springs partially out of the water. This, however, is rare. On these occasions he gorges the bait, the hook, and a foot or two of the chain, without any mastication, and darts off with the treacherous prize with such prodigious velocity that it makes the rope crack again as soon as the coil is drawn out. Much dexterity is required in the hand which holds the line at this moment. A bungler is apt to be too precipitate, and jerk away the hook before it has got far enough into the shark's maw. The secret of the sport is to let the monster gulp down the whole bait, and then to give the line a violent pull, by which the barbed point buries itself in the coat of the stomach. When the hook is first fixed, it spins out like the log-line of a ship going twelve knots.

"The suddenness of the jerk with which the poor devil is brought up often turns him quite over. No sailor, however, thinks of hauling a shark on board merely by the rope fastened to the hook. To prevent the line breaking, the hook snapping, or the jaw being torn away, a running bowline is adopted. This noose is slipped down the rope, and passed over the monster's head, and is made to join at the point of junction of the tail with the body; and now the first part of the fun is held to be completed. The vanquished enemy is easily drawn up over the taffrail, and flung on deck, to the delight of the crew."

A sight of this voracious monster in his own element is never to be forgotten. It has been observed that the word "villain" has never been written in more unmistakable characters on any living creature than the shark. His appearance exhibits every character of ferocity. The head is large; the mouth wide and grasping; but the teeth, the most appalling features of the animal, are remarkable for their power of mischief: there are six rows in the upper jaw, and four in the lower; the teeth are triangular, sometimes two inches in breadth, sharp-edged, and notched like a saw, and as they are so planted in the jaw that each tooth is capable of independent action, being furnished with its own muscles, and as the strength of the jaws is enormous, they form a most terrific and formidable apparatus of destruction.

Although no part of the shark is wholesome for food, the flesh being coarse and leathery, yet it is eaten by the natives of Guinea, after being kept a sufficient time to render it tender. The fins being gelatinous, are used by the Chinese for making a rich soup. The liver yields an abundance of oil which is much esteemed. I have already mentioned the uses to which the skin is applied.

You will be shocked to hear that on some parts of the African coasts there are human beings so depraved and superstitious as to worship this fearful monster, and who believe that a person swallowed by him is sure to go to heaven. Their mode of adoration is thus: The negroes proceed in their boats to offer sacrifices of goats, poultry, and other things. But far more horrible still is the offering of an infant, reared for the purpose until it attains the age of ten. The poor child is bound to a post on a sandy point at low water; as the tide rises the sharks arrive, and the infant is devoured, the parents fully believing that it will thus enter Paradise. We may well ask ourselves if it is possible to find a more atrocious and dismal proof of human depravity!

"Oh, sad estate
Of human wretchedness! So weak is man—
So ignorant and blind!"

The South Sea Islanders had some strange superstitious ideas relative to some of the shark species. Although they would not only kill, but eat certain sharks, the large blue kind (*Squalus glaucus*) were deified by them; and rather than attempt to destroy them, they would endeavour to propitiate their favour by prayers and offerings. Temples, we are informed by Mr. Ellis, in his "Polynesian Researches," were erected, in which priests officiated, and offerings were presented to the deified monsters; while fishermen and others, who were much at sea, sought their favour. Many funny legends were formerly in circulation among the people relative to the regard paid by the sharks at sea to priests of their temples, whom they were always said to recognize, and never to injure. But for the sharks, the South Sea Islanders would be in comparatively little danger from casualties in their voyages among the islands; and although, when armed, they have been known to attack a shark in the water, yet, when destitute of a knife or other weapon, they become an easy prey, and are consequently much terrified at such merciless antagonists.

Mr. Ellis relates a fearful instance of the rapacity of the shark, when a number of chiefs and people—altogether thirty-two—were passing from one island to another in a large double canoe. They were overtaken by a tempest, the violence of which tore their canoes from the horizontal spars by which they were united. It was in vain for them to endeavour to place them upright, or empty out the water, for they could not prevent their incessant overturning. As their only resource, they collected the scattered spars and boards, and constructed a raft on which they hoped to drift to land. The weight of the whole number who were now collected on the raft was so great as to sink it so far below the surface that they sometimes stood above their knees in water. They made very little progress, and soon became exhausted by fatigue and hunger. In this condition they were attacked by a number of sharks. Destitute of a knife or any other weapon of defence, they fell an easy prey to these monsters. One after another was seized and devoured or carried away by them, and the survivors, who with dreadful anguish beheld their companions thus destroyed, saw the number of assailants apparently increasing as each body was carried away, until only two or three remained. The raft, thus lightened of its load, rose to the surface of the water, and placed them beyond the reach of the voracious jaws of their relentless destroyers. The voyage on which they had set out was only from one of the Society Islands to another, consequently they were not very far from land. The tide and the current now carried them to the shore, where they landed, to tell the melancholy fate of their fellow-voyagers.

The natives of Tahiti use hooks made of wood, and of the most formidable character, for shark fishing. These are a foot in length and an inch in diameter. They are such frightful implements that no fish less voracious than a shark would venture to approach them. In some, the marks of the sharks' teeth are numerous and deep, and show the effect with which they have been used.

One of the most sad and thrilling episodes of shark encounters that I have read was published some years since in a work called "Ward's Miscellany." A small schooner called the "Magpie" was cruising between the island of Cuba and the Havannah, in search of pirates. One evening the sea and the air were so calm that the vessel lay on the bosom of the water like a huge animal asleep, with her head towards the shore. The crew were engaged in telling those marvellous stories which seamen believe, and never fail to narrate to each other in their hours of idleness, for such occasionally visit even the mariner afloat. Lieutenant Smith, the commander, who had been on the look-out for the pirate ship as long as twilight enabled him to do so, laid aside his glass and descended into the cabin. All above, below, and around was now lulled as in slumber, for the laugh and the voice of the story-teller had become silent. Presently the mate of the watch observed a small black cloud resting over the land. The cloud was gradually increasing, and although the mate saw no ground to apprehend danger, he thought it right to communicate the fact to his superior officer, believing that the land breeze was about to set in with unusual strength. Mr. Smith commanded him to keep a sharp look out, and he would join him on deck immediately. A moment after, a squall, as strong as it was sudden, burst from the cloud, and just as Mr. Smith had ascended to the deck, the schooner was upset, and immediately sank.

Two of the crew were below, and they went down with her; the others, twenty-two in number, were left struggling with the quiet deep, for the squall had passed, and the sky and sea were again tranquil. It was now discovered that the boat had drifted from the vessel, and floated. A rush was made towards her, and several of the men attempted to get into her on the same side. The consequence was, that she became half full of water, upset, rolled over and over, and at length lay with her keel upwards. Some got across her keel, others supported themselves by holding on to her with their hands, and thus all were for a time safe.

Mr. Smith now reminded the crew that it was impossible for them to remain long in this predicament, and exhorted them to right the boat and bale the water from her. He was immediately attended to; the men on the keel relinquished their seats, the boat was turned over, and two men were ordered into her to bale out the water. This they commenced doing with their hats, and it seemed probable that by perseverance their task would be accomplished. At this moment a man called out that he saw the fin of a shark. Immediately all was confusion; every one endeavoured to save himself, and in so doing rushed into needless danger. Smith begged them to persevere in attempting to clear the boat of water, and directed those not engaged in baling the water to keep splashing with their legs to frighten away the sharks. Again he was attended to; four men were in the boat baling, and the water was rapidly decreasing, when a noise was heard, and more than a dozen sharks darted in amongst them. In the panic which ensued the boat was again upset, and the men were at the mercy of the marine monsters. At first the sharks played about amongst the men, occasionally rubbing against them; but presently a loud shriek arose from one of them—his leg was bitten from his body! The attack was now general; shrieks arose from one and another. Some were torn from the boat, and several sank into the abyss, either through being bitten or from fear.

In this critical moment Lieutenant Smith was not dismayed.

He still gave orders to the crew firmly and coolly, and was still obeyed by them. The boat was again righted, and the baling again commenced, Smith clinging to the stern while he directed and encouraged his crew. For a moment he ceased to splash, while he looked into the boat to see what progress his men were making. At this instant a shark bit off both his legs above the knees. With fortitude scarcely to be believed, he endeavoured to conceal the fact from his remaining crew, but, in spite of all his efforts to suppress it, a deep groan escaped him; he loosed his hold of the boat and was about to sink, when two of his men caught hold of him and placed him in the stern-sheets. Although bleeding and in agony, he still exerted himself for his crew. He expressed his sorrow for their situation, gave them advice affectionately, yet coolly, and ended with these words: "If any of you survive this fatal night, and return to Jamaica, tell the admiral (Sir Laurence Halsted) that I was in search of the pirate when this lamentable occurrence took place; tell him that I hope I have always done my duty, and that I——" At this instant some of the men endeavoured to get into the boat, which was thus drawn on one side, and Lieutenant Smith rolled overboard, and sank to rise no more. The boat was now again upset. Some of the bleeding seamen placed themselves on the keel, but one by one dropped into the ocean. It was at eight o'clock when the "Magpie" sank, and before nine all on board of her were eaten by the sharks or drowned, with the exception of two, who succeeded in righting the boat and getting into her. They immediately began baling, and worked until they were nearly exhausted. The sharks swam round the boat, and endeavoured to upset her, but failing, and perhaps gorged already, at length departed. The men worked at intervals, until the boat was nearly free from water, and then lay down and slept until after daylight. The morning was fine but sultry. The men were hungry, thirsty, and fatigued: they looked around them; an unbroken ocean, a cloudless sky, and a burning sun were all that were within their view. They began to think of the only resource remaining for either—to kill his comrade and devour his flesh. They were men of equal strength, and both had knives. Each, however, seemed unwilling to resort to this horrible expedient except in the last extremity. The man at the stern (for they had separated from each other, in mutual apprehension, by nearly the whole length of the keel) knelt down and prayed, and his comrade followed his example.

As the morning went on they suffered intensely from thirst, and aggravated their sufferings by attempting to allay it with salt water. The madness of despair was beginning to develop itself in one of them when a sail appeared in sight, which afterwards proved to be a brig steering towards them. One flung his jacket in the air, while the other hailed again and again, and sometimes both hailed together, although the brig was at such a distance that it was not possible their cries would be heard. She approached nearer and nearer, and so rivetted were their minds on the brig that hunger and thirst were forgotten in the excitement of hope. The people on board the ship appeared to notice them, but just as they had reason to think that such was the case, she changed her course and hoisted additional sail. Still they attempted to gain their attention, and attempted to propel the boat with their hands; but all was in vain; the ship was becoming every moment more distant, and their chance of release from such a horrible condition, of course, fainter.

At this moment one of the sailors conceived the bold project of swimming to the brig, which was by this time two miles and a half from them. His comrade remonstrated with him, so wild and hopeless did the undertaking appear to him, especially as the fins of sharks were seen again here and there above the water. After a little hesitation, caused by the appeal of his shipmate, and a short prayer, he jumped over. The splash occasioned by his doing so caused the sharks to disappear, and the man in the boat well knew that they were in search of his comrade. Immediately afterwards, three of them passed the boat towards him.

With the greatest anxiety the sailor in the boat watched his messmate: he swam well, kicking and splashing as he went, to frighten the sharks. Once he beheld one of them close to him; but he only swam the faster, and kicked more vigorously. The wind had freshened, the brig was sailing more fleetly, his cries were unheard by the crew, and he began to think he must yield himself a prey to the sharks. At last he saw a man look over the side of the vessel; he held up both his hands, jumped up in the water, and was at length seen. A boat was got out, the brave swimmer was picked up, and was soon joined by his comrade on board the brig. The sharks were defrauded of their prey. The two survivors of the "Magpie" were tried by a court-martial, and as a reward for their perseverance, industry, and obedience to their commander in circumstances of such peculiar peril, promoted to be warrant officers.

To this family of the *Squalidæ*, or *Sharks*, belongs the *Blue* species, to which I have alluded, and which visits our own coasts during the pilchard and herring fishery, but whose chief residence is the Mediterranean. It is about seven feet long. The whole of the upper parts is of a slate-blue colour, and the under side nearly pure white.

The *Hammer-headed* species are distinguished, as the name implies, from each side of the head being extended—hammer-shaped—into a kind of branch, which has the eyes at the outer extremity. Its habits are of the family character, and it never hesitates to attack man when an opportunity offers. The *Smooth Shark* is so named from the smoothness and softer nature of its skin than its other relations; it is about four feet in length, and is a frequent visitor to the British seas. The *Dog-Fish*, the most common of the minor members of the shark family, will be found noticed in a subsequent chapter on "Fishing." The *Spinous Shark*, so named from its "prickles," which resemble those on the stems of a rose-bush, is not, happily, a frequent visitant to British waters, though of inferior size to most of the family, being from four to eight feet. The *Angel-Fish*, or *Monk-Fish*, or *Shark-Ray*, closes our list of the "ocean pirates." The depressed form, rounded head, with the eyes on the upper surface, and the singularly expansive pectoral fins (which may, under the imaginative form of wings, have originated the designation of "angel") distinguish this strange, and, on the whole, uncouth fish, which partakes something of the character of the ray and the shark. It is not unfrequent on our coasts, and attains a considerable size, some weighing a hundredweight. It is a fierce and dangerous fish to contend with, and fishermen tell strange stories of its strength and fury.

The *Greenland Shark*, which abounds in the Northern seas, although smaller than his powerful relative, being usually about fourteen feet long and six to eight feet in girth, partakes of his ferocity, and is a fearful enemy to the whale, whom he frequently worries to death, and feasts upon afterwards, scooping out pieces from his body as large as a man's head. The blubber appears to be a peculiarly "dainty dish" to this Arctic monster, and while the crew of a ship are employed in cutting up a whale, he will come in for his share, and is so greedy for his favourite food that the men consider themselves safe from his gripe. Insensible to pain and tenacious of life as are all the larger sharks, the Arctic member of this ferocious tribe has been proved to be so in a remarkable degree. A few ugly wounds do not spoil his appetite, and even when pierced through the body with a sailor's knife, he does not desert the whale's carcase until his appetite is fully satisfied. Even when the body is cut into parts, the separate portions continue to show signs of life for some time, and it is unsafe to put the hand into his mouth a good while after the head has been separated from the trunk.

The Greenlanders eat the flesh of this fish both fresh and dried, and twist his rough skin into a kind of rope. This shark is known to have seized a native canoe covered with seal-skin (which was probably the attraction) in his mouth from beneath, and by closing his jaws, destroyed both the canoe and its inmate.

The largest of this terrible tribe, the *Basking Shark*, visits our seas occasionally, though most abundant in the tropics. He has been seen off the coast of Scotland, and taken, from his enormous length, for the "sea-serpent," attaining upwards of fifty feet. One of this size was captured some years ago at Kuraci, at the mouth of the Indus. Happily, however, his voracity is not proportioned to his size, being satisfied chiefly with sea-slugs, small fishes, jelly-fish, &c. Pennant mentions a basking shark twenty-six feet in length, taken off Anglesea, from which one hundred and fifty-six gallons of oil were obtained.

You have, no doubt, often heard of the pilot-fish as a guide and companion to the shark in his pursuit of prey. Whether this pretty fish, which is only about a foot in length, really does befriend and assist the ocean monster is not quite certain, but some accounts give an air of probability to the belief. Stevens, one of the first voyagers to the East Indies (1579—1583), alludes to this circumstance in a fanciful manner. Describing the sharks, he says: "These have waiting on them six or seven small fishes, which never depart, with guards (bands), blue and green, round their bodies, like comely serving-men, and they go two or three before them, and some on every side." Dr. Mayen remarks: "We ourselves have seen three instances in which the shark was led by the pilot. When the former neared the ship, the latter swam close to his snout or near one of his breast-fins; sometimes it darted rapidly forwards or sideways, as if looking for something, and constantly went back again to the shark. When we threw overboard a piece of bacon fastened on a great hook, the shark was about twenty paces from the ship. With the quickness of lightning the pilot came up, smelt at the dainty morsel, and instantly swam back again to the shark, swimming many times around his snout and splashing, as if to give him exact information as to the bacon. The shark now began to put himself in motion, the pilot showing him the way, and in a moment he was fast to the hook."

Dr. Bennett, in his "Gatherings of a Naturalist," says: "I have observed that if several sharks swim together, the pilot-fishes are generally absent; whereas, on a solitary shark being seen, it is equally rare to find it unaccompanied by one or more of these reputed guides. The only method by which I could procure this fish was, that when capturing a shark, I was aware these faithful little fishes would not forsake him until he was taken aboard; therefore, by keeping the shark, when hooked, in the water until he was exhausted, or, as the sailors term it, "drowned," the pilot-fish kept close to the surface of the water over the shark, and, by the aid of a dipping-net fixed to the end of a long stick, I was enabled to secure it with great facility."

The pilot-fish, like the mackerel in shape, has five conspicuous tranverse bands round the body, and the general colour is a silvery greyish-blue. It is common in the Mediterranean and abounds in the warmer parts of the ocean.

The ancients gave to the *whales* the benefit of its services. Oppian says:

> " Bold in the front the little pilot glides,
> Averts each danger, every motion guides;
> With grateful joy the willing whales attend,
> Observe the leader, and revere the friend;
> True to the little chief, obsequious roll,
> And soothe in friendship's charms their savage soul."

Making a pet of a shark seems a monstrous idea, but such was really the case some years ago with one of these animals which frequented Port Royal harbour, in Jamaica. It was called "Old Tom of Port Royal," and was fed whenever it approached the ships, but was at length killed by the father of a child which it had devoured. Whilst the shark frequented the port no other fish of his tribe dared to intrude on his domain, where he reigned lord paramount in his watery empire, and had not been known to commit any depredation, except the one for which he suffered.

I think we may consider this as a rather questionable proof as to what lengths the shark may be trusted for domestication; but we must also look upon this animal with a deprecatory indulgence, for even in its voracity it is fulfilling a wise law of Nature; in fact, it is the "scavenger of the ocean," as well as the "pirate." Nothing seems to be rejected by these creatures: offal of the most offensive kind, living as well as dead matter, is greedily swallowed by them. In this manner they are purifiers of the ocean, and, as the Rev. William Kirby observes, they exercise the same functions that the hyænas and vultures and other animals do on earth.

"Another lesson," says the same reverend instructor, "may be learned from the existence of these terrible monsters; for if God fitted them to devour, He fitted them to instruct. The existence of creatures so evil, and such relentless destroyers of His works in the material world, teach us that there are probably analogous beings in the spiritual world; and what occasion we have for watchfulness to escape their destructive fury!"

## CHAPTER IX.

### SEA-HORSES, NARWAHLS, AND POLAR BEARS.

"There we hunted the walrus, the narwahl, and the seal,
Aha! 't was a noble game!
And like the lightning's flame
Flew our harpoons of steel!"

LONGFELLOW.

ALL the shores and borders of the Arctic zone are crowded with amphibious animals, which appear to form an intermediate link between whales and quadrupeds. Among these I will now notice the *Morse* (derived from the Russian *morss*) or *Walrus* (from the Norwegian *hval-ros*, whale-horse), also called by sailors the Sea-Horse. It is a large, shapeless, unwieldy creature, from twelve to fifteen feet in length and eight to ten feet in circumference; the head small, the limbs short, and of an intermediate character between fins and legs. The eyes are small and brilliant; the nostrils are large, somewhat round, and placed on the upper part of the snout or muzzle. The lips are remarkably thick and covered with bristles. The neck is short. The insides of the paws are protected by a rough horny kind of coating, of a quarter of an inch thick; the fore-paws, or webbed hands, are from two to three feet in length, and, being expansive, can be stretched to a considerable width. The colour varies with age; the young are black, they then become brown, and gradually pale, until in old age the walrus is white. The hairs, thick as a crow-quill, together with the long white tusks and fierce-looking eyes, give the animal a most diabolic look as it raises its head above the waves. Previous to the development of the tusks in the young walrus, the front face, when seen at a little distance, bears a striking resemblance to the human countenance; and this appearance seems to have given rise to the fanciful reports of mermen, or mermaids, in the Northern seas. Captain Scoresby mentions that he has seen a sea-horse in such a position and under such circumstances that it was easy to mistake it for a human being. The surgeon of his ship actually reported to him that he had seen a man's head just appearing above water!

The most remarkable feature of the walrus consists in the two teeth or tusks, which are directed downwards from the upper jaw, and are sometimes nearly two feet in length, diverging at their points, and weighing from five to ten pounds. They are of beautiful white bone, almost equal to ivory, and are much employed in the fabrication of teeth, chessmen, umbrella-handles, whistles, and other small articles. The Greenlanders and other people of the North make hunting weapons from them, and domestic tools. These tusks not only serve the animal in procuring its food—which is said to be shell-fish and marine vegetables—but are formidable weapons against its foes. They also enable the walrus to raise its unwieldy bulk upon the ice, when its access to shore is prevented.

The speed of this animal in the water is very great, and a contrast to its sluggish appearance on the ice. Large numbers of them crowd together on shore, and present a curious spectacle. The moment the first lands, so as to be dry, it will not stir until another comes, and urges it forward by beating it with its great tusks; this one is served in the same manner by the next, and so on in succession, until the whole are landed, tumbling over one another in the operation.

In the voyages of the early navigators in the Arctic seas, they found the walrus, hitherto a partially unmolested animal, easy of capture. In 1606, Stephen Bennet, the captain of the "God-speed," a vessel of sixty tons, writes: "We saw a huge morse putting his head above water, making such a horrible noise and roaring, that they in the boat thought he would have sunk it." In another place they found "a multitude of these monsters of the sea lying like hogs upon an heap." They shot at them in vain until their muskets were spoilt and their powder was spent, when "we would blow their eyes out with a little pease-shot, and then come on the blind side of them, and with our carpenter's axe cleave their heads; but for all that we could do, of about a thousand were killed but fifteen." They filled a hogshead with the loose teeth found on the island. The navigators became more expert in their cruel onslaught upon the poor animals, for in a subsequent voyage the same captain relates that in six hours they slew from seven hundred to eight hundred, not only for the sake of the teeth, but boiling the blubber into oil. They also contrived to get on board two young walruses, male and female; the latter died on the passage, but the other reached England, and was taken to Court, "where the King and many honourable personages beheld it with admiration." It soon, however, fell sick and died.

Captain Cook, who was among the first to give anything like a distinct account of this curious animal, relates in one of his voyages:

"We got entangled with the edge of the ice, on which lay an innumerable multitude of sea-horses. They were lying in herds, huddled one over the other like swine, and were roaring and braying very loud, so that in the night, or in foggy weather, they gave us notice of the vicinity of the ice before we could see it. They were seldom in a hurry to get away until after they had been fired at, when they would tumble over each other into the sea in the utmost confusion. Vast numbers of them would follow us, and come close up to the boats, but the flash of a musket in the pan, or even the bare pointing of one, would send them down in an instant." In another part, Cook mentions the wariness of the animals: "We never found the whole herd asleep, one being always on the watch. This, on the approach of a boat, would rouse the next, and the alarm being gradually communicated, the whole herd would speedily awake."

The walrus is hunted chiefly for its oil and tusks; the natives of the northern shores esteem its flesh highly, and it is greedily eaten along with the lard and even the skin. Mr. Lamont calculates that about a thousand walruses are captured yearly in the seas about Spitzbergen, exclusive of the number which sink or die of their wounds.

Though generally of a peaceful and harmless nature, yet when attacked by foes, and especially by man, these huge animals will defend and support each other with remarkable courage and fidelity, fearlessly proceeding to the rescue of an unfortunate associate, and striving even to death for its deliverance. As early as ,1671, Martens, in his "Voyage to Greenland," relates having killed some sea-horses on the ice; "the rest came all about our boat, and beat holes through the sides of it so that we took in abundance of water, and were forced at length to row away because of their great numbers, for they gathered themselves more and more together, and pursued us, as long as we could perceive them, very furiously."

Parry records a similar incident in his Arctic voyage in the "Fury" and "Hecla." A boat's crew proceeded to attack two hundred of these animals, but they made a most desperate resistance; some of them with their cubs on their backs; and one of them tore open the planks of the boat in two or three places.

Captain Phipps (afterwards Lord Mulgrave) in his expedition to the North Pole in 1773, relates that two officers engaged in an encounter with a walrus, who, on being wounded, plunged into the water, and obtained a reinforcement of its fellows, who made a desperate attack on the boat, wresting an oar from one of the men, and had nearly upset her, when another boat came to her assistance.

The affection of the mother for its young is remarkable. Captain Cook, in his third voyage, says:

"We hoisted out the boats, and sent them in pursuit of the sea-horses that surrounded us. Our people were more successful than they had been before, returning with three large ones and a young one. On the approach of our boats towards the ice, they all took their cubs under their fins, and endeavoured to escape with them into the sea. Several, whose young were killed or wounded, and were left floating on the surface, rose again, and carried them down, sometimes, just as our people were going to take them into the boat, and they might be traced bearing them a great distance through the water, which was coloured with their blood. We afterwards observed them bringing them up at times above the surface, as if for air, and again diving under it with a dreadful bellowing. The female in particular whose young had been destroyed and taken into the boat, became so enraged that she attacked the cutter, and struck her tusks through the bottom of it."

Admiral Beechey also gives his testimony to the same effect:

"In the vast sheet of ice which surrounded the ships there were occasionally many pools, and when the weather was clear and warm, animals of various kinds would frequently rise and sport about in them, or crawl from thence upon the ice to bask in the warmth of the sun. A walrus rose in one of these pools close to the ship, and finding everything quiet, dived down again and brought up its young, which it held to its breast by pressing it with its flipper. In this manner it moved about the pool, keeping in an erect posture, and always directing the face of its young towards the vessel. On the slightest movement on board the mother released her flipper, and pushed the young one under water; but when everything was quiet, again brought it up as before, and for a length of time continued to play about the pool, to the great amusement of the sailors."

Man is not the only assailant of the sea-horse. On land its especial foe is the great Polar bear, and between these animals there are often terrible battles. On these occasions the tusks of the walrus stand in good service, for they manage, usually, to beat off the grizly enemy, though at the cost of many severe wounds.

Beechey gives an amusing instance of the cunning displayed by Bruin in his "inquiries" after the walrus:

"One sunshiny day, one of these animals, about ten feet in length, rose in a pool of water not very far from us, and after looking round, drew his greasy carcase upon the ice, where he rolled about for a time, and at length laid himself down to sleep. A bear which had probably been observing his movements, crawled carefully upon the ice on the opposite side of the pool, and began to roll about also, but apparently more from design than amusement, as he progressively lessened the distance that intervened between him and his prey. The walrus, suspicious of his advances, drew himself up preparatory to a precipitous retreat into the water, in case of a nearer acquaintance with his playful but treacherous visitor. On this the bear became instantly motionless, as if in the act of sleep, but after a time began to lick his paws and clean himself, encroaching occasionally a little more upon his intended prey. But even this artifice did not succeed: the wary walrus was far too cunning to allow himself to be entrapped, and suddenly plunged into the pool, which the bear no sooner observed than he threw off all disguise, rushed towards the spot, and followed him in an instant into the water—where I fear he was as much disappointed in his meal as we were of the pleasure of witnessing a very interesting encounter."

At sea, the sword-fish is the most nimble and fiercest enemy of the walrus. We should scarcely imagine from the uncouth and heavy appearance of this animal that it would exhibit any striking traits of intelligence; but it seems that when young it is not difficult to domesticate. Lamont mentions having seen one about the size of a sheep on board a Norwegian vessel, and the most comical *facsimile* imaginable of an old walrus. It had been taken alive after the harpooning of its mother, and was as playful as a kitten. It was a great favourite with all on board, and the only thing that annoyed it was pulling its whiskers.

Another tusky inhabitant of the Arctic seas is the *Narwahl*, or *Monodon*, or what is popularly called the *Sea-Unicorn*, also an animal of the Mammalian order, about sixteen feet long and eight feet in circumference. In appearance the narwahl resembles a small whale, but with the addition of two long, straight, and pointed tusks, like spears, spirally twisted, directed forwards, and differing in length, the left one being about seven feet and a few inches, and the right seven feet. It frequently happens, however, that only one of these tusks grows, and the other, somehow strangled, remains shut up in the bone like a nut. This will account for the appellation given to the narwahl of the "sea-unicorn." These tusks are of a whiter and harder substance than ivory. The Kings of Denmark possess a magnificent throne in the Castle of Rosenberg made of this material.

In former times, when the origin of the horns of this animal was not well known, they were supposed to possess miraculous powers of healing diseases. The monks, in particular, fostered this delusion, and pretended that every ill under the sun could be removed by their power. The narwahl has no true teeth in either jaw; the mouth is small and the lips are stiff, but it is able to catch and swallow so large a fish as the skate, the breadth of which is nearly three times as much as the width of its own mouth. It seems probable, however, that the horn serves them in this need, the fish being pierced with it, and killed before devoured. It is used, also, in digging sea-plants from the rocks at great depths, in order to drive from their retreats the shrimps and other animals on which the narwahl feeds. The tail is about twenty inches long and four feet broad. It has no dorsal or back fin, but in place of it there is an irregular, sharp, fatty ridge, two inches in height, extending between two and three feet along the back, nearly midway between the snout and the tail. The prevailing colour of the animal is bluish-grey on the back, variegated with numerous dark spots, with paler and more grey marks on a white ground at the sides. In old sea-horses the colour is wholly white, or yellowish-white, with dark grey spots. They are quiet and inoffensive in their habits, and swim with great rapidity. When respiring on the surface of the water, after blowing repeatedly, they frequently lie motionless for several minutes with the back and head just appearing above water. When harpooned, they dive to a considerable depth, and on returning to the surface for respiration, are readily killed in a few minutes with the lance. Near the coast they are always seen in flocks in the severest winters. The Greenlanders drive them with their sledges to fissures in the ice, where they are dispatched. The blubber, enwrapping the whole body, is from two to four inches in thickness.

When a number of sea-horses are together, they divert themselves in gambols, when, their horns appearing above the water, as if brandished about like weapons, have a singular effect, and the clattering noise they produce, with a kind of gurgling sound of the animals themselves, would lead one to suppose that some hostile proceedings were going on; but it is merely a playful movement of instruments which, if aggressively employed, would be dangerous. The force with which the narwahl urges its speed may be conceived by the circumstance that its tusk has been sometimes found driven through the planks of vessels.

I cannot leave this part of my subject without a few observations on the most formidable of Arctic animals, the *Greenland Bear*. Although not amphibious, and therefore not strictly within the scope of my arrangement, yet the White Bear, "the tyrant of the cliffs and snows, uniting the strength of the lion with the untameable fierceness of the hyæna," from its capacity of swimming with great facility and power, may be said to exercise some control over the wide domain of the Northern regions, both in ocean and on land. It exercises these capacities especially in the pursuit of its favourite food, the seals. When these latter animals are floating about on loose drift-ice, the bear tries every art of cunning to get at them. It slips into water about half a mile to leeward of its prey, and swims slowly and silently towards them, keeping very little of its head above water. On approaching the ice on which the seals are lying, the bear slips along unseen under the edge of it until close to the hapless victims, when a jump and a few blows of its tremendous paws generally settles the business.

Every Arctic voyager is aware of the fact that the Polar bears are seen on the ice at a great distance at sea, and quite out of sight of land. Captain Sabine states that he saw one about midway between the north and south shores of Barrow's Straits, which are forty miles apart, though there was no ice to be seen on which it could rest itself.

The appearance of the white bear is clumsy and awkward. It is impatient of heat, and seems to have no other residence but the ice, and as it derives nearly all its sustenance from the sea, that would seem to be its proper situation. It is the only known species which is strictly marine in its habits, and differs from others of its kind by having a flat head and a comparatively long neck. It is entirely carnivorous, and animals of the land and sea, the dead and the living, are alike devoured. The floating carcases of whales and other marine animals form a considerable part of its food.

Cartwright relates an instance of its agility in the water. He saw a Polar bear dive into the water after a salmon and kill it in an instant. On land it moves faster than would be supposed from its appearance; when at full gallop its pace is described as a kind of shuffle as quick as the sharp trot of a horse. The fur is silvery white tinged with yellow, close, short, and even on the neck and head and upper part of the back. The sole of the foot, which is very large, exhibits a striking instance of adaptation of means to an end, for it is almost entirely covered with long hair, securing the animal a firm footing on the ice. The claws are black and much curved, thick and short. The length the white bear attains is from seven to eight feet. It has a most fearful aspect from its eyes being covered with a membrane or web, similar to that with which the eyes of birds are provided. The use of this is to protect the sight from the strong glare of the snow. The sense of smell is very acute, and sailors take advantage of this to entrap the animal within reach by burning a herring. When attacked, it rears itself on the hinder feet, and thus exposes itself to the deadly effects of the spear. The affection between the parent and young of the Polar bear is so great that they will sooner die than desert each other in distress. While the "Carcass" frigate, which went out some years ago to make discoveries in the Northern seas, was locked in the ice, the man at the mast-head one morning signalled that three bears were directing their course to the vessel. They had no doubt been invited by the scent of some blubber of a sea-horse that the crew had killed a few days before, which had been set on fire, and was burning on the ice at the time of their approach. They proved to be a she-bear and her two cubs, but the cubs were nearly as large as the dam. They ran eagerly to the fire, and drew out of the flames part of the flesh of the sea-horse that remained unconsumed, and ate it voraciously. The crew from the ship threw great lumps of the flesh of the sea-horse which they had still remaining upon the ice. These the old bear brought away singly, laid every lump before her cubs as she brought it, and dividing it, gave to each a share, reserving but a small portion to herself. As she was bringing away the last piece, the sailors levelled their muskets at the cubs, and shot them both dead; and in her retreat they wounded the dam, but not mortally. The affectionate concern expressed by the poor beast in the last moments of her expiring young was most touching. Though she was herself dreadfully wounded, and could but just crawl to the place where they lay, she carried the lump of flesh she had brought away, as she had done others before, tore it in pieces, and laid it before them; but when she saw that they refused to eat, she laid her paws first upon one, then upon the other, and endeavoured to raise them up: during this her moans were pitiful. When she found that she could not stir them she went off, and when she had got to some distance looked back and moaned; and that not availing to entice them away, she returned, and smelling around them, began to lick their wounds. She went off a second time as before, and having crawled a few paces, looked again behind her, and for some time stood moaning. Finding at length that they were cold and lifeless, she raised her head towards the ship and uttered a growl of despair, which was answered by a volley of musket-balls, and she fell between her cubs, licking their wounds as she died.

Scoresby, in his "Account of the Arctic Regions," mentions a singular instance of sagacity in a mother-bear, who, with two cubs, was pursued across a field of ice by a party of armed sailors. At first she seemed to urge the young ones to increased speed, by running before them, turning round, and manifesting by a peculiar action and voice her anxiety for their progress; but finding her pursuers gaining upon them, she carried, or pushed, or pitched them alternately forward until she effected their escape. In throwing them before her, the little creatures are said to have placed themselves across her path, to receive the impulse; and when projected some yards in advance, they ran onwards until she overtook them, when they alternately adjusted themselves for a second throw.

It is to this maternal attachment of the bear that the poet James Montgomery alludes, speaking of the Greenlanders going

> "In bands, through snows, the mother-bear to trace,
> Slay with their darts the cubs in her embrace;
> And while she lick'd their bleeding wounds, to brave
> Her deadliest vengeance in her inmost cave."

The white bear can make very little resistance when attacked in the water, unless it can lay hold of the boat's gunwale with its paws, to prevent which the sailors endeavour to chop them off. Commander Inglefield says:

"While working our way amongst the ice, a bear was observed swimming among the loose pieces. A boat was lowered, and I proceeded in pursuit, but Bruin swam hard for his life, and we did not succeed in coming up with him till we were some distance from the ship. A shot I put into him with the Minié rifle rendered him desperate, and he turned upon me, swimming and plunging over the brash ice to get at the boat; but the rifle had been discharged and was not prepared for a second shot, and we had not provided ourselves with an axe, a very necessary weapon, to prevent these brutes from getting into the boat, which they always attempt to do when badly hurt. He came within a single yard, when a Colt's revolver was pulled from my breast coat-pocket, and waiting till his nose nearly touched the muzzle, Bruin lay dead, his head falling between his fore legs, and we quietly towed him alongside."

Scoresby relates an amusing instance of a bear climbing into a boat, and sitting down coolly inside it, while the crew whom it had ejected hung on outside until another boat's crew came up and killed it.

The accounts given by the early navigators in the Northern seas of the size, strength, and ferocity of the Polar bear are appalling, but modern experience has considerably modified such impressions. That the animal when pressed hard will attack a man there is no doubt, and it must be very formidable; but it usually makes off when pursued, or when it cannot attain its object by cunning.

In the second voyage to Greenland, in 1595, of William Barentz, one of the hardiest of the Arctic navigators, there is a curious relation of an encounter with a bear. Some of his crew had landed, and as two of his men were lying together "a greate leane white beare came suddenly stealing out, and caught one of them faste by the necke, who, not knowing what it was that tooke him by the necke, cryed out and sayd, 'Who is it that pulls me so by the necke?' Wherewith the other, that laye not farre from him, lifted up his head to see who it was, and perceiving it to be a monstrous beare, cryed out and sayd, 'Oh, mate, it is a beare!' and therewith rose up and ranne away." The animal is said to have instantly bit his head in two, and sucked out his blood, and upon being attacked by a boat's crew of twenty persons, some with pikes and others with muskets, turned furiously upon the assailants, seized one of the men and tore him in pieces, and the rest ran away. The people on board, perceiving what had happened, went on shore to the number of thirty, and attacked the furious animal. The purser shot it in the head between the eyes, but it still retained a hold of the dead man. At length, on seeing it stagger, the purser and a Scotchman drew out their cutlasses, and struck the bear with such force that the weapons were broken, when one William Geysen felled it to the ground, when they contrived to kill it.

It was in pursuit of a bear in the Northern seas that Nelson, who became "the hero of a hundred fights," displayed when a youth the cool courage for which he was afterwards so much distinguished. He was coxswain to his uncle, Captain Lutwidge, in Lord Mulgrave's expedition to the Arctic regions in 1772. In these high Northern latitudes the nights are sometimes clear, and during one of them, notwithstanding the intense cold, young Nelson was missing. Search was made for him in vain, and it was feared he was lost, when at sunrise he was discovered at a considerable distance on the ice, armed with a musket, in anxious pursuit of an enormous bear. The lock of the gun being injured, the piece would not go off, and he had followed the animal in hopes of tiring it, and being able to attack it with the butt-end. On his return, being reprimanded for leaving the ship without leave, and asked what could possibly have induced him to undertake so rash an action, the young sailor replied, with great simplicity, "I wished to get the skin for my father."

I will conclude my observations on the bear by relating to

you that in the reign of Henry III. a large one was brought to London, and lodged, as a prisoner, but in comfortable quarters, in the Tower, where it was visited as an immense curiosity, you may be sure. Two writs of the monarch I have mentioned are still extant, one of which orders the Sheriff of London to pay fourpence a day "for our white bear in the Tower of London and his keeper;" also "to provide a muzzle and iron chain to hold him when out of the water, and a long and strong rope to hold him when he is fishing in the Thames."

## CHAPTER X.

### MINUTE ANIMAL LIFE IN THE OCEAN.

> "Oh, what an endless work hath he in hand
> Who'd count the sea's abundant progeny;
> Whose fruitful seed far passeth that on land,
> And also them that roam the azure sky,
> So fertile be the floods in generation,
> So vast their numbers, and so numberless their nation."
> SPENSER.

TRUE and just are the words of our great national poet; for, as Humboldt informs us, though the surface of the ocean is less rich in animal and vegetable forms than that of continents, still, when its depths are searched, perhaps no other portion of our planet presents such fulness of organic life. Darwin says that our land forests do not harbour so many animals as the low-wooded regions of the ocean, where the seaweeds, rooted to the shoals, or long branches detached by the force of waves and currents, and swimming free, upborne by air-cells, unfold their delicate foliage. The microscope still further increases our impression of the profusion of organic life which pervades the recesses of the ocean, since throughout its mass we find animal existence, and at depths exceeding the height of our loftiest mountain chains. Here swarm countless hosts of minute animals, which, when attracted to the surface by particular conditions of weather, convert every wave into a crest of light. The abundance of these minute creatures, and of the animal matter supplied by their rapid decomposition is such, that the sea-water itself becomes a nutritious fluid to many of the large inhabitants of the ocean.

Even in the bleak and dreary regions of the Northern world the wintry seas are filled with a profusion of animal life. The smaller species, of which the herring may be taken for an example, are found amidst the depths of the Arctic zone in immense shoals; countless millions of creatures of *Beröe*, a genus of *Acalephæ* (from the Greek, signifying "nettles," so named from the stinging power which many of them possess), of higher organization than the *Medusæ*, or jelly-fish, exist here, with globular or oval bodies of a delicate or jelly-like substance, strengthened by bands which are covered with rows of large *cilia* (a peculiar sort of moving organs resembling microscopic hairs), the motion of which is extremely rapid, and is evidently controlled by the will of the little animal. *Jelly-Fish*, *Zoophytes*, &c., swarm also to such an extent as to convert the surface water in some places almost into a kind of soup, which furnishes food not only to small fish, but to whales and animals of the largest growth. Even the colour of the ocean is influenced by the enormous quantity of the organic life it sustains. The application of the microscope—for by far the most numerous of the animalculæ can only thus be traced—shows them to be the cause of a peculiar tinge observed over a great extent of the Greenland Sea. This colour is olive-green, and the water is dark and dense compared to that which bears the common cerulean hue. The portion of the ocean so distinguished amounts to not less than twenty thousand square miles, and hence the number of animalculæ which that space contains is far beyond human calculation. Scoresby estimated that two square miles only would include 28,888,000,000,000,000; and as such an amount is out of conception, he illustrates it by observing that eighty thousand persons would have been employed since the creation in counting it! This green sea may be considered as the Polar pasture-ground, where whales are always seen in the greatest number. The remarks of the eminent navigator and naturalist I have mentioned, on this subject, are so interesting that I will quote them.

"Nothing," he says, "particularly being observed in this kind of water (the Greenland Sea) to give it the remarkable colour it assumes, I at first imagined that this appearance was derived from the nature of the bottom of the sea; but on observing that the water was imperfectly transparent, insomuch that tongues (points of ice projecting nearly horizontally from a part that is under water) of ice, two or three fathoms under water, could scarcely be discerned, and were sometimes invisible, and that the ice floating in the olive-green sea was often marked about the edges with an orange-yellow stain, I was convinced that it must be occasioned by some yellow substance held in suspension by the water, capable of discolouring the ice, and if so, combining with the natural blue of the ocean so as to produce the peculiar tinge observed. For the purpose of ascertaining the nature of the colouring substance, and submitting it to a future examination, I procured a quantity of snow from a piece of ice that had been washed by the sea, and was greatly discoloured by the deposition of some peculiar substance upon it. A little of this snow dissolved in a wine-glass appeared perfectly cloudy, the water being found to contain a great number of semi-transparent spherical substances, with others resembling small portions of fine hair. On examining the substance with a compound microscope, I was enabled to make the following observations :

"The semi-transparent globules appeared to consist of an animal of the *Medusa* (jelly-fish) kind. It was from one-twentieth to one-thirtieth of an inch in diameter. Its surface was marked with twelve distinct patches of dots of a brownish colour: these dots were disposed in pairs, four pairs, or sixteen pairs, alternately composing one of the patches. The body of the animal was transparent. When the water in which it lay was heated, it emitted a very strong odour, resembling, in some respects, the smell of oysters when thrown on hot coals, but much more offensive. The fibrous or hair-like substances were more easily examined, being of a darker colour. They varied in length from a point to one-tenth of an inch, and when highly magnified, were found to be beautifully shaped."

Some of the calculations of the ingenious and clever Scoresby are very curious and instructive. In a drop of water there were fifty of these animalculæ, on an average, in each square of the micrometer-glass of an eight hundred and fortieth of an inch; and as the drop occupied a circle on a plate of glass containing five hundred and twenty-nine of these squares, there must have been in this single drop of water—taken out of the yellowish-green sea, in a place by no means the most discoloured—about twenty-six thousand four hundred and fifty of these animalculæ! Hence, reckoning sixty drops to a dram, there would be a number in a gallon of water exceeding, by one-half, the population of the whole globe! It gives a wonderful conception of the minuteness and vastness of creation, when we think of more than twenty-six thousand animals—living, obtaining subsistence, and moving perfectly at their ease, without annoyance to one another—*in a single drop of water!*

The diameter of the largest of these animalculæ was only the two-thousandth part of an inch, and many only the four-thousandth. The army which Buonaparte led into Russia in 1812, estimated at five hundred thousand men, would have extended—in a double row, or two men abreast, with two feet three inches space for each couple of men—a distance of one hundred and six and a half English miles; the same number of these animalculæ, arrayed in a similar way in two rows, but touching one another, would only reach *five feet two and a half inches!* A whale requires an ocean to sport in, but about one hundred and fifty millions of these animalculæ would have abundant room in a tumbler of water! What a stupendous idea is thus afforded of the immensity of creation, and of the bounty of Divine Providence, in furnishing such a profusion of life in regions so remote from the habitations of men! Even if we consider the number of animals in a space of two miles square as great, what must be the amount requisite for the discoloration of the sea through an extent of, perhaps, twenty or thirty thousand square miles!

If we turn from the Arctic seas to the warmer regions of the ocean, we find the same wonderful profusion of animal life existing in minute forms of infinite variety: small Mollusca (soft animals inhabiting shells); Crustacea (with articulated limbs and hard coverings), and luminous creatures, as *Salpæ*, of which vast gelatinous shoals are met with at sea, associated in a round mass like a chain, transparent, and of beautiful colours, of which, we are told, that during a journey of nearly eight hundred miles, they were thickly abundant throughout the track of the ship in the ocean. Each portion of the vast masses of floating seaweed consists—when carefully examined—of a little densely populated world, being crowded with living beings, all active and full of bustling animation—strange-shaped little fishes, bright sea-slugs, tiny shells of the nautilus tribe, grotesque sea-spiders, and whole gangs of odd crabs, jelly-fish, and transparent shrimps.

"The number of living creatures of all orders," observes Darwin, "whose existence intimately depends on the kelp (marine plants) is wonderful. A great volume might be written describing the inhabitants of one of these beds of seaweed. Almost all the leaves, excepting those on the surface, are so thickly encrusted with corallines as to be of a white colour. We find exquisitely delicate structures, some inhabited by simple hydra-like *Polypi*, others by more organized kinds and beautiful compound *Ascidiæ* (from the Greek *askos*, a bottle or pouch, these little molluscs resembling sacs everywhere closed, except at two orifices). Innumerable crustacea frequent every part of the plant. On shaking the great entangled roots, a pile of small fish, shells, cuttle-fish, crabs of all orders, sea-eggs, star-fish, and animals of a multitude of forms all fall out together. Often as I recurred to a branch of the kelp, I never failed to discover animals of new and curious structures. I can only compare these great aquatic forests of the Southern Hemisphere with the terrestrial ones in the intertropical regions. Yet if in any country a forest were destroyed, I do not believe nearly so many species of animals would perish as would here from the destruction of the kelp. Amidst the leaves of this plant numerous species of fish live which nowhere else could find food or shelter; with their destruction, the many cormorants and other fishing birds, the otters, seals, and porpoises, would soon perish also."

How elevating is the thought that amidst all this prodigious variety and profusion, the boundless extent of which no human mind can conceive, yet the minutest animated particle that is revealed by the microscope is governed by the same laws that regulate the highest objects in creation!

> "Each moss,
> Each shell, each crawling insect, holds a rank
> Important in the scale of Him who framed
> This scale of beings; holds a rank which, lost,
> Would break the chain, and leave a gap behind,
> Which Nature's self would rue."

Very interesting is the study of those curious inhabitants of the ocean, constituting what are termed by naturalists *Acalephæ*, as I have previously mentioned, but which are more commonly known by such names as jelly-fish, sea-blubber, &c., and are sometimes called sea-nettles, the singular characteristics of which I ought to explain to you a little more fully. Most of them were included in the Linnæan genus Medusa, and the name *Medusæ* is still frequently applied to them. They abound in all parts of the ocean, although some are tropical and others belong to cold latitudes. Some are of a large size, reaching to two feet in diameter, and others are very small. They are of an extremely soft jelly tissue, which in most of them, and in all the true Medusæ, is unsupported by any harder substance. The latter comprise various species that shine with great splendour in the water. The South Atlantic abounds with them, and much amusement may be derived in a long sea voyage by observing these beautiful organisms, for endless are the moulds in which prolific Nature has cast them. Some are shaped like a mushroom, others are like ribbons, or globular, flat, or bell-shaped; others, again, resemble a bunch of berries. Their motions are generally slow, their sensations dull, and directed entirely to the procuring of food. They often float without any apparent animation, trusting in the winds and waves to waft them about, and to carry them their food; some keep a little beneath the surface, and propel themselves by contracting their pellucid disks. They have been termed the "living jellies of the deep," and some are endowed with an acrid secretion, which irritates the skin, and has thus caused them to be termed sea-nettles. The poet Crabbe thus characterizes them :

> "Those living jellies which the flesh inflame,
> Fierce as a nettle, and from that the name;
> Some in huge masses, some that you may bring
> In the small compass of a lady's ring.
>
> Figured by hand Divine—there's not a gem
> Wrought by man's art to be compared to them;
> Soft, brilliant, tender, through the wave they glow,
> And make the moonbeam brighter where they flow."

There is one large species common in the Straits of Singapore, dreaded by the Malays on account of the violence of this power. Mr. Adams, surgeon to H.M.S. "Samarang," mentions, in "Belcher's Narrative," the case of a Malay fisherman who was obliged to have his thumb amputated in consequence of the violent inflammation caused by contact with one of these Medusæ.

Sometimes these animals are colourless, and as transparent as crystal; others are embellished with the most brilliant hues, and seem as if adorned with the richest enamel. Stevens, one of the first voyagers to the East Indies (1579—1583), describes the jellyfish he saw in the Gulf of Guinea as "a thing swimming on the water, like a cock's comb, but the colour much fairer, which comb standeth upon a thing almost like the swimmer of a fish in colour and bigness."

Another curious and widely-distributed class of marine animals are the *Annelides*, or *Sea-Worms* (from the Latin *annulus*, a ring), the bodies being composed of rings and joints. Some species are only met with in the high seas, swimming freely, while most of the others are to be found on the sea-shore, burrowing in the sand or mud, or living under stones, or amidst seaweed. A few construct a sheath or case for themselves, in which they ordinarily live, but which are not essential to the existence of the tenant, as they can leave it without inconvenience, and wander at liberty for their food elsewhere. Their bodies are formed of more or less numerous rings, each of which is furnished with feet, which are the chief organs of motion, and are truly wonderful. They are generally in the form of small tubercles, and for the most part are composed of two branches. Their summit or tip is frequently armed with one or more bundles of bristles, which play an important part in the history of the animals. They form an ornamental appendage to the worm, and at the same time are used as organs of defence and offence. Notwithstanding they live in situations in which they are seldom seen by the human eye, yet in some species these organs have a remarkable degree of brilliancy, shining with a metallic lustre and splendour of the richest kind. The common *Sea-Mouse*, for instance, has a very large bundle of them attached to each foot, which are very fine and of considerable length. Gold, azure, purple, and green play on their surface in a thousand reflections, and these rainbow colours are in perfect harmony with the changing reflections and rings of the body. The wing of the butterfly has not received a more brilliant dress than these worms, concealed at the bottom of the waters, and sometimes buried in black and fœtid mud. As Cuvier says, they are brilliant as gold, and changeable to every hue of the rainbow. The colours they present are not surpassed in beauty by the scale-like feathers of the humming-bird, nor by the most brilliant gems. These bristles, however, are as useful as they are ornamental. Surrounded on every side by enemies, usually dwelling in the waters where the worms live, they require powerful weapons of offence for resistance or for securing their prey.

Some species of these worms are armed with a weapon like a harpoon, a lancet, or a knife. Some have an appendage, falchion-shaped, and others a bayonet fixed upon a musket, while others represent the appearance of a barbed arrow. These weapons are used to pierce the bodies of their enemies, and they frequently leave them in the wounds they have made. The celebrated French naturalist, Milne Edwardes, thus describes the harpoon-shaped bristles: "The tubercles of the feet," he says, "from which the barbed arrow-shaped bristles spring, are, in reality, quivers full of arrows, stored there for the use of the animals to protect them from violence," or as Gosse fancifully observes, "You may imagine you behold the armoury of some belligerent sea-fairy, with stores of arms enough to accoutre a numerous host. If you look closely at the weapons themselves, they rather resemble those we are accustomed to wonder at in missionary museums—the arms of some ingenious but barbarous people from the South Sea Islands, than such as are used in civilized warfare.

The number of such-like weapons in these worms is immense. "Let me ask the naturalist," says Dr. Johnston, "to count the number which may be required to furnish the garniture of a single individual. There are worms which have five hundred feet on each side; each foot has two branches, and each branch has at least one spine and one brush of bristles, some of them simple, some of them compound. This individual has, therefore, two thousand spines at least, and if we reckon ten bristles to each brush, it has also twenty thousand of them! Let us look a little further, not merely to the exquisite finish of each bristle, but to the means by which the host is put in motion. There is a set of muscles to push them forth from their port-holes; there is another to replace each and all of them within their proper cases; and the uncounted crowds of these muscles neither twist nor knot together, but play in their courses, regulated by a will that controls them more effectually than any brace; now spurring them to convulsive energy, now stilling them to rest, and then putting them into action with an ease and grace that charm us into admiration, and fix the belief that even these creeping things participate largely in the happiness diffused throughout creation!"

The *Nereids*, which belong to the same class of sea-worms, have a long body, narrowed towards the inferior extremity, and divided into numerous segments, with well-developed appendages, a head, eyes, horns or feelers, and, in general, a large proboscis, armed with a pair of jaws, curved, hooked, and strong, with teeth on the inner margin. Gosse thus describes the *Pearly Nereis*, which is one of the finest and commonest of the kind: "The upper surface is of a warm fawn brown, but the beautiful flashes of rainbow blue that play on it in the changing light, and the exquisite pearly opalescence of the delicate pink beneath, are so conspicuous as to have secured for it the title of 'pearly' *par excellence.*"

Another species of the group of the Nereids, the "*White-Rag Worm,*" a common inhabitant of the shores of our own country, varying from six to ten inches in length, is of a beautiful pearly lustre, exactly similar to that of mother-of-pearl. The foot, when magnified, resembles a horse's hoof, and is a very marvellous piece of Nature's mechanism. This animal swims rapidly in the sea. Another species is of a rich greenish colour, varied with bluish shades, reflecting a metallic lustre, and varying like the hues of the rainbow.

With the tribe of sea-worms I may also mention the *Sea-Leech* or Skate-sucker, so named because the worm lives on fish, and attaches itself chiefly to the skate, from which it is scarcely ever found free. The mouth of this animal is not provided with jaws, so it sucks up the juices of the body of its host by a kind of pumping process.

The *Leaping-Worms*, found on the coasts of Borneo, are curious creatures. Each step in advance to take them causes them to jump in a rapid manner, and in a series of leaps they reach the margin of the water, when it is impossible to capture them. When lying at rest they are scarcely distinguishable from the mud in which they lie. They are wedge-shape in form, about three or four inches long, with flat pointed tails, and broad heads and prominent eyes. The sailors have nicknamed them "Jumping Johnnies."

Other curious marine objects are the *Pteropods* (from Greek words signifying "wing" and "foot"), active, little, energetic molluscs, common almost in every sea. They are the very butterflies of the deep, and from their extreme vivacity would appear to be possessed of acute sensibilities. Insatiate and greedy, they are ever on the move, spinning, whirling, and diving in every direction.

Such is a brief outline, my young friends, and, I am afraid, very imperfect, of some of the minute animal organisms which are found in countless myriads in the ocean. In other chapters you will find notices of the larger inhabitants of the deep; but how slight is our knowledge, even with the acquirements of modern discovery, to give even a slight insight into the mysteries of creation in the vast abyss of waters!

> "Fish in the sea the circling eddies hide,
> And through the trackless deep unseen they sporting glide;
> And, ah! how great the task! for who can know
> What creatures swarm in secret depths below?
> Unnumbered shoals glide through the cold abyss
> Unseen, and wanton in unenvied bliss.
> For who, with all his skill, can certain teach
> How deep the sea—how far the waters reach?"

The existence of animal life at great depths of the ocean is a subject on which some of the most eminent scientific men of our time have been divided; the general opinion having been that living bodies could not possibly sustain the enormous pressure of the waters. Recent discoveries, however, have shown that such opinions are incorrect, and Dr. Carpenter has been able, by his experiments in deep waters, to prove Dr. Wallich's statement that *temperature* and not depth determines the existence and abundance of deep-sea life.

Sir John Ross published in 1819 an account of sea-worms and other animals which had been brought up from great depths, where no life had been supposed to exist, in the Arctic seas; and about thirty years afterwards his nephew, Sir James C. Ross, made similar discoveries in the Antarctic seas. In 1862 Dr. Wallich published his researches in the Atlantic sea-bed, and the results of his soundings, to a depth of seven thousand five hundred and sixty feet, from which he drew up star-fishes, are very curious. "What," he remarks, "mechanical ingenuity failed to achieve, hunger or curiosity achieved; and thus while the sounding apparatus only succeeded in bringing from this depth a number of minute shell-covered creatures, so simply organized as to render them incapable of perceiving or escaping a danger, thirteen star-fishes, ranging in diameter from two to three inches, came up, convulsively embracing a portion of the sounding-line which had been paid out in excess of the already ascertained depth, and rested for a sufficient time at the bottom to permit their attaching themselves to it. These star-fishes arrived at the surface in a living condition, and, what is more extraordinary, continued to move their long spine-covered rays for more than a quarter of an hour afterwards."

Although this description of animal life does not correctly apply to the "minute" objects which form the subject of my present chapter, I have introduced it to show how this discovery has led the way to the very interesting and valuable researches of Dr. Carpenter and other distinguished scientific explorers. I wish that space permitted me to enter more largely into this most interesting subject. Dr. Carpenter effected his dredgings and soundings between the north of Scotland and the Faroe Islands, and many particulars of his valuable discoveries may be found in his lecture at the Royal Microscopical Society. By sending down into the deep, registering thermometers, he was able to show the existence of a warm and a cold area, the former abounding and the other deficient in living forms. It was remarkable that many of the *Forarminfera* (from the Latin *foramen*, "hole," *fero*, "I bear," the designation of a tribe of minute shells) procured from the deep-sea beds, were not dwarfed—as was formerly supposed must be the case from the pressure and other peculiar conditions; on the contrary, many specimens from the warm space were of unusual dimensions. At upwards of three thousand feet, not only was life abundant, but various, including molluscs, crustacea, &c. In one sounding the sand was composed entirely of animals, which could not exist in multitudes without a considerable supply of food: it is supposed that the deep sea must contain myriads of infusoria (microscopic animals) suitable for their support.

SEA-SOUNDINGS, as you may know, comprehend the means employed to ascertain the depth of water beneath a ship or boat. This is essential to discover shoals, or sunken rocks, or when approaching a shore. It was formerly the practice to use for this purpose silken threads twisted together, or the lead and line. What is nautically termed "throwing the lead," is performed by a man standing in the ship's chains. The lead has a cup-like hollow on the lower surface, to which a lump of tallow is attached; and in tolerably shallow water, the seaman sounds with a line of from sixty to one hundred and eighty feet in length, which is marked, at distances of twelve or eighteen feet, by pieces of cloth of different colours. The particles of mud, sand, and shell (if there are any at the bottom) adhere to the tallow, and are brought up with it; by which, not only the depth of water is ascertained by the length of line run out, but the nature of the bottom of the ocean is made out, whether rocky or otherwise. But (as Professor Ansted informs us) this method is only adapted for small depths (within six hundred feet), and improved methods have been adopted of late, by which depths of from two to three thousand feet could be, with tolerable accuracy, determined. The American sounding apparatus of Lieutenant Brooke is now generally employed with great success to obtain proof not only of the depths of the ocean, but the nature of its bottom, even where the distance to be traversed is greater (observes Professor Ansted) than the loftiest peak of the Himalayans, or the Andes, above the sea-level.

The apparatus is a light thin framework, containing a cup and valve for catching and holding the mud or sand of the bottom; and to this is attached a heavy sinker, in such a way, that while perfectly safe to carry down the line, it becomes detached and is got rid of the instant the bottom is reached. There is, therefore, nothing to bring up but the line itself, and the few pounds' weight of framework, with the matters from the bottom of the ocean; and nothing is lost but the sinker—an iron ball of sufficient weight for the purpose. A modification of this apparatus has been made for the use of the British navy, which ensures greater success, and by this means a large number of deep soundings have been made in various parts of the Atlantic, and also in the Indian and Pacific Oceans.

It is to be hoped that with these means of testing accurately the depths of the ocean, new light will be thrown upon its hidden recesses and its animated recluses; and that science will be enabled to pierce

"The dark, unknown, mysterious caves
And secret haunts—
Beneath all visible retired."

## CHAPTER XI.

### THE ROCK-BUILDERS OF THE OCEAN.

" Toil on! toil on! ye ephemeral train,
Who build in the tossing and treacherous main;
Toil on! for the wisdom of man ye mock
With your sand-based structures and domes of rock.
Your columns the fathomless fountains lave,
And your arches spring to the crested wave;
Ye 're a puny race thus boldly to rear
A fabric so vast in a realm so drear!

Ye bind the deep with your secret zone;
The ocean is sealed, and the surge a stone;
Fresh wreaths from the coral pavements spring,
Like the terraced pride of Assyria's king.
The turf looks green where the breakers roll'd;
O'er the whirlpool ripens the rind of gold;
The sea-snatched isle is the home of men,
And mountains exult where the wave hath been."

Mrs. SIGOURNEY.

ONE of the most conspicuous wonders of the vast ocean is CORAL, that most beautiful and precious of its productions, which you have no doubt often remarked, without thinking of the cause of its formation and the extraordinary results to which it gives rise.

No art can imitate the delicate tracery, the rich colour, and the singular forms that coral assumes. It has been called by some writers "The Queen of the Ocean," and no term could be more appropriate. Ehrenberg, the celebrated naturalist, on viewing the coral-beds of the Red Sea, exclaimed, "Where is the Paradise of flowers that can rival such variety and beauty?"

Mr. J. Beete Jukes records his own vivid impressions on seeing some coral-beds in the Pacific:

"I had," he says, "hitherto been rather disappointed by the aspect of the coral reefs, so far as beauty was concerned; and, though very wonderful, I had not seen in them much to admire. One day, however, on the lee side of one of the outer reefs, I had reason to change my opinion. In a small bight (a little bay between two points of land) of the inner edge of the reef was a sheltered nook, where the extreme slope was well exposed, and where every coral was in full life and luxuriance."

Mr. Jukes describes them as of every shape: some delicate and leaf-like; others with large branching stems; and others, again, exhibiting an assemblage of interlacing twigs of the most delicate and exquisite workmanship. Their colours were unrivalled, vivid greens contrasting with more sober browns and yellows, mingled with rich shades of purple, from pale pink to deep blue. Among the branches, covered with their beautiful drapery of ocean vegetation, floated fish of various colours, radiant with metallic green or crimson, or fantastically banded with yellow and black stripes. Patches of clear white sand were seen here and there, for the floor, with dark hollows and recesses. All these, seen through the clear crystal water, the ripple of which gave motion and quick play of light and shadow to the whole, formed a scene of rarest beauty, and left nothing to be desired by the eye, either in elegance of form or brilliancy and harmony of colouring.

I must tell you, however, that it is only in the ocean the glorious homes of the rock-builders are to be seen in perfection, for, immediately after drawing the coral from the water, so rapidly does atmospheric exposure affect them, that it would be difficult to recognize the lovely objects which a moment before were glowing in the still waters.

> "Under spar-enchased bowers
> Bending on their twisted stems,
> Glow the myriad ocean-flowers,
> Fadeless—rich as Orient gems;
> Hung with seaweed's tasselled fringes,
> Dyed with all the rainbow's tinges,
> Rise the Triton's palace walls.
> Pallid silver's wand'ring veins
> Streams like frost-work o'er the stains;
> Pavements thick with golden grains
> Twinkle through their crystal halls."

Such are the grand and mysterious operations of Providence in the depths of the ocean! I will now describe to you the singular animals to whom the accomplishment of these marvels is due; but I must first mention that coral was formerly supposed to be a marine plant. This ancient notion rested not merely on its shrublike form, but from the circumstance that its branches are covered with a soft coating while in the water, but which dries up immediately on its extraction. Marsilli, an Italian naturalist, perceived in 1707 small objects in the coral-cells, which he thought were flowers; but at length Peyssonnel, a French physician at Marseilles, discovered in 1727 that there was life in the coral, and that these assumed flowers were in reality minute animals. Thus, by the aid of the microscope, an object which might be said to belong to mineralogy, and by its trunk and branches to botany, was now admitted to a rank in the animal world. This discovery of Peyssonnel, the result of thirty years' studious research into the nature of coral, was laughed at by many persons at the time and treated as absurd, but Linnæus, the great Swedish naturalist, saw the truth at once, and did not hesitate to place coral at the head of the zoophytes, or animal plants, an appropriate designation, because it indicates at the same time the double nature of the substances.

A common characteristic of these animals is that their mouths are surrounded by radiating tentacles or feelers, appendages by which they attach themselves to surrounding objects, arranged somewhat like the rays of a flower. By this you will understand the term *polypi*, by which these animals are also known, from the

Greek words *polus*, "many," and *pous*, "foot." Of these the individuals of a few families are separate and perfect in themselves, but the greater number of zoophytes are compound beings, or, as I may better explain myself, each zoophyte consists of an indefinite number of individuals, or polyps, connected together.

Now, this polyp is an extraordinary creature, and has a tenacity of life truly remarkable. If you cut off the branch of a tree, or sever the limb of an animal, these parts will wither and decompose by passing into other parts of matter. If you cut a tree carelessly, its natural symmetry is disfigured; if you slit it down its centre, it is destroyed. Animals thus treated die, with the exception of the polyp, for it will put forth new limbs, form a new head or tail, and, if divided, become two separate existences.

"If," remarks M. Trembley, who was a close observer of these animals, "a polyp be cut in two, the fore part, which contains the head and mouth and arms, lengthens itself, creeps, and eats on the same day. The tail part forms a new head and mouth; at the wounded end shoot forth arms; if turned inside out, the parts at once accommodate themselves to these new conditions. If the body were cut into ten pieces, every portion would become a new perfect living animal. A polyp has been cut lengthways at seven in the morning, and in eight hours afterwards each part has devoured a worm as long as itself! How astonishing it is to see a creature so apparently frail in structure, possessing the actions, sensations, and powers of higher organized beings! The stomach is without membrane or cell; the outside surface-cells form a kind of double skin, and the inside consist of a wall of cells running crosswise, with a velvet-like surface, being red or brown grains held together by a sort of gluey substance."

And now let us see how these minute builders of the ocean rocks make their habitations, and form the wonderful coral groves and islands—sometimes hundreds of miles in extent—that we read of.

The various species of these animals appear to be furnished with glands (a set of bodies employed to form or to alter the different liquids in the animal body) containing gluten (the basis of glue), converting the carbonate of lime which is in the ocean, and other earthy matters, into a fixed and hard substance, twisted—as you observe in coral—in every variety of shape.

If you examine a piece of coral with the microscope, you will see that it is covered with a multitude of small pits, which are cells of the most beautiful construction, made with the greatest regularity, and in such a manner that the most experienced builder would pronounce faultless. How this is effected and what peculiar instincts the little toilers of the ocean possess that enable them to construct their dwellings with such mathematical nicety are among those mysteries of Nature we cannot comprehend; but it is certain that large masses of solid rock are framed by these animals, ever working to the music of the waves. "Verily," observes Baker, "for my own part, the more I look into Nature's works, the sooner I am inclined to believe of her even those things that seem incredible." But here we have the *certainty* of Nature's operations: we know that islands and continents are constructed for the habitation of man by these minute animals; that mountains like the Apennines, and regions to which our own country is but trifling in comparison, are the results of their toil. Dr. Mantell remarks, that south-west of Malabar there is a chain of reefs and islets of coral extending four hundred and eighty geographical miles; on the east side of New Holland are unbroken reefs of three hundred and fifty miles long; and between that and New Guinea a coral formation of seven hundred miles in length.

The process by which these great changes are effected is still going on extensively in the Pacific and Indian Seas, where multitudes of coral islands emerge from the waves, and shoals and reefs, where the rock-builders are ever busy, appear at small depths beneath the water.

How truly wonderful it is to know that the Polynesian Archipelago, now one of the great divisions of the globe, has its foundations formed of coral reefs, the spontaneous growth of once living animals! As one generation of the coral-builders dies and leaves its chalky remains, another succeeds, until the mass of coral appears above the ocean, when the formation ceases, for it is only in that element the labourers can live.

> "Ye build! ye build! but ye enter not in,
> Like the tribes whom the desert devoured in their sin;
> From the land of promise ye fade and die,
> Ere its verdure gleams on your wearied eye."

One marvel ceases here, and another commences. "The vegetation of the sea, cast on its surface, undergoes a chemical change; the rains assist in filling up the little cells of the dead animals; the fowls of the air and the ocean find a resting-place, and assist in clothing the rocks; mosses carpet the surface; seed brought by birds, plants carried by the oceanic current, animalculæ floating in the air live, propagate, and die, and are succeeded through the assistance their remains bestow by more advanced animal and vegetable life; and thus generation after generation exist and perish, until at length the coral island becomes a Paradise, filled with the choicest exotics, the most beautiful birds, and delicious fruits."

Here is a glowing theme for the imagination to dwell upon! How wonderful to think that the surface of the globe is being changed by these diminutive living agents; that in tropical climates they are encircling islands with belts of coral, enlarging their coasts, forming stupendous reefs, and working out the plans and the will of the great Architect of the Universe!

"We feel surprised," observes Mr. Darwin, in his "Journal of Researches," "when travellers tell us of the vast dimensions of the Pyramids and other great ruins; but how utterly insignificant are the greatest of these when compared to the mountains of stone accumulated by the agency of various minute and tender animals!"

> "Millions of millions thus from age to age,
> With simplest skill and toil unweariable,
> No moment and no movement unimprov'd,
> Laid line on line, on terrace terrace spread,
> To swell the heightening, brightening, gradual mound,
> By marvellous structure climbing towards the day."

## CHAPTER XII.

### *PERILS OF THE CORAL REEFS.*

> " Five hundred souls, in one instant of dread,
>   Are hurried o'er the deck;
> And fast the miserable ship
>   Becomes a hapless wreck.
> Her keel hath struck on a hidden rock,
>   Her planks are torn asunder,
> And down comes her mast with a reeling shock,
>   And a hideous crash like thunder.
> Her sails are draggled in the brine
>   That gladden'd late the skies,
> And her flag that kiss'd the fair moonshine,
>   Down many a fathom lies."
>
> WILSON.

THE vast coral reefs, which have been described in the preceding chapter, are often the source of great dangers to navigators; and numberless instances have occurred of entire or partial destruction of ships and heavy losses of life in consequence. One case, that happened some years ago in the Indian Seas, nearly proved fatal to the whole crew of a fine large ship called the "Cabalve." The story of this shipwreck, as related in a letter to a friend by one of the surviving officers, is deeply interesting. The vessel was bound for Bombay, and was proceeding on its way at a quick rate, with every feeling of security in those on board, when one morning, between four and five o'clock (the weather being dark and cloudy), an alarm was given of "breakers ahead!" Every effort was instantly made to free the vessel from her dangerous position, but in vain, for she struck on the coral reef, and the shock was so violent that every person was instantly on deck, with horror and amazement depicted upon every countenance at what appeared to be certain destruction. The vessel soon became fixed on the coral reef, and the sea broke over her with tremendous violence, staving in the exposed side, washing through the hatchways, and tearing up the decks.

"We were now," observes the officer alluded to, "uncertain of our distance from a place of safety: the surf broke over the vessel in a fearful cascade; the crew despairing and clinging to her sides to avoid its violence, while the ship was breaking up with a rapidity and crashing noise, which, added to the roar of the breakers, drowned the voices of the officers. The masts were cut away to ease the ship, and the cutter cleared and launched in readiness. When the long-wished-for dawn at length broke upon us, instead of alleviating, it rather added to our distress. We found that the ship had run on the south-east extremity of a coral reef, surrounding on the eastern side those sand-banks or islands in the Indian Ocean, called by the natives Carajos: the nearest of these was about three miles distant, but not the least appearance of verdure could be discovered, or the slightest trace of anything on which we might hope to subsist. In two or three places some rocks in the shape of pyramids appeared above the rest like distant sails, and were repeatedly cheered as such by the crew, until it was perceived that they had no motion, and the delusion vanished. The masts had fallen towards the reef, the ship having fortunately canted in that direction, and the boat was therefore protected in some measure from the surf. Our commander, whom a strong sense of misfortune had entirely deprived of presence of mind, was earnestly requested to get into the boat, but he would not, thinking it unsafe. He maintained his station on the mizzen-topmast that lay among the wreck, the surf which was rushing round the bow and stern continually overwhelming him. I was myself close to him on the same spar, and in this situation we saw many of our shipmates meet an untimely end, being either dashed against the rocks or swept away by the breakers.

"The large cutter full of officers and men now cleared a passage through the mass of wreck, and being furnished with oars, watched the proper moment and pushed off for the coral reef, which she fortunately gained in safety, but they were all washed out of her in an instant by a tremendous surf; yet out of more than sixty persons whom she contained, only one man was drowned. Our captain, seeing this, wished he had taken advice which was now of no use. Finding I could not longer maintain myself on the same spar, and seeing the captain in a very exhausted state, I entreated him to return to the wreck; but he replied that since we must all inevitably perish, I should not think of him, but seek my own preservation. An enormous breaker now burst on us with tremendous violence, so that I scarcely noticed what had occurred to him afterwards, being washed down by successive seas.

"At length, after most desperate efforts, I was thrown on the reef, half drowned and severely cut by the sharp coral, when I silently offered up thanks for my preservation, and crawling up the reef, waved my hand to encourage those who remained behind to make an effort. The captain, however, was not to be seen, and most of the others had returned to the wreck, and were employed in getting the small cutter into the water, which they accomplished, and safely reached the shore. About noon, when we had all left the ship, she was entirely broken up. The whole of the upper works—from the after-part of the forecastle to the break of the poop-deck—had separated, and was driving in towards the reef. Most of the lighter cargo had floated out of her: bales of cloth, cases of wine, puncheons of spirits, barrels of gunpowder, hogsheads of beer, and other articles, lay strewed on the shore, together with a chest of tools. Finding the men beginning to commit the usual excesses, we stove in the heads of the spirit-casks to prevent mischief, and endeavoured to direct their attention to the general benefit. The tide was flowing fast, and we saw that the reef must soon be covered; we therefore conveyed the boats to a place of safety, and filling them with all the provisions that could be collected, proceeded to the highest sand-bank, as the only place which held out the remotest chance of safety.

"Our progress was attended with the most excruciating pain I ever endured, my feet being cut to the bones with the rocks, and my back blistered by the sun, exhausted by fatigue, up to the waist —sometimes to the neck—in water, and being obliged frequently to swim. Seeing, however, that several had reached the highest sandbank, lighted a fire, and were employed in erecting a tent from the cloth and small spars which had floated up, I felt my spirits revived, and had strength sufficient to reach the desired spot, when I was invited to partake of a shark which had just been caught by the people. Having set a watch to announce the approach of the sea, lest it should cover us unawares, I sank exhausted on the sand, and fell into a sound sleep. I awoke in the morning, stiff with the exertions of the previous day, yet feeling grateful to Providence that I was still alive.

"The people now collected together to ascertain who of the crew had perished, when sixteen were missing: the captain, surgeon's assistant, and fourteen seamen. We divided our men into parties, each headed by an officer: some were sent to the wreck and along the beach in search of provisions, others to roll up the hogsheads of beer and butts of water that had floated on shore; but the greater number were employed in hauling the two cutters up, which the carpenters were directed to repair.

"By the time it was dark we had collected about eighty pieces of salt pork, ten hogsheads of beer, three butts of water, several bottles of wine, and many articles of use and value, particularly three sextants and a quadrant. Four live pigs and five live sheep had managed to swim ashore through the surf. We first began upon the dead stock, serving out two ounces to each, and half a pint of beer for the day. Nothing but brackish water could be obtained by digging in the sand. We collected all the provisions together near the tent, and formed a store-house, setting an officer to guard them from plunder, to which, indeed, some of the evil characters were disposed, but as they were threatened with instant death if detected, they were soon deterred. The second night was passed like the first, all being huddled together under one large tent; the more robust, however, soon began to make separate tents for themselves, and divided into messes as on board. A staff was next erected, and a red flag hoisted upon it as a signal to any vessel that might be passing. Of fish there was a great variety, but we had few facilities for catching them; so that, upon the whole, we were nearly half starved. The bank on which we lived was about two miles in circumference at low water; the high tides would sometimes leave us scarcely half a mile of sand, and often approached close to the tents; and if the wind had blown from the westward, or shifted only a few points, we must have been inevitably swept away. Providence was, however, pleased to preserve us, one hundred and twenty in number, to return to our native country. In seven days after our stay upon the barren coral reef, the largest boat was repaired, and the officers thought it advisable to dispatch her for relief to the Isle of France, distant about four hundred miles. The superior officers, finding it impossible to leave the crew, gave the charge of her to the purser. We furnished him with two sextants, a navigation book, sails, oars, and log-line. Six officers and eight men, who perfectly understood the management of the boat, joined him. In four days from leaving the coral reef the cutter reached Mauritius, and three days after the purser returned by the Government vessels the 'Magician' and 'Challenger.' We were taken on board, after having passed sixteen days on the reef, exposed to the greatest distress of body and mind."

Such is a graphic account of a fearful shipwreck on a barren coral reef, from one of the survivors among the crew. You can thus form an idea of the dangers to which seamen are exposed by these colossal works of tiny polyps:

>"For often the dauntless mariner knows
>  That he must sink beneath,
> Where the diamond on trees of coral grows
>  In the emerald halls of death."

## CHAPTER XIII.

### INSTINCT OF THE ROCK-BUILDERS—CORAL FISHERIES.

" Who taught the natives of the field and wood
To shun their poison or to choose their food?
Prescient, the tides and tempests to withstand,
Build on the wave, or arch beneath the sand?"

POPE.

 MUST not omit to tell you that these living atoms, the rock-builders of the ocean, exhibit a wonderful instinct in the construction of their dwellings. To protect these from the violent storms by which the waters of the deep are frequently agitated, they erect a breastwork, which effectually shields them from wind and wave. In the early stages of their operations they work perpendicularly, so that the highest part of the coral wall on reaching the surface is on the windward side, and affords a protection to the busy labourers in their operations. You will be surprised when I inform you that these breastworks, or breakwaters, will resist more powerful seas than if formed of granite, rising as they do frequently from a depth of a thousand or fifteen hundred feet, and adapted in a way that no human skill or foresight could equal to the utmost powers of the heavy billows that continually lash against them.

How wonderful is this instinct and design of self-preservation in insects so exceedingly minute as the coral-workers!

Another observation I may make on this subject is, that in one species a remarkable arrangement is found: the upper openings of the cells in which they live have a vase-like form, shutting with a lid: when the animal wishes to expand itself, it opens the lid like a trap-door, and protrudes itself; and when it re-contracts itself and retreats, the lid falls, and closes the aperture so exactly that the animal is perfectly protected.

The common Red Coral which is used for many ornamental purposes, and is so much admired for its fine colour, is chiefly obtained from the Mediterranean, in some parts of which extensive "fisheries" are carried on. It is brought up from the depths of the sea by means of a kind of grappling apparatus dragged after a boat, the pieces being broken from the bottom by beams of wood which are sunk by weights, and then entangled among hemp. Great care is necessary to preserve the pieces from being lacerated. Red coral has a shrub-like branching form, and grows to the height of about a foot, with the thickness of a little finger. Much of the coral obtained from the Mediterranean is sent to India, where it is much prized by the natives. Many of the arms and horse-caparisons of the Oriental chiefs are studded with this beautiful ornament.

Red coral is also found in the Red Sea, the Persian Gulf, Messina, the Dardanelles, and a few other places. The French and the Sicilians are the only people who make coral-fishing a regular source of interest. As this precious substance requires eight or ten years to come to any perfection by the labours of its industrious architects, the spots where it is fished are divided each into ten portions, and only one of these is fished in the year, so that each may remain to "grow" during the time necessary to bring it to maturity.

Black Coral is most esteemed, but it is scarce: the red, white, and yellow are chiefly used for ornamental purposes, and for a particular plaything, which probably may have amused you when an infant and cutting your teeth. The Pink Coral is esteemed for its scarcity.

The ingenuity of man continually exerted to imitate nature, and frequently with great success, is practised in the fabrication of false coral, made with powdered marble and fish-glue, and coloured with vermilion and red lead.

You will not be surprised to hear, considering its beauty and rarity, that coral was formerly supposed to possess some singular qualities. It was applied to stop bleeding, and Ovid tells us the reason for this belief, and, indeed, how red coral originated. The story will make you smile and wonder how such nonsense could be believed. Perseus, one of the heroes in the mythology of Greece, having cut off the head of Medusa, the only one of the Gorgons who was subject to mortality, laid it on a tuft of growing plants on the sea-side, which, imbibing the blood, became red and petrified. The sea-nymphs marvelled much (as well they might) at the transformation, and amused themselves by breaking off fragments and casting them into the sea. Each piece so thrown became, it is said, the seed of fresh coral.

The ancients considered this ocean treasure as a charm against the sting of a scorpion. Thus Orpheus says:

"The coral, too, in Perseus' story named,
Against the scorpion is of might proclaimed."

Coral beads were anciently worn in India as sacred amulets or charms. The Romans tied little branches round childrens' necks to keep off the influence of the "evil eye," a superstition which had also many believers in the middle ages among our own countrymen, and which still exists in some foreign countries.

Coral was said to preserve houses from the effects of thunderstorms, and to be of much finer colour when worn by men than by women. Even at the present time there are people so credulous as to believe that coral necklaces become pale when the wearer is about to be ill. There is no doubt that coral loses its colour by time and exposure, and this may have given rise to this superstition. The small pointed branches, mounted with a ring at one end for suspension, are extensively manufactured at Naples as "charms;" and Ferdinand I., King of that country, a most bigoted monarch, was a devout believer in their efficacy, and used to point the coral towards any one whom he suspected of having a malicious influence.

Such, my young friends, is a brief, yet, I trust, not uninteresting account of what is essentially one of the "wonders of the ocean," and yet but an atom in a multitude of marvels that no tongue can number and no imagination can conceive: an imprint of Almighty Power—

" One Spirit,—His
Who wore the plaited thorns with bleeding brows,—
Rules universal nature."

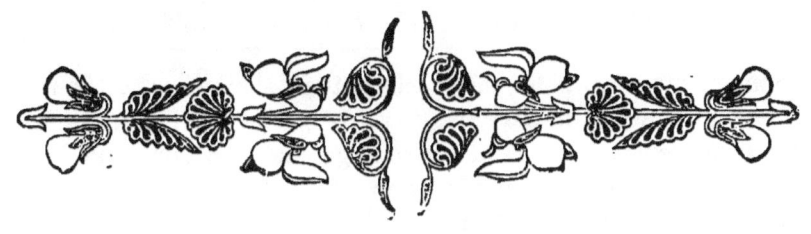

## CHAPTER XIV.

### *PEARLS.*

"Ocean's gems, the purest
Of Nature's works! What days of weary journeyings,
What sleepless nights, what toils on land and sea,
Are borne by men to gain thee!"

AMONG the rare and beautiful objects of creation may be mentioned PEARLS, which rank with the most valuable of precious gems, and are highly prized as ornamental appendages by the rich and the noble in all countries.

While admiring these jewels, you may not know, perhaps, at what perils and cost of life they are obtained, for it is necessary to seek for them in the depths of the ocean, and although the divers employed for this purpose are very strong and expert, still in the Indian Sea and the Eastern Archipelago, where the true pearl-oysters are found, sharks are numerous, and it is necessary to take every precaution against those voracious monsters. This occupation was formerly considered so dangerous that only condemned criminals were thus employed, but many thousand persons now obtain a livelihood by these means in the Persian Gulf and at Ceylon. At one time, when the Dutch had possession of this beautiful island, the number of large pearls obtained there was considerable.

These pearl-divers are a hardy race of men, singularly adapted to their hazardous occupation, and very superstitious; for before commencing operations, they consult the "shark-charmer," a wiseacre who pretends to have the power of preserving his dupes from the angry jaws of the great sea-scourge, and makes a good living by it, the office being handed down from father to son as hereditary. The divers have such confidence in their powers, or spells, that they will not descend to the bottom of the deep without knowing that one of the enchanters is present in the expedition. Two of the "charmers" are constantly employed, one going out regularly in the head pilot's boat, while the other performs certain ceremonies on shore, such as consulting the auguries, which, if auspicious, ensure the divers in their perilous submarine occupations by closing the mouths of the sharks at the word of command. The "charmer" is shut up in a room where nobody can see him, from the period of the sailing of the boats until their return. He has before him a brass basin filled with water, containing one male and one female fish made of silver. If any accident should happen from a shark at sea, it is believed that one of these fishes is seen to bite the other. The divers also say that if the conjuror is dissatisfied, he has the power of making the sharks attack them, on which account he is sure of receiving liberal presents daily.

The Gulf of Manaar, where the pearls are found (and which separates Ceylon from the continent of India on the north-west), abounds in sharks; and, however the divers may consider their lives "charmed," the risks are lessened by the sea-monsters being alarmed at the unusual number of boats, the noise of the crews, and the constant descending of the baskets for the shells. It is not improbable that the dark skins of the divers are also some protection. It seems that the pearl-divers in the Persian Gulf in former times were so conscious of this advantage of colour, that they were accustomed to blacken their limbs in order to baffle their powerful enemy. This is related by Massoudi, one of the earliest of Arabian geographers, who adds, "that the divers filled their ears with cotton steeped in oil, and compressed their nostrils with a piece of tortoise-shell."

The pearl fishery of the Bahrem Islands (in the Persian Gulf) produces a most abundant supply of these ocean gems, the produce of a two months' season sometimes realizing nearly one hundred thousand pounds of our money. Persians are chiefly engaged in this pursuit, and the divers belong to that nation.

The method pursued by the Cingalese divers is very simple. They proceed in boats to the place of operation at the season, which lasts about two months, commencing in February and ending in April. Each boat contains about twenty men, half of whom are divers, while the others row the boats, and assist their companions in reaching the surface of the water after diving. Five of the divers descend at the time, and when they come up, the other five take their turn; for I should tell you that the fatigue and exhaustion of the body is very great in continuing under water; and a minute—in some cases a minute and a half or nearly two minutes—is about the utmost time these men can sustain their breath. Many divers suffer severely from over-taxing their powers of endurance, and bloodshot eyes and spitting of blood are common to them. It is to be hoped that the modern improvements in diving-bells and suitable apparatus for divers will be much more generally adopted than they have been in a few places, that life may be rendered more secure, and other distressing consequences be obviated.

To facilitate the descent of the diver into the water, a stone weighing about twenty pounds is suspended over the side of the boat, with a loop attached to it, in which he inserts his foot; a bag of network is attached to his toes; his right hand grasps the rope, and after inhaling a full breath, he presses his nostrils with his left hand. He now raises his body as high as possible above the water to give force to his descent, and liberating the stone from its fastenings, he sinks rapidly below the surface. As soon as he reaches the bottom, the stone is drawn up, and the diver, throwing himself on his face, collects into his bag as many oysters as he can. This, on a signal, is hauled to the surface, the diver springing to the rope as it is drawn up. The sea, at the oyster-beds, is generally from twenty-four to sixty feet deep. The number of oysters thus collected varies: sometimes several thousand are obtained in one day, and at other times a few hundred only.

The oysters are landed from the boats, and are placed underground to putrefy, and it is amidst such a mass of corruption that the pearl, *"Purest of Nature's works,"* is obtained.

The pearl-fishers in ancient times used to place the shells in vessels filled with salt, and leave them until all the fish were dissolved, the gems remaining at the bottom. The ordinary operation now is, that as soon as putrefaction is sufficiently advanced, the oysters are placed in a trough, and sea-water is thrown over them. They are then shaken and washed. Inspectors stand at each end of the trough, to see that the labourers secrete none of the pearls, and others are in the rear to examine the shells thrown out. The workmen are not allowed to raise their hands to their mouths while washing the pearls, lest they might attempt to swallow some. Sometimes the pearls, instead of adhering to the shells as is usually the case, are in the bodies of the oysters, which are boiled before being thrown aside as useless. The number of pearls in a shell differs: one may contain a considerable number, while hundreds are without any.

To give you an idea of the extent to which the pearl fishery in Ceylon has been carried for several ages, the shore in some parts of the island has been raised to the height of many feet by enormous mounds of shells, millions having been flung into heaps that extend to the distance of many miles.

At the Pearl Islands, near the Isthmus of Panama, the divers use a very simple method of obtaining the oysters. They traverse the bay in canoes that hold eight men, all of whom dive in the water to a depth of from fifty to sixty feet, where they remain sometimes nearly two minutes, during which they collect all the oysters they can in their hands, and rise to deposit them in the canoes, repeating the operation for several hours.

In Sweden the oysters are taken with a pair of long tongs. The fishermen are in small boats, painted white on the bottom, which reflects to a great depth, and enables them to see the oysters and seize them.

The most beautiful and costly pearls are obtained from the East, and are called "Oriental;" the colour of those found in Ceylon is generally a bluish silvery white, but they are met with of several other hues. Those from the Persian Gulf are of great purity and richness. The preparation of the pearls for market occupies a considerable number of the inhabitants of Ceylon. After being thoroughly cleaned, they are rounded and polished with a powder made of the pearls themselves, and arranged into classes according to their various sizes and quality. They are then drilled and strung together, the largest being generally sent to India, where they are highly prized, while the smaller ones are forwarded to Europe. The operation of drilling is a very delicate one, and the black people are very expert in it. It is done with a wooden machine in the form of an inverted cone, in the upper flat surface of which are pits to receive the pearls. The holes are made by spindles of various sizes, which revolve in a wooden head by the action of a bow-handle, to which they are attached. During the operation (which is done by one hand, while the other presses on the machine), the pearls are moistened occasionally, and the whole is done with astonishing rapidity.

My young readers are no doubt anxious to learn how the pearl is formed within the oyster-shell. This is a subject that has been much debated in ancient and modern times. You will be amused by the explanation given by the illustrious Pliny (who died in the year of our Saviour 79), one of the most enlightened of the old philosophers. He says that "the pearl was produced by the dews of heaven falling into the open shells at the breeding-time. The quality of the pearl varied according to the amount of the dew imbibed, being lustrous if that were pure, dull if it were foul; cloudy weather spoilt the colour, lightning stopped the growth, and thunder made the shell-fish unproductive, and to eject hollow husks called bubbles."

The same naturalist also relates a story how the shoals of pearl-oysters had "a king, distinguished by his age and size, exactly as bees have a queen, wonderfully expert in keeping his subjects out of harm's way, but if the divers once succeeded in catching him, the rest straying about blindly, fell an easy prey. Although defended by a body-guard of sharks, and dwelling among the rocks of the abyss, they cannot be preserved from ladies' ears."

These are very pretty and fanciful ideas, as were many fictions of the pagans, and our own poet Moore has alluded to them in one of his sweet melodies:

"And precious the tear as that rain from the sky
Which turns into pearls as it falls in the sea."

Some naturalists have suggested that pearls are the unfructified eggs of the oyster, others that the jewel is a morbid concretion produced by the endeavour of the animal in the shell to fill up holes; the general opinion, however, seems to prevail thus: most shelly animals which are aquatic are provided with a fluid secretion with which they line their dwellings to render them smooth and polished for their tenderly-formed bodies. This fine even lining you must have frequently remarked in shells of every description. The fluid is laid in extremely thin semi-transparent threads, which gives the interior of the shell the beautiful play of colours you must often have observed. Now, to account for the pearl in the shell, I must tell you that small rounded portions are formed in the lining, which are supposed to be the result of accident, such as grains of sand or other substances getting into the shell, and, irritating the animal inside, causes it, by an instinct of nature, to cover the cause of offence, not having the power to remove it. As the fluid goes on regularly to supply the growth and wear of the shell, the prominences continue to increase, and being more brilliant than the rest of the shell, they become a pearl, a composition of carbonate of lime and a little animal matter.

If a pearl is cut tranversely and observed through a microscope, it will be found to consist of minute layers, resembling the rings which denote the ages of certain trees when cut in a similar manner.

Those clever people the Chinese, who are never at a loss for expedients, are in the habit of laying a string with five or six small pearls, separated by knots, inside the shells, when the fish are exposing themselves to the sun. These, after some years, are taken out, and are found to be very large fine pearls. The same ingenious people also introduce into the shell of a mussel different substances, such as mother-of-pearl, the beautiful white enamel which forms the greater part of the substance of most oyster-shells, fixed to wires, which thus become coated with a more brilliant material. Another practice among the Chinese, equally clever, is to serve the purpose of a deception upon the credulous. They place small metal images of their god Buddha in the shells, which are soon covered with a pearly secretion, and become united to the shells. These are sold as miraculous proofs of the truth of their worship. The Chinese are also said to employ a means of procuring pearls artificially by the introduction of shot between the mouth of the animal and its shell.

I must not omit to tell you that the pearl-oyster which has been the subject of my remarks is not the only mollusc which produces pearls: an oyster with a thin transparent shell, which is used in China and elsewhere as a substitute for glass windows, produces small pearls, as also the fresh-water mussel of our own country, pinna, a genus of the same family with the pearl-mussel, and even in limpets.

In reading the history of our own country you will find that pearls were found on its coast in early times. Indeed, the Roman historian Suetonius (who was born about seventy years before the birth of our Saviour) has recorded in his "Lives of the Twelve Cæsars" that the principal motive for inducing Julius Cæsar to invade Britain was the fame of its pearls, and he is said to have taken to Rome, as a trophy of his conquest, a corslet richly adorned with British pearls, which he placed in a temple dedicated to Venus.

The ancients were extravagantly fond of these beautiful jewels: necklaces, bracelets, and earrings were worn in profusion; a string of pearls was estimated by a Roman writer at about eight thousand pounds of our money; the single pearl which Cleopatra dissolved and swallowed was valued at nearly eighty-one thousand pounds; and a similar act of folly is reported in later times, in the reign of our Queen Elizabeth, when Sir Thomas Gresham, one of London's merchant princes, reduced a pearl to powder worth fifteen thousand pounds, and drank it in a glass of wine to the health of his sovereign, in consequence of a wager with the Spanish ambassador that he would give a more costly dinner than the other. Quite as absurd was the notion in former times that powdered pearls were unfailing remedies in all stomach complaints.

Pearls are esteemed according to their size, colour, form, and lustre: the largest, usually about the dimensions of a small walnut, are called "paragons" and are very rare; those the size of a small cherry are next in rarity, and are called "diadem" or head pearls. They receive names also according to their form, whether quite round, semicircular and drum-form, or that of an ear-drop, pear, onion, or as they are otherwise irregularly shaped. The small pearls are termed "ounce pearls," on account of their being sold by weight, and the very smallest "seed pearls."

The largest pearl on record is one, pear-shaped, brought from India in 1620, by Gongibus de Calais, and sold to Philip IV. of Spain. It weighed four hundred and eighty grains. The merchant, when asked by the monarch how he could venture to risk all his fortune in one little article, replied with great tact, "because he knew there was a King of Spain to buy it of him." This pearl is said to be now in the possession of the princely family of Yousoppoff, in Russia.

Runjeet Sing, the former possessor of the famous Koh-i-Noor diamond, had a string of pearls which was considered nearly equal in value to the "Mountain of Light." They were about three hundred in number, and the size of small marbles, all choice pearls, round and perfect both in shape and colour. Two hours before he died he sent for all his jewels, and gave the magnificent string of pearls to a Hindoo temple.

## CHAPTER XV.

### *THE VEGETATION OF THE OCEAN.*

"Call us not *weeds*, but flowers of the sea,
For lovely, and gay, and bright-tinted are we,
Our blush is as deep as the rose of thy bowers,
Then call us not weeds,—we are ocean's gay flowers."

YOU are, no doubt, well acquainted with the voyages of Christopher Columbus, who added a new hemisphere to our globe. He was born in Genoa about the year 1435. This very eminent man was the son of a wool-comber, but having at the age of fourteen taken to a seafaring life, he became the celebrated discoverer of whom you read in every geography and history of the world. However, what concerns the present chapter is to remind you how, in his search for a new world, he encountered one of the greatest marvels of ocean vegetation—a garden of enormous extent in the waste of waters, which perplexed and terrified his timid seamen. "When" as Robertson, in his "History of America," relates, "about four hundred leagues to the west of the Canaries, he found the sea so covered with weeds, that it resembled a meadow of vast extent, and in some places they were so thick as to retard the motions of the vessel. This strange appearance occasioned new alarm and disquiet to the sailors." They imagined that they had now arrived at the utmost boundary of the navigable ocean; that these floating weeds would obstruct their farther progress, and concealed dangerous rocks, or some large tract of land that had sunk, they knew not how, in that place. Columbus endeavoured to persuade them that what alarmed ought rather to encourage them, as it was a sign of their approaching land. At the same time a brisk gale arose, and carried them forward; several land-birds were seen hovering about the ship, and directed their flight towards the west; a whale, also, was seen heaving up his huge form in the distance, which Columbus affirmed was a favourable indication of the neighbourhood of land. The desponding crew resumed some degree of spirit, and began to entertain fresh hopes.

The marine vegetation that threatened to impede the course of the adventurous Columbus was the *Gulf-weed*, so termed from its great abundance in the Gulf of Mexico. The Portuguese call the waters thus covered the "Grassy Sea," for the surface, during several days' sailing, is literally carpeted with the weed. Here the beautiful fishes of the warmer latitudes,

"with fry innumerable, swarm,"

and find a refuge from their relentless pursuers in the ocean; and the whole mass, extending many miles in space, affords food and shelter to an infinity of small marine animals.

In the Atlantic Ocean these sea-weeds cover an expanse of two hundred and sixty thousand square miles, a vast mass of vegetable matter that no other similarly furnished tract of open water is known to produce.

These sea-weeds are occasionally thrown up by currents on our own shores, and you may know them by the cluster of air-vessels that the *Sargassum* or Gulf-weed bears, and which, from their appearance, have given them the name of "tropical grapes."

How marvellous, my young friends, is this vast provision of Nature in the ocean depths for the wants and nourishment of animal life, all created for wise purposes by the Great Being

"Who sleeps not,—is not weary; in whose designs
No flaw deforms, no difficulty thwarts,
And whose beneficence no change exhausts!"

Innumerable animalculæ (small or minute objects, visible or invisible to the naked eye), the chief food of the whale and also of many species of fish eaten by man, derive their sustenance from sea-weeds.  Myriads upon myriads of eggs of fishes find security in this tangled mass of sea-plants, and the young fish are sheltered there until they acquire strength to commit themselves to the water.  It has been remarked that "the vegetable kingdom in the sea is no barren spot in the garden of Nature, but in usefulness and abundance it is not inferior to the most favoured spots on land."  But the character of sea-weeds is very different to land-plants : the former, supported in a liquid of greater specific gravity than themselves, do not require the woody fibres which are necessary for land-plants, except such as support themselves by climbing; and, as they derive their nourishment from the water which covers them, they do not need the continuous vessels which are so necessary to land-plants for their growth and life.  This is explained by the simple experiment of placing one portion of sea-weed in water, and exposing the other part to the air, when the latter will speedily dry and wither, while the former retains its freshness.

Again, the trees, and flowers, and shrubs which adorn our gardens require, as you know, the bright beams of the sun to warm them into life and beauty ; but the plants that thrive in the depths of the ocean are not dependent for their existence on light, for only a feeble ray can reach many of them in their rocky homes far beneath the surface.

Humboldt mentions the fact of a sea-weed of a fine grass-green colour being brought up from a depth of one hundred and ninety-two feet, where it had vegetated, though the light that had reached it could not have been more than that afforded by half the light of an ordinary candle.

Who can conceive the mighty operations of the All-Powerful Creator in the depths of the ocean ?  What transcendent wonders lie hidden in the waste of waters !  Let us imagine to ourselves vast submarine forests, which we know to exist—an almost boundless extent of vegetation, which lives, thrives, and decays, unseen by mortal eyes—and how insignificant is human comprehension!

"Viewing these tribes of sea-weed," says Dr. Greville, in his "Algæ Britannica," "in the most careless way, as a system of subaqueous vegetation, we see the depths of ocean shadowed with submarine groves, often of vast extent, intermixed with meadows, as it were, of the most lively hues, while the trunks of the larger species, like the great trees of the tropics, are loaded with innumerable minute kinds, as fine as silk, or transparent as a membrane."

How singular the contrast, also, between the gigantic "weeds" that line the ocean depths and spread forth their knotted shoots upon the surface of the water, and the small, beautifully coloured, delicate plants that cling to the rocks, and rival in loveliness the choicest flowers of our gardens!

"Art's finest pencil could but rudely mock
The rich, gay sea-weeds 'broider'd on a rock;
And those bright watery rocks, he would explore,
Small excavations on a rocky shore,
That seem like fairy baths, or mimic wells,
Richly embossed with choicest weeds and shells,
As if her trinkets Nature chose."

On the shores of the North Pacific you would see the *Nereocystus*, with a slender stem, upwards of three hundred feet long, bearing at its extremity a large air-vessel six or seven feet in length, shaped as a barrel, and crowned with a tuft of upwards of fifty forked leaves, each thirty to forty feet long, forming the fishing-grounds of the sea-otter, who can seek his prey with greater certainty amidst the shade of the enormous leaves.

In the Antarctic regions the growth of sea-weeds is remarkable. The "*Tree*" sea-weed, according to Dr. Hooker, rises from the ocean with a huge stem or trunk eight or ten feet in height, and the thickness of a human thigh. The ends of the branches give out leaves two or three inches broad, which, when in the water, hang down like the boughs of a willow. Thousands of these aquatic trees, uprooted by the currents, are often mistaken for driftwood, and are collected for fuel. Darwin mentions some sea-weeds that grow on the rocks in the Arctic seas, which, though of prodigious length, instead of being spread along the bottom of the ocean, are in part floated on the surface by means of the numerous air-vessels they contain. These gigantic sea-plants are sometimes fifteen hundred feet in length. So full of air-vessels are they, that they look like a honeycomb.

Dr. Hooker mentions that one species of sea-weed in the Antarctic regions, in its horizontal growth at the surface of the ocean, ranges between two hundred and seven hundred feet in length; and that at the Falkland Islands the beach is lined for miles with entangled cables of this weed, much thicker than the human body.

Opposed to these gigantic marine plants we have multitudes of smaller growth, combining the most delicate, beautiful, and curious characteristics of form and colour. Not to tire your memory with hard names, I will mention a sea-weed you may have probably seen —the *Water Flannel*, which waves backwards and forwards like the pendulum of a clock; and I have no doubt you have often, when at the sea-side, enjoyed the fun of cracking the air-vessels of the *Bladder-weed*, and pulled to pieces the thready weeds that children call "sea-silk." The sea-coasts present an exhaustless variety of pleasure derived from sea-weeds. There you may find the *Whip-lash*, which grows from thirty to forty feet in length, and is used for fish-lines in Scotland. You may have found the *Net-weed*, which spreads its delicate interlaced threads like a web in the water; and you would meet with the feathery *Callithamnion* (a name derived from Greek words signifying "beautiful" and "a little shrub"), one of the most lovely of sea-weeds, of a bright, fine, rosy-red colour; the branches divided like the teeth of a comb. Then there is the *Fern-leaf* sea-weed, another attractive plant, and the splendid *Fan-weed*, representing a collection of hundreds of beautiful little fans, every one of which, if minutely examined, is of exquisite workmanship. On the southern coast of our country you would find a common shore-plant of the tropical seas, the *Peacock's Tail*, another lovely sea-weed. When growing, the fronds are rolled up into cups, while the delicate fibres with which they are bordered reflect the most glorious tints. Then there are the curious *Sea-thongs* or *Girdles*, which you may have often seen on the coast, and which, when taken out of the water and held by the stem, resemble a flag-staff and streamers.

The varieties of form and substance in sea-plants are also highly interesting subjects for contemplation: some are like masses of jelly, others are elastic like India-rubber; many are tough as leather, others firm as wood; some have delicate transparent leaves, others have thick, finely-veined, or nerveless leaves.

The plants of the ocean gardens can vie also in glowing tints with many of our most attractive land-flowers:

> " The Hand which adorned the sweet perfumed parterre
> Did our fringe-like and fanciful dresses prepare,
> As pendent we hang round the coralline caves,
> Or float our light branches beneath the green waves,
> Or twine 'midst the gems of the watery deep,
> Or climb up the rocks, or in modesty creep.
> Could you view all the beauties of which we might boast,
> How varied our forms and our tints on each coast,
> You would surely declare that the boon should be ours
> Henceforth to assume the high title of *flowers*."

The natural colours of many sea-plants are exceedingly beautiful when viewed in their native element; but exposure to the sun and air—unless they are preserved with the greatest care and delicacy—causes them to fade. Those of the red species, which abound chiefly in the temperate zone, acquire their richest tints in the deepest water. The plants of an olive colour are mostly found in the neighbourhood of the tropics, while the green species principally inhabit the Polar seas. But, besides the colours I have mentioned, there are countless varieties of other shades.

Having alluded to the beauty and richness of ocean vegetation, I will now mention its usefulness, in addition to the shelter and nourishment it affords to the inhabitants of the deep—

> " Invisible,
> Amid the floating verdure millions stray."

They soften the currents of rolling waters, and lessen the violence with which the waves would, otherwise, break upon the shores of the land.

## USE OF SEA-WEEDS FOR FOOD.

The distinguished naturalist, Charles Darwin, alludes to the value of sea-weeds to those who traverse the ocean: "I believe, during the voyage of the 'Beagle' and 'Adventure,' not one rock near the surface was discovered which was not buoyed by this floating weed. The good services it thus affords to vessels navigating near this stormy land (Terra del Fuego) is evident, and has certainly saved many from being wrecked."

And now let us consider the use of sea-weeds for food. The value of these in many parts of the world is very great; the Chinese especially are the largest consumers of any nation, and have various ingenious methods of preparing them for the table. *Ceylon Moss*, formerly much esteemed, is the produce of an esculent sea-weed gathered on the western coast of Ceylon, and possesses many nutritious qualities. *Carrageen Moss* is a sea-weed much used for food in Ireland; it is also frequently employed instead of isinglass for making soups and jellies. In Bavaria it serves for clarifying beer. The young stalks of the *Tangle-weeds*, when well boiled and served up with pepper and vinegar, are very wholesome. One species grows to the length of twenty feet.

You may have remarked on the sea-shore a pretty weed resembling in shape the palm of a hand, with leaves like fingers growing around it. This is popularly called *Dulse*, and is eaten both raw and roasted, the taste resembling that of cooked oysters. This is also a favourite food of lobsters, crabs, and other shell-fish. The Icelanders have a particular relish for this sea-weed, and prepare it by drying, when it gives out a white powdery substance, which is sweet and palatable. Cattle are also very fond of dulse, especially sheep, for which reason it is often called "sheep's dulse." These animals seek it eagerly on the sea-shore, and are sometimes carried away by the tide in their eagerness to obtain it. In Kamtchatka it is used for making a fermented beverage.

The marine vegetable called *Laver*, so much esteemed in various parts of England as a relish for the table, is a species of sea-weed, stewed and served as a sauce.

Having alluded to the value of sea-weeds for food, I will now mention their importance to the agriculturist for manure. As every species is applicable for this purpose, you can imagine how almost universal is their use on the coasts of our own country and elsewhere. The harvest of the deep is as anxiously looked for as the crops which gladden the heart of the husbandman on land. In the Channel Islands sea-weeds are used for manure and for fuel, and so highly are they valued, that the farmers there have a proverb "No sea-weed, no corn-yard;" indeed, so precious is the "Vraic," as it is called, that special laws are enforced for its regular collection. The weeds are burnt on the hearth for fuel, and the charred ash serves to fertilize the ground.

The uses to which sea-weeds are applied are, indeed, numerous and important. I will merely mention a few. The ashes of marine plants afford a large quantity of soda salts, and especially the carbonate, such as "Kelp," which is prepared by merely burning certain species of weeds suitable for the purpose, and this was formerly in great request for the manufacture of glass, but now there is a better and cheaper means of getting soda from salt.

According to Pliny, the value of soda in making glass was discovered by a mere accident. A vessel loaded with soda was once driven ashore on the coast of Palestine. The crew landed, and made a fire upon the sands to boil their kettle. They took some lumps of the soda for the kettle to rest upon, without the least idea of what would result. The soda was melted, and, uniting with the sand, formed a rough kind of glass.

But kelp, although superseded in this respect, is valuable from the circumstance that *iodine* (discovered in 1811, by Courtois, in the waste liquors produced in the manufacture of carbonate of soda from the ashes of sea-weeds), which is so necessary in medicine, in photography, and various processes connected with the arts, is chiefly derived from it. Iodine exists in the waters of the ocean and mineral springs, marine shelly animals, and sea vegetation generally, but not to the same extent as in kelp. When heated, iodine rises in a vapour of a violet colour (hence its name, from a Greek word for "violet"), and this is condensed and solidified by a chemical process.

Iodine is found in large quantities in the sea-weeds which cover the rocks for miles round the west coast of Ireland. The average yield of British kelp is said to be ten thousand tons yearly, of the value of forty thousand pounds.

In some of the countries bordering on the Baltic, sea-weeds are used for packing materials and for stuffing articles. The *Ulva Marina* is extensively employed in our own country for the latter purpose. Attempts have been made to manufacture paper from sea-weeds; marine sugar is obtained from several species. The Chinese derive from them a gum for making their lanterns and transparencies, also a varnish, and a size for the manufacture of silk and paper.

You may see in the British Museum fishing-lines made of sea-weed, and used on the north-west coast of America.

## CHAPTER XVI.

### *SPONGES.*

> "First from his lodge dislodged, he thrust apart
> His bellows, and his tools collecting all,
> Bestow'd them careful in a silver chest;
> Then all around with a wet *sponge* he wiped
> His visage, and his arms, and brawny neck."

THUS Homer describes Vulcan making a similar use of the SPONGE (derived from a Greek word "to squeeze") as that in which we now employ it, and showing through how many ages of time that common but valuable material has been known and appreciated, for the great master of epic poetry is supposed to have lived eight hundred years before the birth of our Saviour.

Among ancient nations the sponge was also used as a soft and elastic lining for the brazen helmets of their soldiers, and many other purposes. It is one of the many valuable spoils we take from the ocean, their birthplace and their nourishment; and this leads us to inquire into the nature of these singular productions. It has long been a matter of debate among naturalists whether sponges should be classed among the vegetable or animal kingdoms; they are now generally placed under the order *Zoophyte*, or plant-animals (from two Greek words signifying "animal" and "plant").

Aristotle, the greatest of ancient philosophers, who was born three hundred and eighty-four years before Christ, described the sponge as a stationary or rooted animal; but from other statements he made it is certain that he considered its place as between the animal and vegetable. Some modern naturalists have placed sponges among marine vegetables, and their appearance, if you casually look at them, would seem to justify such an opinion; but the researches of Mr. Ellis, a merchant of London, who made similar branches of natural history a particular pursuit, gave additional interest to this case. In the course of his miscroscopic investigations, he was astonished at discovering that sponges possessed a system of pores (passages of perspiration) and vessels, in which sea-water passed with all the appearance of the regular circulation of fluids in animal bodies, and a seeming purpose of conveying animalculæ (small minute animals) to itself for food.

More recently Dr. Grant gave the result of his experiments on the same subject. The account is so interesting that I will give it in the Professor's own words. "Having," he says, "placed a portion of sponge in a watch-glass with some sea-water, I beheld for the first time the splendid spectacle of this living fountain vomiting forth from a circular cavity an impetuous torrent of liquid matter, and hurling along in rapid succession opaque (cloudy) masses which it strewed everywhere around. The beauty and novelty of such a scene in the animal kingdom long arrested my attention, but after twenty-five minutes of constant observation I was obliged to withdraw my eye from fatigue, without having seen the torrent for an instant change its direction or diminish the rapidity of its course. In observing another species, I placed two entire portions of this together in a glass of sea-water, with their orifices opposite to each other at the distance of two inches. They appeared to the naked eye like two living batteries, and soon covered each other with the materials ejected. I placed one of them in a shallow vessel, and just covered its surface and highest orifice with water. On strewing some powdered chalk on the surface of the water, the currents were visible to a great distance, and on placing some pieces of cork or of dry paper over the orifices, I could perceive them moving by the force of the currents at the distance of ten feet from the table on which the specimens rested."

So interesting are the sponges, which, although ranked as creatures of very low intelligence, yet are by no means the least curious of those manifestations of the Divine Power

> "That built the palace of the sky,
> Formed the light wings that decorate the fly;
> The Power that wheels the circling planets round,
> Rears every infant floweret on the ground;
> That bounty which the mightiest beings share,
> Feeds the least gnat that gilds the evening air."

Every one of my young readers must be conscious of the useful qualities of the sponge, but many are unacquainted with the manner in which and where they are obtained. The finest qualities of sponge come from the Ottoman Archipelago, and form one of the principal articles of commerce with Turkey. The island of Calymnos is the principal station for the sponge fishery, and more than three hundred boats are employed, averaging each about six tons, and carrying six to eight men, of whom two are rowers. The finest qualities are sent in large quantities to our own country, and the common and coarser kinds are forwarded to France, Austria, and Constantinople.

The average depth at which the best sponges are found is about one hundred and eighty feet; those of an inferior quality are brought from a lesser depth. The method of diving is much the same as I have described in the coral-fishing. The diver, who goes head-foremost into the water, takes with him a triangular-shaped stone, to which a strong line is attached to assist him in his descent, and direct him like a rudder to any particular spot. On reaching the bottom, the diver tears off a number of sponges, which adhere in masses to rocks and stones, sometimes to large shells, and are either round, flat, or hollow like a funnel; and then, pulling a line, he is drawn up, with the sponges in his arms, by the rowers. An experienced diver will make from eight to ten dives during the day. The proceeds of the fishery are divided into shares, the divers receiving a whole share, and the rowers two-thirds of a share. Formerly the divers used to sell their sponges by weight, to increase which they put sand into them, a practice still continued, though now sold by quantity.

The sponge in its natural state would not be recognized as that we are accustomed to use daily. In its primitive condition it is covered with a thin dark skin, inside of which there is a liquid like milk, and of the same consistency. If you examined a drop of this liquid by the microscope, it would appear entirely composed of very small transparent grains, nearly of the same size, with some moisture. This jelly matter connects the different parts of the framework of the sponge and lines the various canals or passages. The pores, or apertures for perspiration, are minute openings on the surface, protected by the framework, and into which the water enters in currents, and after traversing the interior passages, is ejected by means of openings which are larger than the pores, and in many species are elevated above the surface. To examine closely the framework or skeleton of the sponge, to which I have alluded, it is necessary to macerate it in hot water, which removes the gelatinous matter, and leaves it in a condition to be examined by the microscope. This framework consists principally of two materials, one animal, the other mineral; the first of a thready, horny, elastic nature, the second (the species most commonly used for domestic purposes) of a flinty or chalk material. The thready portion consists of a light pale-coloured network, with some few exceptions always solid, and varying considerably in size. The mineral portion has little spines, which, if examined with the microscope, show traces of a central cavity or canal, the extremities of which are closed.

How the growth and increase of the sponge is effected affords matter of the deepest interest, and this, like everything else in nature, shows the unerring wisdom of an all-sustaining Providence:

"See through this air, this ocean, and this earth,
All matter quick, and bursting into birth.
Above, how high progressive life may go!
Around, how wide! how deep extend below!

> Vast chain of being! which from God began.
> Nature's ethereal, human, angel, man,
> Beast, bird, fish, insect,—what no eye can see,
> No glass can reach—from infinite to Thee,
> From Thee to nothing."

From the framework or skeleton of the sponge emerge, at certain seasons of the year, a yellow kind of grain, which projects as it increases in size into the cavities of the sponge, and forms the germ or seed of another race; these are egg-like in appearance; and a large portion of its surface becomes covered with little hairs, called *cilia* (eyelashes), from their resemblance to such. These hairs act as oars to the little germ, to convey it away as soon as it falls on the water to some other spot to which it may attach itself. The hairs, after accomplishing their purpose, fall off, leaving the germ to gradually develope into the sponge.

## CHAPTER XVII.

### SHELLS.

" See what a lovely shell,
　Small and pure as pearl,
　　Lying close to my foot.
　　　Frail, but a work divine,
　Made so fairly well,
　　With delicate spire and whorl,
　　　How exquisitely minute,
　　　　A miracle of design!

" What is it? A learned man
　　Could give it a clumsy name.
　Let him name it who can,
　　The beauty would be the same.

" The tiny coil is forlorn,
　　Void of the little living will
　　　That made it stir on the shore.
　　　Did he stand at the diamond door
　　Of his house in a rainbow frill?
　　　Did he push, when he was uncurled,
　A golden foot and a fairy horn
　　Through his dim water-world?"

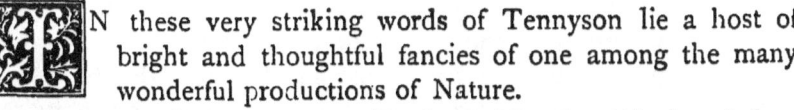N these very striking words of Tennyson lie a host of bright and thoughtful fancies of one among the many wonderful productions of Nature.

"How beautifully," observes Professor Moseley, "is the wisdom of God developed in shaping out and moulding shells, and especially in *the particular angle which the spiral of each species of shell affects*, a valve connected by a necessary relation with the material of each, and with its stability, and the conditions of its buoyancy."

This is shown in many ways, for in the structure of SHELLS there is a general adaptation of the wants of the animal to which they belong. Thus, there are light shells for the floaters and swimmers, strength for the limpets and periwinkles, and other adjustments as needed for others. What can be more wonderful than the apparatus essential to what are commonly called *bivalves*, or molluscous animals protected by two shells? The *hinge* which connects them shows a singular contrivance for the necessities of the animal. It is formed entirely of the inner layer of shell, and consists of either a simple cardinal (from the Latin *cardo*, "a hinge") process, or of serrated projections, or *teeth* as they are called, with corresponding cavities or sockets into which they are inserted. To this hinge is superadded a ligament, the external substance by which the shells are united, which binds the two parts together, and keeps those composing the hinge in their places. This ligament (from the Latin *ligare*, "to tie") is highly elastic, being composed of a number of fibres, parallel to each other and perpendicular to the valves which they connect. When the animal is undisturbed, the elastic ligament keeps the valves open, and the functions are carried on without any effort. When danger is apprehended, or circumstances require it, the adductor (from the Latin *adduco*, "I draw towards") muscle or muscles contract, overcome the resistance of the hinge, and shut the valves close until they may be opened with safety.

Conchology (from the Greek *kogchulion*, "a shell," and *logos*, "a discourse") is, as I need scarcely mention, the science which teaches the arrangement of shells into classes, species, &c. Formerly, these beautiful productions of Nature were looked upon as merely pleasing toys and objects of curiosity, but gradually this innocent trifling came to be viewed in its true light, by some collectors worthy of better employment, who put off childish things and went deeper into the subject. In anticipation of this, shell-collectors began to look upon their treasures as an assemblage of gems, and, indeed, the enormous prices given for fine and scarce shells, joined with the surpassing beauty of the objects themselves, almost justified the view which the possessor took of his cabinet of treasures. But after all, these were mere trinkets, and the study of shells and their inhabitants at length became a science of the utmost importance, not only to naturalists generally, but to the geologist, to whom it is of the greatest value in indicating the difference of strata and their comparative ages.

In Southern Europe some very beautiful shells are found, especially in the Italian seas. Tarento is singularly rich in shells. The Indian seas, more than any other part of the world, abound with the greatest variety of shell-fish, which exhibit a remarkable contrast, comparatively speaking, to the few species found under the parallel latitudes of Africa and America. "It is also a singular fact," observes Mr. Swainson, "that nearly three-fourths of these shells belong to the animals entirely carnivorous, who, to support life, must be continually carrying on a destructive warfare against the weaker animals of their own class."

Many beautiful shells are brought from the coasts of Chili and Panama in tropical America. From the western coasts of Africa are obtained many attractive shells, such as the blood-spotted *Harp*, the sharp-ribbed *Cockle*, &c. The small *Cowry*, well known as a substitute for coin among the barbarous nations of Western Africa, is the same species as that so abundant in the Indian seas.

Passing to Australia, there are found on the coasts many of the most beautiful and rare rolled shells known: the *Snow-spotted* kind being most valued. They have two dark bands on a flesh-coloured ground, the surface being entirely covered with white dots.

Many deep-sea shells are so firm in their structures that they are brought to the beaches, especially of the tropical seas, in an entire state, and are eagerly sought after by collectors. Independent of their shape, colour, and lustre, many of them are valuable, inasmuch as they inhabit the seas at such depths as not to be known in the living state.

The number of shells is far, very far beyond human calculation. An examination of the rocks on our own sea-shore during the summer will prove this in a slight degree. These are so covered with shells that scarcely a pin's point could be introduced between them. Many apparent grains of chalk are in reality microscopic shells and fragments of marine coral, of which upwards of a thousand have been obtained from one pound of chalk.

"The most level and lowest parts of the earth," says Cuvier, "when penetrated to a very great depth, exhibit nothing but horizontal strata, composed of various substances, and containing, almost all of them, innumerable marine productions. Similar strata, with the same kind of productions, compose the hills even to a great height. Sometimes the shells are so numerous as to compose the entire body of the stratum. They are almost in such a perfect state of preservation, that even the smallest of them retain their most delicate parts, their sharpest ridges, and their finest and most tender processes. They are found in elevations far above the level of every part of the ocean, and in places to which the sea could not be conveyed by any existing cause. The summits of the Pyrenees and the Andes, at the height of thirteen or fourteen thousand feet above the level of the sea, present them to our notice."

The sea-banks and coasts are covered with broken shells, of which lime is the ingredient. This generally exists in the state of carbonate, the same as in chalk, common limestone, and marble. Many of the more tender shells and shelly matters are broken by the agitation of the waters, and form a variety of sand which is truly a product of the sea, and forms a valuable manure on land. Great deposits of this article are found on the coasts of Devonshire and Cornwall, and in many other parts of the British coast.

A species of shell, the *Cerithium telescopium*, is so abundant near Calcutta as to be used for burning into lime. Great heaps of it are first exposed to the sun, to kill the animals, and then burnt. In some places they are so plentiful as to be used in road-making. Mobile in America is built on a shell-bank.

It was formerly believed that shells were not only devoid of vessels, but completely without organs, being composed of the transpiration of particles, chiefly carbonate of lime, cemented together by a kind of animal glue. It is now known that shells always possess a more or less distinct organic structure, which in some cases resembles that of the external skin of the higher animals, whilst in others it approaches to that of the true skin.

In the limited space to which my remarks on the subject of this chapter is necessarily confined, I cannot give more than a brief outline of this exceedingly interesting department of science. I must refer my young readers, who desire more extensive information, to the various valuable works which have been published of late by naturalists who have made conchology their especial study. I may briefly observe that what are called the *Testacea* (from the Latin *testa*, "a shell,") comprise animals surrounded with a shelly covering, and may be generally described as of three kinds : those that possess a single shell, of whatever form or character, and hence called *univalves;* those which have two shells, the *bivalves*, or *Conchæ;* and others having more than two shells, or *multivalves*. Of these, the univalves are the most numerous and exhibit the greatest variety of forms, being for the most part regularly or irregularly spiral. Among the most common may be mentioned the *Helix*, or snail genus; the *Paletta*, or limpet; and the *Turbo*, or wreath genus, of which the periwinkle is a species.

The shell of the *Clam*, or *Bear's Paw*, is described as, perhaps, the most ornamental of bivalves, in regard to form, texture, and colour. It comes from the South Seas, and is much used for decorative purposes.

Among the most curious shells is the *Murex*, or *Purple-shell*, so highly valued by the ancients for the exquisite dye it is capable of producing; the *Volute*, or *Mitre-shell*, including the fine polished spiral shells, without lips or perforation, which are often exhibited on chimney-pieces as ornaments, sometimes embellished with dots and with coloured bands. The *Strombus* comprise larger shells, spiral like the volute, but with a large expanding lip spreading into a groove on the left side, and often still farther projecting into lobes or claws, the back frequently covered with large excrescences, in some species called *Cormorant's Foot*.

And now for a few observations on the use and value of shells. Even as mere objects of attraction they tend to raise the thoughts to that great and glorious Being,

> "Our God, omnific, sole original,
> Wise wonder-working wielder of the whole:
> Infinite, inconceivable, immense,"

who has shaped and adapted them to the wants of numberless creatures, of which science at the most can have but a feeble comprehension. "Beautiful," observes Mr. Jesse, "since more exquisite samples of elegance of form and brilliancy of colour cannot be found through the wide range of natural objects, whether organized or inorganized; surprising, when we consider that all these durable relics were constructed by soft and fragile animals, among the most perishable of living creatures. Still more surprising is an assemblage of shells, when we reflect upon the endless variation of pattern and sculpture which it displays; for there are known to naturalists more than fifteen thousand perfectly distinct kinds of shells. Every one of these kinds has a rule of its own, a law which every individual of each kind, through all its generations, implicitly obeys.

"The formation of the shell itself is but an example of a process at work equally in the animal and vegetable kingdoms. A shell, whether simple or complicated in the contour or colour, is the aggregate result of the function operation of numberless minute membranous cells, the largest of which does not exceed one-hundredth of an inch in diameter, and in the majority of instances is less than one-thousandth of an inch. In the cavities of these microscopic chambers is deposited a crystalline carbonate of lime, which gives compactness to the beautiful dwelling-house, or rather coat-of-mail, that protects the tender mollusc. How astonishing is the reflection, that myriads of exactly similar and exceedingly minute organs should so work in combination that the result of their labours should present an edifice rivalling, nay, exceeding in complexity, yet order of detail and perfection of elaborate finish, the finest palaces ever constructed by man!"

Sea-shells perform also an important part in the economy of the universe. Maury remarks on this subject, that shell-fish and various other tribes that dwell far down in the depths of the ocean, although regarded as being so low in the scale of creation, spread over certain parts of the waters "those benign mantles of warmth which temper the winds, and modify more or less all the marine climates of the earth. The sea-breezes and the sea-shells perform their appointed offices, acting so as to give rise to a reciprocating motion in the waters, and thus imparting to the ocean forces also for its circulation. Sea-shells and sea-insects are the conservators of the ocean. As the salts are emptied into the sea, these creatures secrete them again, and pile them up in solid masses, to serve as the bases of islands and continents, to be in the course of ages upheaved into dry land, and then again dissolved by the dews and rains, and washed by the rivers into the seas."

The *use* of shells is multifarious: in China, some descriptions are prepared as medicines; as articles of ornament they were employed in the earliest times. Several perforated shells found in Aquitaine, in France, show that they must have been worn as decorations or charms by primitive races. The custom of using shells as necklaces is common not only among savages, but amongst civilized people at the present day. Nacreous or pearl-like shells are employed for making buttons and other articles; coloured and pearl ones form the ornaments of *papier-maché* work, card-cases, &c. Various small shells are made into flowers and decorations for head-dresses; very beautiful cameos are carved upon some descriptions of shells for brooches, bracelets, ear-rings, and other attractive objects. The *Fountain-shell* of the West Indies is one of the largest known univalve shells, weighing sometimes four or five pounds. Immense quantities are imported from the Bahamas for the manufacture of cameos. The secret of cameo-cutting, Mr. Woodward informs us, consists simply in knowing that the inner stratum of porcellanous shells is differently coloured from the exterior. Some shells are manufactured into spoons, handles for knives, cups, lamps, &c. The purest kind of lime is made from calcined shells, and their use as a manure I have already mentioned.

Mother-of-pearl is the beautiful white enamel, or pearly lining, which forms the greater part of most oyster-shells, but especially the larger ones found in the seas of the Pacific and Indian Oceans.

In the cathedral and some of the churches in Panama the upper portions are studded with pearl shells, which give them a strange and not unpleasing appearance.

Mr. M'Micking, in his "Recollections of Manilla and the Philippines," states that in many of the houses in the capital the outer side of the verandah or corridor is composed of coarse and dark-coloured mother-of-pearl shells, of little value, set in a wooden framework of small squares, forming windows, which move on slides. Although the light admitted through this sort of window is much inferior to what glass would give, it has the advantage of being strong.

The use of spiral shells as trumpets or horns is traced back to the Romans, and they are thus employed by the Africans, the natives of the Eastern Archipelago and New Zealand, and also in Japan. The fine *Trumpet-shell* is found in most warm climates, in the African, the American, and Asiatic seas, also on the coasts of the islands of the South Pacific.

Mr. Ellis, in his "Polynesian Researches," speaking of the Tahitians, observes, "The sound of the trumpet or shell used in war to stimulate in action by the priests of the temple, and also by the herald, and others on board their fleets, was more horrific than that of the drum. The largest shells were usually selected for this purpose, and were sometimes above a foot in length, and seven or eight inches in diameter at the mouth. In order to facilitate the blowing of this trumpet they made a perforation, about an inch in diameter, near the apex of the shell. Into this they inserted a bamboo cane about three feet in length, which was secured by binding it to the shell with fine braid; the aperture was rendered air-tight by cementing the outside of it with a resinous gum from the bread-fruit tree. These shells were blown when a procession walked to the temple, or their warriors marched to battle, at the inauguration of the king, during the worship at the temple, or when a *tabu* or restriction was imposed in the name of the gods. The sound is extremely loud, but the most monotonous and dismal that it is possible to imagine."

This is the shell generally represented by painters in the hands of the "Tritons" or sea-monsters.

In Ceylon shells of a certain kind are used to contain the sacred oil for anointing the priests. On the western coasts of South America there is a species of limpet which attains the diameter of a foot, and the shell of which is employed by the natives as a basin.

Another general application of shells is as weights to nets and barbs for harpoons and hooks.

To shell-fish, as articles of food, I have already alluded with regard to the lobster, crab, oyster, mussel, &c. Mr. Woodward mentions that the "scallops," so called in the London market, or the "queens" at Brighton, or "frills" on the coasts of Dorsetshire and Devonshire—are now almost as much eaten as oysters, but require cooking first. An allied species has received the name of the "St. James's shell." It was worn by pilgrims to the Holy Land. The fossils of this kind, found in the sub-Apennine formation of Italy, were supposed, by early writers, to have been dropped by these devout persons on the road. Parnel says of the "Hermit:"

"He quits his cell, the pilgrim-staff he bore,
And fixed the scallop in his hat before."

Clams — another species of bivalve molluscs — are eaten in North America; while the giant clam of the Indian Ocean, the shell of which often weighs upwards of five hundred pounds, contains an animal sometimes weighing twenty pounds, which Captain Cook found to be very good eating. The rock-limpet is much used by fishermen for bait. In the north of Ireland they are eaten. The whelk is also employed for bait, and many tons' weight of these, cockles, and winkles, are consumed by shell-fish amateurs.

The mention of cockles reminds me of a statement in Drake's "Voyage round the World," the quaint style of which is amusing:

"Our stay being longer than we purposed (in Patagonia), our diet began to wax short, and small mussels were good meat, yea, the sea-weeds were dainty dishes. By reason whereof we were driven to seek corners very narrowly for some refreshing, but the best we could find was shells instead of meat. We found the nests, but the birds were gone—that is, the shells of the cockles on the sea-shore, where the giants had banqueted, but could never chance with the cockles themselves in the sea. The shells were so extraordinary that it would be incredible to the most part, for a pair of shells did weigh four pounds, and what the meat of two such shells might be may be easily conjectured."

The shells called *Porcelain-shells* by the French and Germans are almost entirely composed of lime, are richly enamelled, and are often very beautiful. They are most abundant and attain their largest size in the seas of warm climates. Only a few small species are found on the British coasts. The *Cowry-shell*, to which I have alluded as a substitute for money, is not of great beauty, being yellow or white, often with a yellow ring about an inch long, and nearly as broad as long. In Bengal three thousand two hundred cowries are reckoned equal to a rupee, so that a cowry is equal in value to one-thirty-sixth of a farthing. Yet cowries to the value of two hundred thousand rupees are said to have been imported annually into Bengal. Many tons of cowries are annually imported into England to be used in trade with Western Africa. Of the cowries a very remarkable fact has been stated, that when the animals find their shells too small for the increased dimensions of their body, they quit them, and proceed to the formation of new ones of larger size, and, consequently, more adapted to their wants. As soon as the cowry has abandoned its covering, the hinder part of its body begins to furnish anew the shelly matter which is afterwards condensed on its surface. This secretion is continued until at length the shell appears of the consistence of paper; and the mouth or opening of the shell, which at this period is very wide, soon afterwards contracts to its

proper form and dimensions. The edges are thickened, and form into those beautiful folds or teeth which are so remarkable on each side of the opening of these shells. The porcelain and cowry-shells belong to a family which includes also the shells called *Poached Eggs*, and the *Weaver's Shuttle*, remarkable for its prolongation at both ends.

A well-known shell, distributed over the whole world, is the *Fusus* (from the Latin, "a spindle"), so named from its shape. In Scotland it is called the "roaring buckie," from the continuous sound, as of waves breaking on the shore, heard when the empty shell is applied to the ear. Wordsworth alludes to this "voice" of a shell in some sweet lines:

"I have seen
A curious child, who dwelt upon a tract
Of inland ground, applying to his ear
The convolutions of a smooth-tipp'd shell,
To which, in silence hush'd, his very soul
Listen'd intensely, and his countenance soon
Brighten'd with joy; for murmurings from within
Were heard—sonorous cadence, whereby,
To his belief, the monitor express'd
Mysterious union with his native sea."

In the cottages of Zetland, this shell, generally about six inches long, is used for a lamp, being suspended horizontally by a cord, its cavity containing the oil, and the wick passing through the canal.

The shell of the *Haliotis* (from the Greek *als*, "the sea," and *ous*, "the ear") is very ornamental, and valued, on account of its pearly lining, for adorning *papier maché* articles. These shells, which are very numerous, and some of splendid appearance, come from the tropical seas, and are commonly called, from their shape, "ear-shells," or "sea-ears." One species, however, is found on the southern European coasts, and on those of the Channel Islands. From the warm regions we also obtain the beautiful *Harp-shells*, the delicate and brilliant colours of which render them highly prized; also the *Fountain-shells* to which I have already alluded as used for cameos, and are much esteemed as garden ornaments for their solid and delicately-tinted substance. One of these shells sometimes weighs four or five pounds.

A shell called the *Razor*, a common species of which you may have often picked up on our sea-coasts—some straight, about an inch long and eight inches broad; and another, curved like a sword—attain a large size in the tropical seas, and are of great beauty. They are found in the sands of all seas, except in the cold regions, the *solen*, the name of the inhabitant of this shell, burrowing in the sands, and ascending from its holes by means of the foot, which can be lengthened or contracted at will.

What are called *Top-shells*, from their spiral and very generally top-shape, are frequently found on our coasts, and many of them are very ornamental, but not equal in this respect to the tropical specimens.

From Australia we obtain a large number of the richly decorated *Pheasant-shells*, formerly of great rarity, and expensive, but now comparatively cheap.

The *Wentletrap-shells*, the common kinds of which are found on our own coasts and those of continental Europe, are very pretty: they are spiral, with many whorls or wreaths, deeply divided, and crossed by remarkably elevated ribs. The *true* shells of this species come from the warm seas, and are generally very beautiful. One kind, called the *Precious Wentletrap*, is of such rarity and richness, that it is said to have been sold to shell-collectors at the price of two hundred guineas, but it may now be had for a few shillings. It is nearly two inches in length, snow-white or pale flesh-coloured, with eight separated wreaths. *Trough-shells*, several small species of which are very abundant on our sea-shores, are triangular, broader than long, and the valves equal. Some of them have a very attractive appearance.

## CHAPTER XVIII.

### SUBMARINE SCENERY.

"The water is calm and still below,
  For the winds and waves are absent there,
And the sands are bright as the stars that glow
  In the motionless fields of upper air.
There, with its waving blades of green,
  The sea-flag streams through the silent water,
And the crimson leaf of the dulse is seen
  To blush like a banner bath'd in slaughter!"

PERCIVAL.

IT is in the warm sea regions that the glory of submarine scenery is developed, the great transparency of the water in various places affording an ample view of the magnificent objects which gem the ocean depths. The poet Moore, writing of the Bahamas (the earliest discovery of Columbus), a chain of islands in the Atlantic, remarks on the singular clearness of the water, so that the rocks are seen to a very great depth. "As we entered the harbour," he observes, "they appeared so near to us that it seemed impossible to avoid striking on them." Addressing the Marchioness of Donegal, he says:

"Believe me, lady, when the zephyrs bland
  Floated our bark to this enchanted land—
  These leafy isles, upon the ocean thrown
  *Like studs of emerald o'er a silver zone—*
  Never did weary bark more sweetly glide,
  Or rest its anchor in a lovelier tide."

Dr. Collingwood, in his "Rambles of a Naturalist," describes a scene of marvellous submarine beauty in the China seas. He speaks of Fiery Cross Reef on a day when the sea was so calm that the ship's anchor could be distinctly seen sixty or seventy feet from the surface. Rowing over a two-fathom patch, he allowed the boat to drift slowly, and gazed on the sea treasures beneath him.

"Glorious masses of living coral strewed the bottom; immense globular madrepores (zoophytes); vast overhanging mushroom-shaped expansions; complicated ramifications of interweaving branches, mingled with smaller and more delicate species, round, finger-shaped, horn-like, and umbrella forms, lay in a wondrous confusion; and these were painted in every shade of delicate and brilliant colouring—grass-green, deep blue, bright yellow, pure white, rich buff, and more sober brown; altogether forming a kaleidoscope effect of form and colour unequalled by anything I ever beheld. Here and there was a large clam-shell, wedged in between masses of coral, the gaping zigzag mouth covered with a projecting mantle of the deepest Prussian blue; beds of dark purpled, long spined *echini* (sea-urchins), and the thick black bodies of sea-cucumbers varied the aspect of the sea bottom. In and out of these coral groves, like gorgeous birds in forest trees, swam the most beautifully coloured and grotesque fishes—some of an intense blue, others bright red, yellow, black, salmon coloured, and every hue of the rainbow, curiously barred, and bound, and bearded."

All the deepest colours we are acquainted with are those of hot climates, and all the lightest those of cold ones. The brilliant colour of fishes, shells, and sea-weeds of the tropics, and especially of the Indian and Caribbean Seas, are spoken of with admiration by every navigator.

"To give some idea," remarks Mr. Adams ("Voyage of H.M.S. Samarang"), "of the splendid colour of tropical fishes, I copy from my journal the colour of a species of *Balistes* (cross-bow-fish) taken by us at Sooloo: upper part of the body pale brown, with two broad stripes of deeper brown extending backwards towards the dorsal (back) fin, four well-defined and narrow streaks descending to the end fin, a bright spot of ultramarine round the end; iris golden, a dark greenish-brown margined with deep blue, reaching from beneath the eyes to the pectoral fin; over the eye and summit of the head, a deep blue colour, with a lighter streak running down before the eye to the base of the pectoral fin; a bright blue stripe above the upper lip, reaching to the angle of the mouth; from this point to a little below the pectoral fin, a deep orange-yellow stripe; all below this, and on the stomach, pure dead white; a pale oval mark on the tail; all the fins light semi-transparent."

Wondrously beautiful is the fish thus carefully described, but it is eclipsed, if possible, by the imperial *Chætodon* (from Greek words "I contain," "a tooth"), the generic name of a family of spiny-finned fishes inhabiting the southern seas of China. The singular splendour of this animal will give you an idea of the marvels that exist in the bosom of the deep. Its body is deep blue, marked all over by about thirty-two narrow bands of orange-yellow. The pectoral fins are black, and the entire tail a bright yellow. It is rather a large fish of its kind, sometimes attaining the length of fifteen inches. The tribe to which this fish belongs seems to have been particularly favoured, for Nature seems to have bestowed her brightest ornaments on them with a most lavish hand.

And here, my young friends, let me remark to you—however, diverging somewhat from my present subject—that the glorious beauty of these and other inhabitants of the warm seas, while it pleases the eye and excites admiration, has one drawback, and a very important one too. For the nourishment of man they are not to be compared to the far less showy but more wholesome fishes of the colder waters, which produce the species best suited for food, and very far superior in flavour. Professor Maury states from his own knowledge, that seamen, even after long voyages, prefer their salt beef and pork to a mess of fish, resplendent with all the hues of the rainbow, caught in the warm seas; reminding us of what the poet so aptly says:

> "It is the flavour forms the test of merit,
> Which, when with wholesome qualities combined,
> Forms the intrinsic value of all food.

> If mere exterior is to claim the palm,
> Then must the woodcock to the parrot yield,
> The spotted leopard supersede the deer,
> And dories to the blue-striped wrasse give place."

To the eye of the experienced naturalist, how many, varied, and beautiful are the forms which meet his gaze in the transparent depths of the ocean! Dr. Collingwood describes a magnificent spectacle which he witnessed and declares to be truly a wonder of the deep. This consisted of five or six large salpa-like (gelatinous) bodies, forming an oblique line, each one of a bright and delicate green colour, and with a large rich ruby spot, which shone in the water like carbuncles. Another consisted of a long and delicate chain, which might be compared to a necklace of diamonds set with brilliant rubies, the whole waving gracefully in the currents of the water.

Among these marine gems of the "purest water" which add such splendour to the submarine scenery of the tropics, I may mention, also, the ruby-coloured *Etelis*, a fish allied to the perch tribe—though differing, from possessing strong and long teeth—so named from its colour, which Cuvier compared to the tints of the ruby. The eye of this splendid fish is a conspicuous object, and of a golden orange. The colour of the etelis is bright ruby-red, relieved by stripes of bright golden yellow, which run along the ridges of the scales. But there are numbers of such glorious fishes—shoals

> "Of fish that with their fins and shining scales
> Glide under the green wave, in sculls that oft
> Bank the mid-sea;
>             Or, sporting with quick glance,
> Show to the sun their waved coats dropp'd with gold,
> Or in the pearly shells at ease attend
> Moist nutriment, or under rocks their food
> In painted armour watch."

The Indian Ocean, one of the five grand divisions of the universal ocean, is especially rich in its submarine scenery.

"We dive," says Schleiden, "into the liquid crystal of its waters, and it opens to us the most wondrous enchantments of the fairy tales of our childhood's dreams. The strangely branching thickets bear living flowers. Dense masses of *Meandrinus* (a genus of polyps), and *Astreas* (from the Greek, "a star;" animalculæ which form coral), contrast with the leafy cup-shaped expansions of the *Explanarius*, the variously ramified *Madrepores*, which are now spread out like fingers, now rise in trunk-like branches, and now display the most elegant array of interlacing branches. The colouring surpasses everything: vivid green alternates with brown or yellow; rich tints of purple, from pale red-brown to the deepest blue. Brilliant rosy, yellow, or peach-coloured *Nullipores* overgrow the decaying masses, and are themselves interwoven with the pearl-coloured plates of the *Retipores*, resembling the most delicate ivory carvings. Close by wave the yellow and lilac fans, perforated like trellis-work, of the *Gorgonius*. The clear sand of the bottom is covered with the thousand strange forms and tints of the sea-urchins and star-fishes. The leaf-like *Flustras* and *Escharas* adhere like mosses and lichens to the branches of the corals; the yellow, green, and purple-striped limpets cling like monstrous cochineal insects upon their trunks. Like gigantic cactus-blossoms, sparkling in the most ardent colours, the *Sea-Anemones* expand their crowns of tentacles upon the broken rocks, or more modestly embellish the flat bottom, looking like beds of variegated ranunculuses. Around the blossoms of the coral shrubs play the humming-birds of the ocean—little fish sparkling with red or blue metallic lustre, or gleaming in golden green, or in the brightest silvery tints.

"Softly, like spirits of the deep, the delicate milk-white or bluish bells of the jelly-fishes float through this charmed world. Here the gleaming violet and gold-green Isabelle, and the flaming yellow, black, and vermilion-striped coquette chase their prey; there the band-fish shoots snake-like through the thicket, like a long silver ribbon, glittering with rosy and azure hues. Then comes the fabulous cuttle-fish, decked in all colours of the rainbow, but marked by no definite outline; appearing and disappearing, inter-crossing, joining company and parting again, in most fantastic ways; and all this in the most rapid change, and amidst the most wonderful play of light and shade, altered by every breath of wind and every slight curling of the surface of the ocean. When day declines, and the shades of night lay hold upon the deep, the fantastic garden is lighted up with new splendour. Millions of glowing sparks, little microscopic medusas and crustaceans, dance like glowworms through the gloom. The sea-feather, which by daylight is vermilion-coloured, waves in a greenish phosphorescent light. Every corner of it is lustrous. Parts which by day were dull and brown, and retreated from the sight amidst the universal brilliancy of colour, are now radiant in the most wonderful play of green, yellow, and red light; and to complete the wonders of the enchanted night, the silver disc, six feet across, of the moon-fish, moves, slightly luminous, among the crowd of little sparkling stars."

How like a dream of romance and fairy beauty is this vivid description of submarine scenery in the tropics! What exquisite loveliness exists in those still, transparent waters! far exceeding in richness and colouring the most attractive objects that meet the eye on land. And while only a very small portion of these ocean wonders are unfolded to human gaze, what vast and countless glories are hidden in the great ocean depths to all save Him

"Who guides below, and rules above:
The great Disposer and the mighty King!
Than He none greater, next Him none
That can be, is, or was;
Supreme, He singly fills the throne."

But let us continue these fascinating descriptions from the lectures of Schleiden: "The most luxuriant vegetation of a tropical landscape cannot unfold as great wealth of form, while in the variety and splendour of colour it would stand far behind this garden landscape, which is strangely composed exclusively of animals, and not of plants; for, characteristic as the luxuriant development of vegetation of the temperate zones is of the sea bottom, the fulness and multiplicity of the marine Fauna is just as prominent in the regions of the tropics. Whatever is beautiful, wondrous, or uncommon in the great classes of fish and *Echinoderus*

# THE ASTERIAS OR STAR-FISHES.

(animals which include the sea-urchin and star-fish), jelly-fishes and polyps, and the molluscs of all kinds, is crowded into the warm and crystal waters of the tropical ocean—rests in the white sands, clothes the rough cliffs, clings, where the room is already occupied, like a parasite, upon the first comers, or swims through the shallows and depths of the elements; while the mass of the vegetation is of a far inferior magnitude."

I have, in the chapter on "The Rock-builders of the Ocean," mentioned the wonderful beauty of the coral regions; I will merely add, on this subject, the description given by Mr. Adams ("Voyage of H.M.S. Samarang") of what he witnessed in the clear ocean depths of the tropics.

"I am aware," he cautiously observes, "that persons have been accused of allowing their imaginations to trifle too freely with the reins in describing submarine scenery, but I shall simply state the matter as I found it. *Dentritic* (from the Greek *dentritis*, "like the growth of a tree") *zoophytes*, with their richly slender branches, loaded with innumerable variously coloured polypi, like trees covered with delicate blossoms, uprose from the clear clean bottom of the bay; distinct and characteristic in their specific forms, and contrasting strangely and powerfully with those most apathetic and stone-like combinations of the plant, the animal, and the rock, the *Madrepores*, the *Millipores*, and the *Nullipores*. Flat and immovably extended on the sand, in the bare spots between the corallines, were impassive large blue five-fingered star-fishes, and crawling with an awkward shuffling movement like an *Octopus* (from Greek words, "eight-footed;" a mollusc, whose mouth is surrounded with fleshy appendages which serve as feet), with their snaky arms groping their way among the weeds, and striving to insinuate their writhing forms beneath the coral masses. Fixed flower-like *Actiniæ* (polypi with numerous tentacles) were expanding their flashing petals on the rocks: all contributed to prove that Nature is ever weaving the subtle woof of existence beneath the surface of the waves."

The *Asterias*, or star-fishes, so frequently alluded to in the descriptions of submarine scenery by naturalists, belong to a genus of molluscous worms, and some species you must often have observed on the sea-shore. The most curious of the sea-stars, perhaps, is that called *Caput Medusæ*, or basket-fish, which inhabits most seas, and consists of five central rays, each of which divides into two smaller ones, and these are again divided into two others; the same kind of division and subdivision being continued to a vast extent, and every ray regularly decreasing in size, until at length the ramifications amount to many thousands, forming a beautiful network spread over the water. The colour of the worm varies, being sometimes pale, sometimes reddish, white, and brown. The arms of the star-fishes are furnished on their lower surfaces with suckers, which enable them to crawl along the smoothest rocks.

The madrepores, millipores, and nullipores are polypi, classed by Cuvier in the third family of the *Coralliferi*, including all the numerous species which were for a long time regarded as marine plants, and in which numerous individuals are so united as to form compound animals, for the most part fixed, like plants, by a branched stem, or by simple expansions of a solid substance at the base or in the middle of the group.

No more lovely ornaments of "submarine gardens" could be imagined than the *Anemones*, a name thus applied about a century ago by the indefatigable naturalist, Ellis, who made them the subject of some remarkable investigations, and who remarks that "their tentacles being disposed of in regular circles, and tinged with a variety of bright lively colours, very nearly represent the beautiful petals of some of our most elegantly fringed and radiated flowers, such as the carnation, marigold, and anemone," reminding us of what Du Bartas says, in his quaint poem on the birth of the world, that seas have

> "Pinks, gilliflowers, mushrooms, and many millions
> Of other plants."

You must have frequently seen some of the smaller species of anemones on the rocks of our sea-coast and in aquariums, but to observe these animals in their full bloom of loveliness, we must gaze into the transparent waters of the tropical seas, where they attain their greatest size and beauty, spreading out their delicate tentacles or "feelers," and displaying all the vivid colours which render them so remarkable. The similarity of some of these animal "flowers" to the Flora of the earth is very singular. Hughes, in his "Natural History of Barbadoes," describes some of them as found in a submarine rock-basin:

"In the middle of it there is a fixed stone or rock which is always under water. Round its sides, at different depths, seldom exceeding eighteen inches, are seen at all times of the year, issuing out of little holes, certain substances that have the appearance of fine radiated flowers, of a pale yellow or a bright straw-colour, slightly tinged with green, having a circular border of thickset petals, about the size of, and much resembling, those of a single garden marigold, except that the whole of this seeming flower is narrower at the setting on of the leaves than any flower of that kind."

> "Each following billow lifted the last foam
> That trembled on the sand with rainbow hues;
> The living flower that, rooted to the rock,
> Late from the thinner element,
> Shrank down within its purple stem to sleep,
> Now feels the water, and again
> Awakening, blossoms out
> All its green anther necks."

This reads like a gardener's description of some new and rare plants.

But the elegance and beauty of the anemones belong only to their native element; when left dry by the receding tide, they contract into a jelly-like mass, and the glorious hues that shone through the clear waters of the ocean fade away.

"I once cut off," adds Mr. Hughes, "with a knife which I had held for a long time out of sight near the mouth of a hole out of which one of these animals appeared, two of the seeming leaves. These, when out of the water, retained their shape and colour; but being composed of a membrane-like substance, surprisingly thin, it soon shrivelled up and decayed."

Each species generally selects a peculiar haunt, but they are found in every sea. Some appear suspended from the vaults of submarine reefs; others cover the more exposed sides of rocks with a sort of flower-like tapestry.

One species commonly found on our own coasts, and a gem of the aquarium, is named *Mesembryanthemum* (from *mesembris*, "midday," and *anthemon*, "a flower"), after the fig-marigold, an annual of our English flower-gardens. If you look attentively at one of these animals, you will be struck with its remarkable beauty. Around the margin of the mouth there is a circle of little azure knobs or knots, like turquoise beads. Another British sea-anemone, called the *Crassicornis*, exhibits the most attractive colours—red, varied with white, orange, green, and yellow.

The term applied by naturalists to these very interesting "animal-flowers" is *Actinia* (from the Greek *aktin*, "a ray"), subdivided into a number of genera, and is now the type of a family called *Actiniadæ*.

The sea-anemones are a hungry class, preying especially on small crabs, which they clasp in a fond embrace, and eventually devour. Another peculiarity in these strange and beautiful marine animals is their power of reproducing organs of their own bodies that may have been broken off. Mr. Bennett relates:

"I had once brought to me a specimen of the crassicornis, that might have been originally two inches in diameter, and that had, somehow, contrived to swallow a valve of *Pecten maximus* (a genus of two-shelled molluscs) of the size of an ordinary saucer. The shell, fixed within the stomach, was so placed as to divide it completely into two halves, so that the body, stretched tightly over, had become thin and flattened like a pancake. All communication between the interior portion of the stomach and the mouth was, of course, prevented; yet, instead of emaciating and dying of an atrophy, the animal had availed itself of what had undoubtedly been a very untoward accident, to increase its enjoyments and its chances of double fare. A new mouth, furnished with two rows of numerous tentacula, was opened up at what had been the base, and led to the under-stomach: the individual had become a sort of Siamese twin, but with greater intimacy and extent in its unions."

The anemones I need scarcely further describe to you, except as soft fleshy bodies, with mouths surrounded by several rows of tentacles or feelers, which they expand, contract, and move at will with wonderful ease, shrinking when touched into a solid round mass with a slippery surface, which renders it difficult to remove them without injury.

The singular clearness of the waters of the Red Sea has often been noticed by travellers, as presenting views of submarine scenery of the greatest beauty. Aiton, in his "Lands of the Messiah, Mahomet, and the Pope," says:

"When leaning over the edge of our boat on the smooth surface of the sea, I could distinctly see the pebbles and the pure white sand at a depth even of one hundred and eighty feet. Through the body of the water I could discern the minutest objects at an immense depth. The secrets of the deep thus laid open to me afforded the most magnificent spectacles that could be conceived. In one part I noticed whole forests of pale pink and red coral, spreading forth their luxuriant branches, and imparting a blush to the element in which they grew. How varied, how beautiful was their colouring! a brilliant red or blue, or gorgeous with orange or the deepest black. In one spot they were of a dead white or living purple, in another a bright yellow or crimson, and everywhere fancifully diversified."

It is in the Red Sea also that the strange family to which the *Sea-Slug* and the *Sea-Cucumber* belong are found in great abundance —many of the species exhibiting splendid colours, and making the bottom of the sea, particularly among coral formations, gay and lovely as a garden. Here also are seen the zoophyte *Gorgonias*, the stem of which is usually brown or black, whilst the fleshy parts often exhibit colours of great brilliancy. One species, the *Sea-Fan*, is brought to us as a curiosity. Here are also the *Serpula* (from the Latin *serpo*, "I creep"), a species of ringed animals, like worms, inhabiting a limy tube like that of molluscs, which they attach to rocks and shells in the sea. The wide end of the tube is open, and from this the animal protrudes its head and gills, which expand as beautiful fan-like tufts. They are generally most splendidly coloured. And here also are the *Sertularia*, a genus of zoophytes attached to stones, shells, and sea-weeds, and very beautiful, reminding us of the lines of Southey:

> "And here were coral bowers,
>   And grots of madrepores,
> And banks of sponge, as soft and fair to eye
>   As e'er was mossy bed
> Whereon the wood-nymphs lie
>   With languid limbs in summer's sultry hours.
> Here, too, were living flowers,
>   Which, like a bud compacted,
>   Their purple cups contracted.
>   And now, in open blossoms spread,
> Stretched like green anthers many a seeking head;
>   And arborets of jointed stone were there,
> And plants of fibres, fine as silkworm thread:
>   Yes, beautiful as mermaid's golden hair,
>    Upon the waves dispread;
>   Others, that like the broad banana glowing,
> Raised their long wrinkled leaves of purple hue,
>   Like streamers wide outflowing."

The waters of the North Sea, along the west coast of the Scandinavian peninsula, have been remarked by all observers for being of an extraordinary transparency. "As we passed," says Sir Arthur de Capel Brooke, "slowly over the surface, the bottom, which here was in general a white sand, was clearly visible with its minutest objects, where the depth was from one hundred and twenty to one hundred and fifty feet. During the whole course of the tour I made, nothing appeared to me so extraordinary as the inmost recesses of the deep thus unveiled to the eye. The surface of the ocean was unruffled by the slightest breeze, and the gentle splashing of the oars scarcely disturbed it. Hanging over the gunwale of the boat, with wonder and delight I gazed on the slowly moving scene below. Where the bottom was sandy, the different kinds of asteriæ, echini, and even the smallest shells, appeared at that great depth conspicuous to the eye, and the water seemed in some measure to have the effect of a magnifier, by enlarging the objects like a telescope, and bringing them seemingly nearer. Now, creeping along, we saw, far beneath, the rugged sides of a mountain, rising towards our boat, the base of which, perhaps, was hidden some miles in the great deep below. Though moving on a level surface, it seemed almost as if we were ascending the height under us; and when we passed over its summit, which rose in appearance to within a few feet of our boat, and came again to the descent, which on this side was suddenly perpendicular, and overlooking a watery gulf, as we pushed gently over the last point of it, it seemed almost as if we had thrown ourselves down this precipice, the illusion, from the crystal clearness of the deep, actually producing a sudden start. Now we came again to a plain, and passed slowly over the submarine forests and meadows which appeared in the expanse below; inhabited, doubtless, by thousands of animals, to which they afford both food and shelter,—animals unknown to man; and I could sometimes observe large fishes of singular shape gliding softly through the watery thickets, unconscious of what was moving above them. As we proceeded the bottom became no longer visible; its fairy scenes gradually faded to the view, and were lost in the dark green depths of the ocean."

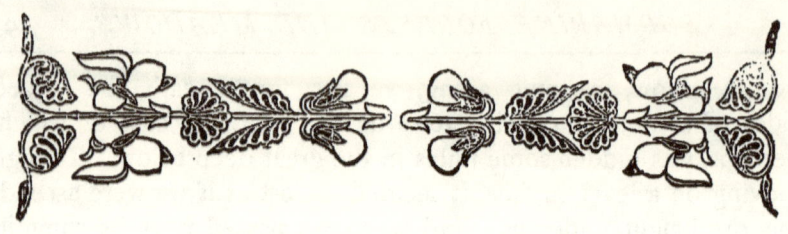

## CHAPTER XIX.

### THE FLOATING NAVIGATORS OF THE OCEAN.

"Spread, tiny nautilus, the living sail,
  Dive at thy choice, or brave the freshening gale!
If unreprov'd the ambitious eagle mount
Sunward, to seek the daylight in its fount,
Bays, gulfs, and ocean's Indian widths shall be
Till the world perishes a field for thee."
WORDSWORTH.

AMONG the most interesting and poetical illustrations of the wonders of the ocean are the singular floating animals, of which the *Nautilus*—called by Byron "the ocean Mab," "the Fairy of the Sea"—will be, undoubtedly, familiar to you from the great beauty of its shell, which renders it a favourite ornament in many houses.

Very pretty stories and verses have been written on the sailing and rowing habits of these curious animals; and their appearance, when seen skimming the water, would strongly favour such ideas. The Dutch naturalist, Rumphius (who died in 1706), writing in the year previous to his decease, and giving an account of the rarities at Amboyna, the principal of the Molucca islands, says, "When the nautilus floats on the water, he puts out his head and all his tentacles, and spreads them upon the water; but at the bottom he creeps in a reversed position, with his boat above him, and with his head and tentacles (feelers) on the ground, making a

THE NAUTILUS.—P. 195

tolerably quick progress. He keeps himself chiefly on the ground, creeping also, sometimes, into the nets of the fishermen; but after a storm, as the weather gets calm, they are seen in troops, floating on the water, being driven up by the agitation of the waves. This sailing is not, however, of long continuance, for having taken in all their tentacles, they upset their boat and so return to the bottom."

Until a comparatively recent period, very little was known of the nautilus; for, although shells were plentifully found on the shores of the warm seas it inhabits, the fish itself, living chiefly at the bottom of the sea, creeping like a snail, or lying in wait for runaway crabs or suchlike food, was difficult to obtain. However, in 1829, a specimen was captured by Mr. Bennett, a naturalist, at the New Hebrides, and the great naturalist, Professor Owen, described the fish in a valuable memoir. The specimen is still preserved in the museum of the Royal College of Surgeons, in London. Little could be known from the shell itself; but here was the tiny navigator of the ocean, that would ride out a storm in which the strongest man-of-war might founder, revealed in all its most curious mechanism; the oars and aërial sails—to which Pope (among many others) alludes in his "Essay on Man,"

"Learn of the little nautilus to sail,
Spread the thin oar, and catch the driving gale,"—

disappearing, to give place to its real method of propulsion.

The *Paper Nautilus* has eight tentacles, and one pair of these expand at their extremities into broad and thin membranes, which, I need scarcely tell you, compose a web of several sorts of fibres, interwoven for the wrapping up of some parts, the fibres giving them an elasticity by which they can contract and grasp the parts they contain—whence the fable received through so many ages, of its sails; the membranous arms of the fish are the organs for secreting and repairing the shells.

The functions of the supposed sails of the paper nautilus were determined by an experiment. One of the "sails" was cut off in several living specimens, the right sail being removed in some, the left in others; and the creatures were then kept in a submarine cage, and supplied with food. Some of them survived the operation for four months, when it was found that the shell had grown only on that side on which the membranous arm had been preserved; thus showing the animal to be the builder of its own habitation, and that the expanded arms do not serve the purposes of sails.

A real rower on the ocean is the beautiful little blue and silver shell-fish, the *Glaucus*, also a tenant of the warm seas, who swims with great swiftness by aid of its conical and oar-like appendages.

A wonderful builder is the nautilus, as you would find if you saw the chambers it fashions for its own accommodation; for the shell is divided into partitions, and as the animal increases in size it forms another and larger apartment proportionate to its growth, leaving the others empty as it proceeds, until, satisfied with its labours, it becomes the occupant of the highest chamber, though still communicating with the cells it has abandoned, by means of a membranous tube which passes through the centre of each, enabling the nautilus, by throwing air or gas into the empty chambers, or by exhausting them of air, to rise or sink into the water at will.

An American writer, O. W. Holmes, has written some very sweet verses on the peculiarity of this nautilus, which you will read with pleasure :

> " This is the ship of pearl, which poets feign
>     Sails the unshadow'd main—
>         The venturous bark that flings
>     On the sweet summer wind its purpled wings
>     In gulfs enchanted, where the syren sings,
>         And coral reef lies bare,
> Where the cold sea-maids rise to sun their streaming hair.

> "Its webs of living gauze no more unfurl,
>     Wreck'd is the ship of pearl!
>         And ev'ry chamber'd cell
>     Where its dim dreaming life was wont to dwell,
>     As the frail tenant shap'd his growing shell,
>         Before thee lies reveal'd—
> Its iris'd ceiling rent, its sunless crypt unseal'd !

"Year after year beheld the silent toil
   That spread his lustrous coil;
      Still, as the spiral grew,
   He left the past year's dwelling for the new,
   Still with soft step its shining archway through,
      Built up its idle door,
Stretch'd in his last-found home, and knew the old no more.

"Thanks for the heavenly message brought by thee,
      Child of the wandering sea,
      Cast from her lap, forlorn!
   From thy dead lips a clearer note is borne
   Than ever Triton blew from wreathèd horn!
      While on mine ear it rings,—
Through the deep caves of thought I hear a voice that sings:

"'Build thee more stately mansions, O my soul,
      As the swift seasons roll!
      Leave thy low-vaulted past!
   Let each new temple, nobler than the last,
   Shut thee from heaven with a dome more vast,
      Till thou at length art free,
Leaving thine outgrown shell by life's unresting sea.'"

How truly wonderful is the intelligence displayed by the tiny nautilus in its chambered dwelling! "These beautiful arrangements," as the late Dean Buckland remarked, "are and ever have been subservient to a common object—the construction of hydraulic instruments, of essential importance in the economy of creatures destined to move sometimes at the bottom, and at other times upon or near the surface of the sea. The delicate adjustments whereby the same principle is extended through so many grades and modifications of a single type, show the uniform and constant agency of some controlling intelligence; and in searching for the origin of so much method and regularity amidst variety, the mind can only rest when it has passed back through the subordinate series of second causes to the great First Cause, which is found in the will and power of a great Creator."

The *Pearly Nautilus*, thus named from the shell being lined with a layer of the most beautiful pearly gloss, inhabits the Indian and Pacific Oceans. Nothing can exceed the pure loveliness of this "gem of the deep;" the interior being white, like the finest porcelain, and streaked with reddish chestnut. It is highly prized in Eastern countries, where it is made into drinking-cups. The Chinese are particularly expert in manufacturing it into various ornaments.

There are other floating navigators of the deep; among others, the *Snail-slime-fishes*, which frequent the Arctic seas, and are found in immense quantities on the coast of Spitzbergen. The shell is the boat of this animal, which it rows through the water by a dip of its raised fins. In this act the open extremity of the shell is its prow, the opposite end occupies the place of a poop, and the margin of the body resembles and performs the office of a keel. Otho Fabricius, in his "Fauna Greenlandica," says, "I have often seen it with admiration and pleasure. He can move in a retrograde manner. When weary with rowing, or when touched, the little boatman contracts his oary fins, and drawing within the shell, sinks to the bottom, where he rests for a short time. Then again he rises upwards, rowing obliquely until the surface is attained, when his course is held in a straight line over the trackless surge. When taken out of the shell, although without injury and in the water, he immediately dies."

Before quitting the nautilus, I may add, that the shells of this "ocean navigator" abound in the coral seas, and are cast on shore in such profusion, that many tons' weight are collected at New Caledonia and the Figi Islands, and are conveyed to Sydney. The young shells, when polished, obtain a high price.

The *Argonaut* differs from the true nautilus, inasmuch as its shell is not divided into chambers, but has one spiral cavity, into which the animal can entirely withdraw itself. From the disproportionate size of the last whorl (a wreath or turning of the spires of *univalves*, or shells of one piece only) it has some resemblance to a canoe, the spire representing the poop. If the waves rise or danger threatens, the argonaut withdraws all its arms into the shell, contracts itself there, and descends to the bottom. The body does not penetrate within the spire of the shell, nor does it adhere to it; at least, there is no muscular attachment, which led to the supposition that it occupied a shell belonging to some other animal. This freebooting stigma does not belong to the argonaut, for experiments have proved that the animal is its own builder, and consequently a rightful tenant of his mansion.

There is a curious and highly interesting floating object to which I would now draw your attention, the "*Sea-Bladder*" (*Physalia pelagica*, from the Greek *physe*, "a bladder"), called by our seamen the "Portuguese man-of-war," and by the French sailors the "galley" or "frigate." This singular zoophyte, or animal-plant, for it combines the two natures, is seen floating, sometimes singly, at other times in vast numbers, in the tropical seas, and attracted the attention of naturalists from a very early period. The notion of its sailing properties may have arisen in consequence of the crest which it has the power of erecting along the ridge of its back, which, when caught by the wind, assumes somewhat the appearance of a natural sail, by means of which it seems enabled to glide over the surface of the ocean. This, however, I should tell you, is not the case, as the creature does not move by this means, nor does it appear to possess the power of imparting any special direction to its course, which is entirely at the mercy of the winds and waves. The body itself, upon which the ridge or crest erects itself, is of a slight half-transparent character, and has somewhat the appearance of an unusually solid soap-bubble, glistening with a more than ordinary amount of various coloured hues.

Mr. Bennett, in his "Gatherings of a Naturalist in Australia," describes this body as of delicate crimson tints, as he saw it floating on the waves. There are also veinings of rich purple, and opaline flashes of azure, orange, and green, changing in colour at every movement; and its long dependent tentacles or feelers are of the deepest purple.

Dr. Collingwood mentions having observed these splendid zoophytes in the Atlantic Ocean, near the equator, sailing by from time to time during the day, and attracting attention by their large size and brilliant colour. "They had the appearance of beautiful prismatic shells, standing upright on a rich blue cushion, the cell being radiated from the base or cushion to the circumference, which was fringed with a rich and bright rose-colour." Dr. Collingwood captured several specimens, and the largest measured in the bladder eight inches, and the greatest vertical circumference ten inches and a quarter. Mr. Bennett says: "The long dependent tentacles or feelers are from four to five feet in length, and are capable of being extended much farther when shot off for the capture of prey."

But the glory of these magnificent objects, so developed in their native element, fades, like sea-weeds, as the zoophyte is taken from its watery home, with the exception of the long tentacles, which retain their colour (dark purple) until decomposition takes place. "There is no rose without a thorn," is a well-known saying; and this gaily-coloured zoophyte has a dangerous stinging property to those who handle it incautiously. Dr. Collingwood relates an instance of a sailor seeing one within reach from a boat, who took it up with his naked hands; the threads or elastic tentacles clung to his arm, causing the man to yell with agony. He was quickly brought on board, and ran about like a maniac, requiring several men to hold him. When secured, and the proper remedies applied, he rolled about for some time groaning with pain; his arm was red, inflamed, and swollen, and remained so for some hours.

Its earliest modern name of "sea-nettle" is derived from that conferred upon this class of marine creatures by Aristotle, in consequence of the burning sting caused by the poisonous tentacles or feelers of several members of this group; a sting which leaves after it a white pimple, like that caused by a nettle.

A remarkable interest is attached to the nautilus from the very remote periods of time to which it can be traced; fossils being found in the most ancient rocks in which shell animals have been discovered, in various parts of the world, living ages before the Flood in temperate and tropical seas. In the London clay, which forms such a large extent of the substratum (under layer of soil) of the great metropolis, lie buried vast numbers of the pearly shells of the nautilus, which, evidently at a great distance of time, found in our own country a congenial climate and home. The largest British specimens of the fossil nautilus occur in the carboniferous limestone, and you may see specimens of these in the British Museum more than a yard in length, and thick in proportion.

In the museum of the Royal College of Surgeons, in London, you may see a specimen of the entire animal, soft parts and shell, of the pearly nautilus: a portion of the shell has been removed to show some of the chambers, and the membranous tube or syphon which traverses them. There is also a specimen of the paper nautilus (*Argonauta Argo*) suspended as when floating, with the expanded membranous arms in their natural position spread over the shell which they form and repair.

Resembling somewhat in appearance the nautilus, the shell being chambered and spiral, but differing otherwise in some respects, was the primitive navigator of the ancient seas, the *Ammonite*, of which the shells now only remain, the most beautiful of all our fossils, and found in almost every country in the world, upwards of two hundred species having been described. The name is derived from a fancied resemblance of its shell to the ram's horn ornaments on sculptured heads of Jupiter Ammon. They are of very different sizes, varying to even three or four feet in diameter. The larger ones were formerly taken for petrified snakes, and were found in great numbers at Whitby in Yorkshire. Sir Walter Scott alludes to this popular superstition in his poem of "Marmion," where the nuns of Whitby exultingly told

> "How of thousand snakes, each one
> Was changed into a coil of stone,
> When holy Hilda pray'd."

The visitors to Whitby are still invited to buy a petrified snake, and to add to their natural appearance, the mouth of the ammonite is carved into a head, and eyes are introduced made of coloured glass.

The ammonite, with a shell a yard across, would have been an animal large in proportion to its body-chamber, and requiring a certain amount of water to be displaced by its shell, to move at ease along the bottom of the sea in search of its food. The shell of the ammonite, though of the same flat character as that of the nautilus, appears to have been much thinner; but, to compensate for this, there were flutings which are seen in the surface, occasioned by the transverse (or crossing from corner to corner) ribs. The round knobs or bosses studding some of the ammonites were like gems on a diadem, adding strength as well as beauty to their form. The whorls or wreaths of the shell were rounder and more in number than that of the nautilus, and the tubes—the hydraulic instinct by which the chambers were supplied with air, or exhausted, for the ascent or descent of the animal—instead of running through the cells like that of the nautilus, went *round* the chambers of the ammonite.

How strange are the vicissitudes of all created things! While some survive the shocks and rents of time, others are known only as fossil memorials of the primitive world. The nautilus still rides on the crest of the ocean waves, but the ammonite—long, long since removed from the element in which it lived—only remains as a petrifaction to tell of its existence in ages before the Flood.

A poet and geologist (Richardson) has alluded to this in some charming verses:

> "The nautilus and the ammonite
> Were launch'd in storm and strife,
> Each sent to float, in its tiny boat,
> On the wide, wild sea of life.

> "And each could swim on the ocean's brim,
> And anon its sails could furl,
> And sink to sleep in the great sea-deep,
> In a palace all of pearl.

> "Thus, hand in hand, from strand to strand
> They sailed in mirth and glee,
> Those fairy shells, with their crystal cells,
> Twin creatures of the sea!

> "But they came at last to a sea long past,
> And as they reach'd the shore,
> The Almighty's breath spoke out in death,
> And the ammonite lived no more.

> "And the nautilus now, in its shelly prow,
> As o'er the deep it strays,
> Still seems to seek, in bay and creek,
> Its companion of other days.

> "And thus do we, on life's stormy sea,
> As we roam from shore to shore,
> While tempest-toss'd, seek the loved, the lost,
> But find them on earth no more."

I must not omit to mention the little floating *Pteropoda* (from two Greek words signifying "a wing" and "a foot"), or *Wing-shells*, the inhabitants of which pass their entire life in the sea far away from any shelter except that afforded by the floating Gulf-weed, and whose organization is peculiarly adapted to that sphere of existence. In appearance they strikingly resemble the fry of the ordinary sea-snails, swimming, like them, by the vigorous flapping of a pair of fins. To the naturalist on shore they are almost unknown, but the voyager on the great ocean meets them where there is little else to arrest his attention, and marvels at their delicate forms and almost incredible numbers. They swarm in the tropical, and no less the Arctic seas, where by their myriads (as Scoresby informs us), the water is discoloured by them for leagues. They are seen swimming on the surface in the heat of the day, as well as in the cool of the evening. In high latitudes they are the principal food of the whale and of many sea-birds.

Another floating inhabitant of the deep is described by Mr. Adams as the beautiful *Ianthina* or *Ocean-Snail*, which is quite blind, and has large horny mandibles (jaws), furnished with sharp, curved, slender teeth. This animal is remarkable for floating shell downwards in the water, and Mr. Adams tells us that the anterior part of the foot forms a shallow cup, which embraces the smooth anterior rounded part of the float. Thus the fish can raise or lower itself in the water at pleasure. When it wishes to bring its head to the surface of the water, this part of the foot is made to glide over the back of the float. The floats are made of a mucous film containing air; and when cut with scissors, the animal descended to the bottom of the vessel in which it was consigned, and did not make a new one.

The nautili belong to a class called *Cephalopoda* by Linnæus, (from the Greek, *kephale*, "head," and *pous*, "foot," so named from the singular attachment of the feet to the head—locomotive organs employed as oars or feet when moving along the bottom of the sea, and consisting of a circlet of muscular arms or tentacles, in addition to which many of this class have fins. To this same definition of Linnæus belong the *Cuttle-fish*, the bony scale on the back of which you must have frequently picked up on the sea-shore, and which is employed for making pounce, tooth-powder, for polishing, and other purposes in the arts.

The common cuttle-fish is abundant on the English coasts. Its skin is smooth, whitish, and dotted with red. It attains the length of a foot or more, and is one of the pests of the fishermen, devouring partially the fish which have been caught in their nets. The eggs of the cuttle-fish are frequently cast on shore clustered together. Singularly interesting is the study of these creatures, which are provided with a means of escaping danger, in their ink-bags, from which they can at will emit a fluid, darkening the water and thus enabling them to get off. This natural ink of the fish is employed in painting; Cicero tells us that it was anciently used for writing with.

Another property possessed by this class of animals is, that if any of its tentacles or feelers are bitten off, which is often the case—the conger eel having a special relish for the dainty morsel—others supply their place, the power of reproduction being given to them. The whale also regales on the cuttle-fish, and the plaice tribe have the same partiality. The most common species form the bait with which one-half of the cod taken at Newfoundland are caught.

The general description of the cuttle-fish may be thus described: the body oblong, or longer than broad, and depressed, sac-like, with two narrow lateral fins of similar substance with the mantle (the outside skin of shell-fish, which covers a great part of the body, like a cloak). There is an internal shell lodged in a sac on the back part of the mantle, somewhat oval and bladder-shaped, being comparatively thick near the anterior end, where it is terminated by a sharp point, affixed, as it were, to its general outline. The whole shell is light and porous, and is formed of thin plates, with intervening spaces, divided by innumerable partitions, and consists chiefly of carbonate of lime, with a little gelatinous and other animal matter, which is most abundant in the internal harder part of the shell. The eyes are very large, and the head is furnished with eight arms, each of which has four rows of suckers and two long tentacles, expanded and furnished with suckers on one side at the extremity. Cuttle-fish are enabled to leap out of the water by the sudden extension, not of their tails, but of their numerous arms, or other processes from their bodies.

In hot climates some of the species of cuttle-fish grow to a prodigious size, and are furnished with a fearful apparatus of arms with suckers, by which they can rigidly fasten upon and convey their prey to the mouth. In the eight-armed species which inhabit the Indian seas these tentacles are said to be no less than nine fathoms in length.

Extraordinary stories have been related of these animals. Pliny mentions the head of one which was as large as a cask, the arms thirty-six feet long. They are described as first darting from side to side in the pools, and fixing themselves so tenaciously to the surface of the stones that great force was required to remove them. When thrown upon the sand, they progressed rapidly in a sidelong shuffling manner, throwing about their long arms, ejecting their inky fluid in sudden violent jets, and staring about with their shining eyes in a grotesque and hideous manner. As food it was highly prized by the ancients, and is still much esteemed in some parts of the world. It is regularly exposed for sale in the markets at Naples, Smyrna, and in the bazaars of India. In a curious Japanese book there is a picture of a man in a boat engaged in catching cuttle-fishes with a spear; and also of a fishmonger's shop in Japan, where a number of enormous cuttle-fishes are represented hanging up for sale.

The Rev. Mr. Stewart relates that at Siho Siho, Pauchi, a queen of one of the Pacific islands, was one day seated in the Turkish fashion on the ground, with a large wooden tray in her lap. On this a monstrous cuttle-fish had been placed, fresh from the sea and in all its life and vigour. The queen had taken it up in both hands and brought its body to her mouth, and by a single application of her teeth the black juices and blood with which it was filled gushed over her face and neck, while the long sucking arms of the fish, in the convulsive paroxysm of the operation, were writhing about her head like snakes. A more disgusting picture of epicurism it would be difficult to imagine.

Columbus describes the mode of fishing with the cuttle-fish pursued in his time by the natives of Santa Marta:

"They had a small fish, the flat head of which was furnished with numerous suckers, by which it attached itself so firmly to any object as to be torn in pieces rather than abandon its hold. Tying a line of great length to the tail of this fish, the Indians permitted it to swim at large. It generally kept near the surface of the water until it perceived its prey, when, darting down swiftly, it attached itself by its suckers to the throat of a fish, or to the under shell of a tortoise, nor did it relinquish its prey until both were drawn up by the fisherman, and taken out of the water."

In this way the Spaniards witnessed the taking of a tortoise of immense size, and Fernando Columbus himself affirms that he saw a shark caught in this manner on the coast of Veragua.

This account, strange as it may seem, has been corroborated by various navigators, and the same mode of fishing is said to be employed on the eastern coast of Africa, at Mozambique, and at Madagascar.

The South Sea Islanders have a curious contrivance for taking the cuttle-fish, which resort to the holes of the coral rocks, and protrude their arms or tentacles for the bait, but remain themselves firm within the retreat. The instrument employed for taking them consists of a straight piece of hard wood, a foot long, round and polished, and not half an inch in diameter. Near one end of this a number of the most beautiful pieces of the cowry or tiger-shell are fastened, one over the other, like the scales of a fish or the plates of a piece of armour, until it is about the size of a turkey's egg, and resembles the cowry. It is suspended in an horizontal position by a strong line, and is lowered by the fisherman from a small canoe until it nearly reaches the bottom. The fisherman then gently jerks the line, causing the shell to move as if it were inhabited by a fish. The cuttle-fish, attracted, it is supposed, by the appearance of the cowry (for no bait is used), darts out one of its arms, which it winds round the shell and fastens among the openings between the plates. The fisherman continues jerking the line, and the fish puts out successively its other arms until it has fastened itself to the shells, when it is drawn up into the canoe and secured.

In conclusion, I will mention that the cuttle-fish belongs to a period before the Flood, like the nautili; their undigested fossil remains are frequently noticed within the ribs of the *Ichthyosauri* and *Plesiosauri* in the limestone rocks, showing that then, as in the present day, to eat and to be eaten was the general law of nature.

## CHAPTER XX.

### *PHENOMENA OF THE OCEAN—ATMOSPHERIC INFLUENCES.*

"Truly great and transcendantly beautiful, O Jehovah! are these Thy works even here below. Framed they are in profound wisdom, disclosing all their charms only to our lens-aided eyes. How grand, then, will be those which—when the glass has been removed in which we see darkly—when this mist of mortality has been scattered—Thou art pledged to reveal hereafter to Thy servants that have worshipped Thee here in sincerity and truth!"

HEDWIG.

THE navigators in the Northern seas have the opportunity of witnessing to perfection some curious phenomena, among which I may mention the *Mirage*, a name given by the French to an optical deception in the atmosphere by which a ship appears as if transferred to the sky. These appearances were regarded by the credulous, in former times, as supernatural; but they are referred to the refractive and reflective properties of the atmosphere. Not only is there an increase in the vertical dimensions of the objects affected, so that low coasts frequently assume a bold and precipitous outline, but objects sunk below the horizon are brought into view with their natural position changed and distorted.

Dr. Hayes, in his "Open Polar Sea," gives the following vivid description of the optical delusion:

"These Arctic skies," he says, "do sometimes play fantastic

tricks, and on no occasion have I witnessed the exhibition to such perfection. The atmosphere had a rare softness, and throughout almost the whole day there was visible a most remarkable mirage, or refraction, an event of very frequent occurrence during the calm days of the Arctic summer. The entire horizon was lifting and doubling itself continually, and objects at a great distance beyond it rose, as if by strange enchantment, and stood suspended in the air, changing shape with each changing moment. Distant icebergs and floating ice-fields, and coast-lines and mountains, were thus brought into view—sometimes preserving for a moment their natural shapes, then widening and lengthening, rising and falling, as the wind fluttered or fell calm over the sea. The changes were as various as the dissolving images of a kaleidoscope, and every form the imagination could conceive stood out against the sky. At one moment a sharp spire, the prolonged image of a distant mountain-peak would shoot up, and this would fashion itself into a cross, or a spear, or a human form, and would then die away, to be replaced by an iceberg, which appeared as a castle standing upon the summit of a hill, and the ice-fields coming up with it flanked it on either side, seeming at one moment like a plain, dotted with trees and animals; again, as rugged mountains, and then breaking up after awhile, disclosed a long line of bears, and dogs, and birds, men dancing in the air and skipping from the sea to the sky. There was no end to the forms which appeared every instant, melting into other shapes as suddenly. For hours we watched the 'insubstantial pageant,' until a wind from the north ruffled the sea, when, with its first breath, the whole scene melted away as quickly as the 'baseless fabric' of Prospero's vision."

Scoresby, during a voyage to the eastern coast of Greenland, was amused by the singular refractive power of the Polar atmosphere. The rugged surface of the coast assumed the form of castles, obelisks, and spires, which here and there were linked together, so as to present the appearance of an extensive city. At other times it resembled a forest of naked trees, and it was easy to conceive colossal statues, porticoes of rich and regular architecture, shapes of lions, bears, horses, &c. Ships were seen inverted, and suspended high in the air, and their hulls often so magnified as to resemble huge edifices. Objects really beneath the horizon were raised into view in a most extraordinary manner. It seems positively ascertained, that points on the Greenland shore, not above three or four thousand feet high, were seen at the distance of one hundred and sixty miles. The extensive evaporation of the melting ice, with the unequal condensation produced by streams of cold air, are considered as the chief sources of this extraordinary refraction.

The same navigator relates that when in the Polar Sea, his ship had been separated for some time from that of his father, which he had been looking out for with great anxiety. At length, one evening, to his astonishment, he beheld the vessel suspended in the air in an inverted position, with the most distinct and perfect representation. Sailing in the direction of this visionary appearance, he met with the real ship by this indication. It was found that the vessel had been thirty miles distant, and seventeen beyond the horizon, where her appearance was thus elevated into the air by this extraordinary refraction.

Sometimes two images of a vessel are seen, the one erect and the other inverted, with their topmasts and their hulls meeting, according as the inverted image is above or below the other.

"The most remarkable instance of mirage I have seen," says Dr. Kelly, "was that in which a vessel, with all sails set, at one moment looked like an immense black chest, no sails or masts being visible. On observing her for a time, the black body seemed to separate horizontally into two parts, and two sets of mingled sails occupied the intervening spaces, with one set of very small sails above. The figures afterwards became more distinct, and three images were clearly discerned. Another vessel changed, also, from the form of a great square flat-topped chest, to five distinct images, the upper with the sails erect, and the two lower double images with their sails rather confusedly intermingled."

Another phenomenon which is seen in its highest perfection in the Polar seas is the *Aurora Borealis*, or the "Northern Daybreak," so named from its appearance in that part of the heavens, and its close resemblance to the aspect of the sky before sunrise.

The lines of James Montgomery on this grand spectacle of nature are very fine:

> "Midnight hath told his hour; the moon, yet young,
> Hangs in the argent west, her bow unstrung;
> Larger and fairer, as her lustre fades,
> Sparkle the stars amidst the deepening shades:
> Jewels more rich than night's regalia gem
> The distant ice-blink's spangled diadem;
> Like a new morn from Orient darkness, there
> Phosphoric splendours kindle in mid-air,
> As though from heaven's self-opening portals came
> Legions of spirits in an orb of flame,—
> Flame that from every point an arrow sends,
> Far as the concave firmament extends;
> Spun with the tissue of a million lines,
> Glistening like gossamer the welkin shines;
> The constellations in their pride look pale
> Through the quick trembling brilliance of that veil;
> Then, suddenly converged, the meteors rush
> O'er the wide south; one deep vermilion blush
> O'erspreads Orion glaring on the flood,
> And rabid Sirius foams through fire and blood.
> Again the circuit of the pole they range,
> Motion and figure every moment change,
> Through all the colours of the rainbow run,
> Or blaze like wrecks of a dissolving sun:
> Wide ether burns with glory, conflict, flight,
> And the glad ocean dances in the light."

During the winter of the Northern Hemisphere, the inhabitants of the Arctic zone, as I have informed you, are without the light of the sun for months together, and their long dreary night is relieved by the light of this meteor, which occurs with great frequency in those regions, and the exceeding beauty of which those who have seen it only in our latitudes can hardly conceive. It is generally described as an immense curtain, waving its folds like the canopy of an ample tent agitated by the wind, and fringed with a border of light of the richest colours and most vivid brilliancy. It is sometimes seen for a few minutes only, or an hour, or through the whole night, and through several nights in succession.

A dingy aspect of the sky in the direction of the north is generally the precursor of the Aurora, and this gradually becomes darker in colour, and assumes the form of a circular segment, surrounded by a luminous arch, and resting at each end on the horizon. Sometimes the blue sky is seen between the cloud and the horizon. After shooting a number of rays or streamers, the dark part of the cloud generally changes and becomes very luminous. The rays continue to be shot from the upper edge, sometimes at some distance, or very close to each other. Their light is very dazzling; bright columns slowly issue upwards from openings in the main cloud, becoming broader as they proceed. When the Aurora attains its full brightness and activity, rays are projected from every part of the arch, and if they do not rise too high, it presents the appearance of a comb furnished with teeth. When the rays are very bright, they assume a green, violet, purple, or rose-colour, giving to the whole a variegated and brilliant effect. The height of the Aurora has been differently estimated, but it has been seldom found to exceed ninety miles; but its geographical extent is enormous. The origin of the phenomenon is yet unexplained, but it is generally supposed to be electrical. Franklin regarded it as the result of a slow and continual discharge of electric fluid from the atmosphere about the poles to the air above; and Sir Humphrey Davy and other electricians noticed the striking similarity between the Northern Lights and electricity discharged through rarefied air.

The Aurora has been observed in almost every part of the world. The ancients regarded its appearance with great terror, as the precursor of dire events; and there is no doubt that the fiery meteors, representing to their imaginations armies fighting in the heavens, and described by many writers as having preceded remarkable occurrences, must have been this phenomenon. The Indians also regarded these lights as the spirits of their fathers roaming through the land of souls. This idea may have originated from the long streaks of light which spread out with inconceivable swiftness, but always appearing to move to and from a fixed point, somewhat like a ribbon held in the hand and shaken.

Other luminous meteors are seen by the navigators of the

Northern Ocean to perfection, arising, apparently, from the refraction caused by the minute and highly crystallized particles of ice floating in the atmosphere. The sun and moon are often surrounded by *Halos*, circles of vapour, tinted with the brightest hues of the rainbow. Arctic voyagers frequently mention the fall of icy particles during a clear sky and a bright sun, so small as to be scarcely visible to the naked eye, and detected by their melting on the skin; and others larger, presenting a remarkably interesting appearance. M'Clintock, in his "Voyage of the Fox," observes: "The snow crystals of last night are extremely beautiful; the largest kind is an inch in length, and its form exactly resembles the end of a pointed feather. Stellar crystals, two-tenths of an inch in diameter, have also fallen; these have six points, and are the most exquisite things when seen under a microscope. In the sun, or even in moonlight, all these crystals glisten most brilliantly, and as our masts and rigging are abundantly covered with them, the 'Fox' was never so gorgeously arrayed as she now appears."

*Parhelia* (from Greek words "near the sun"), or mock suns, in the vicinity of the real orb, shine at once in different quarters of the firmament. They are most brilliant at daybreak, diminish in lustre as the sun ascends, but again brighten at his setting. Sir Edward Parry describes a parhelion of remarkably gorgeous appearance which he saw during a winter's sojourn at Melville Island. It continued from noon until six in the evening. It consisted of one complete halo, with segments of several others, displaying in parts the colours of the rainbow. Besides these, there was another perfect ring, of a pale white colour, which went right round the sky parallel with the horizon, and at a distance from it equal to the sun's altitude, and a horizontal band of white light appeared passing through the sun. Where the band and the inner halo cut each other, there were two parhelia, and another close to the horizon, directly under the sun, which formed the most brilliant part of the spectacle, being exactly like the sun slightly obscured by a thin cloud at his rising or setting.

A singular phenomenon observed on the Arctic seas by Mr. O'Reilly is mentioned in his account of Greenland. The atmosphere had been obscured by a fog, and the sunlight, falling on the mist, formed an ellipsis, strongly illuminated, apparently rising from the surface of the ocean to the upper edge of the mist. The inner edge was pearly white, with the faintest tinge of blue; the middle yellowish, deepening into brown and purple; the outer edge a blackish blue. In the centre of this oval, Mr. O'Reilly, who had ascended into the hurricane-house, saw reflected his whole figure, of a colossal size, the head surrounded by a circle of the brightest rainbow colours.

The sun, for some time before it finally departs for the Arctic winter, and also after its reappearance in spring, tinges the sky with hues of matchless splendour, which far outvie even the glory of an Italian sky. The edges of the clouds near the sun often present a fiery or burnished appearance, whilst the opposite horizon glows with a deep purple, gradually softening into a delicate rose colour of inconceivable beauty.

Another phenomenon which meets the eye of the Arctic navigator is the *Ice-blink;* a peculiar brightness in the atmosphere which is almost always perceptible on approaching ice. It is a stratum of clear whiteness, occasioned evidently by the glare of light reflected obliquely from the surface of the ice against the opposite atmosphere. This shining streak, which looks always brightest in clear weather, indicates to the experienced navigator, twenty or thirty miles beyond the limit of direct vision, not only the extent and figure, but even the quality, of the ice. The blink from packs of ice appears of a pure white, while that which is occasioned by snow-fields has some tinge of yellow.

James Montgomery, in his "Greenland," has, in very beautiful lines, alluded to this phenomenon:

> " 'Tis sunset: to the firmament serene
> The Atlantic wave reflects a gorgeous scene.
> Broad in the cloudless west, a belt of gold
> Girds the blue hemisphere; above unroll'd
> The keen clear air grows palpable to sight,
> Embodied in a flush of crimson light,
> Through which the evening star with milder gleam
> Descends to meet her image in the stream.

> Far in the east, what spectacle unknown
> Allures the eye to gaze on it alone?
> —Amidst black rocks, that lift on either hand
> Their countless peaks, and mark receding land,
> Amidst a tortuous labyrinth of seas,
> That shine around the Arctic cyclades,
> Amidst a coast of dreariest continent,
> In many a shapeless promontory rent,
> O'er rocks, seas, islands, promontories spread,
> The *ice-blink* rears its undulated head,
> On which the sun, beyond th' horizon shrined,
> Hath left his richest garniture behind.
> Piled on a hundred arches, ridge by ridge,
> O'er fix'd and fluid, strides the Alpine bridge,
> Whose blocks of sapphire seem to mortal eye
> Hewn from cerulean quarries of the sky;
> With glacier-battlements that crowd the spheres,
> The slow creation of six thousand years,
> Amidst immensity it towers sublime,
> Winter's eternal palace, built by Time:
> All human structures by his touch are borne
> Down to the dust; mountains themselves are worn
> With his light footsteps: here for ever grows,
> Amidst the region of unmelting snows,
> A monument, where every flake that falls
> Gives adamantine firmness to the walls."

Another phenomenon remarked by Northern voyagers is the *Tide-rip;* a commotion in the waters not unlike that produced by a conflict of tides or of other powerful currents. These sometimes move along with a roaring noise, and the inexperienced navigator expects to find his vessel drifted by them a long way out of his course; "But," observes Maury, "the next day, at noon, he remarks with surprise that no current has been felt. These are signs of the tremendous throes which occur in the bosom of the ocean. Sometimes the sea recedes from the shore, as if to gather strength for a great rush against its barriers. The 'tide-rip' in mid-ocean—the waves dashing against the shore—the ebb and flow of the tides, may be regarded in some sense as the throbbings of the great sea-pulse."

Directing your attention to other latitudes, I will now allude to that wonderful and beautiful object, the *Luminosity of the Ocean*, which prevails frequently throughout the tropical seas.

> "With scarce inferior lustre gleamed the sea,
> Whose waves were spangled with phosphoric fire,
> As though the lightning there had spent their shafts,
> And left the fragments glittering on the field."

This proceeds, as Herschel observes, from a great variety of marine organisms, some soft and gelatinous, and some minute shelly animals. They mostly shine when excited by a blow or by agitation of the water, as when a fish darts along or oar dashes, or in the wake of a ship, when the water closes on its track. In the latter case are often seen what appear to be large lamps of light rising from under the keel, and floating out to the surface, apparently of many inches in diameter. One of the most remarkable of these luminous creatures is a species of *Pyrosoma* (from the Greek "fire" and "body"), a species of shell animals with muff-shaped bodies upwards of an inch in length, which, when thrown down on deck, burst into a glow so strong as to appear like lumps of white-hot iron.

Frederick Martens, one of the early navigators, describes this illumination of the ocean in very expressive terms:

"At night, when the sea dasheth very much, it shines like fire: the seamen call it burning. This shining is a very bright glance, like unto the lustre of a diamond."

Dr. Collingwood, in his "Rambles of a Naturalist," thus alludes to this phenomenon:

"There are few subjects of study more interesting than the luminous appearance presented by the sea under various circumstances. That the sea, the great extinguisher of fire, should be turned into flame—that the darkness of night should be illuminated by the luminous glow which bathes every ripple and breaks over every wave—that globes of light should traverse the ocean, or that lightning flashes should coruscate no less in the billows of the sea than in the clouds of the air—are all facts which seize on the imagination. Nor is the interest lessened by the knowledge that all these phenomena are produced by animals whose home is in the great waters;

that not only do the fiery bodies of large animals give out steady patches of light, but that of the myriad animalculæ with which the sea teems, like motes in a sunbeam, each contributes its tiny scintillation, the aggregate forming a soft and lovely radiance."

Quatrefages, the French naturalist, gives a vivid description of a luminous sea:

"It exhibited to us in all its splendour the glorious phenomena of its phosphorescence. For more than an hour the waters around us seemed to be kindled into a blaze of light, as if they had borrowed some of the hidden fires of Stromboli. The waves, as they broke along the rocky shore of Sicily, encircled it with a glowing band of light, whilst every projecting cliff was circled with a wreath of fire. Our boat seemed as if it were opening for itself a passage through some glowing and fused liquid, whilst in its wake it left a long track of light, each stroke of the oar brightening the bosom of the waves with a broad silver gleam. The water that was taken up in a bucket presented the appearance of molten lead, as we slowly poured it back into the sea. Everywhere over this brilliant surface of calm light myriads of dazzling green sparks and globes of fire were flashing, quivering, and dying amidst the undulations of the waves, and these sparks and globes of fire were so many living beings. At certain times of the year these miscroscopical beings acquire the property of emitting light at each muscular contraction; and hence every movement in these animalculæ is made apparent by a luminous flash."

Mr. Edmonds, in his "Land's End District," alludes to the luminous waters frequently witnessed in Mount's Bay:

"On these occasions," he observes, "particularly when the night is dark, if a fish rise from the calm water, a most brilliant and beautiful effect is produced. Were you, from a boat, to look down into the sea while fishes were darting to and fro, their paths would be luminous, and the deep would be traversed by streams of light as bright and beautiful as those of stars shooting through the sky. If you draw in your fishing-line, it will appear as a line of fire, and the fish at the end of it like a ball of fire coming near you. A net suspended in the sea appears 'like a brilliant lacework of fire,' and the fishes may be seen carefully avoiding it. When fishermen by night wish to know whether any fish are near, they stamp on the bottom of the boat, and instantly, if there are any beneath, they will be seen darting away in all directions. By this means, in some parts of Cornwall, the fishery is pursued by night."

Crabbe has some beautiful lines on this subject:

> "And now your view upon the ocean turn,
> And there the splendour of the waves discern.
> Cast but a stone, or strike them with an oar,
> And you shall flames within the deep explore;'
> Or scoop the stream phosphoric as you stand,
> And the cold flames shall flash along your hand;
> When, lost in wonder, you shall walk and gaze
> On weeds that sparkle, and on waves that blaze."

To these observations I may add the interesting description of this phenomenon, as witnessed in the vicinity of the Plata by the distinguished Darwin:

"One very dark night the sea presented a very beautiful and singular appearance. There was a fresh breeze, and every part of the surface which, during the day, is seen as foam, now glowed with a pale light. The vessel drove before her bows two billows of liquid phosphorus, and in her wake she was followed by a milky train. As far as the eye reached, the crest of every wave was bright, and the sky above the horizon, from the reflected glare of these livid flames, was not so utterly obscure as over the vault of the heavens. As we proceed farther southward, the sea is seldom phosphorescent, probably owing to the scarcity of organic beings in that part of the ocean. The same torn and irregular particles of gelatinous matter described by Ehrenberg seem, in the Southern as well as in the Northern Hemisphere, to be the common cause of this phenomenon. The particles were so minute as easily to pass through fine gauze, yet many were distinctly visible by the naked eye. The water, when placed in a tumbler and agitated, gave out sparks, but a small portion in a watch-glass scarcely ever was luminous. Ehrenberg states that all these particles retain a certain degree of irritability. My observations gave a different result. Having used the net one night, I allowed it to become partially dry, and twelve hours after, having occasion to employ it again, I found the whole surface sparkle as brightly as when first taken out of the water. It does not appear probable, in this case, that the particles could have remained so long alive. When the waves scintillate with bright green sparks, I believe it is generally owing to minute crustacea (hard-covered animals); but there can be no doubt that very many other pelagic (belonging to the deep sea) animals, when alive, are phosphorescent. The phenomenon is the result of the decomposition of the organic particles, by which process the ocean becomes purified."

> "The lamps of the sea-nymphs,
> Myriad fiery globes, swim heaving and panting; and rainbows—
> Crimson, azure, and emerald—are broken in star-showers, lighting,
> Far through the now dark depths of the crystal, the gardens of Nereus,
> Coral and sea-fan and tangle, the bloom and the palms of the ocean."

In the chapter on "Superstitions connected with the Ocean," I have alluded to *Water-spouts*, and the superstitious terror excited by them among the mariners of former times. I will merely offer a few remarks on this subject in connexion with the phenomena of the ocean. I may describe it as an aqueous meteor, occasioned by the action of a whirlwind upon the surface of the sea. The air, revolving rapidly, sucks the water up, and the fluid thus attracted is received by the low and dense clouds, always attendant upon such occasions, through a trumpet-shaped spout, that moves with, and seems to be guided by, the motion of the particular cloud to which it is attached. When fully formed, the water-spouts appear as tall pillars of cloud, stretching from the sea to the sky, whirling round their axes. The sea at the base of the whirling vortices is thrown into the most violent commotion. Falconer, in the "Shipwreck," thus alludes to this phenomenon :

> "Tall Ida's summit now more distant grew,
> And Jove's high hill was rising on the view,
> When, from the left approaching, they descry
> A liquid column towering shoot on high.
> The foaming base an angry whirlwind sweeps,
> Where curling billows rouse the fearful deeps;

> Still round and round the fluid vortex flies,
> Scattering dun night and horror through the skies.
> The swift volution, and the enormous train,
> Let sages versed in Nature's lore explain."

The Greeks applied the term "*prester*" to the water-spout, which signifies a fiery fluid, from its appearance being generally accompanied with flashes of lightning and a sulphureous smell, showing the activity of the electrical principle in the air. Lucretius refers to this in the following terms:

> "Hence, with much ease, the meteor we may trace,
> Termed, from its essence, Prester by the Greeks,
> That oft from heaven wide hovers o'er the deep.
> Like a vast column, gradual from the skies,
> Prone o'er the waves descends it; the vex'd tide
> Boiling amain beneath its mighty whirl,
> And with destruction sure the stoutest ship
> Threat'ning that dares the boist'rous scene approach."

A few minutes suffices in general for the duration of this phenomenon, but several have been known to continue for nearly an hour. In the Mediterranean as many as sixteen water-spouts have been observed at the same time. The principal danger seems to be from the wind blowing in sudden gusts in their vicinity from all points of the compass, sufficient to overwhelm small vessels carrying much sail.

Mr. Ellis, in a cruise amongst the islands of the Pacific Ocean, had, on more than one occasion, a perilous escape from these phenomena. At one time the weather seemed clearing from a previous storm, when one of the native boatmen pointed to a large cylindrical water-spout, extending like a massive column from the ocean to the dark impending clouds:

"It was not very distant, and seemed moving towards our apparently devoted boat. The roughness of the sea forbade our attempting to hoist a sail in order to avoid it; and as we had no other means of safety at command, we endeavoured calmly to await its approach. The natives abandoned themselves to despair, and either threw themselves along at the bottom of the boat, or sat crouching on the keel, with their faces downwards and their eyes covered with their hands. The sailor kept at the helm. Mr. Barff sat on one side of the stern, and I on the other, watching the alarming object before us. While thus employed we saw two other water-spouts, and subsequently a third, if not more, so that we seemed almost surrounded with them. Some were well defined, extending in an unbroken line from the sea to the sky, like pillars resting on the ocean as their basis, and supporting the clouds; others assuming the shape of a funnel or inverted cone, attached to the clouds, and extending towards the waters beneath. From the distinctness with which we saw them, notwithstanding the density of the atmosphere, the farthest could not be many miles distant. In some we could imagine to have traced the spiral motion of the water as it was drawn to the clouds, which were every moment augmenting their portentous darkness. The sense, however, of personal danger and immediate destruction if brought within the vortex of their influence, restrained in a great degree all curious, and what, in other circumstances, would have been interesting observation on the wonderful phenomena around us, the mighty agitation of the elements, and the terrific sublimity of these wonders of the deep.

"The roaring of the tempest, and the hollow sounds that murmured on the ear as the heavy billows rolled in foam or broke in contact with opposing billows, seemed as if deep called unto deep, and the noise of water-spouts might almost be heard, while we were momentarily expecting that the mighty waves would sweep over us. Our prayers were offered to Him who is a very present help in every time of danger, for ourselves and those who sailed with us; and under these or similar exercises several hours passed away. The storm continued during the day. At intervals we beheld, through the clouds and rain, one or other of the water-spouts, the whole of which appeared almost stationary, until at length we lost sight of them altogether, when the spirits of our native voyagers evidently revived."

The natives of the South Sea Islands, although scarcely alarmed at thunder and lightning, are at sea greatly terrified by the appearance of water-spouts. They occur more frequently in the South than in the North Pacific, and although often seen among the Society Islands, are more rarely met with in the Sandwich group. But throughout the Pacific, water-spouts of varied form and size are among the most frequent of the splendid phenomena and mighty works of the Lord which those behold who go down to the sea in ships and do business upon the great waters. They are sublime objects of unusual interest when viewed from the shore; but when beheld at sea, especially if near, and from a small and fragile bark, it is almost impossible so to divest the mind of a sense of personal danger as to contemplate with composure their stately movement, or the rapid internal circular eddy of the waters.

The *Tornado*—which, however, is a general term employed to designate what is called a hurricane or whirlwind—is a sudden and violent storm of wind, accompanied by lightning and heavy torrents of rain, occurring frequently in the Indian Ocean, on the coasts of Africa, and other places in the tropics. While the tornado is passing over a ship, a loud creaking noise, occasioned by the electric fluid descending along the masts, is distinctly heard amongst the rigging. After the squall has passed beyond the ship, the lightning again appears to descend in sheets, as they did on its approach. *Typhoons* have their origin in the ocean to the east of China, immediately about Formosa, Luzon, and the islands immediately to the south, and their course is generally along the coast of China. The body of the storm advances at the rate of twelve miles an hour. It is very probable that typhoons arise from opposing aërial currents, each highly charged with moisture which they have taken up from the oceans they have traversed; and their intensity is aggravated by the large quantity of heat disengaged in the condensation of the vapour of the atmosphere into the deluges of rain which fall during the storm.

The *Trade-Winds*, which are classed under the designation of "constant" winds, probably owe the origin of their name to the facilities afforded to trade and commerce by their constant prevalence and uniform course. They are perpetual in the torrid zone, blowing from the eastward with little variation. They were not known to the ancients, and seem to have been unknown even to modern seamen up to the time of Columbus, who had passed some time at the Canaries, to which the trade-winds extend in summer, and who seems to have conceived a just idea of their extent. On his first voyage, after leaving the Canaries his crew were greatly alarmed at finding that the wind always blew from the north-east and east, and feared they would be prevented by it from returning to their native country. Columbus, however, knew otherwise, and on his return from the newly-discovered islands his tack was north of the trade-winds, in the region of the changeable winds. After the time of Columbus, European navigation extended rapidly in the Atlantic and Indian Oceans, and the trade-winds became gradually known.

Seamen dwell with delight in the region of the trade-winds, not only on account of the favouring gale, but its genial influence, the transparent atmosphere, the splendid sunsets, and the brilliancy of the unclouded heavens day and night. The origin of the trade-winds is ascribed by Halley to the rarefaction produced in our atmosphere by the apparent diurnal progress of the sun. It appears that the heat caused by the sun in the air is strong enough to produce this rarefaction to an extent of about sixty degrees of latitude, as the trade-winds, including what is termed the "region of calms," extend over such a portion of the globe. In this immense space the rarefied air is replaced by the colder and denser air which rests over the region contiguous to that of the trade-winds, and this transportation of air is the trade-wind.

The *Monsoon* (from the Arabic word *mausim*, "a set time" or "season of the year") is a term applied to periodical winds which prevail almost entirely in the northern part of the Indian Ocean. The force with which these winds blow is much greater than that of the trade-winds. It is frequently impossible to stem their violence in any way. Many vessels which have endeavoured to force their way against them have been compelled to give in and to enter the nearest harbour. Other vessels are obliged to change their course, and to reach their destination by following a different track, wide of the straight route, and thus avoiding the monsoon. But although these winds, to vessels which miss the right season, render their voyages long and laborious, yet they greatly favour those of ships that arrive at the right period. It is chiefly by the assistance of the north-east and north-west monsoons that the voyages of merchant vessels bound from Canton to England are accomplished in short periods.

Monsoons, when compared with the trade-winds, exercise a most beneficial and important office in nature, especially in their relation to rain-fall, the fertility of the greater part of Southern Asia being entirely due to them. The shiftings of the monsoons is not all at once, and in some places the time of the changes is attended with calms, in others with variable winds; and particularly those of China, at ceasing to be westerly, are frequently very tempestuous, and such is their violence that they seem to be of the nature of the West India hurricanes. Forbes, in his "Oriental Memoirs," thus describes a scene of this character at sea:

"At Aujengo the monsoon commences with great severity and presents an awful spectacle; the inclement weather continues, with more or less violence, from May to October. During that period the tempestuous ocean rolls from a black horizon, literally of "darkness visible," a series of floating mountains, heaving under heavy summits, until they approach the shore, when their stupendous accumulations flow in successive surges, and break upon the beach. Every ninth wave is observed to be generally more tremendous than the rest, and threatens to overwhelm the settlement. The noise of these billows equals that of the loudest cannon, and, with the thunder and lightning so frequent in the rainy season, is truly awful."

It is not easy to explain the origin of the monsoons: they appear to be only a modification of the trade-winds, produced by the peculiar form of the countries lying within and around the Indian Ocean.

The lightning attending these phenomena is described as fearfully vivid, realizing the description of a storm by Shakespere:

"I have seen
The ambitious ocean swell, and rage, and foam,
To be exalted with the threat'ning clouds;

> But never till to-night, never till now,
> Did I go through a tempest dropping fire.
> Either there is a civil strife in heaven,
> Or else the world, too saucy with the gods,
> Incenses them to send destruction."
>
> " Such sheets of fire, such bursts of horrid thunder,
> Such groans of roaring wind and rain."

Other appalling phenomena that I may mention are *Hurricanes* or *Cyclones;* revolving winds, which appear to originate not far from the west coast of Africa, where they move in a more or less north-westerly course, until they reach the coast of North America, where they begin to turn, and continue to the north-east, the vortex gradually widening, until they are lost in the ocean between Iceland and the British isles. These do not follow a straight line, but adopt a whirling course. The cyclones vary in breadth from fifty to five hundred miles, sometimes contracting, and in that case increasing fearfully in violence.

The direct causes of these terrible atmospheric disturbances are not precisely determined: they may arise from an electric condition of a portion of the atmosphere (indeed, atmospheric changes of every kind seem to be connected with electricity), or the sudden heating of the air over some insulated portion of the African mainland, although there is ground for believing that they are not occasioned by heat alone.

Hurricanes have been more terribly destructive than even earthquakes. The "Great" hurricane which commenced at Barbadoes in 1780, was so termed from its terrible results. The very bottom and depths of the sea seemed to be uprooted, and the waves rose to such a height that forts were washed away, and their great guns carried about in the air like chaff; houses were razed and ships were wrecked, bodies of men and beasts were lifted up in the air and dashed to pieces. At the different islands not less than twenty thousand persons lost their lives on shore; while, farther to the north, the "Stirling Castle" and the "Dover Castle," men-of-war, went down at sea, and fifty vessels were driven on shore at the Bermudas. During a hurricane at Guadaloupe, in January, 1825, a brig was whirled out of the water, and actually blown to pieces in the air. At St. Vincent's, in 1831, the water of the sea was raised to such a height as to flood the streets. The waves broke over cliffs seventy feet high. A very remarkable cyclone, or spiral hurricane, passed over a portion of England and the British and St. George's Channels during the autumn of 1859, destroying an enormous amount of shipping. The cyclone in Calcutta, in 1864, was one of the most awful events on record, of which there is no parallel except that in 1832; but even the latter was not so disastrous in its effects. Upwards of three hundred ships were wrecked or irreparably damaged, and the results on shore were appalling.

> "The mountain waves, passing their 'customed bounds,
> Make direful, loud incursions on the land,
> All overwhelming; sudden they retreat,
> With their whole troubled waters; but, anon,
> Sudden return with louder, mightier force."

The noise of the wind in hurricanes is described by a seaman "as the most tremendous unearthly screech he had ever heard." The electric phenomena that sometimes attend hurricanes are very curious. One captain of a vessel states: "For nearly an hour we could not observe each other, but merely the lightning; and, most astonishing, every one of our finger-nails turned quite black, and remained so nearly five weeks afterwards."

The *Bore*, a sudden and impetuous flow of the tide, is one of the most astonishing sights that can be witnessed on the sea-coast.

> "Mysterious impulse!—from the distant main
> A mighty wave majestic rolls along:
> First like a breezy murmur from afar
> 'T is heard—then dies away; but, as it gains
> With louder swell upon the listening ear,
> A hoarser murmur agitates the calm;
> Till bursting into view, the thund'ring tide,
> Fierce as a mountain cataract, descends
> In a steep torrent."

At stated periods this tremendous tidal-wave comes rolling from the sea, threatening to overwhelm everything that moves on the

## SUBMARINE EARTHQUAKES AND VOLCANOES. 227

beach. In certain parts of the Bay of Fundy the bore is more impetuous and higher—sometimes exceeding eighteen feet—than, perhaps, in any other part of the world. It comes in with such force and rapidity, with a noise resembling distant thunder, as sometimes to dash vessels on the shore. It is said also to overtake deer, swine, and other beasts that feed on the beach, and swallow them up before the swiftest feet among them have time to escape. The swine, as they feed on mussels at low water, are said to sniff the bore, either by sound or smell, and generally dash up the cliffs before it rolls in. The bore is caused by the compression of the mass of advancing waters into a gradually narrowing channel.

Among the most extraordinary phenomena in the universe is the volcanic action at the bottom of seas, by the upheaval of which islands are produced, the form, magnitude, and character of which depend on that of the upheaved mass. In general these islands rise suddenly, and their appearance is attended with all the phenomena that accompany eruptions: they are seen for some time, and then gradually disappear. When the dome, upheaved from the bottom of the sea, breaks at the summit so as to form a crater, a part of the circular rampart is sometimes destroyed, so that the sea enters, and an enclosed bay is formed, where innumerable tribes of coral animals build their cells, as I have explained in the chapter on the "Rock-Builders of the Ocean."

Within the Atlantic Ocean no less than five great, and probably connected, centres of volcanic action exist. Iceland, the Azores, the Canaries, the Cape de Verd, and the West Indian Islands, besides many other points (Ascension, St. Helena, St. Paul's, &c.) at which extinct volcanic phenomena are visible. A remarkable submarine volcanic tract has been recently added to them by M. Daussy, forming a belt about seventy miles from the equator on the south side. In the middle of the seventeenth century there were great and disastrous shocks in the Mediterranean basin.

A series of earthquakes and volcanic eruptions, apparently connected with each other, occurred in 1811 and 1812 in the countries surrounding the Columbian Sea. The subterranean force first tried to open a vent by means of a submarine eruption in the Atlantic.

Shocks of earthquake were for several days felt in the island of St. Miguel, one of the Azores, and on the 30th of January, 1811, large volumes of smoke, with which flames were observed to mingle, were seen issuing from the surface of the sea, at a distance of a few miles from the western coast of the island. They threw up mud, stones, and other matter, which in a short time accumulated, so as to form a small island, which was called Sabrina: this disappeared after a few months in the sea. In 1831 an island rose out of the sea between the town of Sciacca, in Sicily, and the volcanic island of Pantellaria. Before any appearance of a change was observed in the sea, the inhabitants of Sciacca were alarmed by a number of very smart shocks of earthquake, of which two might be called severe. An Italian vessel passing near the place where, afterwards, the island rose out of the sea, observed a great disturbance of the waters at that spot. According to his statement, a considerable space of the surface of the sea was seen rising to an elevation of from eighty to ninety feet above its level; the water appeared to bubble as if boiling, and the phenomenon was attended by a noise like thunder. After this agitation had lasted about ten minutes, the watery mass sank to the sea level, but after some time rose again. These risings of the water were repeated at irregular intervals of ten, fifteen, and twenty minutes. A thick cloud of smoke, which enveloped the whole horizon, issued from the raised mass of water.. The surface of the sea surrounding the raised mass was also considerably agitated, and a number of dead fish were floating about. For several days the atmosphere surrounding the town of Sciacca was dim and foggy, so that it was impossible to see what was going on at sea. On the 12th of July, in the morning, people were surprised at finding on the surface of the sea, in front of the town, a quantity of small porous ashes, which had been carried there by a fresh breeze from the southwest. At the same time a very unpleasant smell of sulphuric hydrogen gas incommoded the inhabitants of the town and the country near. Dead fish, recently killed, were floating in all directions.

Captain Senhouse effected a landing on the island thus formed, took possession of it, and called it Graham Island. He found the form of the crater to approach that of a perfect circle, and to be complete along its whole circumference, excepting for about two hundred and fifty yards on the south-east side, which was broken and low, apparently not above three feet high. The whole circuit of the island he conceived to be from a mile and a quarter to a mile and one-third. In the month of December following the whole island had disappeared.

The island of Santorin, one of the Greek islands called the Cyclades, is one of the most extraordinary instances of submarine volcanic action. During the last two thousand years several new islands have been formed in this locality, and singular phenomena have been exhibited even of late years.

*Earthquakes* are very closely related to volcanoes, although by no means confined to volcanic districts. Instances of this phenomenon at sea are frequently recorded by navigators. In most cases the motion felt on board is compared with that experienced when a ship strikes on a rock under water. During the earthquake at Lisbon, an English vessel, sailing at a distance of about fifty miles from the coast of Portugal, experienced a shock of such violence that a part of the deck was damaged. The captain, much surprised, thought that a great mistake must have crept into his reckoning, and that his vessel had got on a rock. He gave orders to put out the long boat, to save the crew, but he was soon convinced there was no danger. The source whence earthquakes originate, the power by which the ground is convulsed, is withdrawn from our investigation. The eye of the most inquisitive naturalist cannot reach it. The substances which are brought up by earthquakes bear evident signs of having endured the action of fire. It is supposed that these phenomena are produced by the efforts of accumulated elastic vapours to escape from the bowels of the earth.

Another phenomenon I may allude to is the *Red-Fog* or *Shower-Dust*, encountered by vessels at sea occasionally, and especially in the vicinity of the Cape de Verd Islands. What these showers precipitate in the Mediterranean is called "sirocco-dust," and in other parts "African dust," because the winds which accompany them are supposed to come from the Sirocco desert, or some other parched land of the continent of Africa. The dust is of a brick-red or cinnamon colour, and it sometimes comes down in such quantities as to cover the sails and rigging, though the vessel may be hundreds of miles from the land. This dust, when subjected to the microscope, is found to consist for the most part of exceedingly minute animal and vegetable organisms, probably derived from some of the great river valleys of South America, being lifted up in vast clouds of impalpable sands by the fierce gales of the equinox.

## CHAPTER XXI.

### SUPERSTITIONS CONNECTED WITH THE OCEAN.

" I saw the new moon late yestreen
With the old moon in her arm;
And if we go to sea, master,
I fear we'll come to harm."
*Old Ballad.*

IT is not surprising that men accustomed to the monotony of a seafaring life, remote from the educational influences afforded to those on land, with the many wonders of the vast ocean around them, full of strange mystery, which science only can partially unveil; with minds thus generally untutored, and consequently more susceptible to superstitious fancies, it is not astonishing that such persons should be among the most credulous of mankind. It is true that the spread of knowledge in modern times has removed many of the absurd notions peculiar to seamen; but, as a class, they may still be considered among the foremost believers in the supernatural.

From the earliest times the sea has been regarded as the region of fabulous marvels. The ancient mariners performed their voyages in a vague mist of capricious doubts and fancies, omens and prognostics, which excited terror or inspired confidence. Every object that met their gaze was endowed by them with some miraculous agency for good or for evil. Their course over unknown waters, peopled by their mythology with imaginary creatures, would naturally create awe and suspicion.

Horace, lamenting at Virgil's departure for Athens, rebukes the impiety of the first mariner, who ventured, in the audacity of his heart, to go afloat, and cross the briny barrier interposed between nations. He esteems a merchant favoured specially by the gods should he twice or thrice return in safety from a distant cruise. He tells us he himself had known the terrors of the dark gulf of the Adriatic, and had experienced the treachery of the western gale.

Ancient writers are diffuse in the description of prodigies witnessed by mariners at sea, many of which, doubtless originating from simple causes, received the addition of a divine interposition. The sudden breaking up of a dense fog, and the sun shining in undimmed splendour, was attributed to the appearance of Apollo himself, as the saints in later ages were supposed to miraculously intervene for the protection of seamen. Apollonius of Rhodes, the Greek poet, describes the Argonauts (Greek heroes who, under the command of Jason, went in search of the Golden Fleece) as suddenly benighted at sea in broad daylight by a dense black fog. They pray to Apollo, and he descends from heaven, and alighting on a rock, holds up his illustrious bow, which shoots a guiding light farther to an island. The delusions of these pagan times continued through succeeding ages, modified only by the change of religion and a better knowledge of navigation. The direct influence of the heathen deities was transferred in Catholic times to the Virgin and the saints, and this belief under various forms still prevails in some foreign countries, where the divine light of evangelical truth has not pierced, while other phases of superstition still linger among our own sailors as regards omens, good luck, and a number of other senseless notions.

The monks in the middle ages were zealous chroniclers of saintly interpositions at sea. In 1226, we are told, the Earl of Salisbury, while returning to England, was so nearly shipwrecked on his voyage, that everything, including articles of great value, was thrown into the sea to lighten the ship. In the moment of greatest danger, a brilliant taper was seen on the top of the mast, and near to it a damsel of surpassing beauty, who protected the light from the wind and rain. This sight inspired the Earl and the sailors with fresh courage, and the presence was assumed to be that of the Virgin, to whom the Earl, from the day of his knighthood, had ordered a taper to be burnt at her shrine. It is probable, also, that the Earl had bestowed other and more substantial gifts on the Church; and this legend would, probably, excite others to similar benefactions.

Edward III., after the surrender of Calais, on his return to England encountered a violent storm. " Oh, Blessed Virgin ! " he exclaimed, " Holy Lady ! why is it, and what does it portend, that in going to France I enjoyed a favourable wind, a calm sea, and all things prospered with me ; but on returning to England all kinds of misfortunes befall me ?" Of course the monkish historians relate that this expostulation had the desired effect, and the storm suddenly subsided.

The fishermen of Sardinia appear to indulge in a plurality of saints to favour their vocation. Tyndale, in his account of that island, gives an interesting description of the superstitious observances of the sailors.

"Amidst the cheers," he says, " of the men at having made a good capture of fish, a general silence prevailed ; the leader, in his little boat, having checked the hilarity, and assumed a priestly as well as a piscatorial character, taking off his cap—an example followed by all his company—commenced a species of chant or litany, an invocation of the saints, to which an *ora pro nobis* (" pray for us ") chorus was made by the sailors. After the Virgin Mary had been appealed to, and her protection against accidents particularly requested, as the ancients did to Neptune, a series of saints were called over, half of whose names I knew not, but who were evidently influential persons in the fishing department. St. George was supplicated to drive away all enemies of the tunny from the imaginary '*lammia*,' or sorceress, to the real shark or sword-fish. St. Peter was reminded of the holy miracle performed for him by an application to confer a similar miraculous draught on the present occasion, and (perhaps to counterbalance the difficulty in case of his refusal) a petition was offered up to St. Anthony of Padua, imploring him to perform some more of his fishing wonders. St. Michael was complimented on his heavenly influence in these matters, and humbly requested to continue his favours. Not knowing why the latter was mixed up in the affair, I asked one of the men for an explanation. 'St. Michael,' he said, 'was with St. Peter when the latter asked Jesus Christ to go fishing, and that, therefore, he was one of the crew of that boat.' Besides the saints of such undoubted authority and interest in tunny-fishing, the shrines of general saints, as well as local ones, were called over, and a blessing requested for the principal towns and places in the Mediterranean which purchased the fish.

"During these pious appeals, so strange to the ears of a Protestant stranger, the preparations for killing the fish were not forgotten, the men having changed their clothes for the occasion; for by the time the carnage was over, the men were covered with blood, the stain of which it is almost impossible to remove. The change of every jacket, waistcoat, and trousers seemed to produce a corresponding one in the litany; and one might have imagined that the saints presided no less over the old clothes than over the tunnies. The next day, the weather being unpropitious, a fresh invocation of the saints was made in church at vespers, and fishermen and others were assembled to implore a change of wind and a successful fish on the morrow."

The saints in turbulent times took good care of their own honour by miraculous interventions; so we read that during the strife between the Scots and the English in 1335, the fleet of the latter entered the Forth, and committed great ravages on the sea-coast. One of these piratical vessels landed on the island of Auronia, and despoiling a church, carried off a splendid image of St. Columba. While on their return, however (according to a Scotch historian), it took vengeance upon them, for a furious storm arose, and one of the largest ships nearly foundered. Having reached Inchkeith in great distress, and implored the saint's forgiveness, they suddenly found themselves in safety, but not until a vow had been made that the image should be replaced in its shrine.

Among the most conspicuous sea-saints were St. Nicholas, St. Peter, St. Christopher, St. Hermus, St. Barbara, St. Andrew, St. Clement, and St. Anthony of Padua. Of these, St. Nicholas is the present patron of those who lead a seafaring life in Roman Catholic countries (as Neptune was of old), and his churches generally stand within sight of the sea, and are plentifully stocked with votive offerings by seamen. Lambarde, in his "Perambulations of Kent," speaking of St. Nicholas's Chapel, near Hythe, says:

> "This is one of the places
> Where such as had escapt the sea
> Were wont to leave their guifts."

The miraculous powers of this saint seem to have been confined to no particular countries or occasions. A church dedicated to this holy man at Arboja, in Sweden, had, before the Reformation, a richly-carved altar-piece, concerning which a tradition is related that during some foreign war, the inhabitants of a besieged town sewed this splendid work of art in a cow-hide, and sank it in the sea to prevent their enemies from obtaining possession of it. The Danes, however, discovered the spot, but in trying to hoist the weighty load into a ship, they found that it would not move. A wise man suggested that they should call over the names of the great churches in Sweden; "For if," he observed, "you stumble on the name of the patron saint of the altar-piece, it will surely raise itself."

This bright idea was acted upon, and St. Lawrence was invoked, but without effect, the altar-piece sticking as tight as ever. St. Bridget proved as obstinate, likewise half the saints in the calendar, when some one suggested St. Nicholas, and up came the altar-piece like a cork, and was sent to the church of which he was the patron.

Innumerable are the instances of saints who are said to have interposed on behalf of seamen in peril. A comical story is related of a Mahommedan saint. A vessel sprang a leak at sea and was nearly sinking, when the captain vowed with a sincere heart that, should a famous saint and prophet vouchsafe to stop the leak, he would offer up the profits of his cargo, and give a couple of silver and gold models of ships, to his shrine. It is related that at this perilous moment the saint (who was still upon earth) was engaged with his barber, under the operation of shaving, and instantly, in his prophetic character, became acquainted with the condition in which the vessel was placed. Out of kindness he threw away the looking-glass he held in his hand, which flew off to the ship, and sticking to the hole, stopped the leak. On the vessel reaching its destination in safety, the captain brought his offerings to the saint, who told him to restore the looking-glass to the barber. The captain, astonished, and knowing nothing of the miracle, was told to examine his vessel, and found the looking-glass firmly attached to the hole in the ship.

Legends of this ridiculous character are numerous in old writings, and I will now pass on to later superstitions. You have no doubt heard of the "Phantom Ship," which was supposed, when seen by sailors—or rather present in their imaginations only—to foretell disaster. This story originated with the Dutch, and found believers among seamen of all countries. Sir Walter Scott alludes to this spectral illusion as a harbinger of woe:

> "The phantom ship whose form
> Shoots like a meteor through the storm,
> When the dark scud comes driving hard,
> And lower'd is every topsail-yard,
> And canvas wove in earthly looms
> No more to brave the storm presumes!
> Then 'mid the roar of sea and sky,
> Top and top-gallant hoisted high,
> Full spread and crowded every sail,
> The demon frigate braves the gale,
> And well the doom'd spectators know
> The harbinger of wreck and woe."

Water-spouts at sea were regarded in olden times with great terror. Sailors were accustomed to discharge artillery at these moving columns to accelerate their fall, from a fear lest the vessel should be sunk by them. The principal danger, however, arises from the wind blowing in sudden gusts in the vicinity of the spout from all points of the compass, sufficient to capsize small vessels carrying much sail. Another practice was to cut the air with a knife, while reciting some prayers, by which simple enchantment it was supposed the water-spouts would be reduced to submission. If it happened, however, to be in an obstinate mood, two sailors would draw their swords, and strike at each other, in true gladiatorial style, taking care between each blow to make the sign of the cross.

The appearance of lightning playing amidst the masts, spars, and cordage of ships was ominous. A single flame was of evil import, whilst two flames signified a successful voyage, and were termed by the ancients "Castor and Pollux." By the superstition of modern times these electrical phenomena have been converted by the Roman Catholic sailors into indications of the guardian presence of St. Elmo, a patron saint of seamen. During the second voyage of Columbus in the West Indies, a sudden gust of heavy wind came on in the night, and his crews considered themselves in great peril, until they beheld several of these lambent flames playing about the top of the masts and gliding along the rigging, which they held as the assurance that their supernatural protector was near. Fernando Columbus, the brother of the discoverer of the new world, records the circumstance in a manner characteristic of the age in which he lived: "On the same Saturday, in the night, was seen St. Elmo with seven lighted tapers at the topmast. There was much rain and great thunder. I mean to say that those lights were seen which mariners affirm to be the body of St. Elmo; on beholding which they chanted many litanies and orisons, holding it for granted that in the tempest in which he appears no one is in danger."

A similar mention is made of this nautical superstition in the voyage of the great navigator Magellan. During several great storms the presence of the saint was welcomed, appearing at the topmast with a lighted candle, and sometimes with two, upon which the people shed tears of joy, received great consolation, and saluted him according to the custom of the Catholic seamen; but he ungraciously vanished, disappearing with a great flash of lightning which nearly blinded the crew.

It is a cheering instance of human progress that, by the introduction of lightning-couductors into ships, the fearful electric currents which destroyed many noble vessels is now placed under control, and rendered powerless to injure, without the aid of St. Elmo or any other names in the Roman calendar.

Among the ancients it was believed that certain persons had the power of raising tempests at sea. In the "Odyssey," Æolus is described as possessing these attributes, and Calypso, in the same work, is said to have been able to control the winds.

The belief in human agency to influence the ocean was prevalent in the fifteenth century. A curious confession was made in Scotland about the year 1469, by one Agnes Sampson, a reputed sorceress, who avowed that "at the time His Majesty (James VI.) was in Denmark, she took a cat and christened it, and afterwards bound to each part of that cat the chiefest parts of a dead man, and several joints of his body; and that in the night following, the said cat was conveyed into the midst of the sea, by herself and other witches, sailing in their baskets, and so left the said cat right before the town of Leith in Scotland. This done, there arose such a tempest in the sea as a greater hath not been seen, which tempest was the cause of the perishing of a boat or vessel wherein were sundry jewels and rich gifts, which should have been presented to the new Queen of Scotland at Her Majesty's coming to Leith."

Such was the language of a silly old woman, probably extorted by torture from a weak imagination.

King James, in his "Demonology," states "that witches can raise stormes and tempestes in the aire, either on sea or land," which was in answer to Reginald Scot, who in his "Discoverie of Witchcraft" ridiculed the "black art" severely, and he had the advantage of his royal master, the "British Solomon," as he had been equivocally termed, in this and many other statements.

The Evil One was supposed to have a direct influence on the winds and waves.

"Our sailors," writes Dr. Pegge in 1763, "I am told, at this very day—I mean the vulgar sort of them—have a strange opinion of satanic power and agency in stirring up winds, and that is the reason they so seldom whistle on shipboard, esteeming it to be a mockery, and consequently an enraging of the devil."

We should scarcely expect that the mere turning of a stone was supposed to have had an effect in procuring favourable breezes, yet we read that the inhabitants of some parts of the Western Islands had implicit faith in this charm. In the chapel of Fladda Chuan there was a blue stone fixed in the altar, of a round form, which was always moist. It was the custom of any fishermen who were detained on the island by contrary winds to wash this blue stone with water, expecting by this to obtain a favourable wind. So great was the regard paid to this stone, that any oath sworn before it could never be broken. Another mode of these primitive islanders to secure auspicious winds was of a bucolic character, and consisted in hanging a he-goat to the mast-head.

A similar feeling with regard to the efficacy of stones, though for another object, existed amongst the fishermen of Iona. This took the shape of a pillar, and the sailor who stretched his arm along it three times in the name of the Trinity could never err in steering the helm of a vessel. The Finlanders are said to have used a cord, tied with three knots, for raising the wind: when the first was loosed, they could expect a good wind; if the second, a stronger; and if the third, such a storm would arise that the sailors would not be able to direct the ship, or avoid rocks, or stand upon the decks. The French seamen in former days had a comical notion that the spirit of the storm was propitiated by flogging unfortunate midshipmen at the mainmast.

Particular seasons of the year and saints' days were held in superstitious regard among mariners, and peculiar customs were attached to them. The old practice of setting the nets at Christmas Eve was general among the Swedish fishermen. The sailors at Folkestone, in Kent, chose eight of the largest and best whitings out of every boat, when they came home from the fishery. Out of the profit arising from these they made a feast every Christmas Eve. On Allhallow's Even, or the vigil of All Saints' Day, the fishermen of Orkney sprinkled what was called *fore-spoken* water over their boats when they had not been successful. They also made the sign of the cross on their boats with tar. The sailors in the Island of St. Lewis had an ancient custom of sacrificing to a sea-god called *Shony*, at Hallow-tide. They came to the church of St. Malvay, each seaman having his provisions with him. Every family furnished a peck of malt, and this was brewed into ale. A fisherman was selected to wade into the sea, carrying a cup of ale in his hand, and crying, "Shony, I give you this, hoping you will send us plenty through the year."

The fishermen of Finland believed that any among them who created a disturbance on St. George's Day would provoke storms and tempests. At Dieppe, in Normandy, even to a late period, All Saints' Day was religiously observed by the sailors of that port. Those who ventured out to sea on that anniversary were supposed to have the "double sight;" that is, each one beheld a living likeness of himself seated in close contact, or when engaged in any work, doing the same. If the nets were cast out, they were found, on drawing them in, to contain nothing but bones. On the same day, towards midnight, a funeral car was heard driven slowly by a team of eight white horses, preceded by dogs of the same colour. Those who listened might hear the voices of those sailors who had died in the course of the year. Those persons who dared to look at this fearful scene were doomed to die shortly afterwards; so, as the hour approached, every house was barred and windows closed.

The Russian Twelfth Day (18th of January) is devoted to the singular custom of blessing the waters of the Neva, there being no parallel ceremony in any other country, except the practice once observed at Venice of the Doge espousing the sea. On the same day at Constantinople, the Greek Patriarch performs a similar custom by throwing a cross into the sea, and it is said that skilful divers generally succeed in obtaining it before reaching the bottom. The fishermen who dwell on the coasts of the Baltic never used their nets between All Saints' Day and St. Martin's Day, believing that any infraction of this rule would prevent them from getting fish through the whole year. A similar observance, for the same reason, was held on St. Blaise's Day. They also considered sneezing on Christmas Day a favourable omen for the ensuing year.

The fishermen of Hartlepool preserve many old customs, such as Carling and Palm Sundays, and Easter Day. At Christmas the children sing carols, and sword-dancers go about the streets; and on the first Monday after the Epiphany, the stot or fool-plough (a small anchor) is dragged through the town, and donations requested.

Sailors have always had their prejudices with regard to certain days of the week. That ominous day, Friday, so dark-lined to many weak-headed individuals—not only at sea, but on shore— was and is still considered by many mariners a blank day for sailing. A Cornish saying places Candlemas Day as ill omened for sailing. Bishop Hall, speaking of a superstitious man, observes, "he will never set to sea except on Sunday." At Preston-Pans, it seems, that holy day was usually selected for sailing to the fishing grounds: a clergyman of the town preached against this Sabbath-breaking, and the sailors, to prevent any ill befalling them in consequence, made a small image of rags, and burnt it on the top of their chimneys.

*Apparitions* have always been a fruitful source of terror to seamen. A few years ago half a dozen sailors on board a man-of-war took it into their heads that there was a ghost in the ship, and declared *they smelt him*. The captain laughed at them, and called them a parcel of lubbers. A few nights afterwards they were in great terror, saying the ghost was behind the beer-barrels. The captain, annoyed at their folly, ordered a dozen lashes to each of them, which effectually stopped all talk about the spirit. When the barrels were removed some time afterwards, a dead rat was found, which had given rise to the story. Brand mentions that the cook of a vessel belonging to Newcastle died on a homeward passage. One of his legs was shorter than the other, which had given him an odd appearance when he walked. A few nights after the body had been committed to the deep, the captain was alarmed by his mate assuring him that the man was walking on the sea before the ship. The captain certainly saw something that seemed to move as the cook had walked, and ordered the ship to be moved towards the object. The seamen were greatly terrified; but it was soon found that the cause of all the commotion was part of a main-top, the remains of some wreck, floating before them. In the campaigns of the French fleet at Mitylene, the crew of a brigantine are said to have seen the figure of a monstrous and hideous seaman, descend in the waters at Zante, with one of the crew who had defied the Virgin while playing at dice on board.

*Bells* had a superstitious influence on the minds of seamen. It was commonly believed that when ships went down during a storm, the death-bell would be distinctly heard by the drowning crew. During tempests at Malta, it is usual to ring all the bells in the Roman Catholic churches for an hour, that the winds may cease and the sea be calmed. This custom also prevails in Sicily and Sardinia. There is a Cornish legend that the bells of Bottreaux Church were sent by ship, but that when the vessel was in sight of the tower, the blasphemy of the captain was punished by the loss of his ship. The bells were supposed to lie in the bay, and announce by strange sounds the approach of a storm.

A belief is still widely entertained in the virtues of a child's caul (a thin skin covering the head of some children when born) as a preservative against drowning and shipwrecks. In a Plymouth paper, the "Western Morning News," of the 9th of February, 1867, there was a notice to mariners: "For safeguard at sea: a child's caul for sale, price five guineas." The pretended virtues of this object reminds us of what is told of Augustus Cæsar, that he carried a seal's skin about him as a preservative against lightning.

*Rats leaving a ship* are considered indications of misfortune, probably from the same idea that crows will not build their nests upon trees that are likely to fall. A droll story is told of a cunning Welsh captain, whose ship was infested by rats, which he was anxious to get rid of. The vessel was lying in the Mersey, at Liverpool, and hearing that there was another, laden with cheeses, in the basin, he got alongside of her about dusk, and soon saw all the rats attracted by the rich smell of the cheeses into his neighbour's ship, when he quietly had his own removed to a safe distance.

*Omens for good or evil* were derived from birds and marine animals. Shakespere alludes to the halcyon when he says:

> "Disown, affirm, and turn their halcyon beaks
> With every gale and vary of their masters."

The osprey is abundant during the summer along the coasts of North America, and its presence is hailed by the fisherman as the harbinger of summer, with the same feelings of satisfaction as the appearance of the gannet on our own shores.

> "The osprey sails above the sound,
> The geese are gone, the gulls are flying,
> The herring-shoals swarm thick around,
> The nets are launch'd, the boats are plying;
>
> "'Yo, yo, my hearts! let's seek the deep,
> Raise high the song, and cheerly wish her,
> Still as the bending net we sweep,
> God bless the fish-hawk and the fisher!'"

The tern is considered in the same favourable light as the osprey and the kingfisher; but the stormy petrels, the "Mother Carey's chickens" of early times, bring apprehensions of fearful dangers to the seaman, owing probably to the appearance of the birds when several hundred miles from land, apparently untired, and seldom seen resting or eating, together with its ominous colour. Pennant, however, says that the petrel does actually caution mariners of an impending tempest by collecting under the stern of the ship.

> "Thus doth the prophet of good or ill
> Meet hate from the creatures he serveth still;
> Yet he ne'er falters; so, petrel, spring
> Once more on the waves with thy stormy wing."

It is curious to find crows employed in the early ages as guides to mariners. We are told that when Flok, a famous Norwegian navigator, was going to start from Shetland to Iceland, he took on board some crows, *because the mariner's compass was not then in use.* When he thought he had made a considerable part of his way, he threw up one of his crows, who, seeing land astern, flew to it, thus indicating the route. Such was the simple mode of keeping a reckoning and steering their course pursued by the bold navigators of the stormy Northern Ocean.

It is still believed that sea-gulls retiring to land foretell a storm; but the migration of sea-birds generally arises from their security in finding food, such as earth-worms and larvæ, driven out of the ground by severe floods. The fish on which they prey in fine weather in the sea leave the surface and go deeper.

Bourne says that, "seeing *three* magpies augurs a successful voyage;" but this will scarcely hold good with the superstitions respecting the same bird formerly held by seamen. Sir Walter Scott relates that a friend on a journey to London found himself in company with a seafaring man of middle age, in the same mail coach, who announced himself as master of a vessel in the Baltic trade. In the course of conversation the seaman observed, "I wish we may have good luck on our journey; but there is a magpie!" "And why should that be unlucky?" said my friend. "I cannot tell you," replied the sailor; "but all the world agrees that one magpie bodes ill luck; two are not so bad; but three are the Evil One himself. I never saw three magpies but twice, and once I nearly lost my vessel, and afterwards, when I was on land, I fell from my horse and was much injured."

The swan was an omen of fair weather to mariners. Coleridge has immortalized the albatross, as the harbinger of good fortune, in the "Ancient Mariner:"

> " At length did cross an albatross,
>   Through the fog it came;
>   As if it had been a Christian soul,
>   We hail'd it in God's name.
>
> " It ate the food it ne'er did eat,
>   And round and round it flew;
>   The ice did split with a thunder-fit,
>   The helmsman steer'd us through.
>
> " And a good south wind sprang up behind;
>   The albatross did follow;
>   And every day, for food or play,
>   Came to the mariners' halloa!

> "In mist or cloud, or mast or shroud,
>   It perch'd for vespers nine,
> While all the night, through fog-smoke white,
>   Glimmer'd the pale moonshine.
>
> "'God save thee, Ancient Mariner,
>   From the fiends that plague thee thus;
> Why look'st thou so?'  'With my crossbow
>   I shot the albatross!'
>
> \* \* \* \* \*
>
> "And all averr'd I had kill'd the bird
>   That made the breeze to blow:
> 'Ah, wretch!' said they, 'the bird to slay,
>   That made the breeze to blow!'"

The albatross is remarkable for the extent of its wanderings; indeed, it may almost be said to pass from pole to pole, and is seen at a greater distance from land than any other bird. Hence sailors regarded this companion of their voyages with superstitious fondness.

Dolphins, as well as porpoises, when they play about a ship, are supposed to foretell storms. The ancient navigators, however, regarded them in a different light, and believed that they conveyed shipwrecked seamen to shore in times of peril. The story of Arion is well known; and Spenser, in his "Marriage of the Thames and Medway," alludes to this romantic fiction, at the sight of which

> "All the raging seas for joy forgot to roar."

Like many other old pagan fictions, this story was invested by the earlier Christian converts with a deeper, holier meaning; and the dolphin, so constantly recognized in sculptures and frescoes, points, not to the deliverer of Arion, but to Him who, through the waters of baptism, opens to mankind the path of deliverance.

We need scarcely be surprised at the superstitions of seamen in former days, when instances of such gross ignorance and credulity are found among the writers of those times. A belief long prevailed that the barnacle, a well-known kind of shell-fish found adhering to the bottom of ships, would, when broken off, become a species of goose. Several old writers assert this, and more than one from personal observation. The numerous tentacles or arms of the animal inhabiting the barnacle-shell, which are disposed in a semi-circular form and have a feathery appearance, seem to have been all that could reasonably be alleged in favour of this strange supposition.

Carrying dead bodies in ships has always been a sore point with sailors, and the sight of even an empty coffin works upon their prejudices. Such Nelson found was the case, when one was sent to him by a brother officer made of the main-mast of the French ship "L'Orient," to remind the illustrious hero that amidst all the glory that surrounded him he was but mortal. Nelson received the present in a proper spirit, and had the coffin placed in his own cabin in the "Vanguard," but the crew could not bear to have the obnoxious memorial in sight, and it was accordingly ordered to be sent below.

In the Orkneys, mariners on going to sea would consider themselves in the greatest danger if by accident they turned their boat in opposition to the sun's course. In Sweden it is considered a bad omen to turn the prow of a vessel towards the shore, and for any one to say "Good luck" to the fishermen when starting; also, that pins found in a church, and made into hooks, get the best fish. Tackle, they affirm, stolen from a friend or a neighbour, secures better luck than when purchased for money—a species of larceny more profitable to the fisherman than comfortable to his friends.

Sneezing—a potent omen in ancient times—had its portent for good or evil among seamen in former days: a sneeze on the left side, at the moment of embarking, foreboded evil, while a fortunate sneeze on the right side betokened a favourable voyage.

"Good luck" is as much the creed of the fisherman as it is of many superstitious persons on land. Only a few years ago, in a number of the "Banff Journal," it was related that the herring fishery being very backward, some of the fishermen of Buckie dressed a cooper in a flannel shirt with burrs stuck all over it, and in this position he was carried in procession through the town in a hand-barrow. This ridiculous ceremony was done to procure "better luck." It happened, also, in a district where there were several churches, chapels, and schools. The fishermen of the Firth of Forth believe that if they chance to meet a woman bare-footed who has broad feet, when they are going to their vessels, they will have "bad luck," and the same fatality attends the sale of fish for the first time in the day to a person having broad thumbs. It is considered "unlucky" to lose a water-bucket or a mop at sea. Children on board are regarded with favour by seamen as likely to bring good luck; not so a cat, which is sure to turn the scale of chance in the wrong direction. Whittington, however, the renowned "thrice Lord Mayor of London," could not have shared in this superstition, if some old stories are true. To play at cards on board is considered unlucky; at some places boats' crews are changed from time to time for the same reason.

I could multiply these instances by similar absurd delusions, many of which unhappily still prevail; but what I have mentioned will suffice to show you how superstition works upon its votaries, and especially on the sailor,

"Whose eventful life,
Whose generous spirit and contempt of danger,
His firmness in the gale, the wreck, and strife,"

does not exempt him from the failings of credulity, and who, as

"Garrulous ignorance relates,
Will learn it and believe."

## CHAPTER XXII.

### MONSTERS OF THE DEEP.—SEA-DRAGONS.

"A world of wonders, where creation seems
No more the works of Nature, but her dreams."

MONTGOMERY.

THE subject I have chosen for the present chapter is one of the deepest interest, for it carries our thoughts to ages beyond the human mind to conceive, when the ocean, covering an immense expanse of our globe, swarmed with gigantic reptiles in the highest state of development, living in the open sea, and seeking the shore occasionally, crawling along the beach in search of prey.

Those of my young readers who have been to the British Museum must have remarked with astonishment the collection to be seen there of huge fossil marine animals, which is probably the finest in the world, and to such, the observations I am about to make regarding them will have a deeper interest.

The term "fossil" (from the Latin *fossilis*) signifies, in general, anything dug out of the earth, and is applied to the remains of animals and vegetables that have, during the lapse of many ages, become petrified, and preserved in such a state as to enable naturalists to describe what they were originally. Some fossil remains are so small as to require the aid of a microscope to examine them, while others, such as I have alluded to, are of proportions so enormous and of forms so strange as to fill us with awe at such wonderful works of the Almighty Creator.

These reptiles were inhabitants of the ocean thousands of ages past, and from their strength and voracity must have been fearful scourges in that element.

I will tell you how the remains of one of the most curious of these antediluvian monsters were found. Lyme Regis, a seaport in Dorsetshire, became remarkable at the commencement of the present century for the number of fossils embedded in the limestone cliffs, and a native of the place, Mary Anning, who had been engaged from her childhood in searching for what were then popularly called "curiosities," saw in 1811 an immense bone projecting from the ledges of the rocks, and having traced the remains of what she considered an enormous crocodile, she employed some labourers to dig out the blocks of stone in which they were petrified. These remains, placed together, proved to be the skeleton of a marine monster about thirty feet in length, with jaws nearly six feet long. This was an *Ichthyosaurus* (from two Greek words signifying "fish-lizard") of which seven or eight different species may be seen in the British Museum.

You have, no doubt, often been amused and perhaps frightened in your childhood, by the descriptions of dragons and other fearful monsters, which found their way, I am sorry to say, much too frequently in story-books; but you could not imagine a more dreadful-looking creature than this huge sea-lizard, with a head like a crocodile, and the jaws provided with a great number of immense teeth (in some cases one hundred and eighty); the eyes in volume exceeding the size of your own head, and so constructed as to afford a wonderful magnifying power in tracing their prey through the darkness and depth of the ocean.

The body was like that of a fish, with a broad and long tail, and four paddles (instead of feet, like those of the lizard or crocodile), similar to those of the whale tribe, enabling the animal to move, as *they* do, with rapidity through the water; and with such a construction of the breast-arch as enabled it to descend to the bottom of the sea in search of food, which consisted of fishes and reptiles, the remains of which have been discovered with the bones of the animal, thus shewing upon what it subsisted. "When we discover" (wrote the late Dean Buckland) "in the body of an Ichthyosaurus the food which it has engulfed *an instant before its death*—when the intervals between its sides present themselves still filled with the remains of fishes which it had swallowed some ten thousand years ago, or at a time even twice as great—all these immense intervals vanish, and we find ourselves, so to speak, thrown into immediate contact with events which took place in epochs immeasurably distant, as if we occupied ourselves with the affairs of the previous day."

Another huge fossil marine animal, the *Plesiosaurus* (from Greek words signifying "near" and "lizard"), somewhat allied in its structure to the animal I have just mentioned, may also be seen in the British Museum, and the first discovery of the remains of this colossal reptile was also made at Lyme Regis, about the year 1823. This was a most extraordinary creature, with the head of a lizard, the teeth of a crocodile, a neck of enormous length, resembling, on a very enlarged scale, that of a swan, the ribs of a chameleon, a body rounded like that of a great marine turtle, a tail shorter, in comparison with the length of the body, than the Ichthyosaurus, acting the part of a rudder in directing the course of the animal through the water.

The Rev. W. D. Conybeare thus describes the habits of this huge reptile: "That it was aquatic is evident from the form of its paddles; that it was marine is equally so from the remains with which it is universally associated; that it may have occasionally visited the shore, the resemblance of its extremities to those of the turtle may lead us to conjecture: its motion, however, must have been awkward on land, and its long neck may have impeded its progress through the water. May it not, therefore, be concluded that it swam upon or near the surface, arching back its long neck like the swan, and occasionally darting it down on the fish which happened to float within its reach? It may perhaps have lurked in shoal water along the coast, concealed among the sea-weed, and raising its nostrils to a level with the surface from a considerable depth, may have found a secure retreat from the assaults of dangerous enemies."

The Plesiosaurus was scarcely as large as the Ichthyosaurus; some of the species, however, measure from eighteen to twenty feet.

The two animals I have described do not seem to have had, as far as can be judged, a *scaly* covering; but another monstrous reptile of the primitive seas, the *Teleosaurus*—a kind of fossil crocodile inhabiting the seas and rivers of the Old World, the great pirate of the ocean—was armed to the teeth, and clothed with an impenetrable coat of mail both on the back and stomach. This fearful animal was thirty feet in length, the head measuring from three to four feet, with enormous jaws, well defended beyond the ears, sometimes with an opening of six feet, through which they could swallow animals the size of an ox.

The animals I have mentioned were, from their enormous size and voracity, the terror of the primitive seas. After them we have the *Mœsasaurus*, a creature whose remains were first discovered at Maestricht, on the banks of the Meuse, in 1780. This occurred when the knowledge of these ancient prodigies was still in its infancy. One saw in it the head of a crocodile, another that of a whale. A long discussion was terminated by the great Baron Cuvier, who, assisted by the genius of Camper, at length gave a true place in the animal kingdom to the Maestricht wonder. Among those interested in the discovery of these ancient vestiges of creation was an officer of the garrison at Maestricht, named Drouin. He purchased the bones of the animal as the workmen disengaged them from the rock, and formed a collection of fossil rarities at Maestricht, which excited great curiosity. The head, which exceeded six feet in length, was sent to France, and is now in the Museum of Natural History at Paris.

To show you the wonderful anatomical knowledge of scientific men in modern times, I may mention that Cuvier was able to ascertain the character of the entire skeleton of this huge animal from the examination of the jaws and teeth alone, and even from *a single tooth !* This told a history in itself: being without a root, not hollow, as in the crocodile, but solid throughout, and joined to the sockets by a broad bony basis, it became an instrument of enormous strength, and proved how formidable the animal must have been. It had sufficient velocity to overtake and capture fishes of immense size, with which the ancient seas abounded. In length it was about twenty-five feet; the tail was flattened on each side, but high and deep, forming a straight oar of great strength to propel the body.

## CHAPTER XXIII.

### *MARINE PRODIGIES.*

"God quickened in the seas and in the rivers
So many fishes of so many features,
That in the waters we may all see creatures,
Even all that on the earth are to be found,
As if the world were in deep waters drown'd.
For seas, as well as skies, have sun, moon, stars,
As well as air, swallows, rooks, and stares,
As well as earth, vines, roses, nettles, melons,
Mushrooms, pinks, gillyflowers, and many millions
Of other plants more rare, more strange than these,
*As very fishes living in the seas:*
As also rams, calves, horses, hares, and hogs,
Wolves, urchins, lions, elephants, and dogs;
Yea, *men and maids*, and which I most admire,
*The mitred bishop and the cowlèd friar;*
Of which examples, but a few years since,
Were shown the Norway and Polanian prince."

Du Bartas.

THE regions of fable are unbounded; and probably no department of Nature is so prolific in supplying food for the wildest fancies of the imagination than the great unfathomed ocean depths, which conceal so many mysteries.

The ancients had their sea-divinities and monsters in profusion. It is true that the powerful mind of Aristotle, the great father of early philosophy, rejected with disdain the credulous tales and fabulous stories of his age in regard to natural history; but the writings of Pliny, the natural historian, abound in prodigies and absurdities, as also those of Ælian, and other ancient authors. For many centuries a mist of doubt, error, and fanciful credulity prevailed with regard to the inhabitants of the ocean. Even in 1554 a work on fishes by Rondelet, a physician at Montpellier, although written with tolerable exactitude in some particulars, concludes with a chapter illustrated by grotesque figures of certain marine monsters; amongst others, a fish dressed as a monk, and a "bishop-fish" in full pontificals. Where the extraordinary originals, from which these cuts were taken, came from, is not known; but they were probably fabricated in the true Barnum style from the skins of some large species of sharks or rays, by the priests of that period, to excite the superstitious veneration of the people, and persuade them, as Du Bartas, in the quotation at the head of this chapter, wishes us to believe, that even the sea contains bishops and monks.

Until the commencement of the seventeenth century, nothing like a dawn of true light with regard to natural history seemed to strike upon the popular mind. A laborious but very credulous professor at Bologna, Aldrovandus, wrote no less than fourteen folio volumes on the subject, published in 1640; but the true and the false, fable and nonsense, are strangely intermixed. Some of the engravings in these books are very curious, and give an idea of the exaggerative style of their contents. These we have, magnified in every extent, by succeeding writers.

The *Kraken*, described by Pontoppidan in his "Natural History of Norway," is one of the most extraordinary of these wonderful sea-monsters, and claims the peculiar privilege of the wide domain of the Norwegian waters.

"Our fishermen usually affirm," says this writer, "that, when they row out several miles to sea, particularly in hot summer days, they are informed by various circumstances that the kraken is at the bottom of the sea. Sometimes twenty boats get together over him, and when, from well-known indications, they perceive it is rising, they get away as fast as they can. When they find themselves out of danger, they lie upon their oars, and in a few minutes they see the monster come to the surface. He there shows himself sufficiently, though only a small part of his body appears. Its back, *which appears to be a mile and a half in circumference,* looks at first like a number of small islands, surrounded with something which floats like seaweeds; here and there a large rising is observed like sand-banks; at last, several bright points or horns appear, which grow thicker the higher they rise, and sometimes they stand up as high and as large as the masts of middle-sized vessels. It seems these are the creature's arms, and it is said, if they were to lay hold of the largest man-of-war, they would pull it down to the bottom. After the monster has been a short time on the water, he begins slowly to sink again; and then the danger is as great as before, because the motion of the sinking causes such a swell and such an eddy or whirlpool that he carries everything before it."

Such is the description of the fabulous kraken. Divested of its supernatural powers and dimensions, there may be some foundations for these exaggerations in the occasional appearances of huge cephalopods (molluscous animals having the head covered with tentacula or feelers, serving as feet), to the general characters of which the description given of its form and monstrous arms sufficiently agrees. Many such animals are known to exist in some seas, and there are reasons for believing that much larger creatures of the same species exist.

It is a favourite notion of Pontoppidan that from the appearance of the kraken originate those dim traditions of floating islands being observed in the North seas. It has been sought to identify the cuttle-fish of enormous size with the kraken, and stories are told of men having been drawn over the sides of vessels by their enormous arms. In 1834, Captain Neill, of the ship "Robertson," of Greenock, saw the head and snout of a great sea-monster, of which a sketch was taken at the time. It appeared like a vessel lying on her beam-ends. The "Robertson" was hauled up so as to near it, and it was discovered to be the head and snout of a great fish swimming to windward: immediately above the water, its eye was seen like a large deep hole. The part of the head which was above the water measured about twelve feet, and its width twenty-five feet. The snout was about fifty feet long, and the sea occasionally rippled over one part, leaving other parts dry and uncovered. Several records exist in Scotland of the appearance of similar animals to that which have been noticed, but the result appears to infer the existence of some enormous cuttle-fish, possessed of characters which distinguish it essentially from every other creature with which we are familiar. Pliny's vast animal, with prodigious arms, which impeded the navigation of the Straits of Gibraltar, would seem to have had a family likeness to the kraken.

The great *Sea-Serpent* appears to have some analogy to the same monster as I have described, and here again the sapient Pontoppidan raises our eyes in astonishment at his description of this marine prodigy, which he describes as six hundred feet in length, ying in the water in many folds, and appearing like many hogsheads floating in a line at a considerable distance from each other. Such a creature is said to have been seen on the coast of Norway, in 1819, for a whole month, seeming to doze in the sunbeams. In 1822 and 1837, it is said to have reappeared in the same waters. The Americans, not to be outdone by the Norwegians, relate several cases in which prodigious sea-serpents have been seen in the Atlantic, opinions varying as to the length of the animals, averaging from eighty feet to two hundred and fifty yards, making curves "perpendicular to the water, and with eyes brilliant and glistening."

Our own sailors have also their account in the prodigy witnessed in 1848, in the South Atlantic Ocean, not far from the coast of Africa, by the officers and crew of H.M.S. "Dædalus." In the "Illustrated London News" of 28th October, 1848, may be seen engravings of this strange monster, from sketches by Captain McQuhae, the commander of the vessel. According to the account forwarded to the Admiralty, the animal was seen not in bright and fine weather, but with a murky atmosphere, and with a long ocean swell. It was swimming rapidly, and with its head and neck above water, and appeared an enormous serpent, with head and shoulders kept about four feet constantly above the surface of the sea. It passed so close under the lee-quarter of the vessel, that its features were easily recognized. The diameter of

# HUGE SEA ANIMAL SEEN NEAR ST. HELENA. 257

the serpent was about fifteen or sixteen inches behind the head, and the animal was never, during the twenty minutes that it continued in sight, once below the surface of the water. The colour was a dark brown, with yellowish-white about the throat. It had no fins, but something like the mane of a horse, or rather a bunch of sea-weed, washed about its back.

Our great anatomist, Dr. Owen, has expressed much doubt as to the existence of a great sea-serpent, on the ground that no bones or other remains of such recent animal have been found. Notwithstanding this high authority, it may be, however, that many animals in the ocean depths, of this character, are still unknown to us. As some proof of this, I may mention, that nine years after this occurrence, in 1857, a similar creature was seen by the officers and crew of the ship "Castilian," bound from Bombay to Liverpool. This event occurred at six in the evening, about ten miles distant from St. Helena. A monster suddenly appeared in the water. The chief facts are in the captain's (Harrington) own words:

"While myself and officers were standing on the lee-side of the poop, looking towards the island, we were startled by the sight of a huge marine animal, which reared its head out of the water within twenty yards of the ship, when it suddenly disappeared for about half a minute, and then made its appearance in the same manner again, showing us distinctly its neck and head, about ten or twelve feet out of the water. The diameter of the head was about seven or eight feet in the largest part, with a tuft of loose skin circling it about two feet from the top. The water was discoloured for several hundred feet from its head, so much so, that on its first appearance my impression was that the ship was in broken water, produced, as I supposed, by some volcanic agency since the last time I passed the island; but the second appearance completely dispelled these fears, and assured us it was a monster of extraordinary length, which appeared to be moving slowly towards the land. The ship was going too fast to enable us to reach the mast-head in time to form a correct estimate of its extreme length; but from what we saw from the deck, we conclude that it must have been over two hundred feet long. The boatswain and several of the crew who observed it from the top-gallant forecastle, state that it was more than double the length of the ship, in which case it must have been five hundred feet long. Be that as it may, I am convinced that it must have belonged to the serpent tribe : it was of a dark colour about the head, and was covered with several white spots."

Captain Harrington, some time afterwards, strengthened his testimony by that of other persons. The conclusion, however, seems to be that the animal actually seen by the captains of the "Dædalus" and the "Castilian" was, most probably, a species of seal known to inhabit the South Seas.

It has been supposed that large fishes of the *Ribbon* family may have given rise to some of the stories about the great sea-serpent. One was lately captured at the Bermudas, apparently an immature fish, but more than sixteen feet in length, and with a row of long flexible filaments, or slender threads, on the back of the head and anterior parts of the back, which might well represent the *mane* alluded to as an appendage of the serpent prodigy. The fishes of this kind are inhabitants of great depths in the ocean, and this may account for the rarity of their appearance. One species belongs to the Northern Seas, where the appearance of the sea-serpent has been particularly recorded; others belong to the warmer regions. It may be that these fishes attain to a length that would corroborate the assertions of those who have seen the sea-serpent, making a due allowance for exaggeration under such novel circumstances.

Mr. Adams, naturalist of H.M.S. "Samarang," writing of Sooloo and the Molucca Archipelagoes, remarks : "I have often witnessed the phenomenon which first gave origin to the marvellous stories of the great sea-serpent, namely, lines of rolling porpoises, resembling a long string of buoys often extending a hundred yards. These account for the so-named protuberances of the serpent's back. They keep in close single file, progressing rapidly along the surface of the water by a succession of leaps, part only of their uncouth forms appearing to the eye."

The serpent in the sea was, at one time, a very general superstition among the heathens, for we find in Isaiah xxvii. 1 : "In that day the Lord with His sore and great strong sword shall punish leviathan the piercing serpent, even leviathan that crooked serpent; and He shall slay the dragon that is in the sea."

In the prose "Edda," a collection of Scandinavian mythology dating from the thirteenth century, there is a story how Thor, the second in rank of the Northern deities, went to fish for the Midgard sea-serpent. It is curious as showing the origin of the popular delusions of the Northern people revived, as we have seen, by Pontoppidan and others, with regard to the kraken and the monstrous serpent. Thor went out of Midgard under the disguise of a young man, and came at dusk to the dwelling of a giant called Hymir. Here he passed the night, but at break of day, when he perceived that the giant was preparing his boat for fishing, he arose and dressed himself, and begged Hymir to let him row out to sea with him. The giant answered that a puny stripling like he was could be of no use to him, and would not venture so far, or remain out so long at sea as he was accustomed to. Thor declared that he would, and felt so enraged at the surly manners of the giant, that he was inclined to let his mallet ring on the head of the savage, but he stifled his wrath, and asked Hymir what he meant to bait with. Hymir told him to manage that for himself, and Thor went up to a herd of oxen belonging to the giant, wrung off the head of one of them, and returning with it to the boat, put out to sea with Hymir. Thor rowed aft with two oars, and with such force that his companion, who rowed at the prow, saw with surprise how swiftly the vessel was driven forwards. He then said that they were come to the place where he usually angled for flat-fish, but Thor would not stop, but rowed on until Hymir cried out that there would be danger from the great Midgard serpent. In spite of these remonstrances, however, it was some time before Thor would lay down his oars. He then took out a fishing-line, exceedingly strong, furnished with a powerful hook, on which he fixed the bull's head, and cast the line into the sea. The bait soon reached the bottom; the huge serpent greedily caught at it, and the hook stuck fast in his palate. Stung with the pain, the monster tugged so violently that Thor was obliged to hold fast with both hands by the oar-pegs; but his wrath now waxed high, and assuming all his divine power and colossal dimensions, he pulled so hard at the line that his feet forced their way through the boat and went down to the bottom of the sea, whilst with his two hands he drew up the serpent. A dreadful scene now took place, Thor darting looks of fierce anger at the monster as it reared its head, spouting out floods of venom upon him. When Hymir saw the serpent he turned pale and trembled with affright, as we may reasonably suppose; and finding himself sinking with the boat, drew out his knife and cut the line, on which the serpent sank again under water. Thor, however, launched his mallet at the monster, and some say struck off its head at the bottom of the sea, while others affirm that the monster still lives in the depths of the ocean. Thor then struck Hymir such a blow with his fist that the giant fell dead headlong into the water; and the god, wading through the ocean with rapid strides, came to land again.

The old Northern writers, like many others of a credulous character, were endowed with very elastic imaginations, and saw most matters through powerful magnifiers. One of this class was Olaus Magnus, Archbishop of Upsal, about the middle of the sixteenth century, who wrote an account of various sea-prodigies. One chapter in his book is "On many kinds of Whales." "Some," he says, "are hairy, and of four acres in bigness: the acre is two hundred and forty feet long and one hundred and twenty broad." Another kind "hath eyes so large that fifteen men may sit in the room of each of them, and sometimes twenty or more; his horns are six or seven feet long, and he hath two hundred and fifty on each eye, as hard as a horn, that he can stir stiff or gentle, either before or behind." The worthy prelate has another chapter, of "Anchors fastened on Whales' Backs," in which it is stated, "the whale hath upon his skin a superficies like the gravel that is by the sea-side, so that ofttimes, when he raiseth his back above the water, sailors take it to be nothing else than an island, and land upon it, and they strike piles into it, and fasten them to their ships; they kindle fires upon it to boil their meat, until at length the whale, feeling the fire, dives down suddenly into the depth, and draws forth man and ship after him unless the anchor breaks."

Olaus tells of fish on the coast of Norway of most horrible form, having very black square heads of ten or twelve cubits, with huge eyes eight or ten cubits in circumference, the apple of the eye being red and fiery-coloured, which in the dark nights and the deep waters appears to fishermen like a burning lamp; and on the head there being hair, like long goose-feathers, hanging down in manner of a beard. One of these sea-monsters will easily drown many great ships with their mariners.

In another chapter of "The Whirlpool and his Cruelty against the Mariners," Olaus treats it as a stupendous fish. "The whirlpool or prister is of the kind of whales, two hundred cubits long, and very cruel. This beast hath a large and round mouth like a lamprey, whereby he sucks in his meat or water, and will cast such floods above his head that he will often sink the strongest ships. He will sometimes raise himself above the sail-yards, and cruelly overthrow the ship like any small vessel, striking it with his back or tail, which is forked, wherewith he forcibly binds any part of a ship when he twists it about." Olaus affirms that a war-trumpet is the fit remedy against him, by reason of the sharp noise, which he cannot endure, or the sound of cannon, with which he is more frightened than by a cannon-ball, "because this ball loseth its force by the water, or wounds but a little his vast body, being hindered by *a mighty rampart of fat*."

The archbishop concludes his strange histories with an observation that no one would be rash enough to controvert, that in the great deeps "there are many kinds of fishes that seldom or never are seen by man."

The belief in *Mermaids* and *Mermen*, prevalent through the remotest ages, was also especially strong in the Scandinavian countries, and some traces of the delusions still linger on some of the out-of-way coasts of the Northern seas. A very high antiquity is claimed for these mythic creatures. Ancient history abounds with notices of them. One was called by the Babylonians *Odakon*, and is regarded by Selden as identical with Dagon (from the Hebrew *dag*, "a fish"), the national god of the Philistines, so frequently mentioned in the Scriptures. It is always represented on medals as half fish and half woman, but the Hebrew writers speak of it as a masculine being. In the excavations of Khorsabad, M. Botta found a figure of Odunes, a creature half man and half fish. At the excavations at Nimroud, Mr. Layard discovered a gigantic figure with a fish's head as a cap, and the body of the fish depending over the shoulders. On the coins of Ascalon is figured a goddess, above whose head is a half-moon, and at her feet a woman with her lower extremities like a fish. It is singular (observes Mr. Gould) how the prevalence of the tales of mermaids exists among Celtic nations, indicating these water-nymphs as having been originally deities of the people. The Peruvians had also their semi-fish gods. These form the types of those imaginary creatures, the subjects of ancient poetry, the Tritons, who were represented as half men and half fish, having power to calm tempests; and probably, too, of the Syrens, whose songs were said to lure the unhappy seamen to destruction.

Innumerable are the stories that are told of mermaids and mermen: they have been made the subject of numberless songs by ancient and modern bards. Shakespere alludes to the vocal powers of these mythic creatures:

> "I heard a mermaid on a dolphin's back
> Uttering such dulcet and harmonious breath
> That the rude sea grew civil at her song."

Our own Laureate inquires

> "Who would be
> A mermaid fair?
> Singing alone,
> Combing her hair
> Under the sea,
> In a golden curl,
> With a comb of pearl,
> On a throne?"

In the "Speculum Regale," an Icelandic work of the twelfth century, is the following description of a mermaid: "A monster is seen also near Greenland, like a woman as far down as the waist; long hands and soft hair, the neck and head in all respects like that of a human being. The hands seem to people to be long, and the fingers not to be parted, but united by a web like that on the feet of water-birds. From the waist downwards this monster resembles a fish, with scales, tail, and fin. This prodigy is supposed to show itself more especially before heavy storms. The habit of this creature is to dive frequently, and rise again to the surface with fishes in its hands. When sailors see it playing with the fish, or throwing them towards the ship, they fear they are doomed to lose several of the crew; but when it casts the fish, or, turning from the vessel, flings them away from her, the sailors take it as a good omen that they will not suffer loss in an impending storm. The monster has a very horrible face, with broad brow and piercing eyes, a wide mouth, and double chin."

Pontoppidan, from whose "History of Norway" I have already largely quoted, records the appearance of a merman, which was deposed to on oath by several observers. "About a mile from the coast of Denmark, near Landscrona, three sailors, observing something like a dead body floating on the water, rowed towards it. When they came within seven or eight fathoms, it still appeared as at first, for it had not stirred; but at that instant it sank, and arose almost immediately in the same place. Upon this, out of fear, they lay still and let the boat float, that they might the better examine the monster, which by the help of the current came nearer to them. He turned his face and stared at them, which gave them an opportunity of examining him narrowly. He stood in the same place seven or eight minutes, and was seen on the water above breast-high. At last they grew apprehensive of some danger, and began to retire, upon which the monster blew up his cheeks and made a kind of lowing noise, diving away from view. In regard to his form, they declare that he appeared like an old man, strong limbed, with broad shoulders, but his arms they could not see. His head was small in proportion to his body, and had short black curled hair, which did not reach below his ears. His eyes lay deep in his head, and he had a meagre face with a black beard. About the body downwards this merman was quite pointed like a fish."

Many of the so-called mermaids exhibited in a stuffed condition from time to time have proved sometimes clever, but more frequently bungling "shams." Among the latter may be classed the exhibition of the famous American, Barnum, a few years since, which proved to be the combination of the head of a monkey with the tail of a fish! The probability is that all the stories about these prodigies have originated in the appearance of seals, walruses, to which I have already alluded, and to what are called the herbivorous cetacea, from their living on sea-plants, and which consists amongst others of the manatee of the West Indies, the dugong of the Eastern seas, and the stellerus, an inhabitant of the Polar regions.

I will briefly describe these animals. The best-known species of the *Manatee*, or Lamantin, or Sea-Cow, is found in the West Indies and on the western coasts of tropical America. These sometimes attain a length of twenty feet, and a weight of three or four tons, and they live chiefly in shallow bays and creeks, and in the estuaries of rivers. The skin is very thick and strong, and is almost destitute of hair. The fingers can be readily felt in the swimming paws, and, connected together as they are, possess considerable power of motion, whence the name manatee (from the Latin *manus*, "a hand"). This animal is usually found in herds, which combine for mutual protection when attacked, placing the young in the centre. When one is struck with a harpoon, the others try to tear it out. The females show great affection for their young.

The *Dugong*—numbers of which frequent the coasts of Ceylon, allured by the still waters and the abundance of sea-weeds—is, perhaps, one of the most likely representatives of what is considered a "mermaid" that could be found. There is a rude approach to the human outline in the shape and attitude of the mother dugong while suckling her young, holding it to her breast by one flipper while swimming with the other, the heads of both being above water; and when suddenly disturbed, diving and displaying her fish-like tail. These, together with her habitual demonstrations of strong natural affection, might readily give rise to the fable of the mermaid.

Megasthenes records the existence of a creature in the ocean near Taprobane (Ceylon), with the aspect of a woman; and Ælian, adopting and enlarging on his information, peoples the seas of Ceylon with fishes having the heads of lions, panthers, and rams; and, stranger still, in the form of satyrs! Statements such as these must have had their origin in the hairs which are set round the mouth of the dugong, somewhat resembling a beard. The Portuguese cherished for a long time their belief in the mermaid; and the historian of the proceedings of the Jesuits in India gravely records that seven of these monsters, male and female, were captured at Ceylon in 1560, and carried to Goa, where they were dissected by the physician to the Viceroy, and "their internal structure found to be in all respects similar to the human!" A dugong, killed at Ceylon in 1847, measured upwards of seven feet in length, but specimens considerably larger have been taken.

The female dugong, or sea-cow of Sumatra, will follow her young to the death, and is usually taken with them. The sea-calves have a short, sharp, pitiable cry, which they frequently repeat, and, like the stricken deer, are also said to shed tears, which, according to Sir Stamford Raffles, were carefully bottled by the common people, and preserved as charms to secure affection.

Only one species of the *Stellerus*—of the same genus as the two I have mentioned—has been known, about twenty-five feet in length, a native of the Polar seas, and never observed since the middle of last century, so that it is supposed to be extinct. The characteristic features of this animal would lead one to suppose, also, that it may have contributed to the misconceptions about the mermaid.

Mr. Rimbault, in "Notes and Queries," remarks that the exhibition of strange fishes appears to have been at its height in the reign of Elizabeth. Shakespere twice alludes to it: once in the "Winter's Tale" (Act IV., Scene 3), where Autolycus says: "Here's another ballad of a fish that appeared upon the coast on Wednesday, the fourscore of April, forty thousand fathoms above water, and sung this ballad against the hard hearts of maids. It was thought she was a woman, and was turned into a cold fish, for she would not exchange flesh with one that loved her. The ballad is very pitiful, and as true;" and again in the "Tempest" (Act II., Scene 2). A printed notice, dated 1566, has for its title "The Description of a Rare or rather Most Monstrous Fishe, taken on the East Coast of Holland, the 17th November, Anno 1566," with a woodcut of the fish, and underneath the following lines:

"The workes of God, how great and strange they be!
A picture plaine, behold, heare you may see."

Two years later there is another printed notice of "a moste true and marvellous straunge wonder, the lyke hathe seldom been seene, of xvii monstrous fishes, taken in Suffulke, at Downam Brydge, within a myle of Ipswiche, the xi daye of October, in the yeare of our Lorde God 1568." Stow, in his "Annales," gives a particular description of this "wondrous draught of fishes," some of them being "eight and twentie foote in length at least."

Wolfe, in 1586, printed a broadside containing an account of a monster fish found in the stomach of a horse! The registers of the Stationers' Company contain an entry in 1604 of "a strange reporte of a monstrous fish that appeared in the form of a woman from the waist upwards, seene in the sea."

Even in 1822, a so-called mermaid was publicly exhibited in London, which continued to be shown to the curious in these matters for many months, but the monster was found to have been constructed of the members of various animals, dexterously put together. Some amusing lines appeared at the period, which I will transcribe:

"Come, mistress mermaid, tell us, for you've seen
    The deeps and things proud Science pines to see;
 Be kind, and say if you have ever been
    In worlds the poets deck with imagery.
 Say, as you floated on the green sea's billow,
 Didst e'er see Neptune's car, or Amphitrite's pillow?

"Now, are there really coral caves below,
    Or beds of amber, or of precious stone,
 To which the blushing Nereids languid go
    In idle hours to recline upon?
 And are there fays to fan them while they're dreaming,
 Whose wings seem like two diamonds' purest gleaming?

" Come, tell the truth, for none, dear mermaid,'s by,
    To stop you short, or tweak you by the nose,
Or contradict you should you tell a lie,
    As you the secrets of the deep disclose.
Therefore be candid, and declare this minute
The wonders of the sea, and all that's in it.

" Alas! you're dumb, and cannot even say,
    As quick you speed from giant sea to sea,
How many sharks you've numbered in a day,
    Or, if you fought them, or thought it best to flee.
Quite mute you are, and quite absurd the notion,
For thee to pump for secrets of the ocean.

" Farewell, dumb thing! perhaps the next we find
    So long a time may not require to woo,
'T will speak, perchance, and haply prove most kind,
    And tell us all we've useless sought of you—
Rare information yielding on the morning
She's clapped within the glass case you're adorning."

*Lewis Frese*

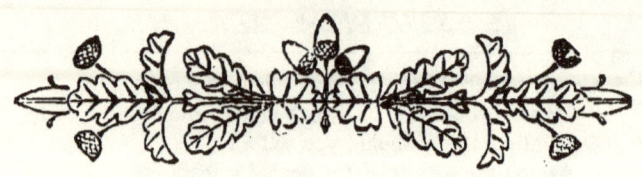

## CHAPTER XXIV.

### MODES OF FISHING IN VARIOUS COUNTRIES.

"A thousand names a fisher might rehearse
Of nets intractable in smoother verse."

OPPIAN.

THE use of nets for entrapping the finny inhabitants of the deep date from the earliest periods. Besides the frequent mention of them in the Holy Scriptures, we find illustrations in the bas-reliefs of Assyria, Greece, and Rome, and in the mural or wall paintings of Egypt. The latter nation delighted in fishing, and, not contented with the abundance afforded by the Nile, they constructed in their grounds spacious sluices or ponds for fish, like the *vivaria* of the Romans, where they fed them for the table, and amused themselves by angling. The fishermen, who composed one of the sub-divisions of the Egyptian castes, generally used the net in preference to the line. The ancients entertained a number of prejudices relative to the wholesomeness or injurious qualities of certain fish. The priests in Egypt were prohibited from eating fish of any kind. For fear of leprosy, the people also were forbidden the use of any fish not covered with scales. Moses adopted the same principles with the Jews: "Whatever hath fin or scales in the water in the seas, them shalt thou eat; whatever hath no fins or scales in the waters, that shall be an abomination to you."

The Greeks and Romans used nets; trawling at sea was also a

favourite mode of angling, and harpoons were in general use, by means of which many large fish were secured. Some mosaics discovered at Palestrina represented men engaged in taking fish out of a reedy decoy by means of small hand-nets. Arrian, in his "Indian History," mentions a people on the coasts of the Persian Gulf, who had nets capable of covering a quarter of a mile of sea, not made of twine, for hemp and flax were unknown in the land, but of the inner bark of palm trees, being, in fact, papyrus nets.

In the dialogues composed by Elfric to instruct the Saxon youths in the Latin language, which are yet preserved to us in the Cottonian manuscripts, a fisherman is asked how he secures his prey, and he answers, "I ascend my ship and cast my net into the river; I also throw in a hook, a bait, and a rod;" which shows that in the earliest periods of our own country, nets of various kinds were employed for entrapping fish; indeed, although St. Wilfrid is said to have taught the people of Sussex the use of the net (probably an improved kind), such means have been employed in different ways from remotest times. One remark I may add to this, that until recently fishing-nets have always been made by hand, and generally the thread has been a more or less thick twine of hemp or flax, the thickness of the twine and the size of the mesh depending upon the kind of fish for which it was made; recently, however, great improvements have been made in the manufacture of nets, and machinery of the most beautiful minute kind has been invented for the purpose.

A great variety of nets are in use among fishermen, but the principal are the *seine, trawl,* and *drift* nets. The first is a very long but not very wide net, one side of which is loaded with pieces of lead, and consequently sinks; the other, or upper, is buoyed with pieces of cork, and is consequently kept on the surface of the water. Seines are sometimes upwards of a thousand feet in length. When stretched out they constitute walls of network in the water, and are made to enclose vast shoals of fish. The trawl is dragged along the bottom of the sea by the fishing-boat; and the drift-net is like the seine, but is not loaded with lead, and is usually employed for mackerel fishing. In the two fishery exhibitions at

Arcachon and Boulogne in France, a few years ago, a number of curious implements for the capture of the inhabitants of the deep were shown. In one corner were curious tongs for taking eels. Long stretches of netting for the sardine fishery, woven with thread so fine that it might be used for the manufacture of ladies' hose, were festooned over a division of the buildings. At another place was a leech-lifter, and near it were deadly traps for taking crabs and lobsters. From the roofs hung stretches of Scotch-made herring-nets, by far the best of their kind; and with such a wall of meshes floating in the sea as these nets present to the fish, each stretch being about a mile long, and with a fleet of a few hundred boats nightly centred on some well-known fishing-ground, the wonder is, not that fishes are scarce and dear, but that a single herring could escape. In the two exhibitions I have mentioned there was shown an array of fishing machinery truly wonderful for ingenuity of construction and power of capture.

In 1864 an attempt was first made to fish by the electric light at Dunkirk. A magneto-electric machine was afterwards employed. The light was constant at one hundred and eighty feet under water, and it extended over a large surface. As soon as the submarine lantern was immersed, shoals of fish of every description came to sport in the illuminated circle, while the fishermen outside it spread their nets from the boats. The light illuminating the deep sea, the fish arriving in shoals, attracted by the fictitious sun, the boats at the edge of the lighted circle, the deep silence interrupted only by the grating of the electro-magnetic machine, formed altogether an imposing sight.

Before I leave this part of my subject I may mention a curious nvention stated in Rymer's "Fœdera," for which Charles I. granted a patent in 1632 to a physician, "for a fish-call or looking-glass for fishes in the sea, *very useful for fishermen to call all kinds of fishes to their nets.*"

A singular method of getting fish is that in which other animals are employed for the purpose. Birds are thus trained by the Chinese. Falcons are not more sagacious in the pursuit of their prey in the air than in another element. They are called *alvoau,* and are about the size of a goose, with grey plumage, webbed feet, and have a long and slender bill, crooked at the point. Their faculty of diving, or remaining under water, is not more extraordinary than that of many other fowls that prey upon fish, but the wonderful circumstance is the docility of these birds in employing their natural instinctive powers at the command of the fishermen who possess them, in the same manner as the hound, the spaniel, or the pointer submit their respective sagacity to the huntsman or the fowler. The number of these birds in a boat is proportioned to the size of it. At a certain signal they rush into the water and dive after the fish, and the moment they have seized their prey, they fly with it to their boat, and though there may be a hundred of these vessels together, the birds always return to their own masters; and amidst the crowd of fishing-junks which are sometimes assembled on these occasions, they never fail to distinguish that to which they belong. When the fish are in great plenty, these astonishing purveyors will soon fill a boat with them, and will sometimes be seen flying along with a fish of such size as to make the beholder suspect his organs of vision; and such is their sagacity that when one of them happens to have taken a fish which is too large for a single falcon, the rest immediately lend their assistance. While they are thus labouring for their masters, they are prevented from paying any attention to themselves by a ring which is passed round their necks, and is so contrived as to frustrate every attempt to swallow the least morsel of what they take. They eat thankfully what is afterwards given them in reward. One of the old domestic sports of the Earls of Menteith, in their island home of Talla, was fishing with geese. A line with a baited hook was tied to the leg of a goose, which was made to swim in water of proper depth. A boat well filled escorted this formidable knight-errant. A marauding fish would take hold of the bait, and put his mettle to the test. A combat ensued, in which, by the display of both contending heroes of much strength and agility, the goose always came off victorious, and would drag his prisoner to the boat in triumph.

No nation on the earth puts in practice a greater variety of modes for catching fish than the Chinese. One method is to nail on each side of long narrow boats a plank two feet broad, covered with white shining japan, and placed by a gentle inclination so that its lower edge just touches the surface of the water. This device is used at night, with the intent that the reflection of the moon should increase its deceptive influence; and whether the fish which are sporting around are dazzled by the splendour, or merely mistake the lustrous plank for the sparkling water, it is impossible to say, but in their moonlight gambols great numbers either fall on the plank and are secured, or fairly vault into the body of the boat.

In some places the Chinese soldiers have acquired the dexterous art of shooting fish with bows and arrows. To the arrow a long piece of packthread is attached, by means of which, when the fish is pierced, it is drawn to hand. In other places the muddy bottom is so replenished with the finny tribes, that men standing up to the waist in the water strike them with sticks. Besides these various devices, another is in general use, and consists in stretching out a net on four pieces of bamboo suspended by a long pole.

The South Sea islanders are expert fishermen, and their methods for the capture of the finny tribe are numerous, and some very ingenious. They have, as Mr. Ellis informs us, a singular mode of taking a remarkably timorous fish, which is called the *needle*, on account of its long sharp head. A number of rafts are built, each about fifteen or twenty feet long, and six or eight wide. At one edge a kind of fence or screen is raised four or five feet by fixing the poles horizontally one above the other, and fastening them to upright sticks placed at short distances along the raft. The men on the raft go out at a distance from each other, enclosing a large space of water, having the raised part or frame on the outside. They gradually approach each other till the rafts join, and form a connected circle in some shallow. One or two persons then go in a small canoe towards the centre of the enclosed space, with long white sticks, which they strike in the water with a great noise, and by this means drive the fish towards the rafts. On approaching these the fish dart out of the water, and in attempting to spring over the raft, strike against the raised fence on the outer side, and fall on the surface of the horizontal part, when they are gathered into baskets or canoes on the outside. In this manner great numbers of these and other kinds of fish, that are accustomed to spring out of the water when alarmed or pursued, are taken with facility. Fishing-nets are remarkably well made, and those for casting are used with great dexterity, generally as the islanders walk along the beach. When a shoal of small fish appear, they throw the net with the right hand, and sometimes enclose the greater part of them.

Next to the net the spear is most frequently used. This is darted at the fish, sometimes with one hand, but more frequently with both, and very successfully. When fishing on the reefs, they wear a kind of sandal made of closely-netted cords of the cloth plant, to preserve their feet from the edges of the shells, the spikes of the sea-urchins, &c.

"I have often," observes Mr. Ellis, "when passing across the bay, stopped to gaze on a group of fishermen standing on a coral reef or rock, amidst the roar of the billows, and the dashing surf and foam that broke in magnificent splendour around them. With unwavering glance they have stood, with a little basket in one hand and a pointed spear in the other, striking with unerring aim such fish as the violence of the wave might force within their reach."

The shell, or shell and bone, hooks, are curious and useful, answering the purpose of hook and bait, the small ones being made circular, and bent so as to resemble a worm; but the most common one is that used in catching dolphins, albicores, and bonitos. The shank of the hook is made with a piece of the mother-of-pearl shell, five or six inches long and three-quarters of an inch wide, carefully cut and finely polished, so as to resemble the body of a fish. A barb is fastened by a firm bandage of finely-twisted flax; to the lower part of this the end of the line is securely fastened. When taken out to sea, the line is attached to a strong bamboo cane about twelve or fifteen feet long. When a shoal of fish is seen, the natives who angle, sit in the stern of the canoe, and hold the rod at such an elevation as to allow the hook to touch the edge of the water, but not to sink. When the fish approach it, the rowers ply their paddles briskly, and the light bark moves rapidly along. The deception of the hook is increased by a number of hairs or bristles being attached to the end of the shell, so as to resemble the tail of a flying-fish. The victims, darting after and grasping their prey, are at once secured. During the season two men will sometimes take twenty or thirty large fish in this way in the course of the forenoon.

The most ingenious method, however, of taking these large fish is by means of a *mast*. A pair of ordinary-sized canoes is usually selected for this purpose, and the lighter and swifter the more suitable they are esteemed. Between the fore-part of the canoes a broad, deep, oblong kind of basket is constructed with the stalks of a strong kind of fern, interwoven with tough fibres of a tree: this is to contain the fish that may be taken. To the fore-part of the canoes a long curved pole is fastened, branching in opposite directions at the outer end; the foot of this rests in a kind of socket fixed between the two canoes. From each of the projecting branches lines with pearl-shell hooks are suspended, so adjusted as to be kept near the surface of the water. To that part of the pole which is divided into two branches strong ropes are attached; these extend to the stern of the canoe, where they are held by persons watching the seizure of the hook. The *tira*, or mast, projects a considerable distance beyond the stern of the canoe, and bunches of feathers are fastened to its extremities. This is done to resemble the aquatic birds which follow the course of the small fish. As it is supposed that the bonito follows the birds with as much ardour as it does the fishes, when the fishermen perceive the birds they proceed to the place, and usually find the fish. The undulation of the waves occasions the canoe to rise and sink as they proceed, and this produces a corresponding action in the hook suspended from the mast; and so complete is the deception that if the fish once perceives the pearl-shell hook, it seldom fails to dart after it, and if it misses the first time is almost sure to be caught the second. As soon as the fish is fast, the men in the canoe, by drawing the cord, hoist up the mast and drag in the fish, suspended as it were from a kind of crane. When the fish is removed the crane is lowered, and as it projects over the canoe the rowers hasten after the shoal with the greatest speed.

These and a variety of other methods of fishing are pursued by daylight, but many fish are taken by night. Sometimes the fishery is carried on by moonlight, occasionally in the dark; but fishing by torchlight is the most picturesque. The torches are bunches of dried reeds firmly tied together. Sometimes the natives pursue their nocturnal sport on the reef, and hunt the hedge-hog-fish. Large parties often go out to the reef, and it is a beautiful sight to see a long line of rocks illuminated by the flaring torches. These the fishermen hold in one hand, and stand with the poised spear in the other, ready to strike as soon as the fish appears.

The Indians on the coasts of the Pacific have also a singular mode of taking the *Candle-fish* or *Eulachon*, a most valuable acquisition to their domestic comforts. Immense shoals approach the shores in summer, and are caught in moonlight nights, when they come to sport on the surface of the water, which may often be seen glittering with their multitudes. The Indians paddle their canoes noiselessly amongst them, and catch them by means of a monster comb or rake—a piece of pine-wood from six to eight feet long, made round for about two feet of its length at the place of the hand-gripe, the rest flat, thick at the back, but having a sharp edge at the front, where teeth are driven into it, about four inches long and an inch apart. One Indian, sitting in the stern, paddles the canoe; another, standing with his face to the bow, holds the rake firmly in both hands, the teeth pointing sternwards, sweeps it with all his force through the glittering mass, and brings it to the surface teeth upwards, usually with a fish, and sometimes with three or four, impaled on each tooth. This process is carried on with wonderful rapidity. This fish, although not larger than a smelt, enjoys the distinction of being probably the fattest of all animals, comparatively speaking: to boil or fry it is impossible, as it melts entirely into oil. Even in a dried state the Indians use it as a lamp, merely drawing through it a piece of rush pith as a wick, and the fish then burns steadily until consumed. By a peculiar mode of preparation, these fishes are preserved as a winter food, and notwithstanding their great fatness, they are said to be of an agreeable flavour. Drying is accomplished without any cleaning, the fish being fastened on skewers passed through their eyes, and hung in the thick smoke at the top of sheds in which wood fires are kept burning. They are then stowed away for winter.

Turning to other countries, we will now glance at the *White Porpoise* fishing in the St. Lawrence, one of the largest rivers in North America, issuing from Lake Ontario, and falling into the Gulf of St. Lawrence. The animal I have mentioned is a species of whale, and is chiefly common in those quarters, being valuable for its oil, which gives a brilliant light only surpassed by gas, and its skin, which is manufactured into leather which has no equal for quality. The fish was formerly taken in enclosures made of light and flexible poles fixed in the beach, within which the porpoise pursued the small members of the finny tribe during high tide, and where, its appetite once satisfied, it became heavy and almost asleep from gluttony, and seemed to forget for several hours the dangers that surrounded it as the tide went out. The fishermen, silent, and on the look-out on the cliff, having seen that the waves had retreated, give the signal: two or three light skiffs (either bark or wooden canoes), manned by three or four expert rowers, appear upon the waves, which they scarcely touch with their oars. Standing in the bow of each of these canoes, a man with bare and muscular arm, a steel spear in his hand, intently follows with his eye the track of the fish, indicating the course to be taken, whether to the right or left, and strikes the mortal blows. Often after one of these vigorous strokes, which are enough to kill the largest porpoise, the spearsman may be seen, when he does not strike aright, urging on the pursuit for a new contest of speed between his skiff and the wounded animal: sometimes the blood which reddens the surface of the water indicates the course to be followed, and sometimes the sound of the subdued breathing of the porpoise, which comes to the surface of the water to breathe, throwing up a stream which descends in the form of a curve. The porpoise might break through this fence of flexible poles, eighteen or twenty inches apart, but it is afraid, and returns by the way it came: a new stroke is given, but it is by a harpoon which has a rope attached to it. The struggle becomes more intense and exciting. The paddle at the stern of the frail skiff is alone put in requisition. It is now the boatman's turn to display his skill. The animal leaps out of the water, stops, dives, and turns about in every way; a white foam rises on each side of the boat, and its progress, hitherto so swift, is suddenly stopped; the animal is fatigued by its wound, wants to breathe, but fear keeps it below the water, and immediately the man in the bow rolls up at his knee the line which he had allowed to run out, and the boat is brought silently forward towards the victim. Again he stands up and with one hand brandishes his spear, while with the other he suddenly pulls the rope, inflicting fresh wounds: the fish once more leaps, but this time is the last, for a vigorous blow aimed at the spine between the head and neck is fatal.

Another plan is to use nets for entrapping the porpoise. The weight of one of these fishes is about two thousand five hundred pounds: the largest are sometimes four thousand pounds, and these are about twenty-two feet long and fifteen in circumference.

I may remark here that the flesh of the common porpoise was formerly much esteemed in our own country, and was reckoned fit for the royal table. Among the singular directions for the management of the household of King Henry VIII., we find among the dainty dishes to be "set before the king" a porpoise, "and if too big for a horse-load, an extra allowance to be given to the purveyor." In the time of Queen Elizabeth it was still used by the nobles of England, and was served up with bread-crumbs and vinegar.

A curious mode of fishing the *Gar-fish* or *Sea-Pike*, in the Ionian Islands, is mentioned by Mr. Yarrell. A small triangular raft is formed of three pieces of bamboo, each a foot and a half long; a little thwart is inserted, in which a small mast is fixed; it is then rigged with a sail, &c., in imitation of the boats of the country. The fisherman, taking his station on a projecting rock, with deep water alongside, and an off-shore breeze, commits his little raft to the wind, carrying with it a line of about two hundred feet in length. A float is fixed at about every six feet, and from each float depends a fine hair-line with a baited hook. When the fish bites it draws the bait down violently once, and then seems to resign itself to death. The fisherman waits till ten or twelve are hooked; he then hauls in his raft, relieves it of its freight, and again launches it for another cruise. Fifty or sixty are sometimes caught in this way during half an hour.

The gar-fish is not uncommon on our coasts, and is abundant in the Baltic. It attains a length of two or three feet. The upper parts of the body are of a dark greenish-blue mackerel tint, and a curious circumstance is that its bones are green. Mr. Couch remarks that when this fish is taken by the hook, it mounts to the surface often before the fishermen have felt the bite, and there, with its slender body half out of the water, struggles with the most violent contortions to wrench the hook from its hold.

In various chapters of this book I have already mentioned the mode of capturing the large inhabitants of the deep—the whale, the seal, the shark, sea-unicorn, and others. I must not omit another important fish of large dimensions, the *Tunny*, sometimes nine feet in length and upwards of a thousand pounds in weight, and belonging to the Mackerel family. This fish is found in the Mediterranean and the Atlantic Ocean, but chiefly in the former, where this particular fishery is of great importance, and constitutes one of the greatest branches of Sicilian commerce. The fish appear at the latter end of May, at which time the *tonnaire*, as they are called, are prepared for their reception. This is a kind of aquatic castle, formed, at a considerable expense, of strong nets fastened to the bottom of the sea by anchors and heavy-laden weights. The *tonnaires* are fixed in the passages amongst the rocks and islands that are most frequented by the tunny-fish. Care is taken to close with nets the entrance into these passages, except one small opening, which is called the "outer gate." This leads into the next compartment, which we may term the "hall." As soon as the fishes have entered here, the fishermen who stand sentries in their boats during the season shut the outer entrance, which is done by letting down a small piece of net, portcullis-fashion, which effectually prevents the tunnies from returning by the way they came. The inner door of the "hall" is then opened, which leads to another compartment, and by making a noise on the surface of the water the tunnies are soon driven into it. As soon as the whole have been got into this compartment, the inner door of the "hall" is again closed, and the outer entrance is opened to receive more fishes. The last compartment of network is called the " chamber of death." This is composed of stronger nets and heavier anchors than the others.

As soon as a sufficient number of tunny-fish has been collected here, the slaughter begins. The fishermen attack the poor defenceless animals on all sides, who dash the water about in their efforts to escape, but are at length subdued, and yield themselves a prey to their conquerors.

"There is something," says Mr. Badham, a witness of this fish massacre, " extremely exciting in seeing the wholesale capture of a herd of these great black fish, intermixed, as they generally are, with the forms of many of their large congeners, and occasionally with a sword-fish or a dolphin besides; and no one ever left the spot after one of these enormous hauls without feeling that, however superior the whale fishery may be in enterprise, it cannot yield its votaries half the pleasures or charms of these scenes."

A very questionable kind of pleasure, however, I think it must be to many, to see the agonies and the butchery which must necessarily take place on these occasions.

The *Sturgeon* fishery is carried on to a very considerable extent in the Russian dominions on the coasts of the Caspian and Aral Seas. They are caught in an enclosure formed by large stakes, representing the letter Z repeated several times. These fisheries are open on the side nearest the sea, and closed on the other, by which means the fish, ascending in its season up the rivers, are caught in these narrow angular retreats, and are easily killed. The Hon. Captain Keppell, describing the method of catching sturgeon in the fishery of Karmaizack, says :

"Two persons are in each boat; one (generally a female) rows, while the other hauls in the fish. The instruments used consist of a mallet and a stick, with a large unbarbed hook at the end. Every fisherman has a certain number of lines. One line contains fifty hooks; these are placed at regular distances from each other; they are without barbs, sunk about a foot under water, and are kept in motion by small pieces of wood attached to them. The sturgeon generally swims in a large shoal near the surface of the water, and upon being caught by one hook, he generally gets entangled with one or two others in his struggles to escape. Immediately on our arrival the boats pushed from shore. Each fisherman proceeded to take up his lines. On coming to a fish he drew it with his hooked stick to the side of the boat, hit it a violent blow on the head with the mallet, and, after disengaging it from the other hooks, hauled it into the boat. On every side the tremendous splashing of the water announced the capture of some huge inhabitant of the deep."

The sturgeon belongs to a numerous species inhabiting both sea and fresh water—those of the former, and the largest kind, being especially plentiful in the Caspian and Black Seas, where they attain a length of from twenty to twenty-five feet, and have been known to weigh nearly three thousand pounds. The flesh has the appearance and consistency of veal, and was highly esteemed by the ancients. Pliny states that it was brought to table with much pomp, and ornamented with flowers, the slaves who carried it being also decorated with garlands and accompanied with music.

In England, when caught in the Thames and within the jurisdiction of the city, it is reserved for the Sovereign as a "royal fish." In the "Illustrated London News," for the 15th of April, 1860, is a notice of a fine sturgeon thus taken, and forwarded to the Queen at Windsor by order of the conservators of the river.

The famous *caviare* of the Russians is made from the roe of the sturgeon, freed from its membranes, washed in vinegar, and dried in the open air. It is then salted, put into a bag and pressed, and finally packed in small barrels for sale.

The principal fishery of the *Conger Eel* in our country is upon the Cornish coast. They are chiefly caught by what are termed "bulters," which are strong lines, several hundred feet long, with hooks about eight feet apart, baited with sand-launces, pilchards,

## DIFFERENCE BETWEEN SEA-CONGERS AND EELS.

or mackerel. The bulters are sunk to the ground by a stone fastened to them. Sometimes such a number of these are tied together as to reach to a considerable distance. It is not unusual for a boat with three men to bring on shore from one to two tons as the produce of a night's fishing, the conger being caught most readily at night.

On some of the French coasts the conger fishery is still more abundant than in Cornwall.

The great sea-conger has so great a resemblance to the common eel, the inhabitant of our rivers and ponds, that many persons believed the former was merely an eel of larger growth; but the difference may be readily discerned. The conger, whether large or small, has always the snout and upper jaw projecting beyond the lower one; whilst the fresh-water eel is remarkable for its protuberant lower jaw. The tail is also more lengthened and pointed, the dorsal fin commencing much nearer the head, and the teeth of the upper jaw, although slender, placed so close together as to form a cutting edge. The internal structure of these fishes differs more widely, the conger having a great many more bones than the eel, particularly towards the tail, and in possessing a greater number of vertebræ (the spine or backbone).

The common conger of our coasts is a large fish, sometimes exceeding ten feet in length, and weighing upwards of a hundred pounds, but its ordinary dimensions are from five to seven feet. It is entirely a marine species, although frequently found in the mouths of rivers, its object being, it is thought, that of feeding on the fish that ascend or descend the stream. Of these it devours large quantities, not objecting to crabs and shell-fish, which the strength of its jaws permits it to masticate without difficulty. The smaller kinds of fish it swallows entire, and thus fortified by good nourishment, it becomes a formidable adversary when hauled into the boat by a fisherman's line, or found among the rocks, where it is sometimes left by the retiring tide. Pennant says: (in his time) "fishermen are very fearful of large congers, lest they should endanger their legs by clinging round them; they therefore kill them as soon as possible."

I believe this is not a matter of complaint in *our* time. The conger, however formidable, also finds a dangerous adversary in the spiny lobster of the Mediterranean Sea, which is said to enter into a fierce battle with the conger, and generally becomes the victor, from the superiority of its weapons of defence, the claws, which lacerate and wound the monstrous eel, proving the death summons.

The conger, when properly cooked, has a most delicious flavour, but somehow or other there is a great antipathy to the fish, as being, probably, too much of the serpent form; but travellers in Cornwall find a conger-pie delicious, and those persons who have visited the Channel Islands will not easily forget the delicious soup that is made from this fish. Even as far back as the reign of Queen Elizabeth, there was a singular mode of *curing* congers in Cornwall, which was merely to slit them in half, and without any further preparation to hang them up in a kind of shambles erected for that purpose: such parts of them as were not *gone*, were considered fit for use, and exported to Spain and Portugal.

The *Sand-Eel* fishery, although of a very primitive character, being mostly carried on with spades, shovels, three-pronged forks, rakes, and in fact any implement of a *raking* character at hand, is very exciting and amusing. I have often in the Channel Islands (Guernsey) enjoyed this amusement, which usually takes place on a clear moonlight night. Large shoals are observed frequently swimming near the shore, and it often happens that, instead of retiring with the ebbing tide, they dig into the sand (whence their name), and remain there until the water covers them again. Advantage is taken of this, and hundreds of men, women, and children set to work with the readiest implements they can find, and the scene becomes very animated. When dug from the sand the fish leap about with singular velocity, and the gathering of them affords a fine amusement to the younger parties, who are commonly the most numerous and eager in this pursuit. It is remarkable with what ease and rapidity these slender and delicate-looking fish penetrate the sand, even when it is of a pretty firm texture. They are a favourite meal with many, and are sometimes salted and dried; but their principal use is as bait for the capture of more valuable fishes, there being scarcely any other found to answer the purpose so effectually. This well-known fish scarcely ever exceeds seven or eight inches.

The *Mackerel* belongs to the same family as the tunny-fish, which I have just described, but is a comparatively small member as regards size, being usually about fourteen inches long and about two pounds in weight. This beautiful fish (as you may have remarked, a vivid green and blue) is readily caught by bait, and particularly when the bait — which is usually a piece from one of its own kind—is moved quickly through the water. The boats engaged for this fishing are often under sail. Besides the line, drift-nets and seines are employed. The size of the mesh is one inch and one-sixth from knot to knot when the twine is wet, or in the square, from one corner to another. A row of corks runs along the head-line, and the lower border is left suspended by its own weight. The number of nets in each boat depends upon its size. A boat of Yarmouth may carry eleven score of nets, and as these are fastened in length to each other, they will extend to a distance of a mile and three-quarters. More than a hundred boats assemble at Plymouth during the season, and a wide extent of sea is consequently swept by the nets. These are shot across the course of the tide twice between evening and morning; for fish avoid the nets during the day, and scarcely less so during very dark nights. This latter circumstance is caused by the light produced in the sea by luminous animals, which then appears most conspicuous; and hence a hazy atmosphere is judged beneficial. The use of lights is employed in some countries. Bloch, in speaking of the mackerel fishery, says, that at St. Croix, on the approach of night, when the sea is smooth, they prepare their torches, and hold them as close to the water as possible. The fish soon show themselves, and rise above the surface, when the nets are immediately shot, and soon taken in with abundant success.

When the shoal of mackerel approaches the land the seine comes into operation. This consists of a single net, which, on the east coast of Cornwall, is about seven hundred feet in length, and seventy in depth at the middle. The full size of the mesh from corner to corner is two and three-quarter inches at the sides, which is the same dimension allowed to the drift-net; but for about two hundred feet of the hollow, the size of the mesh is lessened to two and a half inches, to prevent the fish from being hung in the meshes; for if this should happen, the net would not be raised from the bottom, and fish and net would be lost. Shoals of mackerel are rapid in their motion, and exceedingly uncertain, as well as easily alarmed. They rarely stay long at the surface, and when they sink below it is doubtful in what direction they may again appear. The whole proceedings are, therefore, full of excitement, and great haste is employed to enclose them in the circle of the seine.

The mackerel is a favourite article of food, but its flesh soon changes; and a capture that might have proved valuable, may be rendered worthless if the fishes are not at once sent to the market. A principal object of the French fishery is to prepare the mackerel salted for use at home, for which purpose they are immediately stored in bulk on board the boats. In the west of Cornwall, also, considerable numbers are salted, chiefly for the use of miners, who seem to prefer salted fish to even the fresh that abound in the finest condition in their markets.

It was formerly supposed that great migrations of mackerel took place, but it is now believed, as in regard to the herring, that they merely leave the deep water and approach the coast for the purpose of spawning. The mackerel is of less importance than the herring fishery. It is a restless, ever-wandering rover, and unlike the herring in its habits in that respect. It is found in large numbers in the Mediterranean.

The Yarmouth boats have occasionally realized a sum of thirty-five thousand pounds in a season from the sale of mackerel. The average consumption in London alone has been estimated at twenty-five millions. The south coast of England—wherever there is a range of beach suitable for seining—the neighbourhood of Brighton, and a considerable sweep of the coast to the west of Portland, are well known as excellent fisheries for mackerel.

Let us now turn to other fish, and perhaps the *Herring* fishery affords one of the best illustrations of British enterprise. We must now proceed to the Norfolk coast, for it is there that this most valuable fish is found in the greatest abundance, perhaps more so than in any other part of the world. The name of the fish is derived from the German *heer* "an army," in reference to the vast shoals in which they arrive. The herrings appear on the Norfolk coast in the last week of September for the purpose of spawning, and are then in the best condition to become the food of man. Having fulfilled this obligation of nature, they return to their former haunts about the commencement of December. A few, however, may be found at other periods of the year, particularly about midsummer; and, although small, they are much esteemed for their delicate flavour. The Yarmouth herring has less oil than the Scotch herring, but is unrivalled in point of quality. It seldom measures more than fourteen inches in length, in girth six inches and a half, and it weighs about nine ounces. The vessels employed by Yarmouth in this fishery are usually decked boats, of from forty to fifty tons burthen, and carrying a crew of ten men. Besides the boats belonging to the town, there are many others called "cobles," which come from Scarborough, Filey, and other northern ports. Each fishing-boat is provided with from sixty to one hundred nets, each net about fifteen yards long upon the rope, fastened by small cords called "seizings." These nets are floated by corks placed at intervals of a few feet from each other; the warp which supports the whole is frequently a mile in length, and is borne up by small buoys. The nets themselves are usually made in four parts or widths, called "lints," one being placed above another, and so forming a wall in the sea, against which the fish are invited to drive their heads.

This fishing is carried on during the night only, it being supposed that the stretching of the nets in the day-time would drive away the shoal. In the dusk of the evening the nets are thrown over the side, and the boat is then steered under an easy sail, or allowed to drift with the tide until daylight, when the nets are hauled in. A single boat has sometimes, in one night, taken twelve or fourteen *lasts* of herrings, each "last" numbering ten thousand fish, or, by the fisherman's calculation, thirteen thousand two hundred; but it often happens that a boat does not obtain more than this quantity during the season. The average catch for each boat is about thirty "lasts" (three hundred thousand); but a boat has been known to bring in the enormous quantity of two hundred and sixty-four thousand herrings *at one time.* Like all fisheries, the result is very uncertain. "It is a curious and bountiful provision of nature," remarks Dr. Lankester, "that forces the herring, and other fish usually distributed through the deeps, to congregate together, and visit our shores in such immense abundance, at a time when they are in the highest perfection, and when most fitted for human food."

The herring dies as soon as it leaves the water, hence the phrase "as dead as a herring." The fishes are therefore salted as soon as caught, and when the boat has reached land they are brought to shore, and carried to the fish-house in "swills," which are open coarse wicker baskets. Arrived at the fish "office," the herrings, after being sufficiently salted, remain on a floor for twenty-four hours if intended to be slightly cured, or for ten days if intended for the foreign market; they are then washed in large vats filled with fresh water; "spits" (pieces of wood about four feet long and of the thickness of a man's thumb) are passed through their heads or gills, and they are then hung up in rows to the top of the building. Wood fires are then kindled under them, and are continued day and night, with slight intermissions to allow the fat and oil to drop, until the fish are sufficiently cured, which, if they are intended for the foreign market, is at the end of fourteen days, but if for home consumption, three or four days suffice. The first are called "red" herrings, from the deep colour which they acquire, and the others are known as "bloaters." When cured, the herrings are taken down and placed in barrels, which contain each about seven hundred fish. From thirty to forty thousand barrels are sent yearly from Yarmouth to the towns on the Mediterranean coasts. The annual supply of herrings at Billingsgate Market is estimated at one hundred and twenty thousand tons, valued at one million two hundred pounds sterling! The greatest enemy to the herring fishermen is the dog-fish, which, in pursuit of the herring, frequently becomes entangled in the nets, and does great damage to them in endeavouring to escape.

The herring fisheries sometimes suffer very considerably from the ravages of this fish, the popular name of some of the smaller species of shark, owing this designation to their habit of following their prey like dogs hunting in packs. These predaceous fishes are seldom abundant when the herrings are in a compact body; but sometimes they commit great destruction when a shoal is first drawn in near land. They have been known to consume as many herrings as would fill a dozen barrels out of one boat's nets in the course of an hour. They are also very destructive to the nets when they get entangled, their hard fins tearing them to pieces. In like manner they make sad havoc with other fishes. Occasionally only a few escape with their heads, the tails of others are snapped off, and pieces bitten out of the belly. A cod-fish sometimes comes up a mere skeleton, stripped to the bone on both sides.

The *Dog-fish* attains a length of three or four feet, and is found in the Atlantic, the Mediterranean, and the South seas. One of the most abundant species on our coasts is the common dog-fish, which sometimes appears in prodigious numbers, twenty thousand having been taken at Cornwall at one time in a net, and the fishermen of the Orkneys and Hebrides, where they are much used for food, sometimes load their boats to the water's edge with them.

Another voracious enemy of the herring (and the pilchard) is the *Hake*, a member of the Cod family, with the same predatory instincts. It is sometimes three or four feet in length, coarse in quality, but valuable as a "stock" fish. It is generally taken by lines, like cod and ling, but in the spawning season, when it keeps near the bottom, it is sometimes caught by trawl-nets.

Allied to the herring, but differing in some respects, being nearly equal in size, but rather thicker, and the lines of the back and belly being straighter, the scales also being larger and fewer, is the *Pilchard*, a fish also of immense importance in our British fisheries, and plentiful on the coasts of Devonshire and Cornwall. These fish congregate in deep waters, within limits extending from the Scilly Isles, as far, sometimes, as the Irish, Welsh, and Cornish coasts. A portion strikes the land north of Cape Cornwall, and turns in a north-easterly direction towards St. Ives, constituting its summer fishery. The great bulk passes between the Scilly Islands and the mainland. To look from Cape Cornwall, or from any of the high lands of St. Just, and see this immense moving mass of fishes, extending as far as the eye can reach, approaching the shores, and reddening the waters, is a sight of great interest and beauty, and such as would repay any exertion to witness.

The seine or net used in St. Ives Bay for capturing pilchards is nearly twelve hundred feet long, and nearly sixty feet in depth. More than two hundred and fifty of such nets are kept at St. Ives, each having its own boat to carry it. Every seine or net-boat, when its turn arrives, is attended by one or two tow-boats with stop-nets, and also by a smaller boat called the "follower," used principally for carrying the men to and from the larger boats. When the *huers* or sentinels stationed on the hills perceive a shoal of pilchards, they immediately signal to their respective boats, and by signs give the necessary directions for their capture. They are enabled to do this by observing on the water a reddish hue, like that of sea-weed (very different from their colour out of water), and the denser the shoal of fish, the deeper is this hue. As soon as the seine-boat and tow-boat are within reach of the shoal, they start for the same point in opposite directions, and are rowed rapidly round the fish, while the nets which they carry are being shot or cast into the sea. When the seine and the stop-net meet, they are immediately joined, and form a complete circular wall round the pilchards about eighteen hundred feet in circumference, and reaching from the surface to the bottom, the nets being kept in a vertical position by corks strung on their head-ropes and leads on their foot-ropes. This net-work enclosure, with all its contents, is then warped towards the shore into the securest part of the bay, out of the reach of the strong tidal current, and there moored with anchors so placed as to keep it as open or as nearly circular as possible. Within this large net a small one, called the tuck-net, is introduced at low water, so that the fish are raised to the surface, dipped up in baskets into the boats, taken to shore, and carried in barrows to be cured and salted. The St. Ives seine fishery does not differ materially from that in Mount's Bay, except that in the latter place, owing to the greater depth of water, the nets are about thirty feet deeper, and they are also longer. Besides the method of capturing pilchards with deep nets in shallow water in the daytime, there is a far more common mode in Cornwall of taking them in shallow nets, in deep water, by night. As these drift-nets are always spread in the open sea, where they might be destroyed by vessels sailing over them, their head-ropes are sunk about eighteen feet below the surface, and kept suspended at that depth by cork buoys fixed at regular intervals. By this contrivance, not only are the nets preserved, but larger quantities of fish are taken. These nets, each with a driving-boat attached, are left to go with the wind or tide all the time the net remains in the water.

As soon as the pilchards caught by the seine or drift-nets are landed, some are sold in the neighbouring towns and villages, and the rest, when cured and placed in barrels, are exported to the Mediterranean, where, during Lent, they are much sought after.

The method of curing the pilchards is very simple. They are placed in cellars, and women are employed in arranging them in layers, with salt between. After remaining in bulk about five weeks, during which oil and other matters drain from them, they are put into troughs of water, washed quite clean, and then carefully laid in casks, where they are subjected to heavy pressure for about a week. The oil thus expressed flows out from holes at the bottom or crevices in the sides of the untightened casks, and as this reduces their contents, more fish are added, until each cask, when the pressure is removed, weighs at least four hundredweight. The capital employed in the Cornish pilchard fishery amounts to at least two hundred and fifty thousand pounds, and affords employment to about ten thousand persons.

The *Sprat* was formerly considered by naturalists to be the young of the herring, as well as that of the pilchard: it is now generally admitted to be a distinct species. This fish comes into season in November, and continues so all the winter months, during which the sale, especially in London, is immense. About five hundred boats are annually employed in the sprat fishery. So great is the abundance sometimes, that thousands of tons are sold to farmers for manure. Most fish are caught on dark and foggy nights.

The *Whitebait*, little fishes from three to six inches in length, the delicious flavour of which you may have often enjoyed, are caught by means of bag-nets, sunk four or five feet below the water. They are very abundant in many parts of the British coasts, particularly in the estuary of the Thames in spring and summer, when they arrive in shoals to deposit their spawn. For several months they continue to ascend the river with the flood tide, and descend with the ebb tide, not being able to live in fresh water. Greenwich and Blackwall are celebrated for whitebait dinners. It was formerly supposed that this fish was the young of the shad, or sprat, but is now regarded as a distinct species.

The *Sardine*, a fish of the same genus with the herring and pilchard, smaller than the latter, abounds in the Mediterranean, and is found also in the Atlantic Ocean. The sardines of the west coast of France, which are largely imported into our country, are generally young sprats, and sometimes young herrings. This "sardine" fishery is a great business in France, and especially at Concarneau, where as many as thirteen thousand men aid in the fishery. This is conducted in a way remarkable for the extravagance it involves. The sprat fisheries on the British coast—indeed, all our net fisheries—are carried on in the most primitive way; but the French have made it a "bait" fishery, and use the roe of the cod, which is brought at a considerable expense from the North seas for the purpose. The fish are gutted, beheaded, sorted into sizes, and washed in sea-water, then dried on nets or willows; they are then placed in a pan, kept over a furnace, and filled with boiling oil. The fish are plunged into the cauldron, two rows deep, arranged on wire gratings. They are afterwards placed to drip, the oil being carefully collected, after which they are packed in the tin boxes you have so often seen. It is said that, besides the quantity exported, as many as four millions are annually prepared for the home market.

I need not enter into any particulars about the *Cod* fishery on the banks of Newfoundland, which presents nothing new or very interesting except in the value attached to every part of this valuable fish. The tongue of the cod, whether fresh or salted, is a great delicacy; the gills are used as baits in fishing; the liver, which is large and good for eating, also furnishes an enormous quantity of oil, now much esteemed for consumptive patients; the swimming-bladder furnishes an isinglass; the head is eaten, and the Norwegians give it, with marine plants, to their cows, to produce a greater quantity of milk; the vertebræ, the ribs, and the bones are given by the Icelanders to their cattle; even the intestines and eggs are eaten. The coast of Iceland abounds in fish, especially of the cod tribe, and this abundance has not only from a very early time supplied the inhabitants with their chief food, but enabled them to procure other necessaries. As the principal fishings begin on the Newfoundland coast, at the Feroe Islands, in Norway, and in Iceland at the same time, it seems evident that the cod is not a migratory fish, but a dweller where it finds its food. The Icelanders fish chiefly from open boats, and sometimes from decked ones. Only the largest boats, with six or twelve oars, are used in the cod fishery, and in these the natives often go out many miles to sea in the depth of winter to fish. They are a most hardy set of mariners. Their mode of capturing the cod is either by small drift-nets, deep-sea or hand lines, and the ordinary long line. The fish caught by the net are different from those taken by the line, being more plump, with smaller heads. The number of Iceland boats employed in the cod fisheries average nearly five thousand, and the number of persons employed exceeds ten thousand.

"The modern cod-smack," says Mr. Bertram, "usually carries from nine to eleven men and boys, including the captain. The line is chiefly used for the purpose of taking cod or haddock. Each man has a line of three hundred feet in length, and attached to each of these lines are one hundred 'snoods,' with hooks already baited with mussels, pieces of herring, or whiting. Each line is laid 'clear' in a shallow basket or 'skull;' that is, it is so arranged as to run freely as the boat shoots ahead. The three hundred feet line, with one hundred hooks, is called in Scotland a 'taes.' If there are eight men in a boat, the length of the line will be two thousand four hundred feet, with eight hundred hooks (the lines being tied to each other before setting). On arriving at the fishing-ground, the fishermen heave overboard a cork buoy with a flag-staff affixed to it, about six feet in height. The buoy is kept fixed by a line reaching to the bottom of the water, and having a stone or small anchor fastened to the lower end. To this line, called the 'pow-end,' is also fastened the fishing-line, which is then paid' out as fast as the boat sails. Should the wind be unfavourable, the oars are used. When the line is all out the end is dropped, and the boat returns to the buoy. The pow-end is hauled up, with the anchor and fishing-line attached to it. The fishermen then haul in the line with whatever fish may be on it. Eight hundred fish might be taken (and often have been) by eight men in a few hours by this operation. Many a time the fish are eaten off the line by the 'dog' (dog-fish) and other enemies, so that a few fragments and a skeleton or two remain to show that fish have been caught. The fishermen of 'deck-welled cod-bangers' use both hand-lines and long lines. The cod-bangers' tackling is, of course, stronger than that used in open boats. The long lines are called 'grut lines' or great lines. Every deck-welled cod-banger carries a small boat on deck, for working the great lines in moderate weather. This boat is also provided with a well, in which the fish are kept alive till they arrive at the banger, when they are transferred from the small boat's well to that of the larger vessel."

London alone requires an annual supply of five hundred thousand cod-fish, which is one of the best fish our seas afford. The London market was formerly supplied with cod from the "Doggerbank," an extensive flat sandbank in the middle of the German Ocean, between England and Denmark; but of late years the fish have increased on our own coasts to such an extent that London is now almost entirely supplied from the coasts of Lincolnshire and Norfolk.

The *Haddock*, which has a striking family resemblance to the cod, is taken both by trawl-nets and lines, and being in great esteem by fish-eaters for the excellence of its flavour, we ought to be pleased that the fish is so partial to our own coasts, where it appears in vast shoals at particular seasons. Fishermen sometimes find haddocks and other fishes caught in their lines reduced to mere skin and skeleton by the *Hag*, one of the species allied to the Lamprey family, resembling an eel or worm, and a perfect anatomist in its way. It is believed to enter by the mouth of the haddock, and thus prey upon it: the fish thus treated is called a 'robbed' fish. As many as six hags have been taken out of a single haddock, and they are also said to make their way into fishes through the skin, and are hence sometimes called "borers." It is supposed, however, that the hags are swallowed by fishes, and, in retaliation, work out their insides.

The *Coal-fish*—a relative of the cod, with a very vulgar name, derived from its black coat, but a fish of really handsome form, and about two or three feet in length—takes a bait with extraordinary eagerness: when a boat falls in with a shoal, they may be kept beside it by being thus attracted till the whole are captured. It is abundant in all Northern seas, and is taken on the British coasts. In many parts of Scotland they are well known to juvenile anglers, who take them in plenty from the end of piers, often with a rude tackle and almost any kind of bait. In the winter-time (according to Mr. Low), while the fry of this fish is in the harbour of Orkney, it is common to see five or six hundred people, of all ages, fishing for them with small angling-rods about six feet long, and a line a little longer; but with this simple apparatus they kill vast numbers. The whole harbour is covered with boats.

Other members of the cod family are caught much in the same manner as their representative, and are very valuable as food, especially the *Ling*, which is found abundantly on our own coasts. The sounds (air-bladders) are pickled, and the roes are preserved in brine, and eaten as food, or used as a means of attracting fish by throwing it about the nets, as is often done by French fishermen. The *Common Hake*, a fish sometimes measuring three feet, is also plentiful on the English and Irish coasts, and very voracious. When enclosed in a net with pilchards—as frequently happens on the Cornish coast—it gorges itself with them: Mr. Couch has seen seventeen pilchards taken from the stomach of a hake of ordinary size. It is to this species, and the common cod when dried and salted for exportation, to which the name of "stock" fish is usually applied. Forty thousand hakes have been landed on the shores of Mount's Bay in Cornwall in a single day, and the quantity captured on the Irish coast is immense. Galway Bay is sometimes called the "Bay of Hakes" from the numbers of that fish taken.

The *Turbot*, an especial delight of fish epicures in all times, is taken, with other flat fish, by lines and hooks, the fishermen going out in parties of three to a "coble," each man carrying his long line, the united ends of which are a league in length, and draw after them fifteen hundred baited hooks; these lines, as they are to lie across the current, can only be shot twice in twenty-four hours, when the rush of the water slackens as the tide is about to change. The Italians christen the turbot the "sea-pheasant," from its flavour. The Romans were particularly fond of this dainty, and frequent allusion to its size occur in their writers; thus:

> "Great turbots and late suppers lead
> To debt, disgrace, and abject need."

> "The border of the broadest dish
> Lay hid beneath the monster fish."

But the size mentioned by the ancient writers is of a fabulous character. However, it sometimes attains a weight of between seventy and ninety pounds. It is now chiefly obtained by beam-trawling, a triangular purse-shaped net about seventy feet long, usually having a breadth of about forty feet at the mouth, and gradually diminishing to the end of the net, which is about ten feet long, and of nearly uniform breadth. The turbot is of all the flat fishes the most valuable. The *Brill* belongs to the same tribe, as well as other less important fishes. The turbot is shorter, broader, and deeper than almost any other kind of flat fish. It generally keeps close to the bottom of the sea, and is found chiefly on banks where there is a considerable depth of water. Some of the banks in the German Ocean abound in turbots, as the Doggerbank, and yield great quantities to the London market.

Of *Soles*, the annual London consumption is estimated at one hundred millions, which are taken exclusively by the trawl, for by no other mode of capture could a thousandth part of the supply be obtained.

In proportion to the benefits derived from the spoils of the *Turtle*, the shell of which is so ornamental and useful in the arts, the ingenuity of man has been sharpened by his eagerness to acquire them. The modes by which the people of Celebes take them are by the harpoon and net, or by falling on the females when they resort to the strand to lay their eggs. The turtle is turned on its back, when, unable to turn again, it lies helpless. It sometimes also falls into the hands of the dwellers on the coast through means of their fishing-stakes, into which it enters like the fish, and from which it can find no outlet. It is then killed and robbed of its upper shield; but, as the shells adhere fast to each other, and would be injured by being torn off, the usual plan is to wait a few days, by which time the soft parts become decomposed, and the shells are removed with little trouble. When the turtles lie floating on the sea either for the purpose of sleep or respiration, the fishermen approach them quietly with a sharp harpoon, carrying a ring at the butt-end, to which a cord is attached. The harpooner strikes, and the wounded animal dives, but is at last secured by the cord. In the South Seas, skilful divers watch them when so floating, and getting under the animals, suddenly rise, and so seize them. Mr. Darwin describes a curious method of capturing turtles which he witnessed at Keeling Island in 1836:

"I accompanied," he remarks, "Captain Fitzroy to an island at the head of the lagoon: the channel was exceedingly intricate, winding through fields of delicately-branched corals. We saw several turtles, and two boats were then employed in catching them. The water is so clear and shallow, that although at first a turtle quickly dives out of sight, yet, in a canoe or boat under sail, the pursuers, after no very long chase, come up to it. A man standing ready in the bows at this moment dashes through the water *upon the turtle's back;* then clinging with both hands by the shell of the neck, he is carried away until the animal becomes exhausted, and is secured. It was quite an interesting sight to see the two boats thus doubling about, and the men dashing into the water to secure their prey."

But the most singular mode of capturing turtles is that practised on the coasts of China and the Mozambique, by the aid of living fishes trained for the purpose, and thence named "fisher-fishes." The fish is a species of remora (sucking-fish), and the islanders who use it are said to proceed in the following manner :

They have, in their little boat, tubs containing many of these fishes, the top of whose head is covered with an oval plate, soft and fleshy at its circumference. In the middle of this plate is a very complicated apparatus of bony pieces disposed across in two regular rows, like the laths of Persienne blinds. The number of these plates varies from fifteen to thirty-six, according to the species: they can be moved on their axis by means of particular muscles, and their free edges are furnished with small hooks, which are all raised at once like the points of a wool-card. The tail of each of the trained fishes in the tubs is furnished with a ring for the attachment of a fine but long and strong cord. When the fishermen perceive the basking turtles on the surface of the sea, knowing that the slightest noise would disturb the intended victims, they slip overboard one of their fish tied to the long cord, and pay out line according to their distance from the turtles. As soon as the fish perceives the floating reptile, he makes towards it, and fixes himself so firmly to it that the fishermen pull both fish and turtle into the boat, where the fish is very easily detached from its prey, and the turtle is secured.

*Crabs,* which belong to the highest order of *Crustaceans* (from the Latin *crusta,* "a hard covering"), are taken by traps—baskets which readily permit an entrance, but not their escape, and which are baited with meat or animal garbage of some kind—or pots, or caught in the holes of the rocks at low tide with a rod and hook. You are no doubt well aware of the pugnacious instincts of these animals, which require very careful handling when found on the rocks or the sea-shore. Their fighting propensities are not confined to other prey, but they have fierce encounters among themselves, by means of their formidable claws, with which they lay hold of their adversary's legs, and dexterously amputate them.

The *Hermit Crab* is one of the most curious of this numerous family. A more daring little burglar could not be found than this animal, appropriating to its own use the shells of whelks and periwinkles, after basely dislodging and killing their lawful owners. It is curious to see this crab busily parading the sea-shore, dragging its old incommodious habitation behind it, unwilling to part with it until another and more convenient one is found. It stops first at one shell, turns it, passes by, then goes to another, looks at it attentively for a time, and then tries it. Not being found suitable, it resumes the old one, and in this manner frequently changes, until at length it finds one light, roomy, and commodious; into this it enters and takes up its abode. Frequently two of them will have a severe contest for possession, and a fierce fight ensues. With such very bad instincts and unscrupulous habits, it is not surprising that the hermit-crab should be a very suspicious animal. On the slightest alarm it retires into its shell, guarding the entrance to it with its largest claw. The structure of the animal renders it equal to most emergencies. The part which in the lobster becomes a fan-like expansion at the end of the tail, is an appendage to the hermit crab for firmly holding on by the shell, and so tenacious is the hold that it may be torn to pieces, but cannot be pulled out. As they increase in size, the hermit crabs are compelled to enter on a fresh career of crime. The ancients were well acquainted with the predaceous habits of this little marauder. Oppian writes:

> "The hermit-fish, unarm'd by nature, left
> Helpless and weak, grow strong by harmless theft;
> Fearless they stroll, and look with panting wish
> For the cast crust of some new-covered fish,
> Or such as empty lie, and deck the shore,

> Whose first and rightful owners are no more.
> They make glad seizure of the vacant room,
> And count the borrow'd shell their native home;
> Screw their soft limbs to fit the winding case,
> And boldly herd with the crustaceous race.
> Careless they enter the first empty cell;
> Oft find the plaited whelk's indented shell;
> And oft the deep-dy'd purple, forc'd by death
> To stranger fish the painted home bequeath.
> The whelk's etch'd coat is most with pleasure worn,
> Wide in extent, and yet but lightly borne.
> But when they, growing, more than fill the place,
> And find themselves hard pinch'd in scanty space,
> Compelled, they quit the roof they lov'd before,
> And busy search around the pebbly shore,
> Till a commodious roomy seat be found,
> Such as the larger shell-fish, living, own'd.
> Oft cruel wars contending hermits wage,
> And long for the disputed shell engage;
> The strongest here the doubtful prize possess,—
> Power gives the right, and all the claim confess."

**Crabs** are inhabitants of almost all seas. The different kinds vary much in the form of the *carapace*, or back, which in some is round, or nearly so; in others longer than broad; in some prolonged in front into a kind of beak, &c.; also in smoothness or roughness, with hairs, excrescences, or spines; in the length of the legs, &c. The *King Crab*, an inhabitant of tropical seas, is a remarkable species, having a tail which forms a long and powerful dagger-like spine, sometimes exceeding in length the whole body. Some of these crabs exceed two feet in length, and in the Asiatic islands the spine is often used for pointing arrows; in tropical America the shell is used as a ladle. At Labuan and Singapore Dr. Collingwood met with a new species of crab, the "*Pill-maker*." It is a small creature of its kind, many being the size of large peas. Its habit is to take up particles of sand in its claws, deposit them in a groove beneath the thorax, and afterwards eject them as pellets or pills from its mouth, after having extracted what nutriment they may contain.

The crab (as also the prawn) may be quoted as exercising the virtue of conjugal affection to the highest degree, for the male takes hold of his mate, and never quits her side, swimming with her, crawling about with her; and if she is forcibly taken away, the faithful animal will seize hold of and endeavour to retain her.

Mr. Gosse mentions a curious example of instinctive stratagem in a crab on the shores of the Pacific, about six inches in circumference, which covers itself with decaying vegetable rubbish, mud, sand, &c., and thus lies in ambush for its passing prey. It maintains a sluggish character until taken into the hand, or otherwise alarmed, when it becomes very active. The spines upon its body to retain the rubbish, the short but strong claws easily concealed, the eyes placed at the end of long footstalks, curving upwards and thus raised above the mass, show the beautiful adaptation of its structure to its habits.

*Prawns* in general form resemble lobsters, cray-fish, and shrimps, but belong to a family remarkable for a long saw-like beak projecting from the carapace or back. There are many species, and some of those inhabiting the warm seas attain a large size. Many of them are semi-transparent, and have very fine colours. The common prawn, which forms so great a luxury to our breakfast-table, is from three to four inches in length, is generally taken in the vicinity of rocks at a little distance from the shore, and osier baskets—similar to those employed for catching lobsters—are employed for their capture, and nets.

*Shrimps*, as you no doubt well know, are generally taken by nets in the form of a wide-mouthed bag, stretched by means of a short cross-beam at the end of a pole, and pushed along by the shrimper, wading up to the knees in water. Sometimes a net of larger size is dragged along by two boats. The common shrimp is about two inches long, and the short beak readily distinguishes it from the prawn. When alarmed, it buries itself in the sand by a peculiar movement of its fan-like tail.

Dr. Collingwood mentions a new species of shrimp, which he discovered in the warm seas, of a deep violet colour (those on our own coasts are of a greenish-grey colour, dotted with brown), and with a claw of remarkable construction.

"I placed it," he says, "in a basin of water with a small crab, whose appearance appeared violently to offend it. Whenever the crab came in contact with the shrimp, the latter produced a loud sound, the explanation of which is as follows: the shrimp possessed two claws—one large and stout, and the other long and slender. When irritated, it opened the pincers of the large claw very wide, and then suddenly closed them with a startling jerk. When the claw was in contact with the bottom of the basin, a sound was produced as if the basin were struck; but when the claw was elevated in the water, the sound was like the snap of a finger, and the water was splashed in my face."

Dr. Collingwood called this animal the "trigger" shrimp, from the action of this claw resembling that of a pistol trigger. If only put upon half-cock, this trigger closed without noise.

How wonderful are the means that the Omnipotent Creator has provided (as in all things) for the protection of the shelly inhabitants! The hard covering accommodates itself to their growth, and at the same time is sufficiently light as not to interfere with the movements and functions of the interesting tenant. All the various tribes of shell-bearing animals are thus defended from the injuries and attacks to which their situation exposes them. Thus, some are protected by multivalve, or more than two formed tubular shells, the tenant protruding its organs at the summit, which is defended by the lid, consisting of more than a single piece; in the univalve, or one shell, the animal protrudes itself at the sides, and has no valve, as in the common barnacle. The bivalves, or animals of two shells, bury themselves in the sand, perforate rocks, or suspend themselves by the byssus, or thready filaments; others, again, as the oyster, fix themselves to any convenient substance.

In the common *Periwinkle* (a molluscous, or soft-shelled animal), the mouth of its shell, as you are, no doubt, quite aware, is closed by a horny covering; this is called the "patch," which is attached to the foot, or rather neck, by its convex or lower surface: this is the lid, as you must have remarked.

You all know the *Mussel*, belonging to the molluscous animals, and the common species of which are very abundant on our own coasts, and are much used as bait by fishermen. As an article of food it is much consumed in our own country, but especially so on the Continent. The French people are remarkably clever in their method of cultivating this shell-fish by artificial means. About four miles from Rochelle there may be seen a wonderful mussel "farm," which has been a source of considerable profit for hundreds of years. The mussels are grown on frames of basket-work carefully made, and are larger and of finer flavour than the natural fish. I will tell you how this ingenious plan originated. The particulars are related in a pamphlet published at La Rochelle in 1847. In the year 1035, an Irish bark loaded with sheep was thrown in a heavy storm on the rocks near Esnande, on the coasts of Saintonge, and the only person on board who was saved was the captain, named Walton, who amply repaid the services which had been rendered him, for, having saved some of the sheep from the wreck, he crossed them with the animals of the country, and thus produced a fine race, which is still known under the name of the "marsh sheep." He next devised a kind of net, which was stretched a little above the level of the open sea, where it caught large flocks of shore-birds which skim the surface of the water at twilight or after dark. In order to render these nets thoroughly effective, it was necessary to go to the very centre of the immense bed of mud where these birds seek their nourishment. Walton discovered on examining the poles which supported his nets, that they were covered with mussel-spawn. He then increased the number of the poles, and, after various attempts, constructed his first artificial mussel-bed, or *bouchot*, as it is termed. At the level of the lowest tides, he drove into the mud stakes that were strong enough to resist the force of the waves, and placed them in two rows about a yard distant from one another. This double line of poles formed an angle whose base was directed towards the shore and whose apex pointed to the open sea. This palisade was roughly fenced in with long branches, and a narrow opening having been left at the extremity of the angle, wicker-work cases were arranged in such a manner as to stop any fishes that were being carried back by the retreating tide. Walton had thus combined in one a sort of fish preserve, with a bed for the breeding of mussels. The plan soon became very popular, and the beds were extended in every direction.

The little mussels that appear in the spring are called *seeds*, and are scarcely larger than small beans till towards the end of May; but at this time they rapidly increase, and in July they attain the size of a full-grown bean. They are then fit for transplanting, and are placed in bags, made of old nets, which are set upon the fences that are not quite so far advanced into the sea. The young mussels spread themselves all round the bags, fixing themselves by means of those silky filaments or threads, called byssus, which you have no doubt noticed, and by which the little animals attach themselves to rocks or other substances. In proportion as they grow or become crowded together within the bags, they are cleared out and distributed over other poles lying somewhat nearer the shore, whilst the full-grown mussels, which are fit for sale, are planted on the beds nearest the shore. It is from this part of the mussel-beds that the fishermen reap their harvests, and every day enormous quantities of freshly-gathered mussels are transported in carts or on the backs of horses to La Rochelle, whence they are sent to all parts of France.

As an instance of utility, the common mussel maintains the long bridge across the Torridge river, near its junction with the Taw, at the town of Bideford in North Devon. At this bridge the tide runs so rapidly that it cannot be kept with mortar. The corporation therefore keep boats employed to bring mussels to it, and the interstices of the bridge are kept filled with them. The bridge is supported against the violence of the tide by the strong threads of the byssus which these mussels fix to the stonework.

While on this subject I may allude to oyster farming, which is also carried on extensively in France, and is a thriving business in our own country. There is a very great demand for oysters, on the Continent especially; and as the fish may be kept out of water for a few days without any harm, or can be kept in tanks, and be artificially fed until such time as it is wanted for the table, a large number of fishermen have of late years taken to the rearing and fattening of oysters. There are few places now on the shores of France where oyster culture is not carried on in some one of its various methods: there are places for keeping them alive until wanted, *parcs* for breeding them in, places for fattening them, or pits for *greening* them. The difference between English and French oyster farming is not great, but the little that there is is of great importance to the economy of a large oyster farm. The new oyster farms which have been laid down in England of late years are all upon the French plan, and are very successful. An immense oyster business is done in France, Paris alone requiring a daily supply that in the course of the season is said to amount to *one hundred millions*, and the large provincial towns all consume in proportion. Countless numbers are, besides, exported cured, prepared, and pickled. A little branch taken from the oyster-beds contains several thousands, and common tiles placed in the *parcs* are covered with hundreds of them. The Ile de Ré is one of the most famous oyster-rearing places, and here may be seen a few thousand oyster-*parcs*, and also a few hundred fattening-ponds, and hundreds of thousands of oysters in all states of growth, from the size of a pin's head to a crown piece. The South of England Oyster Company have breeding-grounds close to the village of Havant, on the north-west shore of Hayling Island. At the opposite extremity of this, at the entrance of Chichester Harbour, the first great experiment in oyster culture was made, and with favourable results, the supply of spat or seed in their breeding-beds having been almost unlimited. The oysters are laid down on shingles, and hurdles placed over them. The sides of the hurdles are soon covered with young oysterlings, the largest of which are about the size of a sixpence, the smallest the size of a pin-head, and the greater number exceed a silver fourpenny piece.

Most oysters cast their spawn towards the close of the spring or in the beginning of the summer, as in the month of May. The spawn is by the fishermen called "spat," and in size and figure each resembles the drop of a candle. As soon as cast, or thrown off, these embryo disks adhere to stones, old oyster-shells, pieces of wood, or whatever substance comes in their way; a limy secretion issues from the surface of their bodies, and in the course of twenty-four hours, begins to be converted into a shelly substance. It is two or three years, however, before oysters acquire their full size; in fact, the oyster is said not fit to be eaten until five or six years old.

The *Scallops*, which are a tribe belonging to the oyster, possess the power of leaping out of the water at pleasure to the distance of half a yard; when elevated they open their shells, and eject the water within them, and then falling back into the water, close them with a loud snap.

The gigantic *Clama*, or clam-shell, resembles the oyster. One species found in the Indian Ocean has been found weighing between five and six hundred pounds.

The enemies of the oyster are many. The sea-crab seats itself upon the shell, and drills a little hole in his back, and so kills him. On the sea-shore bushels of shells are found quite riddled with holes by this crab. The star-fish was known in ancient times to prey upon the oyster. Oppian says:

> "The prickly star-fish creeps on with fell deceit,
> To force the oyster from his close retreat.
> When gaping lids their widen'd void display,
> The watchful star thrusts in a pointed ray
> Of all its treasures spoils the rifled case,
> And empty shells the sandy hillocks grace."

The drum-fish—in weight about thirty pounds, and about two feet long—swallows oyster and shell; sometimes two or three pounds of shells are found in the stomach of this fish. The star-fishes *hug* the oyster, and wrap their five rays about him, but the embrace is one of death to the poor victim.

It is not surprising that the inhabitants of the ocean should feed partly on shell-fish; but it is curious to find animals strictly terrestrial preying upon them. Monkeys are said to descend to the sea to devour what shell-fish they may find on the shore. The ourang-outangs, according to Gernelli, feed in particular on a large species of oyster; and, fearful of inserting their paws between the open valves lest the animal should close and crush them, they first place a tolerably large stone in the shell, and then drag out their victim with safety. Monkeys are no less ingenious. Dampier saw several of them take up oysters from the beach, lay them on a stone, and beat them with another until they had demolished the shells. Even the fox, when pressed by hunger, will eat mussels and other bivalves; and the raccoon when near the shore lives much on them, particularly on oysters.

A curious anecdote appeared in "Bell's Weekly Messenger," of 7th January, 1821. A tradesman at Plymouth, having placed some oysters in a cupboard, was surprised on finding in the morning a mouse caught by the tail by the sudden snapping of the shell. At Ashburton, a Mrs. Allridge had placed a dish of Wembury oysters in a cellar. A large oyster soon expanded its shell, and at the instant two mice pounced upon the "living luxury," and were at once crushed between the valves. The oyster, with the two mice dangling from its shell, was for some time exhibited as a curiosity. A better natural mouse-trap could not be imagined. Carew, in his "History of Cornwall," tells of an oyster that closed on *three* mice.

Among birds the molluscs have many enemies. Several of the duck and gull tribes derive a portion of their subsistence from them. The pied oyster-catcher derives its name from this habit. Several kinds of crows likewise feed upon shell-fish. Vultures and aquatic birds detach shell-fish from the rocks.

I may add, that although the consumption of oysters in England is not so great as in France, as already mentioned, from thirty to forty thousand bushels of "natives," as those raised in artificial beds are called, are consumed annually in London alone; and, in addition to these, fully one hundred and twenty thousand bushels of sea-oysters are also sold there.

The *Lobsters* (which belong to the *Crustacea* or hard-shelled animals), the common species of which is so plentiful on the rocky coasts of our own country, and most parts of Europe, are generally, as I have stated, taken in traps, sometimes made of osier twigs, also by nets, sometimes pots, always baited with animal garbage, and in some countries by torchlight, with the aid of a wooden instrument which acts like a forceps or a pair of tongs. They are also taken by the hand, but this requires dexterity, for the claws are powerful weapons of defence: one is always larger than the other, and the pincers of one claw are knobbed on the inner edge, those of the other are serrated. It is more dangerous to be seized by the serrated ("like the teeth of a saw") than by the knobbed claw. A great authority on fish matters, Mr. Bertram, says:

"I once heard a clergyman at a lecture describe a lobster as a standing romance of the sea; an animal whose clothing is a shell, which it casts away once a year, in order that it may put on a larger suit; an animal whose flesh is in its tail and legs, and whose hair is in the inside of its breast; whose stomach is in its head, and which is changed every year for a new one, and which new one begins its life by devouring the old. An animal which carries its eggs within its body, until they become fruitful, and then carries them outwardly under its tail; an animal which can throw off its legs when they become troublesome, and can in a brief time replace them. Lastly, an animal with very sharp eyes placed in movable horns."

The London market alone requires two millions and a half of crabs and lobsters annually. Large numbers are sent from the Scottish coasts. The west and north-west coasts of Ireland abound with fine lobsters, and *welled* vessels bring from them supplies for the London market of ten thousand weekly. A large number of lobsters is brought from Norway, as many as thirty thousand arriving from that country in a single day, conveyed in wells on board steam vessels, and kept in wooden reservoirs, some of which may be seen on the Essex side of the Thames. In order that the great mass of lobsters may be kept on their best behaviour in these reservoirs, the great claw is rendered paralytic by means of a wooden peg driven into a lower joint: however cruel this may seem, it prevents them from tearing each other to pieces, so pugnacious are the animals. A good-sized lobster, we are informed by Mr. Bertram, will yield about twenty thousand eggs; and these are hatched (being so nearly ripe before they are abandoned by the mother) with great rapidity, it is said in forty-eight hours, and grow quickly, although the young lobster passes through many changes before it is fit to be presented at table. During the early period of growth it casts its shell frequently. This wonderful provision for an increase of size in the lobster is, observes Mr. Couch, perfectly surprising. It is indeed astonishing to see the complete covering of the animal cast off like a suit of old clothes, when it hides, naked and soft, in a convenient hole, awaiting the growth of its new crust or coat. Lobsters and crabs change their shell about every six weeks during the first year of their age; every two months during the second year; and afterwards the changing of the shell becomes less frequent, being reduced to four times a year. Previously to putting off their old shell they appear sick, languid, and restless. They acquire an entirely new covering in a few days; but during the time they remain defenceless they seek some lonely place, lest they should be attacked and devoured by such of their brethren as are not in the same weak condition. In casting their shells, it is difficult to conceive how the lobsters are able to draw the flesh of their large claws out, leaving the shells of these entire and attached to the shell of the body. The fishermen say that previous to this operation the lobster pines away till the flesh in its claw is no thicker than the quill of a goose, which enables it to draw its parts through the joints and narrow passage near the trunk. The new shell hardens by degrees.

It is supposed that the lobster becomes reproductive at the age of five years. . Lobsters are very voracious; they are also full of fighting propensities, and have frequent combats among themselves, in which limbs are often lost; but the limb is soon replaced by the growth of a new one, rather smaller than the old one. In the water lobsters can run nimbly on their legs or small claws, and if alarmed, can spring tail foremost to a surprising distance as swift as a bird can fly. Fishermen can see them pass about thirty feet, and, by the swiftness of their motion, suppose they may go much farther. When frightened, they will spring from a considerable distance to their hold in the rocks, and will force their way into an entrance barely sufficient for their bodies to pass.

Like some of the crabs, lobsters are said to be attached to particular parts of the sea.

> "In shelly armour wrapt, the lobsters seek
> Safe shelter in some bay or winding creek;
> To rocky chasms the dusky natives cleave,
> Tenacious hold, nor will the dwelling leave.
> Nought like their home the constant lobsters prize,
> And foreign shores and seas unknown despise.
> Though cruel hands the banished wretch expel,
> And force the captive from his native cell,
> He will, if freed, return with anxious care,
> Find the known rock, and to his home repair."

In some parts of the Continent the fishermen endeavour, by making violent noises, to drive the fish into their nets; but these are so cunning, that when surrounded by the net, the whole shoal will sometimes escape, for if one of them springs over it, the rest will follow like sheep. This circumstance was noticed by Oppian (a Greek poet, born in Cilicia about the year 200):

> "The mullet, when encircling seines enclose,
> The fatal threads and treacherous bottom knows;
> Instant he rallies all his vigorous powers,
> And faithful aid of every nerve implores;
> O'er battlements of cork up-darted flies,
> And finds from air th' escape that sea denies."

The Danish fishermen have a similar mode of taking the horn-fishes, called "green-bone" from the colour of their bones. They are timid, and afraid of the nets, and when the shoals approach, the fishermen commence a regular bombardment with stones, and so frighten them into their meshes.

A writer in "Notes and Queries" mentions a similar practice in Wales.

"The fishermen," he observes, "commenced their operations at every ebbing of the tide, by stretching a seine across the river, several hundred paces above the coast; and whilst drawing it towards the sea, they incessantly disturbed the water by beating the surface, as well as hurling into it the heaviest stones they could poise. The affrighted fish made at once for the sea, which, however, they could not reach except by passing through the intervening shallows. Here they were pursued by dogs trained for the purpose, and clubbed or speared by the men. I have frequently seen from one to two hundred fine fish, weighing from ten to twenty pounds each, taken in this extraordinary way."

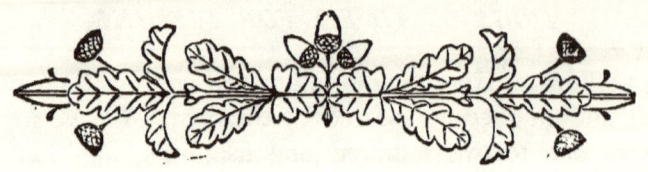

## CHAPTER XXV.

### ODDS AND ENDS ABOUT FISHES.

" Flat-fish, with eyes distorted, square, ovoid, rhomboid, long;
Some cased in mail, some slippery-back'd, the feeble and the strong;
Soft-finn'd, and armed with weapons to poison, stab, or maul;
Their baby-brood who educate to drum, shrill, grunt, and call;
Who build at sea, who bed on shore, who ox-like chew the cud,
Who crest the waves with liquid light, or ink the sable flood,
Who numb the boatman's sinewy arm—on azure wings who soar;
Pelagians from the open sea, and tribes that hug the shore;
Sedan'd on poles, or dragg'd on hooks, or poured from tubs like water,
Gasp side by side, together piled in one promiscuous slaughter."

*The Fish-market at Naples.*—BADHAM.

THE description I have quoted (so ingeniously presented by the Rev. Mr. Badham) of fishes inhabiting the Mediterranean Sea, corresponds entirely with the strange and varied character ascribed to them by ancient and modern writers. I will, however, before alluding to any particular species of fishes, give a brief outline of their nature generally. From the earliest ages fishes were most extensively used as articles of diet, and at the present time they form a considerable portion of the food of mankind generally. In some countries they were the only money of commerce, and dried fish were paid as current coin. Mythological honours were rendered to them by the ancients; and in the case of sharks, as I have mentioned in the chapter on "The Pirates of the Ocean," they are deified on the African coasts. Fish have been perpetuated in coins and sculptures, from which many of the species in ancient use can still be traced.

Fishes people the ocean with their shoals, and serve to keep in check the innumerable creatures of still lower construction, while they themselves are held in check, and afford sustenance to millions which have been placed in our system above them. In *form* they are the most varied beings in creation, and the most inventive fancy could scarcely imagine a shape or appearance to which a resemblance would not be found. They are of hideous or loathsome bulk or the most graceful form, and of gorgeous and resplendent colours; all wondrously adapted to the different modes of obtaining their food, whether by stealth or deceit, strength or swiftness. The general form of a fish is admirably adapted to its native element. In all fishes which require swiftness to secure their prey, the *tail* is the great organ of motion. The absence of any neck gives the advantage of a more extensive and resisting attachment of the head to the body, the greater proportion of which is left free for the play of the muscular masses which move the tail. In the chapter on the "Monarchs of the Ocean" I have explained this wonderful power of the tail in the whales. Besides serving as the rudder or paddle, it is the tail of the fish that enables many of them to make those leaps out of the water to which I have frequently alluded in these pages. From the enormous whales and sharks to the small stickleback, this power seems to belong to the greater number of fishes.

The *fins* on the upper surface of the fish serve to balance the body; those on the lower surface to turn it, to move it slowly, and to keep it suspended in strong currents; but in all these movements the assistance of the tail is observable.

Some of the fins of fishes are vertical, constituting a kind of keel or rudder; those on the back are named *dorsals* (from the Latin *dorsum*, "a back"); behind the vent and under the tail, *anal;* and at the extremity of the tail they form *caudals* (from the Latin *cauda*, "a tail"). They differ in number, size, and the nature of the rays which support them, being sometimes spiny, and in other cases soft and articulated. Those corresponding to arms or wings are the *pectorals* (from the Latin *pectus*, "the chest"), invariably fixed behind the gills.

Paley, in his "Natural Theology," thus sums up the actions of the fins of fishes: "The pectoral, and more particularly the ventral (belonging to the stomach) fins serve to raise and depress the fish: when the fish desires to have a retrograde motion, a stroke forward with the pectoral fin effectually produces it; if the fish desires to turn either way, a single blow with the tail the opposite way sends it round at once; if the tail strike both ways, the motion produced by the double lash is progressive, and enables the fish to dart forwards with an astonishing velocity. The result is not only in some cases the most rapid, but in all cases the most gentle, pliant, easy, animal motion with which we are acquainted. In their mechanical use, the anal fin may be reckoned the keel; the ventral fins, the outriggers; the pectoral fins, the oars [and, we may now add, the caudal fin, the screw-propeller]. And if there be any similitudes between those parts of a boat and a fish, observe," adds Paley, "it is not the resemblance of imitation, but the likeness which arises from applying similar mechanical means to the same purpose."

Another powerful aid to the buoyancy of fishes is the *air* or *swimming-bladder*, which Paley describes as "a philosophical apparatus in the body of an animal." It is easy to see at the back-bone of the herring and other fishes a shining pearly-looking membrane, almost enveloped by the roe or milt of the fish. This is the air or swimming-bladder; and it is of this, as found in the sturgeon, the carp, the ling, and many other fishes, when dried and prepared by certain processes, that the substance called *isinglass* is manufactured.

It is the swimming-bladder that serves the fish for rising or sinking in the waters; but in such fishes as reside at the bottom of the sea or never come to the surface, this bladder is almost always wanting. How truly wonderful is this provision of nature! As Paley remarks, "it would be very worthy of inquiry to know by what method an animal which lives constantly in water is able to supply a repository of air."

The *bodies* of fishes are nearly the same specific gravity as the water in which they live, owing to the great quantity of fat they contain, so that very little effort is required to keep them at any given height, and their ascent or descent in the water.

The *circulation of blood* is peculiar. There is but a single heart in fishes, that is, a heart consisting of only two cavities; and these correspond not to the left heart of mammals or birds, but to their right or pulmonic heart.

*Respiration* is carried on by means of the gills, which take the place of lungs, and consist of a large number of blood-vessels, placed near the forward extremity of the animal, and protected by a bony case or covering, often defended by strong spines. The gills are placed in immediate communication with the heart. Water, which is impregnated with atmospheric air, entering at the mouth, is forced out again by the apertures at each side of the neck, and thus maintains almost a constant stream or rush through them, entering and again expelled at intervals. When fishes are taken from the water, the delicate thready structure of the gills immediately collapses; when exposed to the air, a kind of suffocation ensues, and death is the result. This is the general principle of respiration in fishes, but in some cases the structure varies.

The *smell* of fishes in some species is remarkable: they scent their prey at a great distance, and the very perfection of this function is often fatal to them. Some fishes are so allured by scents, that by smearing the hand over with them, and immersing it in water, fishes (not *sharks*, let us hope) will often flock towards the fingers, and may easily be taken. Fishermen have the habit of making their bait more attractive by steeping it in some strong-smelling ingredient. On the American shores, the fishermen use putrid or damaged fish as bait for mackerel. They are thrown into a box-hopper, in which a cylinder studded with knives is made to revolve by a crank. This is called the "bait-mill," and by its aid the contents are reduced to a kind of paste, which is thrown into the sea to attract the fish, which are then caught by lines with hooks, having a piece of polished pewter attached as a lure. In all fishes, *nostrils* or external openings are very apparent, and in these the nerves of smell are distributed.

*Taste* in fishes (as in animals who almost invariably swallow their food without mastication) cannot be very acute, since their tongue is in great part bony, and is often furnished with teeth and other hard coverings.

The organ of *touch* is in general as imperfect as that of taste: without prolonged members, and flexible fingers capable of grasping, they can scarcely explore the forms of objects by any other means than by their lips. Certain little fleshy tendrils which some fishes possess may supply the imperfections of touch in the other organs.

The bodies of most fishes are covered with small brilliant plates of a horny nature called *scales*, but in some kinds these are wanting, as in the turbot and others, in place of which are found bony protuberances in some species, and in others a very smooth skin without scales, and covered with a thick gelatinous secretion from the body. The scales consist of a substance chemically resembling the composition of bones and teeth. They usually overlap each other like tiles. Some are very thick, forming a kind of armour.

In general, fish have large *eyes*, and in particular, the pupil is very broad and open, as might be expected in creatures who require great powers of vision in the deep, where light penetrates but scantily. The eyes have no real eyelids, the skin passing over them mostly in a transparent form, to admit light; and they are sometimes opaque or dense. Some varieties of fish, whose eyes are fixed on the upper surface of their bodies, cannot see what prey they swallow; others have no outward indication of an eye. "No tear moistens, nor eyelid shelters or wipes the surface: the eyes of fish are only representations of that beautiful and animated organ which is found in the superior class of animals."

"The *teeth* of fishes," says Professor Owen, "whether we study them in regard to their number, form, substance, structure, situation, or mode of attachment, offer a greater and more striking series of varieties than do those of any other class of animals. In number they range from zero to countless quantities. In the sharks and rays the teeth are supported by the upper or lower jaws, as in most quadrupeds; but many other fishes have teeth growing from the roof of the mouth, from the surface of the tongue, from the bony hoop or arches supporting the gills, and some have them developed from the bone of the nose and the base of the skull." In all fishes the teeth are shed and renewed not once only, as in mammals, but frequently during the whole course of their lives.

Fishes have but small occasion for the sense of *hearing*, "being condemned to reside in the empire of silence, where all around is mute." In most fishes the auditory parts are buried in the skull, and send no process to the surface.

Singular stories, however, are told of fishes being sensible to the sound of music. Ancient writers—Ælian and Aristotle—mention some fishes, and particularly skates, who are attracted in this manner. Two men embark in a boat, one with a musical instrument and the other with a net, and by this music the fishes become so entranced as to be taken easily. A somewhat similar mode is said to be practised by the boatmen of the Danube, who use bells for the purpose. Carp have been known to distinguish the sound of a bell, and the voice of their keeper when called to be fed.

The *brain* of fishes is remarkably small in proportion to the size of the animal, the quantity of nerves arising out of it, and the size of the cavity which contains it. The space thus left vacant is often filled with oil or fat.

Some fishes are not altogether indifferent to the fate of their brood. I have already alluded to the attachment of the mammalian order for their young. Some fishes leave the depths of the ocean, and deposit their spawn in the shallows, where the young fry are comparatively safe from the voracity of their numerous enemies. Some build nests for their young, as I shall further explain in this chapter.

The *eggs* of fishes are generally deposited on the surface of the water, where they float during the period of their development.

It is in the Northern seas that fishes display their most astonishing fecundity—not so much in the variety of species as in the multitude of individuals of a species; and the ocean nowhere else produces an abundance of fish approaching to the myriads of herring and cod in that quarter.

The *uses* to which fish are applied are numerous. They afford a valuable manure when they are to be had in plenty. Fishery-salt is also a great fertilizer. Pretty ornaments are made from fish-scales, as brooches, bracelets, &c.; the eyes of fishes are also employed by the makers of shell flowers for imitating buds. Mock pearls are made from an essence obtained by scraping the scales off the bleak (a fresh-water fish) and the whitebait. The natives of the north-west coast of America make from the entrails of fishes bracelets, fishing-lines, thread, work-bags, head-dresses, and needle-cases; fish-hooks and needles are made of the bones.

I have already alluded to isinglass, which is made from the dense membrane which forms the air-bladder of the sturgeon and other fishes. Oil, as you know, forms a staple article of commerce. The dog-fish is caught principally for the oil from its liver—a large fish yielding about a barrel-full. The skin of this fish is used to refine liquors, clear coffee, &c. In several of the chapters in this book I have mentioned other and important uses to which fishes in various ways are applied.

Our ancestors were firm believers in the curative properties of certain fish. I can only mention a few of these strange notions. Pickled herrings were applied to the soles of the feet in fevers; pilchards were in great request for swellings of the gums and legs; the flesh of the tunny was considered an antidote to poison; the teeth of thornbacks, bruised in a mortar, were used for sore eyes; the gall for complaints of the ear; the bones of the sturgeon were reduced to powder and applied in rheumatic cases; oyster and mussel-shells ground to powder were also employed.

Wonderful is the property of several species of fish of inflicting electric shocks so severe as to produce exhaustion and numbness of the nerves exposed to its action. "That God," says Kirby, "should arm certain fishes, in some sense, with the lightning of the clouds, and enable them thus to employ an element so potent and irresistible as we do gunpowder, to astound, and smite, and stupefy, and kill the inhabitants of the water, is one of those wonders of an Almighty arm which no terrestrial animal is gifted to exhibit."

The *Torpedo*, popularly named by fishermen "numb-fish" and

"cramp-fish," a genus of fishes of the Ray order, is a living electrical machine, which has the power of striking its enemies even at a very considerable distance. Fishermen constantly witness evidences of the singular faculty of this fish. As soon as it enters their net, they are made aware of the fact by the shocks which are transmitted through the tackle by which it is suspended. These have been known to be sufficiently violent to compel the men to let go when they are drawing their nets, and thus allow the whole haul to fall back into the sea. The ancients were aware of this singular property in the fish. Oppian says:

> "The hooked torpedo ne'er forgets its art,
> But soon as struck begins to play its part,
> And to the line applies its magic sides;
> Without delay the subtle power glides
> Along the pliant rod and slender hairs,
> Then to the fisher's hand as swift repairs.
> Amazed he stands: his arm of sense bereft,
> Down drops the idle rod; his prey is left.
> Not less benumb'd than if he'd felt the whole
> Of frost's severest rage beneath the Arctic pole."

A poet's license is here exercised, but it is, nevertheless, true that a shock is equally inflicted by the torpedo, whether the fish is touched by the naked hand or by the medium of a stick. The *Torpenididæ*, as this family is termed, has been divided into a number of genera. They have a short and not very thick tail, cylindrical towards the end, and in outward appearance somewhat resemble a skate, and have nearly the same habits. Two species of the torpedo are occasionally found on the southern coasts of England, the common, or *Marmorata*, which sometimes attains a large size, weighing a hundred pounds; and the *Nobiliana*, which is more rare. They are readily distinguished by the spiracles behind the eyes, which are round and fringed at the edges in the former, and perfectly smooth in the latter. These and other species are found more plentifully in the Mediterranean. Mr. Badham states "that when the torpedo is disposed to 'astonish' any one, she furnishes to a careful observer the following premonitory indications of her intentions: the back—which, unlike that of the cat—is gibbous and raised when she is in good humour, flattens as she waxes angry, till the convex surface, gradually drawn in, becomes at length slightly concave; and at the same time the eyes, remarkably prominent during the repose of the creature, are retracted far back in the orbits. These are the precursory signals that the phials of her wrath are to be poured forth; the shock then instantly follows, and the fish as suddenly swells out again, recovering its usual form, generally to prepare for a new attack. These shocks follow in rapid succession: she sometimes inflicts forty or fifty broadsides in the course of one minute, and they are sufficiently powerful to destroy, as by lightning, small animals exposed to their influence."

Cuvier describes the electric apparatus of this fish to consist of a series of honeycomb-looking cells, filled with a thickish gelatinous fluid, and abundantly supplied with nerves, situated between the gills and the head of the fish.

The electrical organs are two in number. The number of cells varies according to the size of the fish: thus, in each organ of one fish were counted four hundred and seventy, and in another large fish one thousand one hundred and eighty-two. This natural electricity can be drawn from the fish by means of a conductor, and a shock is felt through a circuit formed by several persons joining hands.

The *Electric Eel*, little inferior to the torpedo in its "shocking" properties, is an inhabitant of the fresh waters of the tropical seas. The *Thunder-fish* of the Arabs—which also communicates a powerful electric stroke—belongs to the Nile and the rivers of Central Africa.

A remarkable power of *stinging* is possessed by some of the inhabitants of the deep. What is called the *Trygon*, or *Sting-Ray* (one species of which, the *Fire Flaire*, is found in our seas), is able to inflict severe wounds by its muscular and flexible tail, which it winds round the object of attack, and with the sword or spine at its base, pierces and lacerates. This weapon is armed with rows of serrated teeth at each side, every tooth of which is a small saw. "The worst and most dangerous wound, however," remarks Mr.

Badham, "is when the elastic tail dashes the apparatus, saws and all, into an unfortunate fisherman's thigh (as has frequently happened, in spite of the ordinary precautions), dragging it out again to make a new lunge before the unhappy victim has had time to escape; and so expert is this fish in this small-sword exercise, and so swiftly does stroke follow stroke, that persons who have seen it in operation report that, but for the spoutings of fresh blood, and the larger display of raw surface, they would have declared the weapon motionless all the time. The terrible sufferings inflicted by this atrocious caudine weapon—which is borne by four other colossal skates, as well as by the sea-eagle—has caused it to be regarded with as much superstious reverence by fishermen as was the tail of his music-master, Chiron, by the youthful Achilles."

The *Sting-Ray* fish attains a colossal size in the Mediterranean. " He possesses an enormous pair of fins, which, stretching out from either side of the body, offer a striking resemblance to a pair of wide-spread wings; and he has, moreover, a detached head, terminating in a porrect (extended) process, like a beak, and a large pair of piercing bright eyes," whence the origin of its appellation of " sea-eagle."

The *Great Weever* or *Sting-Bull*, and the *Little* or *Viper Weever*, possess the same formidable properties as the stinging ray. Both are found on our coasts, the former being about a foot long, and the other about four or five inches. Though of such small dimensions, these fishes are troublesome to encounter. The fins are spiny, and the gill-cover is furnished with a strong and sharp spine, which is directed backward, but is capable of being made erect to meet an enemy. This they use by a sudden bending of the body. Pennant states that the little weever buries itself in the sand, watching for its prey, leaving only its snout exposed, and if trod upon, it immediately uses its weapon with great force.

I have, in the chapter on "The Floating Navigators of the Ocean," alluded to the stinging powers of the *Physalis*, or "Portuguese man-of-war." It is a common trick with sailors to make a novice pick up one of these beautiful creatures, and then enjoy his discomfiture.

The *Acanthuri*, (from Greek words signifying "a spine," and "tail"), tropical fishes, some of which are remarkable for beauty of form and variety of colours, possess also a power of inflicting dangerous stings or wounds, which has obtained for them the name of "doctors" from our sailors, on account of the severe wounds they inflict on such as handle them unwarily. They have teeth trenchant and notched, and a strong spine at each side of the tail as sharp as a lancet, whence they are also called lancet-fishes. With these weapons they defend themselves with courage and success against the largest of their assailants. Many other fishes possess the same power of inflicting stings and wounds: living a life of constant warfare in the deep, Nature has bestowed upon them means of defence and for procuring their prey.

"It is worthy of observation," remarks Mr. Gosse, "that, with very few exceptions, the immense population of the ocean is carnivorous. The principal circumstance that regulates the choice of diet among fishes seems to be the power of mastery. Of terrestrial creatures, a very large number are peaceful, never, under ordinary circumstances, willingly taking the life of even the most helpless around them; but the sea is a vast slaughter-house, where nearly every inhabitant dies a violent death, and finds a grave in the maw of his fellow. Yet let us not arraign the providence of God, as if it were cruel and unkind: a sudden termination of existence is the most merciful mode, as far as we can conceive, by which the overflow of animal life could be checked."

As James Montgomery says:

> "'T was wisdom, mercy, goodness that ordain'd
> Life in such infinite profusion—Death
> So sure, so prompt, so multiform to those
> That never sinn'd, that know not guilt, that fear
> No wrath to come, and have no heaven to lose."

A very interesting family of fishes, for the peculiar properties which they possess, are the *Sucking-fishes*—remarkable for having the ventral fins united under the surface of the body to form the apparatus which distinguishes them. To this family belong the *Sea-Owl Snail*, and one or two British species, including the *Lump-sucker*.

## THE REMORA OR SUCKING-FISH.

This animal has a grotesque and clumsy form, but the colours which ornament it are very fine, combining various shades of blue, purple, and orange. It attains a tolerably large size, about nineteen inches, weighing sometimes seven or eight pounds. Its sucker is so powerful that a pail, containing some gallons of water, has been lifted, when one of these fishes contained in it was taken by the tail.

To this family Cuvier also referred the far-famed *Remora;* noticing, however, the different position of the sucking disc, and other important distinctions, on account of which a very different place is now assigned to it. The use of the sucking apparatus is, however, much the same—that of attaching the animal to fixed substances, so that it may remain and obtain its food, where otherwise it would be swept away by the current.

The remora (from the Latin *remoror*, "I delay") was the subject of much imaginative terror to the ancients, who believed that it had the power to impede or stop the course of a ship. Oppian says:

> "The seamen run confus'd, no labour spared,
> Let fly the sheets, and hoist the topmast yard;
> The master bids them give her all the sails,
> To court the winds and catch the coming gales;
> But though the canvas bellies with the blast,
> And boisterous winds bend down the cracking mast,
> The bark stands firmly rooted on the sea,
> And all unmov'd as tower or towering tree."

Pliny writes: "Why should our fleets and armadas at sea make such turrets on the walls and forecastles, when one little fish (see the vanity of man!) is able to arrest and stay, perforce, our goodly and tall ships?"

These are droll fancies; but, tested by fact, the adhesive powers of this fish are very remarkable, great weights being dragged by it, and retaining its hold with a bull-dog tenacity, even submitting to be torn to pieces before it will relinquish its hold. It is frequently seen among other fishes in the Atlantic, attaching itself to some one or other by its sucker, and often, also, to the rudder or bottom of a ship.

The length of the Mediterranean remora is about eighteen inches, and the length of the head is nearly one-fifth of the proportion of the whole fish. Feeding principally on the small animals diffused throughout the waters of the ocean, it probably receives a sufficiency of food even when attached to a moving object, as a ship or large fish, merely by opening its mouth, which has a very wide gape.

Belonging to a distinct family, but employing its mouth as a powerful sucker, is the *Sea-Lamprey*, a species resembling eels in the rounded shape of the body and a certain similarity of habits. The mouth is circular, armed with hard tooth-like processes, and provided with a flexible lip. So great is the power of suction which it possesses, that a stone has been raised by it out of the water, weighing ten or twelve pounds, and yet the fish measures but from two to three feet.

The historical renown of the lamprey is very great. It was the favourite dish of the Romans, who kept the fishes in ponds at a great expense. The best lampreys were procured from Sicily as presents to the reigning emperors and high officials. A hundred pieces of gold were sometimes paid for them.

A horrible story is told of Pollio, a friend of Augustus Cæsar, who, on the supposition that lampreys fed on human flesh were more delicate, ordered his slaves, when accused of the slightest fault, to be thrown into his fish-pond. This cruelty was discovered when one of his servants broke a glass in the presence of the Emperor, who had been invited to a feast. The master ordered the slave to be seized, but he threw himself at the feet of the Emperor, and begged him to interfere, and not suffer him to be devoured by the lampreys. On examining into the matter, the Emperor, astonished at the barbarity of his favourite, caused the fish-ponds to be filled up.

In the annals of our own country, you are, no doubt, aware that one of our English monarchs died from eating lampreys to excess:

"Henry First willed of a lampreye to ete,
But his leches [physicians] him vorbode vor yt was a feble mete."

Respecting this fish, Mr. Couch tells us there is another use to which the mouth or sucker is applied. The whole of its interior arch is studded with rows of teeth, each one of which, on a broad base, is furnished with one or two apparently reversed points, and these teeth which are most remote and concealed are larger than others, and more effectually crowded with these points. For simply biting they are useless, but when the breadth of the mouth is brought into contact with the surface of a fish on which the lamprey has laid hold, by producing a vacuum these roughly-pointed teeth are brought forward so as to be able to act on it by a circular motion; and the limited space of the captive prey is thus rasped into a pulp and swallowed, until a hole is made which may, perhaps, penetrate to the bones, and from the torture of which the most strenuous exertion of the victim cannot deliver it. This is frequent on the mackerel and on other fishes, as the gurnard, coalfish, cod, and haddock.

It was an old custom for the corporation of the city of Gloucester to present to the reigning Sovereign a pie of lampreys yearly, but this practice has long ceased.

The "Mail-Cheeked" or *Gurnard* group of fishes offer some very interesting subjects for notice, including a considerable number of species, all characterized by sharp projecting cheeks, and heads cased in armour of bony plates, among which I may mention the *Flying Gurnard*, the *Sea-Scorpion*, the *Father-lasher*, and the pugnacious little *Stickleback*, with the fresh-water species of which you are no doubt perfectly familiar.

The name "gurnard" is derived from the growling grunting noise which these fishes make, by means of the throat and gills, when taken out of the water, and which has obtained for one species the name of "piper." The Romans used to call the latter "lyres," rather, perhaps, on account of their fancied resemblance to an ancient lyre, than to the very unmusical sound they emit. Many of the gurnards are distinguished by beauty of colour: two of the most common species on our own coasts are the rose-red, about fifteen inches in length, and the grey, which is spotted with brown, black, and yellowish-white.

The *New Zealand Gurnard*, about eighteen inches in length, is a splendid fish: the upper part is brownish-red, the fins are very large and of an emerald green, broadly bordered with azure blue, and having an oval patch of velvety black beautifully relieved with snow-white spots.

The *Sea-Scorpion* differs from its land namesake, the possessor of one solitary but dangerous tail-sting, the head of the fish being surrounded with goads and prickles, which render it a formidable enemy to contend with, by swelling out its cheeks and gill-covers to a large size, realizing Ovid's description of it,—

"Scorpœna's poison'd head, beset with spines;"

excepting that the stings, beyond inflicting a smart pain, are not venomous. Some of these animals are remarkable for their ugliness, and others exhibit very fine colours. They abound in the warm seas, and are often taken on our own shores, sometimes exceeding a foot in length.

The *Marine Sticklebacks*, which are thus named from the spines which arm their back, ventral fins, and other parts, are inhabitants of the seas in cold and temperate regions, and are curious little animals, a kind of Lilliputian warriors armed at all points for warfare, protected at the sides by shell-like plates, and with spears that play terrible havoc among the crustacea and small animals on which they feed. They are objects of peculiar interest from the beauty of their colours, which they change in a remarkable manner. They are excessively pugnacious and predatory in their habits, the larger species eating the smaller, and destroying the eggs and fry of fishes to a prodigious extent. Mr. Couch relates of the fifteen-spined stickleback, about six inches in length,—sometimes called the "sea-adder,"—"that it keeps near rocks and stones clothed with sea-weeds, among which it takes refuge upon any alarm. Though less active than its brethren of the fresh water, it is scarcely less rapacious. On one occasion I noticed a specimen engaged in taking its prey from a clump of sea-weed, in doing which it assumed every posture between the horizontal and perpendicular, with the head downwards and upwards, thrusting its projecting snout into the crevices of the stems, and seizing its prey with a spring. Having taken this fish with a net, and transferred it to a vessel of water, in company with an eel three inches long, the latter was attacked and devoured head foremost; not, indeed, altogether, for the eel was too large a morsel, so that the tail remained hanging out of the mouth, and it was obliged to disgorge the eel partly digested."

A writer in "Loudon's Magazine" relates some interesting observations on the fighting propensities of these animals when confined in a tub of water:

"A few at first are turned in, and swim about in a shoal, apparently examining their new habitation. Suddenly one will take possession of a corner of a tub, or, as it will sometimes happen, of the bottom, and will instantly commence an attack on its companions; and if any of these venture to oppose its rule, a regular and most furious battle ensues. The two combatants swim round and round each other with the greatest rapidity, biting, and endeavouring to pierce each other with their spines, which on these occasions are projected. I have witnessed a battle of this sort which lasted several minutes before the other would give way; and when one does submit, imagination can hardly conceive the vindictive fury of the conqueror, who, in the most persevering and unrelenting way, chases its rival from one part of the tub to another until fairly exhausted with fatigue. They also use their spines with such fatal effect that, incredible as it may appear, I have seen one, during a battle, absolutely rip an opponent quite open, so that it sank to the bottom and died. I have known three or four parts of the tub taken possession of by as many other little tyrants, who guard their territories with the strictest vigilance, and the slightest invasion invariably brings on a battle."

It is pleasing to add for the honour of the sex that the females take no part in these ferocious proceedings; a redeeming feature in the belligerents, however, is the care which they take in building their nests, and watching over the welfare of the females and their eggs. You may not have heard of nest-building fishes, and, indeed, although the ancients were acquainted with this instinct in some fishes, it was not until 1838 that modern naturalists proved this by the discovery of a stickleback-nest by Mr. Edwards. These animals collect small pieces of straw or stick, with which the bottom of the nest is laid among water-plants, and these they cement together by a transpiration from their own bodies, which forms a thread through and round them in every conceivable direction. The thread is whitish, fine, and silken. The sides of the nest are made after the bottom.

Not many fishes are yet known as nest-builders. The *Goramy*, a native of the China seas, forms at the breeding-season a nest by interlacing the stems and leaves of aquatic grapes. Both male and female watch these nests for a month or more with great vigilance, violently driving away every other fish until the spawn is hatched. The *Gobies*, or *Sea-Gudgeons*, have similar instincts. Many, however, are known not to construct nests. *Salmon* and others exhibit an approach to the nest-building habit, in making a place for their eggs in the sand or gravel.

I must now notice the *Flying Gurnard*, remarkably distinguished from the others of the family to which it is allied by the great size of its pectoral fins, which are long enough, and their webs sufficiently broad, to sustain the fish in the air during its long flying leaps out of the water. These fins, however, are very different in appearance from those of the flying-fish (*Exocetus*, "fishes out of the water"), which belongs to another family. The flying gurnard is an inhabitant of the warm seas; one species is common in the Mediterranean, and is sometimes fifteen inches in length. Its flight is said not to extend more than about forty yards, but it sometimes rises high enough to fall on the decks of large ships. At particular times, and especially on the approach of rough weather, in the night numbers of them may be seen by the phosphoric light which they emit, making their passages in apparent streams of fire.

*Flying-fishes* have the power of raising themselves out of the water, and continuing suspended in the air until their fins become dry, by which means they escape some of their marine enemies, such as the dolphin and many others.

> "So fishes rising from the main,
> Can soar with moisten'd wings on high;
> The moisture dried, they sink again,
> And dip their wings, again to fly."

But they run the gauntlet of the long-winged sea-birds, which seize them in the air; and between themselves and their swimming and flying enemies, they furnish one of the most singular sights in the warm seas of the tropics. One species of the Exocetus (*volitans*) sometimes visits our own coasts, and are said to "leap" more than two hundred yards in distance, and upwards of twenty feet in height. Although these fishes are called "flying," their action has more resemblance to a long and vigorous leap than the flight of birds. Mr. Bennett remarks that birds have an elegant, fearless, and independent motion; while that of the fish is hurried, stiff, and awkward, more like a creature requiring support for a short period.

Moore addresses in some sweet lines the flying-fish:

"When I have seen thy snowy wing
O'er the blue wave at evening spring,
And give those scales of silvery white
So gaily to the eye of light
(As if thy frame were formed to rise
And live amid the glorious skies);
Oh! it has made me proudly feel
How like thy wings' impatient zeal
Is the pure soul that scorns to rest
Upon the world's ignoble breast,
But spreads the plume that God has given,
And rises into light and heaven.

"But when I see that wing so bright
Grow languid with a moment's flight,
Attempt the paths of air in vain,
And sink into the waves again;
Alas! the flatterer's pride is o'er:
Like that awhile the soul may soar,
But erring men must blush to think,
Like thee again the soul may sink.

"O Virtue! when thy clime I seek,
Let not my spirit's flight be weak;
Let me not, like this feeble thing,
That spreads awhile its splendid wing,
Just sparkle 'midst the solar glow,
And plunge again to depths below;

> But when I leave the grosser throng
> With whom my soul hath dwelt so long,
> Let me in that aspiring day
> Cast every lingering stain away,
> And panting for thy purer air,
> Fly up at once and fix me there."

**Very** curious are the statements regarding what have been called "musical" fish, but how far such a title is warranted is doubtful. It is known that many fishes, notwithstanding their being characterized as mute, are remarkable for giving utterance to a peculiar sound called "drumming." This is very perceptible in the famous *Maigre* of the Mediterranean, the *Umbrina* of the Romans, a fish which swims in groups, and often utters a low bellowing sound beneath the water, which is heard from a depth of one hundred and twenty feet, and is rendered stronger by placing the ear upon the gunwale of the boat.

Lieutenant White, of the American service, in his "Voyage to the China Seas," published in 1824, relates that being at the mouth of the Cambodia, his crew and himself were extremely astonished by hearing certain unaccountable sounds from beneath and around the vessel. These were various, like the bass notes of an organ, the sound of bells, the croaking of frogs, and a pervading twang which the imagination might have attributed to the vibrations of some enormous harp. For a time the mysterious music swelled upon them, and finally formed an universal chorus all around; but as the vessel ascended the river, the sounds diminished in strength, and soon altogether ceased.

Humboldt was witness to a similar fact in the South Sea, but without suspecting the cause. Towards seven in the evening the whole crew were astounded by an extraordinary noise, which resembled that of drums which were beating in the air. It was at first attributed to the breakers. Speedily it was heard in the vessel, and especially towards the poop. It was like a boiling, the noise of the air which escapes from fluid in ebullition. The sailors began to fear there was some leak in the vessel. It was heard unceasingly in all parts of the vessel, and finally, about nine o'clock, **it ceased altogether.**

It would, as Baron Cuvier has observed, form a curious matter of research to ascertain by what organs these sounds are produced at so great a depth, and without communication with the exterior air. The illustrious naturalist further remarks that such of the *Sciænidæ* (the Maigre family) as are the most remarkable for the faculty in question, have the swimming-bladder very large and thick, furnished with extremely strong muscles, and are, in several species, provided with more or less complicated prolongations, which penetrate between the intervals of the ribs. But what renders the phenomenon more unaccountable is that these swimming-bladders have no communication with the intestinal canal, nor, in general, with any part of the exterior.

The interpreter belonging to Lieutenant White's ship stated that the marine music which had so much surprised the crew was produced by fishes of a flattened oval form, and which possess the faculty of adhering to various bodies by their mouths. This fish might have been the *Pogonia*, which produces much more sound than any of the other Maigre tribe to which it belongs, on which account it is sometimes called the "drum-fish." Schœff reports of them that they will assemble round the keel of a vessel at anchor, and serenade the crew. Some of the species attain a large size, one hundred pounds or more, and are excellent for the table.

Sir James Emerson Tennant, in his account of Ceylon, states: "In the evening when the moon had risen, I took a boat and accompanied the fishermen to the spot where musical sounds were said to be heard issuing from the bottom of a lake, and which the natives supposed to proceed from some fish peculiar to the locality. I distinctly heard the sounds in question. They came up from the water like the gentle thrills of a musical chord, or the faint vibrations of a wine-glass when its rim is rubbed by a wet finger. It was not one sustained note, but a multitude of tiny sounds, each clear and distinct in itself, the sweetest treble mingling with the deepest bass. They came evidently and sensibly from the depths of the lake, and appeared to be produced by mollusca, and not by fish."

Sounds somewhat similar are heard under water at some places on the western coast of India, especially in the harbour of Bombay.

At Caldera, in Chili, musical cadences are said to issue from the sea near the landing-place: they are described as rising and falling fully four notes, resembling the tones of harp-strings, and mingling, like those at Batticuloa, until they produce musical sounds of great delicacy and sweetness. The animals from which they proceed have not been identified at either place, and the mystery remains unsolved.

> "And a music wild and slow,
>   Ever o'er the curved shells
> Wanders with a fitful flow,
>   As the billow sinks or swells;
> Now to faintest whispers hushing,
> Now in louder cadence gushing,
>   Waken from their pleasant sleep
> All the tuneful Nereid throng,
> Till their notes of wreathéd song
> Float in magic streams along,
>   Chaunting joyaunce through the deep."

Among the foremost of "queer" fish I may mention the *Sea-Devil*, a most inharmonious name, but which seems to have been given to it on account of its hideous, strange, and uncouth appearance. A species of this extraordinary fish of the Skate family frequents Kingston harbour in Jamaca, where they are seen floating on the surface, or swimming just beneath the water. In the eleventh volume of the "Edinburgh Philosophical Journal" is an account by Lieutenant Lamont, of the Ninety-first Regiment, of the escape of a devil-fish and the capture of another at Port Royal. The lieutenant had been called to the beach by seeing a multitude assembled to look at one of these fishes floating past. His curiosity turned to surprise when he saw, flapping on the water, about twenty yards from the shore, a large dark-coloured mass, whose shape and size he could not immediately determine, but which seemed prodigiously big beyond anything he could conceive, since it so much exceeded all he had ever seen or heard of fishes. The boats were started off to pursue it, and it was harpooned, but no sooner was the monster struck than it made off with amazing velocity, towing the boat of the harpooner after him. A succession of boats now came up. These strung themselves on to the harpooner one after another, striking each a harpoon as the boats came up. They consecutively formed a long line, but such was the force of this fish that all the boats were drawn out ten miles to sea. Night was drawing on. To bring the chase to a close, another harpoon was struck into the monster, when it made one convulsive effort to get away, and broke loose, carrying away eight or ten harpoons and pikes, leaving every one astonished at the success of its escape.

Another devil-fish was not so fortunate, and Lieutenant Lamont gives the history of its capture within the harbour, which the animal traversed up and down, dragging with such velocity the boat from which it had been struck, that the other boats following could not overtake the fish. Its struggles were tremendous, plunging into the midst of the boats that at length surrounded it, darting from the surface to the bottom of the water, and then rising swiftly, dashing the foam about on every side, and rolling round and round to extricate itself from the poles and lines. Unable to get away, it swam off, towing all the boats after it, and then laid itself at the bottom of the water. From this position the stretch and strain of all the boats' crews could not move it. Slackening their efforts gradually, the monster rose again to the surface, when a shower of musket-balls and pikes riddled it through. Until this capture was effected, it was believed that a sea-devil was beyond the might of human art and strength. The dimensions of this fish were not more than half that of the common size, being only fifteen feet in width. A man, however, entered the mouth with ease, the space being two feet and a half. The weight of the fish was so great, that, with difficulty, forty men with two lines attached to it dragged it along the ground.

A devil-fish taken at Barbadoes required seven yoke of oxen to draw it.

In the account of the fish taken in Delaware Bay (remarks the Hon. Richard Hill in an interesting article on the subject of the devil-fish in the "Intellectual Observer," to which I am indebted for the present notice of this curious creature), it is stated that drawing a boat after it with the celerity of a whale when harpooned, it caused a wave to be raised on each side the trough of the sea, several feet higher than the boat; that during the scuffle the vast fins of the fish lashed the sea with such vehemence that the spray rose to the height of thirty feet, and rained dropping water around, to the distance of fifty feet, and yet the measurement of this fish was only half of those generally seen, being only eighteen feet in breath. Three pairs of oxen, one horse, and twenty-two men, all pulling together, with the surges of the Atlantic to help, could barely convey the monster to the dry beach.

The monstrous skate said by Père Labat to have been observed by the natives of Guadaloupe, and described as fourteen feet broad, and ten feet from the head to the commencement of the tail, with the tail fifteen feet more, altogether twenty-five feet long, was no doubt a kindred species of the devil-fish; and the monster spoken of by the early voyagers as suffocating the pearl-divers in the water, and known by the name of *Manta*, was a similar animal.

Surprising stories are related of these fishes. Le Vaillant speaks of three that he saw in the Atlantic—one so large that it seemed fifty or sixty feet wide; they all three carried each on his horns a white fish about half a yard long, which appeared to be stationed there on duty as sentinels, to keep watch for the safety of the "devils," and to guide their movements: that these sentinels passed over their backs when they rose too high, and repassed under them until they descended deeper, disappearing and being seen no more for a time, but reappearing and resuming their post as sentinels when the fish again ascended to the surface.

Among other "queer" fish, I may mention the *Fishing Frog*, or *Angler*, belonging to the "Wristed" family (so named from the prolongation of the wrist-bones, forming a kind of arm, supporting the pectoral fin on a kind of hand), and one of the most extraordinary and repulsive-looking animals that inhabit the deep.

"Let the reader imagine," says Mr. Badham, "a gigantic tadpole blown out to the size of a porpoise (sometimes, indeed, much larger, for Pontoppidan mentions one of twelve feet long, and several writers describe individuals of seven feet and upwards), with an immense head, and a mouth extending on either side far beyond the width of the body, opening to view a capacious den, ragged throughout with hooked and mobile teeth, a triple tier in the upper, and an equal number in the lower jaw, the palate, tongue, fauces, pharynx, and far down the throat, glistening with a like display of ivory fangs; unfishy orbs resembling those of the "stargazer" (the "priest-fish," so named from the whites of its eyes looking constantly heavenward), planted high in the forehead; a scaleless skin, which is reeking, cold, and clammy; its surface, from near the tail to the corners of the mouth, as crawling with long wriggling carunculated (fleshy) appendages, like so many worms in agony; the flesh "boggy" to the touch, save where it is padded out with an enormously distended liver, or just over the branchial (apertures for the passage of water from the gills) cavity; a pantry constantly replenished with provisions; add to all these a large pair of Caliban-hand-like fins, planted close under the throat; a fierce malevolent aspect, and an ungainly mode of wallowing, rather than swimming, through the brine, and it will be apparent, even from this very imperfect sketch, that such a fish scarecrow could not fail to arrest attention, even had there been no other claim to regard than his portentous ugliness."

Such is an admirable description of this marine monster. Of its boldness and voracity many anecdotes are related. A fisherman had hooked a cod-fish, and whilst drawing it up he felt a heavier weight attach itself to his line. This proved to be a frog-fish of a large size, which he compelled to quit its hold by a heavy blow on the head, leaving its prey still attached to the hook. In another instance one of these fishes had seized a conger eel which had taken the hook; but after the latter had been engulfed in the enormous jaws, and perhaps in the stomach, it struggled through the gill-aperture of its captor, and in that situation both were drawn up together.

"I have been told," says Mr. Couch, "of its swallowing a large ball of cork employed as a buoy to a bulter or deep-sea line. These fishes sometimes abound, and a fisherman who informed me of the circumstance noticed seven of them at one time on the deck of a trawl-boat."

It has also been stated that when this fish is captured in a net, its rapacious appetite is not in the least diminished, but it generally devours some of its fellow-prisoners.

The sea-frog, as it can live longer out of water than most other fish, is said to pass some of its time on shore. The naturalist, Rondolet, tells a curious story of one being found on land holding a fox fast by the leg. The cunning quadruped, outreached for once by a fish, had put his foot into the mouth of the sea-frog, who, instantly closing upon it, held it fast as in a trap till next morning, when Rondolet surprised them in this strange position.

The name of "angler" given to this singular fish is derived from its habit of crouching close to the ground, and stirring up with its fins the sand or mud. In the obscurity thus produced the animal moves its appendages, tentacles or feelers, in various directions, by way of attracting as a bait; and the small fishes approaching to examine or seize them are soon conveyed to the capacious jaws of the angler. Nature has added to this provision for obtaining food, inasmuch as a filament shooting up close to the upper lip of the fish carries upon its extremity a little membrane or flag, of brilliant metallic lustre, which, it is supposed, the angler uses as a means of alluring its prey ; and the relative position of the flag, the eye, and the mouth favour such a purpose. The upper part of the body is brown, inclining to dusky, and the lower parts are white. The sea-frog is common in the Northern Ocean and the Mediterranean ; it is also taken sometimes on the British coasts.

In the chapter on the "Monarchs of the Ocean," I have alluded to the *Saw-fish* and the *Sword-fish* as formidable enemies to the whale; but it is not merely on their fellow-inhabitants of the deep that these powerful fishes exercise their aggressive propensities. Some singular instances are related of their attacking even the "wooden walls" that glide tranquilly through their watery domain.

Captain Wilson, of the Halifax packet, states:

"Being in the Gulf of Paria, in the ship's cutter, I fell in with a Spanish canoe, manned by two men, then in great distress, who requested me to save their lines and canoe, with which request I immediately complied, and going alongside for that purpose I dis-

*Lewis Foster*

covered that they had got a large saw-fish entangled in their turtle-net, which was towing them out to sea, and but for my assistance they must have lost either their canoe or their net, or perhaps both, which were their only means of subsistence. Having only two boys with me at the time in the boat, I desired them to cut the fish away, which they refused to do. I then took the bight of the net from them, and with the joint endeavours of themselves and my boat's crew, we succeeded in hauling up the net, and to our astonishment, after great exertions, we raised the "saw" of the fish about eight feet above the surface of the sea. It was a fortunate circumstance that the fish came up with the belly towards the boat, or it would have cut the boat in two.

"I had abandoned all idea of taking the fish, until, by great good luck, it made towards the land, when I made another attempt, and having about three hundred feet of rope in the boat, we succeeded in making a running bowline-knot round the saw of the fish, and this we fortunately made fast on shore. When the fish found itself secured, it plunged so violently that I could not prevail on any one to go near it; the appearance it presented was truly awful. I immediately went alongside the Lima packet, Captain Singleton, and got the assistance of all his ship's crew. By the time they arrived the fish was less violent. We hauled upon the net again, in which it was still entangled, and got another three hundred feet of line made fast to the saw, and attempted to haul it towards the shore; but although mustering *thirty hands*, we could not move it an inch. By this time the negroes belonging to Mr. Danglad's estate came flocking to our assistance, making together about one hundred in number, with the Spaniards. We then hauled on both ropes for nearly the day, before the fish became exhausted. On endeavouring to raise the fish it became most desperate, sweeping with its sword from side to side, so that we were compelled to get strong ropes to prevent it from cutting us to pieces. After that, one of the Spaniards got on its back, and at great risk cut through the joint of the tail, when animation was completely suspended. It was then measured, and found to be twenty-two feet long and eight feet broad, and weighed nearly five tons."

An East Indiaman was attacked by a sword-fish with such prodigious force as to drive its "snout" completely through the bottom of the ship, and must have been destroyed by the leak had not the animal been killed by the violence of its own exertions, and the sword remaining embedded in the wood. A fragment of this vessel, with the sword fixed firmly in it, is preserved as a curiosity in the British Museum.

Several instances of a similar character have occurred, and one formed the subject of an action in the courts of law so recently as 1868, brought against an insurance company for damages sustained by a vessel from the attack of one of these fishes. It seems the "Dreadnought," a first-class mercantile ship, left a foreign port in perfect repair, and on the afternoon of the third day a "monstrous creature" was seen sporting among the waves, and lines and hooks were thrown overboard to capture it. All efforts to this effect, however, failed: the fish got away, and in the night-time the vessel was reported to be dangerously leaking. The captain was compelled to return to the harbour he had left, and the damage was attributed to a sword-fish, twelve feet long, which had assailed the ship below water-line, perforated her planks and timbers, and thus imperilled her existence on the ocean.

Professor Owen, the distinguished naturalist, was called to give evidence on this trial as to the probability of such an occurrence, and he related several instances of the prodigious strength of the "sword." It strikes with the accumulated force of fifteen double-handed hammers; its velocity is equal to that of a swivel shot, and it is as dangerous in its effects as a heavy artillery projectile would be.

Oppian describes the sword-fish when attacked:

> "He summons to his instant aid
> The oft-tried prowess of his trusty blade;
> Selects some boat, and runs his puissant sword
> Full many an inch within the fatal board."

## CHAPTER XXVI.

### *BEAUTIFUL FISHES.*

"Shoals
Of fish that with their fins and shining scales
Glide under the green wave, in sculls that oft
Bank the mid-sea;
Or, sporting with quick glance,
Show to the sun their waved coats dropped with gold."

IN remarking upon beautiful fishes, it would be quite out of the limits of a small publication like the present to attempt more than a bare mention of a few species of the ocean inhabitants which possess, in a special degree, the attributes to which this term may be applied. Among the most prominent of beautiful fishes is the *Dolphin*, which, however, belongs to an extensive family, including the porpoise, grampus, &c., and animals which, on account of their large size, are commonly called whales. The Atlantic species of the dolphin (the *Exquisitis* of Linnæus) exhibits the general form of these fishes, and their colouring, so remarkable for the variation of its tints; a play of vivid green and gold and silver being spread over it in various lights, and changing as it dies.

"Parting day
Dies like the dolphin, whom each pang embues
With a new colour as it gasps away,
The last still loveliest till 't is gone—and all is grey."

Falconer, in the "Shipwreck," thus describes the death of the dolphin after it has been struck by the harpooner:

> "On deck he struggles with convulsive pain;
> But while his heart the fatal javelin thrills,
> And fleeting life escapes in sanguin'd rills,
> What radiant changes strike th' astonished sight
> With glowing hues of mingled shade and light!
> No equal beauties gild the lucid West,
> With parting beams o'er all profusely drest;
> No lovelier colours paint the vernal dawn,
> When Orient dews impearl th' enamelled lawn,
> Than from his sides in bright suffusion flow,
> That now with gold empyreal seem to glow,
> Now in pellucid sapphires meet the view,
> And emulate the soft celestial hue,
> Now beam a flaming crimson to the eye,
> And now assume the purple's deeper dye.
> But here description clouds each shining ray:
> What terms of art can Nature's power display?"

There are, however, many other fish that change colour before they die. "I have seen," remarks Mr. Adams, "species of the cat-fish change from a warm and glowing smalt during the last pangs to a dull leaden hue, losing at the same time the delicate pinky tinge of the sides and abdomen. The common sucking-fish, from a brown, bright, shining, blackish colour, changes even in the water to a leaden hue, and as it dies assumes a tan-colour, which grows paler by degrees and turns to a dingy white."

When swimming near the surface of the water, and glittering beneath the light of a cloudless sky, the dolphins appear clothed in the richest gold, and to have the starry lustre of the topaz and sapphire. Two species have been named, from the variety and vividness of their tints, the "sea-peacock" and the "blue-fish."

The true dolphin has the snout prolonged into a rather slender beak, whence the French have applied to it the name of "the goose of the sea." It was very differently regarded and designated by the ancients, who looked upon it as a sacred fish, and dedicated it to Apollo, who was worshipped at Delphi with dolphins for his symbols. The name is given to one of the fairest provinces of France—Dauphiny, from which the heir-apparent of the throne formerly derived his title of "Dauphin."

Wondrously beautiful, indeed, are these gay inhabitants of the seas, especially when seen playing and springing from the water, when they assume the curved shape that is not natural to them, but which old painters and sculptors have always given them:

> "Upon the swelling waves the dolphins show
> Their bending backs, then swiftly darting go,
> And in a thousand wreaths their bodies throw."

They are, however, very voracious animals, and are said to prey not only on other fishes, but their own species. The flying-fish in particular comes in for a share of their pursuit. Captain Basil Hall gives a vivid description of their operations:

"Shortly after observing a cluster of flying-fish rise out of the water, we discovered two or three dolphins ranging past the ship in all their beauty, and watched with some anxiety to see one of those aquatic chases of which our friends, the Indiamen, had been telling such wonderful stories. We had not long to wait, for the ship, in her progress through the water, soon put up another shoal of these little things, which, as the others had done, took their flight directly to windward. A large dolphin, which had been keeping company with us abreast of the weather gangway, at the depth of two or three fathoms, and, as usual, glistening most beautifully in the sun, no sooner detected our poor dear little friends take wing than he turned his head towards them and, darting to the surface, leaped from the water with a velocity little short, as it seemed, of a cannon-ball. But, although the impetus with which he shot himself into the air gave him an initial velocity greatly exceeding that of the flying-fish, the start which his fated prey had got enabled them to keep ahead of him for a considerable time.

"The length of the dolphin's first spring could not be less than ten yards, and after he fell we could see him gliding like lightning through the water for a moment, when he again rose and shot forwards with considerably greater velocity than at first, and, of course, to a still greater distance. In this manner the merciless pursuer seemed to stride along with fearful rapidity, while his brilliant coat sparkled and flashed in the sun quite splendidly. As he fell headlong on the water at the end of each huge leap, a series of circles were sent far over the the still surface, which lay as smooth as a mirror.

"The group of wretched flying-fish, thus hotly pursued, at length dropped into the sea; but we were rejoiced to observe that they merely touched the top of the swell, and scarcely sank in it; at least, they instantly set off again in a fresh and more vigorous flight. It was particularly interesting to observe that the direction they now took was quite different from the one in which they had set out, implying but too obviously that they had detected their fierce enemy, who was following them with giant steps on the waves, and now gaining rapidly upon them. His terrific pace was, indeed, two or three times as swift as theirs, poor little things!

"The greedy dolphin, however, was fully as quick-sighted as the flying-fish which were trying to elude him, for whenever they varied their flight in the smallest degree, he lost not the tenth part of a second in shaping a new course, so as to cut off the chase; whilst they, in a manner really not unlike that of the hare, doubled more than once on their pursuer. But it was soon too plainly to be seen that the strength and confidence of the flying-fish were fast ebbing. Their flights became shorter and shorter, and their course more fluttering and uncertain, while the enormous leaps of the dolphin appeared to grow more vigorous at each bound. Eventually, indeed, we could see, or fancied that we could see, that this skilful sea-sportsman arranged all his springs with such an assurance of success that he contrived to fall at the end of each just under the very spot on which the exhausted flying-fish were about to drop. Sometimes this catastrophe took place at too great a distance for us to see from the deck exactly what happened; but on our mounting high into the rigging, we may be said to have been in at the death, for then we could discover that the unfortunate little creatures, one after another, either popped right into the dolphin's jaws as they lighted on the water, or were snapped up instantly afterwards.

"It was impossible not to take an active part with our pretty little friends of the weaker side, and accordingly we very speedily had our revenge. The middies and the sailors, delighted with the chance, rigged out a dozen or twenty lines from the jibboom-end and spritsail-yard-arms, with hooks baited merely with bits of tin, the glitter of which blesso resem much that of the body and wings of the flying-fish that many a proud dolphin, making sure of a delicious morsel, leaped in rapture at the glittering prize."

The dolphin, however, in turn becomes the prey of other fishes, and especially of the *Fox-Shark*, or *Sea-Fox* as it is sometimes called, a genus of sharks containing only one known species, belonging to the Mediterranean Sea and the Atlantic, and occasionally seen on our own coasts. This powerful fish attains a length of thirteen feet, including the tail-fin, which is remarkably long, nearly half the dimensions of the animal, and which, as a weapon of offence, is very formidable. The furious lashing of this appendage has obtained for this fish the popular name of "thresher." A whole herd of dolphins will take flight at the first splash of this tail, and even the grampus, the largest of the dolphin family, and, it is said, a formidable adversary of the whale, comes off badly in an encounter with the fox-shark.

Some species of the family of Sea-Breams are remarkable for their great beauty. The *Spanish* is very abundant in the Mediterranean, and is sometimes seen on our own coasts. It attains the length of about fourteen inches. Its colours, when first taken out of the water, are most splendid, being a beautiful red carmine-colour on the back, passing to rose-colour on the sides, with a silver tinting on the abdomen, and the fins are rose-coloured. These lovely hues soon disappear after death, and a sombre yellow prevails.

Nearly allied to this family are the *Gilt-heads* (so named from a half-moon-shaped golden spot between the eyes), inhabitants of the warm seas, and very beautiful in colours; the back being a deep blackish-blue, the sides yellowish, with golden tints; violet and gold being the prevailing decorations.

The numerous and interesting Mackerel family include many species remarkable for rich colouring. The common *Mackerel* itself, which is described in the chapter on "Methods of Fishing," is, as you are aware, a very beautiful fish, with its brilliant blue and green tints, besides its elegant form. The *Dory*, or *John Dory* as it is popularly called, is said to derive its name from the golden tint that prevails over it when taken from the water; *jaune*, in

French being "yellow," and *doré*, "golden." Along the shores of the Mediterranean, where this fish abounds, it is called among other names "St. Peter's Fish," from a legend that the apostle obtained from it the coin to pay the tribute money, and that the impression of his two fingers marks the species to the present day; a distinction, however, which is claimed also for the haddock. The dory is very common on some parts of our coasts. The prevailing colour of the body (which is oval) is an olive-brown tinged with yellow, reflecting in different lights blue, gold, and white. When the fish is taken, the varying tints of these different colours pass in rapid succession over the body. Though flat in form, the fish swims erect, and both surfaces being thus equally exposed to the light, are alike of a coppery hue.

The *Boar-fish*, a relative of the dory, is of inferior pretensions as regards shape and colour, the mouth having some resemblance to the snout of a hog, which doubtless originated the name. The eyes are very large and prominent, and the body of a pale carmine-colour, with orange bands on the back.

But the glory of the Mackerel family, at least, for splendour of appearance, is the *Opah*, or *King-fish*, an inhabitant of the seas of high northern latitudes, and occasionally found on the British coasts, sometimes five feet long and one hundred and fifty pounds in weight. The colours are, indeed, magnificent. The whole back is of a steel blue, which, on the flanks, becomes rich green, reflecting in different lights purple and gold, and a lovely rose-colour on the abdomen. Numerous oval spots, some milk-white, others of a beautiful silvery lustre, adorn this groundwork, while small ones ornament the head. The gill-covers are very brilliant, and the iris of its large eye is of a beautiful golden colour: all the fins are vermilion.

Among marine members of the Perch family, I may mention the *Red Mullet* as very beautiful in its delicate rose-colour, striped with yellow; which colours, however, soon fade after death.

"On fish a different fate attends, nor reach they long the shore
Ere fade their hues like rainbow tints, and soon their beauty's o'er."

It was one of these mullets which was so celebrated among the

Romans for the excellency of its flesh, its great beauty, and the extravagant prices it brought. In the days of Horace this fish was valued in proportion to its size, not because the larger were better, but (as happens in the fashionable world frequently in our own time) because they were procured with greater difficulty. Enormous sums were paid for these fishes. Juvenal tells us,

"The lavish
Six thousand pieces for a mullet gave,
A sesterce for each pound,"

amounting altogether to a sum of nearly fifty pounds of our money, whilst, according to Pliny, a consul named Asinius Celer gave a sum equal to nearly sixty-five pounds of our English currency for a single fish of this kind; an infatuation we can only feel paralleled by the "tulip mania" of former days. Neither did the extravagance of these people end even here, for Seneca informs us they were so exceedingly fastidious about the freshness of this fish that, according to the luxurious habits of those days, rich epicures kept aquariums in their dining-rooms, so that the fish could be taken out alive under the table: one reason, besides the freshness of the fish, being, that the guests might see them change their colours when they were dying. In these feasts they revelled over the expiring mullet, while the bright red colour of health passed through various shades of purple, violet, blue, and white, as life gradually ebbed and convulsions put an end to the revolting spectacle. They also put these devoted fishes into crystal vessels filled with water, over a slow fire upon their tables, a refinement of cruelty which required an "imperial" Humane Society to see after.

The *Basse* or *Sea-Perch* is an elegant fish, with chaste and pleasing colours, the upper parts grey with bluish tints shading into silvery white; tolerably common on the coasts of the south of England during the summer. The armed *Enoplessus*, another member of the Perch family, very abundant in the New Holland seas, is remarkable for its chaste colouring, the ground-shade being of a silvery grey, relieved by eight narrow black bands, which either entirely or in part surround the body. The fins have a yellowish tint. It is about eight or ten inches in length. The *Two-banded*

*Diploprion*, an inhabitant of the coast of Java, also claims the same relationship: the colours are a fine reddish-yellow, relieved by two crossing bands of black; length of the fish about six inches. Another genus is the Mediterranean *Apogon*, about the same length as the last-named fish, but of far more brilliant colours. The prevailing hue is a crimson red, paler on the lower parts, with three deep black markings. The whole surface of the body is covered over with small black spots or dots.

To the same extensive family belong the *Lettered Seranus*, a beautifully-marked fish, found on the coasts of the Mediterranean. The general ground-tint of the skin is a reddish-orange, sometimes inclining to olive, and shading to a pale tint on the lower parts. The back is banded, as in the perch, with dull brown bands, but the most showy marks are the narrow irregular lines of rich blue which run on the nose below the eyes and on the cheeks, which assume the form of written characters (hence the name "lettered"). The ground-colour of the fins is grey, spotted sometimes with reddish-orange, and sometimes with purple. The *Spined Seranus*, belonging also to the warm seas, is of a brilliant red or scarlet, which on the sides assumes a golden tint, and on the belly becomes pale or almost silvery. Upon the sides of the head are three bands of golden yellow, and on the forehead are bands of bronzed green: the fins are tinted with red and yellow. This fish in length is generally from five to seven inches.

The *Beautiful Plectropoma*, also of the Perch family, merits its name from the lovely colours it exhibits. This fish inhabits the tropical seas, and some species are unusually lovely. The ground-tint of the body is olive, crossed by six bands of olive black. A line of blue surrounds the orbit; the fins are tinted with olive and yellow, the pectorals sometimes with a delicate rose-colour. This fish is about four or five inches in length. A formidable rival in point of beauty, however, is the *One-spotted Mesoprion*, of the same family, a native of the American seas, and as remarkable for the elegance of its form (length about fourteen inches) as the richness and lustre of the colouring. The back, upper part of the head, and cheeks are of a rich steel blue, the lower part of the cheeks and

# CURIOUS INSTINCT OF THE ARCHER-FISHES. 345

sides of a rich rose-colour, and the belly silvery; the whole body is striped with seven or eight bands of a golden colour. The dorsal fin has three yellow bands on a rose-coloured ground, and the others are gamboge yellow. The colouring is subject to a considerable variety in tint, from golden orange to silvery. The *Golden-tailed Mesoprion* is of similar richness.

What is called the "Scaly-finned" family of fishes is a large one, containing about one hundred and fifty species, most of which, however, frequent the Indian and Polynesian seas, and are conspicuous for their splendid colouring. It has been observed that if the "feathered" tribes of the warm regions are bedecked with the most brilliant and gorgeous hues, the neighbouring oceans contain myriads of the finny race which in this respect excel them. Upon the first of the three groups of this family especially, Nature has most profusely lavished these splendid ornaments. The purple of the iris, the richness of the rose, the azure blue of the sky, the darkest velvet black, and many other hues are seen commingled with metallic lustre over the pearly surface of the resplendent group, which, habitually frequenting the rocky shores at no great depth of water, are seen to sport in the sunbeams as if to exhibit to advantage their gorgeous dress.

In the chapter on "Submarine Scenery" I have described the *Chætodon* (from the Greek *cheô*, "I contain," and *odontus*, "a tooth,") one of the most beautiful of this family of fishes. Another animal ranged with the "scaly-fins" is the *Archer*, a fish about six or eight inches in length, which, when it perceives a fly or other winged insect hovering over the surface or settled on a twig, propels against it with considerable force a drop of liquid from its mouth, so as to drive it into the water; in attacking an insect at rest, it usually approaches cautiously, and very deliberately takes its aim. It is said to be an amusement with the Chinese in Java to keep this fish in confinement in a large vessel of water, in order that they may witness its dexterity. They fasten a fly or other insect to the side of the vessel, when the fish aims at it with such precision that it rarely misses its mark. This Javanese fish is called the *Chelmon rostratus*. Another genus—the *Toxotus jaculata*—

shoots its watery deluge to the height of three or four feet, and strikes with unerring aim the insect attacked.

"The family of the 'Riband-shaped Fish' includes," says Mr. Swainson, "the most singular and extraordinary fishes in creation. The form of the body when compared to fishes better known is much like that of the eel, the length being in the same proportion as the breadth; but then it is so much compressed that these creatures have obtained the popular name of 'riband-fish,' 'lath' or 'deal-fish.' The body, indeed, is often not thicker, except in its middle, than is a sword; and being covered with the richest silver, and of great length, the undulating motion of these fishes in the sea must be resplendent and beautiful beyond measure. But these wonders of the mighty deep are almost hidden from the eye of man. These meteoric fishes appear to live in the greatest depths, and it is only at long intervals and after a succession of tempests that a solitary individual is cast on the shore, with its delicate body torn and mutilated by the elements on the rocks."

According to this authority, the Mediterranean has hitherto produced the largest proportion of this small family; but it is distributed from the Arctic regions to the sunny shores of India. The *Onion-fish*, whose body peels into flakes like that bulb, the delicate soft *Banner-fish*, and the beautiful *Scabbard-fish*, all belong to this family. The length of the latter splendid species is sometimes not less than five feet. We may conceive a large and broad riband of silver swimming with undulatory motion through the water, and in its progress shedding the most beautiful shining reflections. The iris is the colour of silver, and the fins are transparent or yellowish-grey.

The Goby family include some very beautiful fishes. The *Gemmous Dragonet*, so named from the brilliance of its colours, is one of the finest of its species. The prevailing hue is orange; the back and cheeks have bright lilac spots, bordered with violet; the dorsal fins are orange, beautifully striped, and spotted with lilac, violet, and black. This fish is about a foot in length, and is not an unfrequent visitor to our coasts.

The *Ocellated Blenny*, or *Butterfly-fish*, belonging to a section of the Goby family, is remarkable for the singular appearance of its ornamented dorsal fin. It attains the length of six inches, and abounds in the Mediterranean. The general colour is pale brown, with patches of reddish-brown; the spot on the dorsal fin is of a dark red-brown colour, with a slight indication of light brown around it.

The family of the "Wrasses," or "Old Wives of the Sea"—as they are commonly called—include some very beautiful species, and are distinguished by their elegant, regular, and oval form. The *Rainbow* is remarkable for the beauty of its colouring, as the name would imply: it is the ornament of the markets on the coasts of the Mediterranean, for the various colours of the fish do not yield in their brilliancy and beauty to the most lovely fishes of tropical seas. The summit of the head and back is of a rich brown, mixed with blue and red; beneath this brilliant tint there is a broad band, with a denticulated margin of orange red; below this band, and at the origin of the gill-ray, the middle portion of the side is coloured by a deep blue band. This marking extends to near the tail in a band of ultramarine blue. An ultramarine streak of the loveliest hue arises at the angle of the mouth, crosses the cheek, and is prolonged in fainter hues along the inferior border of the deep blue marking of the side. The dorsal fin is of an olive-colour, mixed with red, having the margin light blue.

These beautiful fishes frequent rocky shores which are covered with marine vegetation.

The *Parrot-fish* belongs to this numerous family, deriving its name partly from a fancied resemblance in their jaws to a parrot's bill. These fishes are remarkable for their brilliant colours, some of them being of wonderful splendour. One species, found in the Mediterranean, is supposed to be the famous *Scarus* of the ancients, of whose *ruminating* powers extraordinary accounts have been related. Oppian speaks of the scarus as frequenting rocks covered with sea-weed, and assigns to it the possession of a voice:

> " Here scarus dwells, the only kind that dare
> To form shrill sounds, and strike the trembling air,
> To pensive silence doom'd, no other fish

> Can speak his wants or tell his secret wish.
> Thrice o'er their food the wanton scarus eat,
> With pleasure the luxurious toil repeat;
> Like sheep on grassy meads, or fatt'ning kine,
> They chew the cud, and on the taste refine."

It is well known that some fishes possess a power identical with rumination: carp, tench, and bream afford the best evidence of this action. The *Goldsinny*, another member of the Wrasse family, a fish from four to seven inches, is strikingly beautiful, being of a rich pink or rose-colour, intermixed on the sides with golden yellow, with darker transverse bands on the back; the fins rosy pink mixed with yellow.

Another finny brilliant is the *Wrasse Rock-fish*, in form something like a perch, with the back more straight: the colours are generally very vivid, especially those of tropical seas. The *Ballan Wrasse* is common on the rocky coasts of our country, and attains a length of about eighteen inches. It is bluish-green, and all the scales margined, more or less broadly, with orange red.

"Nature," observes a French naturalist, "has not conferred upon the fishes of this family either strength or power, but they have received as their share of her favours, agreeable proportions, great activity of fin, and are adorned with all the colours of the rainbow."

The family of the "Pipe-mouthed fishes" (characterized, as the name implies, by a tubular muzzle) has an attractive representative in the *Trumpet-fish*, or *Sea-Snipe*, a remarkable-looking fish, not uncommon in the Mediterranean, but a rare visitor on our coasts. The colour of the back is red, that of the sides being rather lighter; the sides of the head are of a silvery hue, tinged with a golden colour; all the fins are greyish-white. The young are seen near the shore in autumn, shining with a brilliant silvery lustre, not having as yet acquired the golden-red hue of the adult fish. The sea-snipe is small, not extending beyond a few inches.

To this same family (the pipe-fishes) belongs the *Hippocampus*, or *Sea-horse*, which is, perhaps, more remarkable for the singularity of its form—the upper parts having some resemblance to the head and neck of a horse in miniature (hence its name, from the Greek *ippos*, a "horse," and *kampe*, "crookedness")—than for any ornament or colour, although these are not wanting. The singularity of this fish is in the shape and disposition of the plates on the tail, which are such as to admit of its being easily curved inwards, and by the aid of which the animal twists itself around the stems of marine plants, waiting in that position with its head free, ready to dart at any passing object which it desires to make its prey.

For beauty of colouring, irrespective of shape and other repulsive peculiarities, I may mention the *Chimæra*, or *Rabbit-fish*, an animal little known, as it frequents the deep recesses of the ocean, and is only an occasional visitant of our coasts. In Norway, however, it is more common, and receives the name of "gold and silver fish," from the resplendent colours which form the ground of the body, set off by dark spots. It is also called by the Norwegians the "sea-rat," from the form of the tail, and "king-fish," from a thready filament, terminating in a tuft, which is found on the head of the male. The colours are very beautiful: the upper parts dark brown, varied with yellowish-brown and silvery; the lower parts bright silver; the eyes large, green, and brilliantly lustrous, so much so, that the Mediterranean fishermen called this fish the "cat." The form of the fish does not correspond with the vivid colours I have mentioned, the repulsive shape of the head, and the rat-like tail, giving it an appearance somewhat allied to sea-monsters.

In concluding these brief notices of a few out of the multitude of beautiful fishes which give a charm and loveliness to the element in which they live, I would have you remember that these works of a beneficent Creator are intended to raise our thoughts in reverent admiration to that Holy Being, who made all things for our comfort and delight:

> "Beauty was lent to nature as the type
> Of heaven's unspeakable and holy joy,
> Where all perfection makes the sum of bliss."

"The inhabitant of the waters, generally speaking, knows no attachments, has no language, no affections; feelings of conjugality or paternity are not acknowledged by him; ignorant of the art of constructing an asylum, in danger he seeks shelter beneath the rocks or in the darkness of the deep; his life is silent and monotonous. The cravings of voracity alone influence his instinct sufficiently to teach him some kind of obedience in his movements to external signs. Although so small a share of enjoyment and intelligence is their lot, fish are, nevertheless, adorned by the hand of Nature with every kind of beauty: variety in their forms, elegance in their proportions, diversity and vivacity in their colours— *nothing is wanted to attract the attention of man, and indeed it seems as if that attention was the principal object Nature wished to excite.* The splendour of every metal, the blaze of every gem, glitter on their surface; iridescent colours, breaking and reflecting in bands, in spots, in angles, or in undulating lines, always regular, symmetrical, graduating or contrasting, but always with admirable effect and harmony, flashing over their sides: for whom else have they received such gifts, they who at most can barely perceive each other in the twilight of the deep; and if they could see distinctly, what species of pleasure could they receive from such combinations?"

## CHAPTER XXVII.

### TREASURES RECOVERED FROM THE OCEAN.

> "What wealth untold
> Far down, and shining through their stillness, lies!
> Thou hast the starry gems, the burning gold,
> Won from ten thousand royal argosies!"
>
> HEMANS.

WHAT an immense mass of treasures have been sunk during various ages in the depths of the ocean! Year after year the loss of richly-freighted vessels have added to the prodigious stores of buried wealth, and it would be impossible to calculate in any degree the riches which have been thus lost to the world.

Shakspere, in describing the dream of the hapless Duke of Clarence, a prisoner in the Tower, thus alludes to these submarine spoils:

> "Methought I saw a thousand fearful wrecks,
> A thousand men that fishes gnaw'd upon,
> Wedges of gold, great anchors, heaps of pearl,
> Inestimable stores, unvalued jewels,
> All scatter'd in the bottom of the sea.
> Some lay in dead men's skulls; and in those holes
> Where eyes did once inhabit, there were crept
> (As if in scorn of eyes) reflecting gems,
> That woo'd the slimy bottom of the deep,
> And mocked the dead bones that lay scatter'd by."

During the recent wars of our country, the navies of the Continental powers, Spain, France, and Denmark, were almost annihilated, and our own losses amounted to an enormous sum, a large number of stately vessels being battered to pieces and consigned to the bottom of the deep.

"In every one of these ships," observes Sir Charles Lyell, "were batteries of cannon constructed of iron and brass. In each ship were coins of copper, silver, and often many of gold, capable of serving as valuable historical monuments; in each were an infinite variety of instruments of the arts of war and peace, many formed of materials, such as glass and earthenware, capable of lasting for indefinite ages, when once removed from the mechanical action of the waves, and buried under a mass of matter which may exclude the corroding action of sea-water."

But the dangers of naval warfare, however great, may be exceeded by the storm, the hurricane, the shoals, and other perils of the deep. Numbers of richly-freighted vessels have thus perished. "Millions of coin have been sometimes submerged in a single ship, and on these—when they happen to be enveloped in a matrix capable of protecting them from chemical changes—much information of historical interest will remain inscribed, and endure for periods indefinite. In almost every large ship, moreover, there are some precious stones set in seals, and other articles of use and ornament, composed of the hardest substances in nature, on which letters and various images are carved—engravings which they may retain when included in subaqueous strata as long as a crystal preserves its natural form." Such are some amongst the rich and curious objects which the ocean retains, or, at some future period, in a manner that we cannot foresee, may be reclaimed.

The mind of man—always fertile in expedients—has been engaged from very remote times in recovering spoils from the ocean. The "diving-bell"—the original rude notion of which dates from the first half of the sixteenth century—is not the earliest intimation of means used for the recovery of ocean "spoils." The ancient "divers," as we learn from classic writers, were wonderfully expert in their vocation; and in remote ages they were kept in ships to assist in raising anchors, and goods thrown overboard in times of danger; and by the laws of the Rhodians they were allowed a share of a wreck proportioned by the depth to which they had gone in search of it. In the latter part of the seventeenth century the diving-bell was employed in the recovery of lost treasure. At the overthrow of the Armada in 1588, some of the Spanish ships were sunk near the Isle of Mull, on the western coast of Scotland, with an immense amount of riches. Several attempts were made to recover this wealth; the result, however, was merely productive in obtaining a few cannons.

One of the most curious efforts of this kind, in after-years, led to the founding of a noble family, the representative of which is the present Marquis of Normanby. William Phipps, the son of a blacksmith, was born in America in 1650. His father was James Phipps, who had been a working gunsmith at Bristol. At the age of eighteen, young Phipps bound himself for four years to a ship-carpenter at Boston, and soon mastered the art, and established himself as a ship-builder. At length he took to trading, and made a voyage to the Bahamas, where he had heard that a Spanish ship had been wrecked with great treasure on board. He appears to have been partially succeessful in recovering some of the valuables, for he was enabled to make a voyage to England. He had obtained information that there was somewhere in the neighbourhood of the Bahamas another Spanish wreck, " wherein was lost a mighty treasure hitherto undiscovered;" and having a strong impression on his mind that he was destined to be the discoverer, he hoped to be able to persuade some persons of wealth in England to advance the necessary funds, and, although comparatively unknown, to get himself appointed to conduct the search under a commission from the Government.

The plan seemed so plausible that Charles II. gave him a ship, and furnished him with everything for the undertaking. In the "Algier Rose," a frigate of eighteen guns and ninety-five men, he set sail, and arrived at New England. He sought for the sunken treasure in vain; but I must tell you that Phipps was a man of no ordinary character, or he could not have eventually achieved his wonderful success. No difficulties turned him from the object of his pursuit. Once his men, despairing of the undertaking, rose in mutiny, and assembling on the quarter-deck with drawn swords, demanded that he should join with them in running away with the ship, and take to piracy, which was at that time a fashionable mania with loose seamen, who delighted especially in the buccaneering pleasures of the South Seas. Phipps, like every great mind, saw at once the necessity for prompt action, and being a powerful man, he rushed in amongst them, buffeting some with his fists, and eventually reducing the whole to submission. He had, however, an obstinate set to manage, and so resolved to return to England, though convinced that the "spoils of the ocean" were still to be had. He endeavoured to obtain another vessel from James II., who was then on the throne, but as he failed in this, he opened a subscription for private assistance. At first he was laughed at, but at length the Duke of Albemarle, son of the celebrated General Monk, took part in it, and advanced a considerable sum, to enable him to make the necessary preparations for a new voyage.

Phipps soon collected the remainder, and in 1687 set sail in a ship of two hundred tons burthen, to try his fortune once more, having previously engaged to divide the profit according to the twenty shares of which the subscription consisted. On arriving at the spot, the banks of Bahama, on the north side of Hispaniola, where he felt persuaded the sunken treasure lay, he employed the various instruments he had invented for submarine descent (amongst others, the diving-bell is traditionally ascribed to him), but, at first, without success. He had brought a tender with him, and at Port de la Plata had had a large cotton tree hollowed out into a canoe. This and the tender were now anchored in the neighbourhood of the shoals, which were known by the name of the "Boilers," and rose to within two or three feet of the surface of the water. For a long time the men sent in the canoe could make nothing of all "their peeping into the boilers," but at length one of them, looking down into the calm water, perceived a plant or weed, called a "sea-feather," growing, as he thought, out of the rock, and desired one of the Indians to dive and fetch it up, that they might not return to their master empty handed. The diver, bringing up the feather, reported that he had seen a large number of great guns in the water. On further diving, the man brought up a lump of silver, worth from two to three hundred pounds. The story goes on to say that the men fixed a buoy to mark the spot where the discovery was made, and returning to the ship, slipped the mass of silver under the table at which they sat down with the captain, who at length saw it, and cried with some "agony," "Why, what is this? Whence comes it?" And then, with changed countenances, they told him how and where they got it. "Then," said Phipps, "thanks be to God: we are made!"

All hands now set to work vigorously, and in a short time thirty-two tons of silver were raised. Upon much of the coined metal a crust like limestone had gathered, several inches thick, which they broke open with iron instruments contrived by Phipps for the purpose, when whole bushels of rusty pieces-of-eight would come tumbling out. There were also great quantities of gold, precious stones, and pearls. The treasure thus recovered from the ocean by Phipps and his men is stated to have amounted to about three hundred thousand pounds sterling; and, provisions failing, they were obliged to leave before they had completely rifled the sunken ship, and a considerable amount of treasure was obtained by other vessels after their departure.

On the return of Phipps to England some persons endeavoured to persuade the King to seize both the ship and cargo, under the pretence that on the project for the expedition sufficiently accurate information had not been given, but the King answered that Phipps was an honest man, and that he and his friends should share the whole among them had he returned with double the value. The fortunate adventurer was knighted, and the Duke of Albemarle, who was so largely benefited, showed his gratitude by giving him a gold cup valued at a thousand pounds. Phipps returned to America in 1688, having been appointed Sheriff of New England. On his way he made another visit to the sunken treasure-ship, and obtained a handsome addition to his fortune. Honours came thick upon him. He was appointed Governor of Massachusetts, and died in his forty-fifth year in London, in 1693.

This affair was attended with such good consequences to the

Duke of Albemarle that he obtained from the King the governorship of Jamaica, in order to try his fortune with other ships sunk in that neighbourhood, but nothing came of this. In England several companies were formed, and obtained exclusive privileges of fishing up goods on certain coasts by means of divers. The most considerable of these was that which in 1688 tried its success at the Isle of Mull, and at the head of which was the Earl of Argyll. The divers went down to the depth of sixty feet under water, and brought up gold chains, money, and other articles, though of no great value.

Of the use of the diving-bell in recovering property from wrecks, the operations upon that of the "Royal George" afford an example which is no doubt well known to you. On 29th August, 1781, this magnificent ship of 108 guns, described as the best sailer, carrying the tallest masts, the squarest canvas, and the heaviest cannon in the service, while under repair at Portsmouth was heeled over too much, and water entering the port-holes, she filled and went down in three minutes, with all on board—Admiral Kempenfeldt, Captain Waghorn, officers, crew, about three hundred women and children who were temporarily on board, guns, ammunition, &c. So sudden was the fearful calamity, that a smaller vessel lying alongside the "Royal George" was swallowed up in the gulf thus occasioned. Of eleven hundred souls on board, nine hundred at once found a watery grave; the rest, including the captain (Waghorn), escaped.

Cowper wrote an elegy on this mournful event:

> " Toll for the brave!
> The brave that are no more!
> All sunk beneath the wave
> Fast by their native shore."

The "Royal George" was the subject of many submarine operations. During the three months which immediately followed the disaster, several divers succeeded in bringing sixteen guns out of the ship by means of the diving-bell. In 1817, after the ship had been submerged thirty-five years, it underwent a thorough examination by men who descended in a diving-bell. It was found to be little more than a ruinous pile of timber-work, the guns, anchors, spars, and masts having fallen into a confused mass among the timbers. She was too dilapidated to be raised in a body. In 1839 General (then Colonel) Pasley devised a mode of discharging enormous masses of gunpowder by means of electricity, so as to shatter the wreck, and thus afford an opportunity for divers to bring up the heavier valuables. The value of the brass guns fished up was equal to the whole cost of the operations, and a serious obstruction to navigation removed.

Independently of the valuable native productions which are found at the bottom of the sea, such as pearls, corals, sponges, &c., the recovery of lost treasures from ships wrecked, makes it an object of importance to be able to descend to the bottom, and remain there long enough to execute the operations necessary for this purpose. But without the assistance of some mechanical apparatus, it is very little that even the most practised divers can perform. Much ingenuity has been devoted from an early period to the contrivance of apparatus for submarine explorations. Machines which in some degree included the principle of the diving-bell were suggested, contrived, and sometimes used to recover property sunk in the sea. At length, in the sixteenth century, the diving-bell itself was invented and used, and improvements were subsequently made by Dr. Halley, Spalding, Farey, Smeaton, and other eminent scientific men, by which persons can remain for a considerable time under water.

The invention of a diving apparatus, however, dates from a much more remote period. In 1538 two Greeks are said to have descended in a machine to the bottom of the sea, in the presence of Charles V. It is, however, due to Halley that he invented a machine for diving, constructed on the principles of science. It was made of wood and covered with lead. The air that was vitiated by respiration escaped from the chamber through an air-cock, and the pure element was supplied by barrels which descended and ascended alternately on both sides of the bell, like buckets into a well. These barrels, lined with lead, each contained about thirty-six gallons of condensed air, and acted in some measure like two lateral lungs for the diving-bell, with which they were connected by leather tubes. As soon as one of these air-casks was empty they let down another of them. Halley himself relates that in 1721 by the aid of this engine he was able to descend, with four other persons, into water sixty feet deep, and to remain there an hour and a half. Occasionally the water entered, and threatened to invade the interior of the bell: under these circumstances he repulsed the enemy by pouring three or four barrels of air on his head. On reaching the bottom he opened the air-cock, through which the fluid already breathed had to make its escape, and the impure air forced its way out with so much violence that the surface of the sea was quite stirred up and covered with foam.

The glory of having been the first to apply the diving-bell to the works of submarine architecture is due, however, to Smeaton, the great engineer, who in 1779 used it to repair the piles of Hexham Bridge. He also introduced various alterations in the form and appliances of the apparatus. About 1788 he was the first to construct a diving-bell of cast iron; but the peculiar characteristic of his machine was the application of the air-pump, which, as it were, breathed for the benefit of the divers, freeing them from the necessity of personally looking after the supply of the vital fluid. This improved diving-bell was afterwards employed by all the marine engineers.

One of the largest diving-bells ever constructed you may have seen at the Polytechnic Institution. It is of cast iron, five feet high, and weighs three tons: air is supplied to the bell by two air-pumps. The principle of the diving-bell will be easily understood by floating a piece of lighted candle or a wax match on a cork, and then covering it with a tumbler, and pressing it downwards. The candle will descend below the level of the surrounding water, and continue burning for a short time, although the tumbler is completely immersed. This is explained by the air in the tumbler, having no vent, remaining in it, and preventing the water from occupying its place; so that the cork and candle—though apparently under water—are still floating, and surrounded by the air in the tumbler. The candle continues burning until the oxygen of the air is exhausted, and then it goes out, as would the life of a man under similar circumstances.

I will relate to you the case of John Day, who perished in 1774 from an ignorance of these simple facts. This person was a millwright, and although somewhat ingenious, did not comprehend that fresh air is the first necessity of existence. He fancied that he had invented a plan by which he could remain below water, at any depth and without any communication from the air, for at least twenty-four hours, returning to the surface whenever he thought proper. His machine was merely a water-tight box or compartment attached to an old vessel by screws. After entering the box, and carefully closing the hole of entrance, the vessel was to be sunk, and Day, being provided with a wax taper and watch, would at the time appointed disengage his box from the vessel by drawing the screws, and thus rise to the surface. A place in Plymouth Sound, one hundred and thirty-two feet in depth, having been selected, the vessel was towed thither; and Day, provided with a bed, a watch, a taper, some biscuits, and a bottle of water, entered the box which was to be his tomb. It was then tightly closed, according to his directions, and the vessel to which it was attached sank to the bottom, from whence neither it nor the unfortunate man ever arose.

The difference with regard to submarine operations in the diving-bell, and a person furnished with the diving-dress, is that the "bell" diver is confined by a prison of cast iron and glass, whilst the diver in his diving-dress is able to move about just as he pleases at the bottom of the sea. It seems that about the year 1721, one John Lethbridge constructed an apparatus somewhat resembling the diving-dress of the present day. It was like a cask with two holes for the arms, and a glass loophole through which to see all that went on in the water. The diver, in order to work, had to lie down upon his breast. The modern diving-dress is made of India-rubber cloth; a strong metal helmet, with round pieces of plate-glass in front, rests upon a pad on the shoulders; the air is supplied to this helmet from above in the same manner as for the diving-bell, but instead of the waste air passing out below, a second tube carries it up. Leaden weights are attached to the side of the diver, and thus he may descend a ladder and walk about below. He carries with him one end of a cord communicating with the assistants above, and upon pulling this as agreed upon, makes a series of signals. The diving apparatus is more adapted even than the diving-bell to certain submarine operations.

By the aid of the diving-bell an enormous amount of treasure has been recovered from the depths of the ocean; and at the present time operations are being carried on in different parts of the world with this object. In 1799 the British ship "Lutine," freighted with an enormous amount of money, varying from one to two millions, foundered off the sand-banks on the north-west coast of Holland, and the greater portion of that treasure still lies buried with but sixty feet of water over it. The "Lutine" was bound to a port in the Zuyder Zee, and a portion of the money on board was a subsidy for the English troops who were then serving under the Prince of Holland against France. There were also the crown jewels of Holland, which had been sent to this country to be reset and polished. The ship, in making for the entrance of the Zuyder Zee, encountered a fearful storm, was driven on a sand-bank, and foundered, all her officers and crew, except one man, perishing. The survivor, however, only lived a few hours. He was picked up by some Dutch boatmen, who found him floating on some spars, and after stating the facts of the dreadful wreck, he died. Nearly two hundred persons perished in the ill-fated vessel. After much exertion the sunken wreck was discovered lying in sixty feet of water, but no attempt was made to recover the sunken treasure for one or two years. The Dutch Government offered a reward of eight thousand pounds for the recovery of the crown jewels, which, with other inducements held out in England, led to a company being formed, which commenced operations, and in a few years they recovered about one hundred and sixty thousand pounds. In addition to this, and within the past few years, another sum of twenty thousand pounds has been obtained from the wreck by other companies, and the project of obtaining the whole of the missing treasure is not abandoned.

Whitstable, famous for its oysters, has also earned a certain renown from possessing a diver of particular eminence, John Gann, whose amphibious career, extending over many years, is remarkable. Among the exploits of this worthy and his "diving" companions, I may mention the recovery of one hundred thousand pounds from the wreck of the "Lady Charlotte," a ship which had gone down to the bottom of the sea. The Whitstable divers were also at work for some time on the coast of Ireland, in a place where a Spanish vessel had sunk, in which they discovered a large number of dollars. This money had been originally enclosed in a barrel, but the wood had perished at the bottom of the sea, and the hoops of the barrel were displaced; nothing was left but the pieces of coin, and these, gathered in a lump, still retained the form of the cask.

An American "Submarine Company" undertook the raising of the vessels and other materials sunk by the Russians in the harbour of Sebastopol during the Crimean war, and also dispatched an expedition to the Caribbean Sea, to search for the treasures in a sunken Spanish frigate, the "San Pedro." According to official documents, this vessel when she went down contained a million of Spanish dollars and a million and a half in gold. The wreck was discovered; and, after removing a vast amount of deck material, the divers penetrated into the deck-room, where they found gun-carriages, four magnificent brass cannons, silver dollars, and other valuable articles covered with mud. Several gold watches were here taken out; and the divers came to the conclusion that, when driven to the forward part of the ship, the bulk of the treasure would be found. Here they expended their efforts, and the result was the recovery of an immense sum of money, almost equal to the amount that was supposed to have been in the vessel.

During the war of succession in Spain, at the commencement of the eighteenth century, England and Holland allied themselves with the Emperor of Austria against Louis XIV. of France and Philip V. of Spain. The latter powers were in great want of resources for the prosecution of the war, and were expecting daily a fleet of Spanish ships from the Indies, freighted with an enormous amount of treasures in money, gold and silver ingots, and rich merchandise. A French fleet of fifteen vessels left Brest to meet the famous "galleons" and escort them as far as Cadiz. The united squadrons were seen by the English and Dutch vessels, and vigorously pursued into Vigo Bay, 22nd October, 1702, where they were so hotly attacked that the Spanish and French commanders determined on burning and sinking the treasure-ships to prevent their being taken. The "Almirante," the Spanish admiral's ship, and her consorts, were accordingly sent to the bottom of the ocean with all their immense wealth, and have remained immersed in the port of a poverty-stricken nation during the whole time of the Bourbon occupation. Hardly had the ex-Queen Isabella been driven from the throne of Spain, when a Spanish banker long settled in Paris made overtures to the government of Madrid for recovering some of the buried treasures; and, on condition of handing over nearly half of the riches that might be recovered, M. Périere was permitted to commence operations. From late accounts it seems that the undertaking has prospered: after nineteen days' search made with large diving-bells, the remains of fifteen ships were discovered at the depth of a few hundred feet. On knocking a hole into the side of the "Almirante," some ingots, plate, and valuable arms were found by the divers. The further researches for these "submarine treasures" will be deeply interesting.

## CHAPTER XXVIII.

### SEA-BIRDS.

> " Watchful and agile, uttering voices wild
> And harsh, yet in accordance with the waves
> Upon the beach, the winds in caverns moaning,
> Or winds and waves abroad upon the water,
> Some sought their food among the finny shoals,
> Swift darting from the clouds, emerging soon,
> With slender captives glittering in their beaks.
> These in recesses of steep crags constructed
> Their eyries inaccessible, and trained
> Their hardy broods to forage in all weathers."

IN the chapter on "Superstitions Connected with the Ocean" I have alluded to a few marine birds which are considered by seamen as good or evil portents in their passage over the ocean. I will now briefly describe some of the more prominent sea-birds which perform their part in the economy of nature, and derive their chief sustenance from the finny inhabitants of the ocean. They constitute a very extensive family all over the world, ever on the alert to indulge their fishing propensities, and voracious in their appetites; so that the poor fishes, what with numberless foes in their own element, with sea-birds continually on the watch to prey upon them, together with all the ingenious arts practised by man to ensnare them, cannot lead the happy and peaceful life which some fanciful writers have imagined them to enjoy.

Many, many miles out at sea the oceanic birds are seen pursuing their predatory instincts, ever restless and untiring, while, nearer shore, thousands in summer seek precipitous coasts and headlands as breeding stations.

> " Watchful and agile, uttering voices wild
> And harsh, yet in accordance with the waves
> Upon the beach."

In winter others, scarcely less numerous, flock from their more northern homes, and fill our bays and marine inlets.

Le Vaillant describes an interesting spectacle which met his gaze after mounting a rock at Saldanha Bay, near the Cape of Good Hope.

"All of a sudden there rose from the whole surface of the island an impenetrable cloud, which formed, at the distance of forty feet above our heads, an immense canopy, or rather sky, composed of birds of every species and of all colours: cormorants, sea-gulls, sea-swallows, pelicans, and, I believe, the whole winged tribe of that part of Africa, were here assembled. All their voices, mingled together and modified according to their different kinds, formed such a horrid noise that I was obliged every moment to cover my head to give a little relief to my ears. The alarm that we spread was so much the more general among the innumerable legions of birds as we principally disturbed the females, which were then sitting. They had nests, eggs, and young to defend. They were like furious harpies let loose against us, and their cries rendered us almost deaf. They often flew so near us that they flapped their wings in our faces, and, though we fired our pieces repeatedly, we were not able to frighten them; it seemed almost impossible to disperse the cloud."

Many of the precipitous rocks and islands of our own country present greatly exciting spectacles at the breeding season. Myriads of ocean birds,

> " Ranged in figures, wedge their way,
> Intelligent of season, and set forth
> Their airy caravan. High over seas
> Flying, and over lands, with mutual wing
> Easing their flight. The air
> Floats as they pass, fanned by unnumbered plumes."

Certainly not the least interesting of marine birds is the *Gull* *(Larus)*, belonging to a very numerous family *(Laridæ)*, which includes also the squas, terns, petrels, shearwaters, albatrosses, noddies, skimmers, and others, all preying chiefly on fishes and mollusca, together with animal garbage of every kind. From the latter circumstance Buffon calls the gulls "the vultures of the ocean." Several of this family are the most oceanic of all birds, being seen hundreds of miles out at sea, apparently unwearied and restless. The gulls have very powerful wings, flying with ease against the roughest storms. In fine weather they fly high in the air, descending with great rapidity to seize the fishes on the surface of the water, or diving slightly for herrings and small fish within reach. Their plumage being close and thick, they are good swimmers. They have a close resemblance to the terns, or "sea-swallows," as they are sometimes called, but the bill is stronger, and the upper mandible much more curved towards the end. The symmetry and strength of the gulls are remarkable, showing how Nature has adapted them in every particular for all the purposes of their predatory instincts.

"Let the reader," remarks Mr. Frank Buckland, "examine the pectoral or breast muscles of the next gull he kills: he will find them one solid mass of firm, hard muscle, admirably adapted to sustain and work the wings. What models of beauty and lightness are those wings! The bones are composed of the hardest possible kind of bone material, arranged in a tubular form, combining the greatest possible strength with the greatest possible lightness. If we make a section of the wing-bone of a gull, or, better still, of that of an albatross, we shall find that it is a hollow cylinder, like a wheat-straw; but, in order to give it still further strength, we see many little pillars of bone about the thickness of a needle extending across from side to side; these buttress-like pillars are in themselves very strong, and do not break easily under the finger. Again, at the top of the bone we find two or three holes, which communicate with the interior; through these, when the bird is alive, pass tubes, which are connected with the lungs; so that, when the bird starts for a flight, he fills his wing and other bones with air, causing them to act something like a balloon on each side of him. This explains one of the chief reasons why man will never be able to fly: his arm-bones are filled with marrow, which he cannot by any means get rid of, should he be ever so anxious to fly like a bird."

Some of the larger gulls are very expert in breaking the shells of the molluscs on which they feed, by taking them up to a sufficient height in the air, and dropping them on a rock. Audubon, the American naturalist, mentions an instance in which a gull, finding the shell not broken by the fall, carried it up a second and a third time, and dropped it from a loftier height, by which its purpose was effected. Gulls are able to support hunger for a long time. An instance is related of one being kept without food for nine days, and yet retained a considerable degree of strength. When their prey is before them, they dart at it with such violence that they will swallow both bait and hook, and split themselves on the point placed by the fisherman under the fish which he presents to them.

The selfishness and rapacity exhibited by some larger members of the gull family have been often observed; the *Glaucous* is a notable instance, and is called by the Dutch sailors the "Burgomaster," from the tyranny which in virtue of its size and strength it exerts over most of the smaller birds of the Northern seas, compelling them to relinquish the fish they have taken; bad qualities, shared in a like degree by the *Parasiticus Gull*. Mr. Lamont, in his account of Spitzbergen, describes these marine bashaws very amusingly:

"None of these birds ever seemed to take the trouble of picking up anything for themselves, but as soon as they observe any other gull in possession of a morsel which he is not able to swallow outright, they dash at him and hunt him through the air until the victim is obliged to drop whatever he has secured, and the ravenous burgomaster appropriates and swallows it himself. I have watched many of these nefarious transactions, and the result is always the same: the small gull turns, and twists, and doubles, and dodges, screaming all the time so pitifully that one would think he expected to lose his life instead of his dinner, but at last he is compelled to give up possession, and the burgomaster then ceases to molest him."

Sailors are very fond of playing off a joke upon the gulls, which are always hovering about ships. They take three or four pieces of sail-twine about six feet in length; these are tied together in the middle, and to the end of each a small piece of blubber or fat is attached tightly, and then thrown into the sea. A gull comes and swallows one piece, another then sees there is plenty to spare, and swallows the next; perhaps a third gull takes possession of another; but as they are all attached by the sail-yarns, whenever they try to fly away one or the other is compelled to disgorge his share; and this is continued, to the tantalizing suspense of the poor gulls, and the great fun of the sailors. This may be a confirmation of the old popular term applied to persons easily duped, but in most cases the gull shows great wariness and cleverness, especially in escaping from its insatiable enemy the heron.

The glaucous gull is an occasional visitor to our shores from its habitat in Northern Europe. One was shot at Galway during the "famine" year in Ireland (1846). A soup kitchen had been established within some distance of the coast, and each day the stately-looking fellow left its maritime domain, and attracted by the smell, sailed about the vicinity of the soup. Many of the poor famished peasants regarded it with an unfavourable eye, not being accustomed to observe a white bird of such dimensions floating in the air, and uttering its hoarse cries overhead, as if laughing at their misery.

Another inhabitant of the cold regions is the *Iceland Gull*, smaller in size, and elegant in shape. Some species of this family are remarkably beautiful: one of the smallest, the *Larus minutus*, or "Little Gull," from the Arctic shores, has a lovely roseate tint overspreading the white under-plumage. The *Black-headed Gull* abounds on our shores during autumn and winter, and is a fine bird, familiar and unsuspicious in its habits, and additionally interesting from the circumstance that this species was protected by the Druids, and was figuratively adopted as an emblem connected with the Deluge, and formed an important feature in their ceremonies:

> "Screams round the arch-druid's
> Brow the sea-mew white
> As Menai's foam."

The *Great Black-backed Gull*, distinguished also by the appellations of the "Goose Gull," "Grey Gull," and "Parson Gull," the latter name arising from the contrast between the black back with the snow-white of the under-plumage, is a large and handsome bird. To every frequenter of the coast the stately and graceful form of this bird is well known, and whether observed in summer, when quietly sunning itself on the strand, or in winter amidst the conflicting war of elements, steadying itself in the eddying blast, it cannot fail to excite admiration. At no time more attractive than when observed during hazy, foggy weather, a black-backed gull, looming through a cloud, with its immense sweep of wing (often exceeding five feet), increased by the state of the atmosphere to a giant size, almost reminds us of the albatross.

The *Herring*, or "Silvery Gull," is distinguished by the spotless purity of its plumage, and ranks among the most beautiful of the gulls that frequent our shores, and has been called the "feathered dervishes of the air" from their rapid and gyratory mode of flying.

"White bird of the tempest—ah, beautiful thing!
With the bosom of snow, and the motionless wing."

The *Kittiwake* is, with the exception of the "black-headed," the smallest of our common gulls, and during the summer the most frequent visitor on our coasts. Almost exclusively maritime in its habits, it never ventures inland like the other species, but contents itself with the food that it obtains on the sea.

Before leaving the family of gulls, I may mention that these seabirds were formerly considered among the delicacies of a rich man's table. They are thus mentioned in the "Household Book" of the fifth Earl of Northumberland, begun in 1512, where they are charged at one penny or three half-pence each; but in more dainty and modern times the flesh of gulls is considered hard and ill-tasted, and the people whom necessity obliges to make use of it, hang up the body by the feet for some time that the oil may run out.

The *Skuas* are ranked by naturalists in successive order *(Lestris)* after the gulls, who find in them determined antagonists. Armed with a powerful bill, the skua is capable of doing much mischief. It is related that one of these birds, which had received a slight injury in the wing-joint, was taken, and sent by the captain of a vessel on shore, in charge of a sailor, with instructions that the bird should be killed and stuffed. The sailor opening the basket in which it was confined rather hastily, the skua dashed ferociously at him, striking with its bill and buffeting with its wings, drawing blood with every successive stroke it made, until at last the sailor drew out his clasp-knife in self-defence, but so determined was the bird, that had not a table-cloth been thrown over it, the contest would have been of long duration.

The pugnacity of the skua is remarkable. No sooner does a skua observe an eagle within its domains than it makes a violent attack upon him. Mr. Drosier relates a very interesting anecdote on this subject. He was standing at the foot of the loftiest hill in Foula, Shetland: "an eagle was returning to his eyrie, situated on the face of the western crags, in appearance perfectly unconscious of approaching so near to his inveterate foe, as, in general, the eagle returns to the rocks from the sea without even crossing the smallest portion of the island. As I was intently observing the majestic flight of the bird, on a sudden he altered his direction and descended hurriedly, as if in the act of pouncing. In a moment five or six skuas passed over my head with astonishing rapidity, their wings partly closed and perfectly steady, without the slightest waver or irregularity. The gulls soon came up with the eagle, as their descent was very rapid, and a desperate engagement ensued. The short bark of the eagle was clearly discernible above the scarcely distinguishable cry of the skuas, who never ventured to attack their enemy in front, but taking a short circle around him, one made a desperate sweep or stoop, and striking the eagle on the back, darted up again almost perpendicularly. This cowardly attack was imitated by each of the other gulls, and continued some time, the eagle wheeling and turning as well as his ponderous wings would allow, and evidently harassed unmercifully, until I lost sight of the combatants among the rocks."

The *Petrels* are among the most interesting of marine birds.

The name is said to be derived from the circumstance that besides the faculty of swimming, they possess that of supporting themselves on the water by striking very rapidly with their feet, which has caused them to be compared to St. Peter walking upon the water. These birds are to be seen in all seas of the globe from one pole to the other, and are the inseparable companions of mariners during their long navigations, following the vessels in great flocks to pick up any garbage thrown into the water. Their flight is almost always performed by hovering, and without presenting apparent vibrations. They drop promptly on their prey, which seems to consist chiefly of the blubber or fat of whales, mollusca, marine worms, and the spawn of fish. Neither the habits of the petrels, nor the structure of the bill adapt them for fishing. They have the faculty of spouting oil, as a means of defence, in the face of any one who may attempt to take them. Persons not aware of this fact have lost their lives by falling into the sea or down precipices.

The *Storm-Petrel*, the bird of ill omen among mariners, as I have already remarked in another chapter, is about the size of a house-swallow, in length six inches, and the extent of the wings thirteen inches. The whole body is black except near the tail, some feathers of which are white. The ancients believed that the petrel hatched its eggs beneath its wing, as at all seasons and in every sea they had been remarked flying, whilst their appearance on land was never noticed:

"The bird of Thrace,
Whose pinion knows no resting-place."

It is true that the petrels do not quit the sea except at the time of laying, and for the purpose of making their nests upon very precipitous rocks, where they feed their young on half-digested animals. They retire there during the night, and utter a most disagreeable cry, resembling the croaking of a reptile.

The *Terns* or "Sea-Swallows" have remarkably long wings and slender bills; the tail is forked, and the plumage generally is of a delicate pearl-white, with more or less black upon the head. The terns are continually on the wing, and although web-footed, are not seen to swim; they rest but seldom, and only on the land, feeding for the most part on small fish and mollusca, which they seize upon the surface of the water, but they also catch aërial insects. In flying they send forth sharp and piercing cries. The most elegantly formed of the terns is that called the "Roseate," the mantle of which is a pale tint, the under-parts of a rosy hue. Mr. Selby tells us that on the Farne Islands it breeds abundantly. "When intruding on the nest, the bird showed great anxiety, approaching so near that we knocked one or two down with a fishing-rod used by the keeper of the lighthouse for fishing from the rocks. All the terns are very light, the body being comparatively small, and the expanse of wings and tail so buoys them up that when shot in the air they are sustained, their wings fold above them, and they whirl gently down like a shuttlecock." The species are numerous and occur in both hemispheres.

The *Skimmers*, although possessing much of the general habits of the terns, are distinguished by the singular form of the bill, the upper mandible of which is considerably shorter than the other. They skim over the surface of the ocean with great swiftness, and scoop up small marine insects.

The *Albatross*, whose habitual dwelling is the Austral Ocean, from the Cape of Good Hope as far as New Holland, belongs to the genus *Diomedia*, and is the most powerful and bulky of the whole family. The extent of their outspread wings is enormous, yet their flight, except in stormy weather, is by no means lofty: like all the rapacious birds of the ocean, they are most voracious. They devour fish with so much gluttony that often one-half of the body remains outside of the bill until the part which is swallowed, being dissolved by digestion, leaves a passage for the rest. They are often gorged to such a degree as to be unable to fly, or to escape the boats which pursue them. Although the flesh of the albatross is hard and rank, yet sailors contrive to render it eatable, when they are in want of fresh provisions, by taking off the skin, and soaking the body in salt for four and twenty hours, then boiling it, and eating it with some strong sauce.

In spite of the strength and powerful bill of the albatross, it is by no means warlike, and will remain on the defensive against some of the gull tribe which harass them, and to escape such attacks they plunge their body into the water. They experience some difficulty in rising to their flight, and then strike the water rapidly with their feet and clap with their wings; but after this impulsion the wings remain developed, and they do nothing but balance themselves alternately from right to left, shaving the surface of the water with rapidity, and plunging in their heads now and then in search of food to a certain depth.

The *Divers* (*Colymbidæ*) are great destroyers of fish, and expert in their method of getting supplies, as their name would suggest. Indeed, they are said to dive with such celerity that they often evade a shot directed against them, sinking at the very moment the flash appears. These birds cannot support themselves on land except in a position nearly vertical, and by the assistance of their wings, which thus act as oars. Sometimes they fall with their stomach flat on the ground, and have some difficulty in raising themselves up. They are seen in our climates only when the rivers and ponds of cold countries are frozen, and they return to their homes in the north after the thaw. They undergo a periodical change of plumage in one form or another. The *Red-throated Diver* is tolerably common around the coasts, entering the mouths of rivers after shoals of sprats, &c. The *Great Northern Diver*, a remarkably handsome bird, occurs on our shores during winter, frequenting the vicinity of the oyster-scalps, and is there well known to the fisherman from its loud and monotonous call. Leemius remarks of the Laplanders, that if a person hears the cry of any of the divers in spring, and while fasting, the milk from his flocks will not curdle for the whole year. Vigilant and shy, if pursued, it exerts its admirable locomotive powers, and advances with immense speed. Nature has provided means of escape and safety to the divers in the flattened form of the body and the wonderful mechanism of the foot, the membrane of which can be closed preparatory to each stroke.

From the divers we are easily led to the family of the Auks (*Alcadæ*), by means of the *Guillemots*, ocean birds to which the attribute of stupidity has been applied, but probably without sufficient reflection on their peculiar conformation, the wings being short and narrow so that the bird can scarcely flutter; the legs also from their position are quite unfit for the purpose of walking; and the natural element of the bird is only on the bosom of the sea, where it swims with the greatest swiftness, and even dives below the ice.

The *Common* is the only one of the British guillemots that can be called abundant, the others being comparatively rare, and some only straggling visitants. It is found around all our coasts, to the Shetland and Orkney islands, and also around the shores of temperate Europe. When near their breeding-places at the proper season, they assemble in thousands, at times blackening the sea.

"Sitting closely along a ledge of rock," observes Mr. Watters, "no matter how elevated above the sea, they impart all the appearance of being ranged in file, or, as they have been compared by the Manxmen, resembling an apothecary's shop — the even ledges of the rock, the shelves, and the birds the pots; whilst on the least alarm the entire range of the birds sweep downward in a line to the sea. Such successful divers are they, and rapacious feeders, that twenty-five herring fry have been counted in the stomach of a single bird. Congregated in parties of from eight to thirty, they evince the utmost amiability towards each other, fishing and winging their way in small flocks to and from their breeding haunts."

The *Great Auk* is an inhabitant of Northern Europe, and has been rarely captured on our coasts. Of considerable size, its power of progression is limited only to the water, the shortness of its wings rendering it incapable of flight, and from the backward position of its legs, it stands erect and stately. Breeding in remote northern latitudes, the eggs are obtained with great difficulty. The length of the bird is said to be from thirty inches to three feet; the bill, four inches long, is black with transverse furrows, the grooves white. In the dress of winter the chin, throat, and sides of the neck are white. The *Razor-bill Auk* is nearly equally abundant with the guillemot on all our coasts, breeding in the same manner together on rocks, and appearing off our shores during the winter in small parties.

The *Puffin*, or "Sea-Parrot," so named from the bill, which, in comparison with the size of the bird, is strongly developed, is a summer visitant to our shores, repairing to them for the purpose of incubation. It sometimes breeds in fissures of the rocks; but its most general resort is in holes and burrows, either formed by itself or supplied by rabbits, if they happen to be inhabitants of the same locality. On the Bass Rock, the holes in the ruins of the old fortifications afford a retreat. The puffin is used as an article of food by various island and northern tribes in whose vicinity they breed. They are caught by stretching a piece of cord along the stony places where they chiefly assemble, to which nooses are attached.

The *Penguins* occupy habitually the most northern points and islands of Europe, of Asia, and of America; but they cannot remain at sea, except in calm weather. When the tempest surprises them far from shore, great numbers of them perish. Though they usually only shave the surface of the water in flying, they can elevate themselves to a certain height. By night they retire into the clefts of rocks and caverns. In their tottering walk they seem to rock from one side to the other. Their food consists in crustaceous animals, and they also live on shell mollusca and small fish, which they take in diving. They make their nests in holes on the seacoasts, which they enlarge with their bills and feet. These birds are very singular in their habits. Darwin, in the "Voyage of the Adventure and Beagle," relates:

"One day, having placed myself between a penguin and the water, I was much amused by watching its habits. It was a brave bird, and until reaching the sea it regularly fought and drove me backwards. Nothing less than heavy blows would have stopped him: every inch gained he firmly kept, standing close before me, erect and determined. When thus opposed, he continually rolled his head from side to side in a very odd manner, as if the power of vision lay only in the anterior and basal part of each eye. This bird is commonly called the 'jackass penguin,' from its habit while on shore of throwing its head backwards, and making a loud, strange noise, very like the braying of that animal; but while at sea and undisturbed, its note is very deep and solemn, and is often heard in the night-time. In diving, its little plumeless wings are used as fins, but on the land as front legs. When crawling (it may be said on four legs) through the tassocks, or on the side of a grassy cliff, it moved so very quickly that it might readily have been mistaken for a quadruped. When at sea and fishing, it comes to the surface for the purpose of breathing with such a spring, and dives again so instantaneously, that I defy any one at first sight to be sure that it is not a fish leaping for sport."

One of the greatest destroyers of fish is the *Cormorant*, belonging to the family *Pelicanidæ*, or "Pelicans," and the common species of which is widely distributed, extending around the whole coasts of our mainlands and islands, constructing their nests, on the summits of rocks most generally, of sea-weeds or materials collected on the waters. The bird is not easily approached at sea, but gets out of harm's way by flight, not by having recourse to diving, like so many of the true aquatic tribes: the flight, powerful and overland, is performed at a great height. When swimming, it is easily distinguished by its long upright neck. So keen in fishing is the cormorant that advantage has been taken of the circumstance to train it for that purpose in the manner hawks are trained for fowling, a tight collar being put round the throat, to prevent the swallowing of the prey. A bird of this species kept by Colonel Montague was extremely docile, of a grateful disposition, and by no means vindictive. He received it by coach after it had been four and twenty hours on the road; yet, though it must have been hungry, it rejected every sort of food he could offer to it, even raw flesh; but, as he could not procure fish at the time, he was compelled to cram it with meat, which it swallowed with evident reluctance, though it did not attempt to strike him with its formidable beak. After seeing it fed he withdrew to the library, but was surprised in a few minutes to see the stranger walk boldly into the room, and join him at the fireside with the greatest familiarity, where it continued, dressing its feathers, until it was removed to the aquatic menagerie. It became restless at the sight of water, and when set at liberty, plunged and dived without intermission for a considerable time, not capturing, or even discovering, a single fish; and, apparently convinced there were none to be found, it made no further attempt for three days.

The dexterity with which the cormorant seizes its prey is incredible. Knowing its own powers, if a fish is thrown into the water at a distance, it will dive immediately, pursuing its course under water in a direct line towards the spot, never failing to take the fish, and that frequently before it falls to the bottom. The quantity it will swallow at a meal is astonishing: three or four pounds twice a day are readily devoured, the digestion being excessively rapid. If, by accident, a large fish sticks in the gullet, it has the power of inflating that part to the utmost, and while in that state the head and neck are violently shaken, in order to promote its passage. In the act of fishing it always carries its head under water, in order that it may discover its prey at a greater distance and with more certainty than could be effected by keeping its eyes above the surface, which is agitated by the air, and rendered unfit for visional purposes. If the fish is of the flat kind, it will turn it in the bill, so as to reverse its natural position, and by this means only could such be got within the bill. If it succeeds in capturing an eel—which is its favourite food—in an unfavourable position for gorging, it will throw the fish up some height, dexterously catching it in a more favourable one as it descends. The cormorant lives in perfect harmony with the wild swan, goose, various sorts of duck, and other birds; but to a gull with a piece of fish it will instantly give chase.

Mr. Glennon relates: "Several years ago I took a pair of these birds from a nest among the rocks of Howth (Ireland), and kept them for nearly two years, by which time they had attained their full growth. They were pleasant pets enough, unless when pressed by hunger, when they became outrageous and screamed most violently; when satisfied with food, they slept, roosting on a large trough placed for holding water. But woe to the man or beast attempting to approach them when hungry. It happened once that a gentleman's servant went to look at them while in this state: he wore a pair of red plush breeches that immediately attracted the attention of the birds, which I had been in the habit of feeding with livers and lights; the consequence was they made such a furious attack that I had to run to his assistance with a stick, and could not beat them off without the greatest difficulty. Their attack on cats, dogs, and poultry, if unprotected, was always fatal. They fought at once with their bills, wings, and claws, screaming frightfully all the time. In fact, the cause of my parting with them was their having destroyed a fine Spanish pointer: he had incautiously strayed into the place where I kept them, and they immediately flew at and attacked him in front and rear. His loud howling brought me to his aid, when I was astonished to find they had got him down, and before I could rescue him from their fury, they had greatly injured him in one of his shoulders, so much so that he afterwards died of the wound."

The Druids believed the appearance of a cormorant during the celebration of their mysteries was an evil omen:

"Slowly the cormorant aims his heavy flight,
Portending ruin to each baleful rite."

Milton describes the arch-fiend, who—

"On the Tree of Life—
The middle tree, the highest there that grew—
Sat like a cormorant."

The *Pelican*, being furnished with a peculiar organ for storing up its prey, would seem to be still better adapted than the cormorant for being trained to fish. Labat mentions that the Indians adopt this practice, and dispatch a pelican in the morning, after having stained it red, and that it returned in the evening with its bag full of fish, which it was made to disgorge.

The sac or bag of the pelican is an elastic flesh-coloured membrane, which hangs from the lower edges of the under mandible, reaching the whole length of the bill to the neck, said to be capacious enough to hold about four gallons of water. The bird has the power of contracting the bag by wrinkling it up under the mandible, so that it is scarcely visible; but after a successful fishing, it is incredible to what extent it is frequently distended. It preys chiefly on the larger fish, with which it fills its capacious pouch in order to digest them at leisure. Paley, in his "Natural Theology," has made this wonderful attribute of the pelican one of the many arguments of the great Creator's power.

The great stretch of wing in the pelican, extending to eleven or twelve feet, and consequently double that of the swan or the eagle, enables it to support itself a long time in the air, where it balances itself with great steadiness, and only changes its place to dart directly downwards on its prey, which rarely escapes; for the violence of the dash, and its wide-spread wings, by striking and covering the surface of the water, make it boil and whirl, and at the same time stun the fish, and deprive it of the power of escape. When the pelicans are in flocks they act in concert, and, forming a great circle which they diminish by degrees, they thus enclose the fish, and all, at a certain signal, strike the water at the same moment, and amidst the disorder thus occasioned they plump in and seize their prey. These birds spend in fishing the hours of the morning and evening, when the finny tribe are most in motion, and they choose the places where they are most plentiful.

The pelican belongs more to warm than cold climates. It is very common in Africa and in some parts of Asia; it is met with also in America and in the southern parts of Australia. It perches on trees, but does not nestle there, constructing on the ground a nest a foot and a half in diameter, furnished internally with soft sea-plants.

The flesh of the pelican was forbidden to the Jews as unclean. It has an ill taste, and in America is used for its oil. The pouches of these birds have also been used to hold tobacco, and this skin, when dressed, is very soft.

To the pelican tribe also belongs the *Gannet*, "Solan Goose," much larger than the gulls, from which they may be distinguished at a distance by a greater length of neck, the intense whiteness of the plumage, and the black tip of their wide-spreading wings. The mode in which the gannet fishes is peculiar. "In flight," remarks the Rev. C. A. Johns, "it circles round and round, and describes again and again a figure of eight, at a varying elevation above the water, in quest of herrings, pilchards, and other fishes, whose habit it is to swim near the surface. When it has discovered a prey, it suddenly arrests its flight, probably closes its wings, and descends with a force sufficient to make a *jet d'eau* visible two or three miles off, and to carry it many feet downwards. When successful, it brings its prize to the surface, and devours it without troubling itself about mastication. If unsuccessful, it rises immediately and resumes its hunting. It is sometimes seen swimming, perhaps to rest itself, for I did not observe that it ever dived on these occasions. My companion told me that the fishermen on the coasts of Ireland say that if this bird be chased by a boat when seen swimming, it becomes so terrified as to be unable to rise. The real reason may be that it is gorged with food. He was once, he told me, in a boat on the Lough, when a gannet being seen a long way off, it was determined to give chase, and ascertain whether the statement was true. As the boat drew near, the gannet endeavoured to escape by swimming, but made no attempt to use its wings. After a pretty long chase the boatman secured it, in spite of a very severe bite which it inflicted on his hand. It did not appear to have received any injury, and when released on the evening of the same day, swam out to sea with great composure. A fisherman at Islay told me that in some parts of Scotland a singular method of catching these birds is adopted. A herring is fastened to a board, and sunk a few feet deep in the sea. The sharp eye of the gannet detects its prey, and the bird, first raising itself to an elevation sufficient to carry it down to the requisite depth, pounces on the fish, and in the effort penetrates the board to which it is attached. Being thus held fast by the beak, it is unable to extricate itself. Frequently also gannets are caught in the herring-nets at various depths below the surface. Diving after the fish, they become entangled in the nets, and are thus captured in a trap not intended for them. They perform good service to fishermen by indicating at a great distance the exact position of the shoals of fish."

Some idea may be formed of the fishing exploits of the gannet from what Buchanan states, that one hundred and five millions of herrings are destroyed annually by these birds at St. Kilda. They are summer visitors to our coasts, and although from their power of flight they seem to be widely scattered, yet their real stations or breeding-places are few and local. The Bass Rock, St. Kilda, and Ailsa Craig have long existed as the Scotch localities; while Lundy Island on the coast of Devon, and the Skelig Isles in Ireland, are less-known English and Irish stations.

It is on the Bass Rock, in the Firth of Forth, that they assemble in countless multitudes, and present an extraordinary sight to the beholder, nestling upon their eggs, greeting their mates on their arrival from the sea, or quarrelling if one happens to intrude a little too near another. Troops of birds in adult, changing, and first year's plumage, pass and repass, sailing in a smooth noiseless flight. The great proportion build on the ledges of the precipitous face of the rock, but a considerable number also place their nests —generally made carelessly of a few dried stalks of sea-weed, rudely put together—on the summit near the edge, where they can be walked among; there the birds are very tame, allowing a person to approach them, but when a foot is held out aggressively they will bite at it.

Most, if not all, of these breeding stations are rented from the proprietors, the rent being paid chiefly by the feathers. The young geese are killed and cured. The inhabitants of St. Kilda, the most western of the Hebrides, are said to consume twenty-two thousand of the young birds every year, besides eggs. The gannet is easily kept in confinement, though the required supply of fish renders its keep expensive. It is indifferent alike to cold or stormy weather; the air-cells which give lightness to the body are developed in an extraordinary degree. Montague remarks "the gannet is capable of containing about three full inspirations of my lungs, divided into nearly three equal portions, the cellular parts under the skin on each side holding nearly as much as the cavity of the body. In the act of respiration there appears to be always some air propelled between the skin and the body, as a visible expansion and contraction is observed about the breast, and this singular conformation makes the bird so buoyant that it floats high on the water, and does not sink beneath the surface, as observed in the cormorant and shag."

The *Hooper* or *Wild Swan* is the most common of its species in our country, being a general winter visitant. The length to the end of the toes is five feet; to that of the tail, four feet ten inches; extent of wings, seven feet three inches; and weight from thirteen to sixteen pounds. The lower part of the bill is black; the base of it, and the space between that and the eyes, is covered with a naked yellow skin; the whole plumage in old birds is of a pure white, the down being very soft and thick. The cry of the wild swan is very loud, and may be heard at a great distance, from which the name of "Hooper" is derived. When they fly high, and numbers of different ages and sexes are mingled together, their notes are far from disagreeable.

Belonging to the family of the *Falconidæ* are birds of the eagle kind, which fish on their own account, robbing others of their prey when they can, and pursuing nearly the same method of dashing from a height upon the fish in the water. The *Great Sea-Eagle* is a distinguished member of this predatory family, measuring in length three feet, and in extent of wings six feet six inches. This bird often presents a fine feature in the wild and desolate landscape. Its most favourite haunts in Britain are the northern coasts of Scotland, where the headlands reach a stupendous height, are perpendicular on the face, and where the shelves and ledges selected for breeding or roosting-places are secure from aggression either from above or beneath. Here the sea-eagle resides constantly at one season, or he finds a safe shelter during the night, after his more extended hunting excursions. Here he is monarch of all he surveys; amidst the numerous sea-fowl, his companions, his pale grey-tinted plumage and outspread tail being conspicuous when opposed to the dark green sea or the deep and rich shades of many of these splendid precipices. Although of great size and imposing aspect, it is less elegant than the golden eagle, and inferior in courage and activity to many of the smaller species of the tribe. When standing, its postures are by no means graceful, but the keenness of its bright and fierce eye enlivens its appearance, and under excitement it throws itself into beautiful and picturesque attitudes, drawing back its head, and erecting the narrow and pointed feathers of the neck.

Besides a fondness for fish—in capturing which, however, the sea-eagle is not half so dexterous as the osprey—the bird is such a predaceous intruder on the farm-yard, that in the Hebrides a fierce war is waged against him.

"The farmers of the isles of St. Kilda," remarks Mr. Magillivray, "proceed to their extermination, some carrying coils of rope, others bundles of dry heath and burning peat, and ascend to the brow of the mountains, where the fissured and shelved precipice hangs over the foamy margin of the Atlantic. Strings of gannets, cormorants, and guillemots are seen winding round the promontories, while here and there over the curling waves is seen hovering a solitary gull. They have reached the brink of the cliffs, over which the more timid scarce dare venture to cast a glance, for almost directly under their feet is the unfathomed sea, heaving its heavy billows some hundred feet below the place to which they cling. The eagles are abroad, sailing at a cautious distance in circles, uttering wild and harsh screams, and as they sweep past displaying their powerful talons. One of the men fastens the rope to his body, passing it under his arms, and securing it upon his breast by a firm knot. The rest dig holes with their heels in the turf, and sitting down in a row, take firm hold of the cord. The adventurer looks over the edge of the cliff, marks the projecting shelf which overhangs the eagle's nest, and is gradually lowered towards it, bearing in one hand the bundle of heath with the cord attached to it, and the peat burning in the middle, and with the other pushing himself from the angular projection of the rock. At length he arrives on the shelf, and calls to those above to slacken the rope, but keep fast hold of it. Then creeping forwards, and clinging to unstable tufts of vegetation on the sides of the rock, he looks downwards and ascertains the precise position of the nest, in which are two eaglets covered with down, skeletons of fishes, birds, and lambs heaped around them. At sight of the human face—which to their imagination is anything but divine—the young eagles shrink back in terror, cowering beneath the projecting angle that partly roofs the nest. Their enemy now retreats, disposes the bundle of heath in a loose manner, blows the peat into a flame, and partially encloses it. Once more he approaches the brink, casting an anxious eye towards the old eagles which are wheeling in short circles and uttering confused and piercing cries; then blowing the flame, kindles the bundle of combustibles, and rapidly lowers it right into the nest. The young birds scream and hiss, throwing themselves into attitudes of defence. The heath smokes and crackles, and at length blazes into full flame; then the sticks, sea-weeds, wool, and feathers of the nest catch fire, and the ascending column of smoke indicates to the ropemen above that the deed is doing. Flames and smoke conceal the young birds from the avenger's gaze, but he stirs not until they have abated, and he sees the huge eyrie and its contents reduced to ashes. He then calls to his friends, who tighten the rope, and preparing himself for the ascent, is hauled up, encountering no small danger from the fragments which are loosened from the rock, and the difficulty of keeping his face and breast from the ragged points which project from the cliff. Birds have feelings as well as men, and those of the eagle are doubtless acute, for the old birds wheel and scream along the face of the rock for many days in succession, and as by this time the summer is far advanced, they form no new nest."

But the king of winged fishers is the famous *Osprey*, the "Fishing Eagle" *par excellence*, or "Fishing Hawk," as it has been variously named, a bird remarkable among the rapacious kind for the peculiar adaptation it enjoys for fishing. The wings of the male osprey are sixty inches in length, the body being twenty-three; the female, however, is larger, but does not differ much in colour, which is generally in the upper parts a deep brown, beautifully glossed with light purple, the margins and tips of the feathers being pale brown or brownish-white. The osprey finds a worthy antagonist in the white-headed eagle.

"Elevated," remarks Wilson, " on the high dead limb of some gigantic tree that commands a wide view of the neighbouring shore and ocean, the white-headed eagle seems calmly to contemplate the motions of the various feathered tribes that pursue their busy avocations below: the snow-white gulls slowly winnowing the air; the busy sand-pipers coursing along the sands; trains of ducks streaming over the surface; silent and watchful cranes, intent and wading; clamorous crows; and all the winged multitude that subsist by the bounty of this vast liquid magazine of Nature. High over all these hovers one whose actions instantly arrest all the attention of the observer. By his wide curvature of wing and sudden suspension in air he knows him to be the osprey, the "fish-hawk," settling over some devoted victim of the ocean. His eye kindles at the sight, and balancing himself with half-opened wings on the branch, he watches the result. Down—rapid as an arrow from heaven—descends the distant object of his attention, the roar of its wings reaching the ear as it disappears in the deep, making the surges foam around. At this moment the eager looks of the eagle are all ardour; and levelling his neck for flight, he sees the osprey once more emerge struggling with his prey, and mounting in the air with screams of exultation. These are the signals for our hero, who, launching into the air, instantly gives chase, soon gains on the fish-hawk; each exerts his utmost to mount above the other, displaying in the struggle the most elegant and sublime aërial evolutions. The unencumbered sea-eagle rapidly advances, and is just on the point of reaching his opponent, when, with a sudden scream, probably of despair and honest execration, the osprey drops his fish; the eagle, poising himself for a moment, as if to take a more certain aim, descends like a whirlwind, snatches it in his grasp before it reaches the water, and bears his ill-gotten booty to the woods."

In the same picturesque and elegant language Wilson describes the fishing habits of the osprey:

"On leaving its nest, it usually flies direct until it reaches the sea, then sails round in easy curving lines, turning sometimes in the air as on a pivot, apparently without the least exertion, rarely moving its wings. Suddenly it checks its course as if struck by a particular object, which it seems to survey for a few moments with such steadiness that it appears fixed in the air, flapping its wings. This object, however, it abandons, and is again seen sailing round as before. Now its attention is again arrested, and it descends with great rapidity, but before it reaches the surface shoots off on another course, as if ashamed that a second victim had escaped. It now sails at a short distance above the surface, and by a zig-zag descent, and without seeming to dip its feet in the water, seizes a fish, which, after carrying a short distance, it drops and probably yields up to the bald eagle, and again ascends by easy spiral circles to the higher regions, where it glides about with all the ease and majesty of its species. From hence it descends like a perpendicular torrent, plunging into the sea with a low rushing sound, and with the certainty of a rifle. In a few moments it emerges, bearing in its claws the struggling prey, which is always carried head-foremost, and having risen a few feet above the surface, shakes itself as a water-spaniel would do, and then seeks land. If the wind blows hard, and its nest be in a quarter from whence it comes, it is amusing to see with what judgment the osprey beats up to windward; not in a direct line, but, like an experienced navigator, making several successive tacks to accomplish its purpose.

The ospreys watch and pursue fish with as much avidity as the true eagles hunt their game on the land; and Nature, as I have remarked, has provided them with the means for so doing. Fish are slippery, and therefore its claws are long and much curved, its toes nearly of equal length, and capable of being applied in the most effectual manner, in pairs, two and two opposite each other. It must also possess considerable power, and therefore its legs are strong and muscular, and to prevent its being inextricably entangled the claws are smooth and rounded, so that they can, if necessary, be readily withdrawn. The animals on which it feeds live in the water, ordinarily beyond its reach, coming occasionally to the surface; the bird, therefore, has a comparatively slender form, with very long wings, so as to enable it to remain without fatigue sailing or hovering over the water until an opportunity of pouncing occurs. To prevent its plumage from being injured by its sudden immersion into the water, the feathers of the lower surface are rather more compact and considerably shorter than in eagles and most other birds of the family, and those of the leg are short all round, whilst most other species have a large tuft of short feathers. The structure of the wings is also curious: in the osprey they are very long, yet length is not of itself an indication of great speed so much as the power of easy suspension in the air and of continued flight. The osprey requires to hover long over the waters, often over the open sea at some distance from land, sometimes for hours together before an opportunity for pouncing on its prey occurs. Its form, therefore, is as light as is compatible with strength.

> "True to the season, o'er our sea-beat shore,
> The sailing osprey high is seen to soar,
> With broad unmoving wing, and, circling slow,
> Marks each loose straggler in the deep below—
> Sweeps down like lightning, plunges with a roar,
> And bears his struggling victim to the shore."

I have now to notice another family, the *Phaeton* or *Tropic Birds*, so named because, from their habitual residence under the burning zone, bounded by the tropics, they seem attached to the chariot of the sun, to use a classical metaphor. From this climate they remove but little, and their appearance indicates to seamen their approaching passage under this zone, from whatever side they may arrive. Still, they advance seaward many hundreds of miles.

The *Frigate-Bird* is the representative of this species, the swiftest ranger of the ocean, whose extended wings measure a width of seven feet. How this bird treats the unfortunate "booby" (also a fish-hunter) is described by Mr. Gosse, who says:

"Every one who has read the romantic narratives of the old voyagers is familiar with the name of the booby, so termed by seamen from its apparent stupidity and familiarity, suffering itself to be knocked down by a stick, or taken by the hand when it alights, as it often does, on the spars or shrouds of a vessel. This habit seems quite unaccountable. Many birds have manifested a similar fearlessness of man when first discovered, but have soon learned the necessity of precaution; but the booby *will* manifest the same unnatural tameness after being long accustomed to the cruelty of man. It does not arise from helplessness, as it is a bird of powerful wing, like its relative the common gannet; neither is it a sufficient explanation to affirm, as is sometimes done, that it arises from a peculiar difficulty in rising to flight after alighting, because it is not unfrequently caught in the air by the hand, so incautiously does it approach man. Notwithstanding this apparent stupidity, the booby is a dexterous fisher. Hovering over a shoal of fishes, he eagerly watches their motions, turning his head from side to side in a very ludicrous manner. He presently sees one of the unwary group approach the surface: down he pounces like a stone, plunging into the waves, which boil into foam with the shock. Nor fails he to seize the scaly victim, with which he emerges into the air, and soon it is lodged whole in his capacious stomach. But the frigate-bird has watched the proceeding, and instantly betakes himself to the pursuit. Sweeping down upon the unfortunate booby, he compels him to disgorge the fish which he has just swallowed, and which, long before it can reach the water, is seized and again devoured by the oppressor.

The frigate-bird neither swims nor dives; the seamen even believe that it sleeps on the wing: whether this be so or not, there is good evidence that the same individuals will remain in the air for several successive days; they are never known to alight on a vessel. Though the chase of the booby is so usual as to be considered one of its constant means of dependence, yet it also fishes for itself; precluded, however, from plunging into the sea, it can take only such as, like the flying-fish, leap into another element. With such success, however, does it attack these, that it has been seen to snap up three in succession in the course of a few minutes."

The frigates fly with great rapidity, and brave the tempests by shooting above their region and remaining balanced in the air until they can alight upon some rock to rest, for the length of their wings would prevent them from rising either from the waves or the ground. Their sight must also be remarkably piercing to enable them to discover, at such distances as quite escape our vision, the places where pass the flying-fishes, their chief relish. Instead of precipitating their head foremost, like birds which have the faculty of diving, the frigate holds its neck and feet in a horizontal direction, striking the upper column of air with its wings, then, raising and fixing them one against the other above its back, it darts on its prey with such address and velocity that it rarely escapes. The tropic birds, like the cormorant, perch on the highest trees, and make their nests in the holes of precipitous rocks or in the hollows of trees. The young, while in the nest gathered up in a ball and covered with a down of the most brilliant white, have a resemblance to powder-puffs. Of the long tail-feathers—sometimes twenty-four inches—the Otaheitans make plumes for their warriors.

The *Boobies* have been met with in every sea and in every quarter of the globe. They fly with the neck extended, the tail spread out, and the wings almost motionless. Their cry participates of those of the goose and raven. They remove much less from land than the frigate-birds.

In concluding these necessarily brief remarks on marine birds, I am glad to mention that the beneficial effects of the "Sea-Birds Preservation Act"—a Parlimentary Act of the greatest importance, for giving the persecuted birds a chance of hatching and rearing their young in peace and safety—has already manifested most successful results. The wholesale destruction of these beautiful and useful birds called loudly for some repressive measures on their behalf. One essential benefit gained by the wholesome guardianship of the sea-birds during their breeding season is that they now come with every confidence and in great numbers into our harbours and bays, and do incalculable good as indefatigable removers of nuisances, removing garbage of all descriptions, which, if allowed to float on the water or fester between tide-ways, would occasion dangerous maladies.

## CHAPTER XXIX.

### *THE SENTINELS OF THE SEAS.*

"The rocky ledge runs far into the sea,
   And on its outer point, some miles away,
  The lighthouse lifts its solid masonry,—
   A pillar of fire by night, of cloud by day.

" Even at this distance I can see the tides,
   Upheaving, break unheard along its base,
  A speechless wrath that rises and subsides
   In the white lip and tremour of the face.

" And as the evening darkens, lo! how bright
   Through the deep twilight of the purple air
  Beams forth the sudden radiance of its light,
   With strange unearthly splendour in its glare!

" Not one alone; from each projecting cape
   And perilous reef along the ocean's verge,
  Starts into life a dim gigantic shape,
   Holding its lantern o'er the restless surge.

   \*    \*    \*    \*    \*    \*

" And the great ships sail outward and return,
   Bending and bowing o'er the billowy swells,
  And ever joyful as they see it burn,
   They wave their silent welcomes and farewells."

                                      LONGFELLOW.

THERE can be no object, my young friends, more suggestive of pleasant thoughts, of home, of peace, and security, than a lighthouse. Whether placed upon a headland overlooking a wide expanse of ocean, or on a rock lashed by the foaming billows, it is a welcome sight to the traveller returning to his native country after a long absence, and it is a grateful object to those who are leaving home for distant regions, who, after leaving port, can trace for many miles the friendly light, the last visible connection that unites their thoughts to those who are left behind.

The absence of the lights that stream over the heaving waters would indeed be a calamity; indicative, probably, of war's fatal struggles, when a nation dreading hostile invasion would seek to foil their enemies by extinguishing these lights, and thus leaving them to the perils of shoals and quicksands, of breakers and the rocks. Without these glimmering lights it would be impossible to guide a ship through the perilous ocean; commerce would languish, and all the civilizing influences encouraged by trade would be lost.

The earliest allusion to lighthouses or "beacons" to guide the mariner on his sea-journey, date from a remote period. Homer—who is supposed to have lived before the year 776 preceding the birth of our Saviour—alluding to the shield of Achilles, beautifully describes the flash of a beacon-light in some solitary place, as seen by seamen leaving their friends, in verses which contain ample proof of the existence of such a provision for the mariner's safety in the poet's time.

From ancient historians we learn that navigation made its first efforts in the Mediterranean Sea and the Arabian Gulf; in these places the first operations of commerce by water were carried on. The voyages of the Egyptians and the Phœnicians (the most ancient seafaring people mentioned in history) were made in the Mediterranean. Their trade, however, was not confined to the countries bordering upon it; but by acquiring possession of ports in the Arabian Gulf, they extended the range of their commerce, and are represented as the first people of the West who opened a communication by sea with India. For a long period the art of navigation lay in a dormant state: the invention of the compass had not given confidence to the mariner. The Arabians and the Chinese, the early Greeks and Romans, steered cautiously along the coast, stretching out so far at sea as not to lose sight of land,

and as they shaped their course in this timid manner their mode of reckoning was defective.

There is some reason for believing that the lighthouses or sacred towers of antiquity were dedicated to the heathen gods, and that sacrifices were made in them to appease the raging storm and to pray for the safety of the mariner. These light-towers are also said to have been used as naval schools, in which astronomy and the art of navigation were taught. These buildings are described as having been of stone, sometimes of large dimensions, with a kind of altar within, covered with a plate or brazen dish. These towers were numerous; almost every promontory had its lighthouse or temple. In the fortifications of the early ages, the fire-tower was a prominent portion of the buildings. In Italy especially, where the sea-shore formed the point of attack for pirates, watch-towers were erected, from which grates for holding the fuel were suspended by night. The watchmen of these towers by day were provided with large sea-conches or shells, which they frequently sounded, to warn the mariner of his situation, and to alarm the country in case of invasion.

The oldest lighthouse on record is the celebrated *Pharos*, erected on the Egyptian coast, which, being very low land, and exposed almost entirely to the west winds coming up the Mediterranean from the vast Atlantic, must of necessity have made the port of Alexandria very dangerous. This lighthouse was erected three hundred years before the birth of our Saviour, by the order of Ptolemy Philadelphus (a great patron of learning and the arts), for the convenience of the Phœnician merchants who constantly traded with Egypt.

The island of Pharos, upon which the lighthouse was erected, was said, in the time of Homer, to be one day's sail from the Delta (a triangular portion of Lower Egypt comprised between the two main branches of the Nile, and so called from its resemblance to the Greek letter D, △); whereas, since the foundation of Alexandria, it was only a mile in distance, and was even joined to the mainland by a mole or artificial embankment having a bridge at each end.

This tower, if statements are true, was justly entitled to the honour claimed for it as one of the seven wonders of the world. It is stated to have been five hundred and fifty feet in height, and the cost of erection was equivalent, in our money, to one hundred and fifty-four thousand four hundred pounds. The architect was Sostratus, the constructor of many public buildings in Alexandria. The lighthouse consisted of several storeys, one raised above the other, each decorated with columns, balustrades, and galleries made of the finest marble and of the most exquisite workmanship. It has been said that Sostratus furnished the galleries with large mirrors, by which shipping could be seen at a considerable distance. A fire was kept constantly burning on the summit, and, according to Josephus, the Jewish historian, the light was seen at the distance of three hundred stadii (about forty-two British miles).

In more modern times the Turks erected two forts on the points occupied by this Pharos, one of which was the site of the far-famed lighthouse.

The celebrated colossal statue of Apollo at Rhodes is said to have supplied the purpose of a lighthouse. This figure was of bronze, and a period of twelve years is stated to have been employed in constructing it by Chares, of Lindus, three hundred years before the Christian era. The expenses of erection amounted to a sum estimated in our money at nearly fifty-eight thousand pounds. The gigantic size of this figure may be conceived from the account given, that few men were able to encompass one of its thumbs with their arms. The Rhodians placed this brazen sentinel at the entrance of their port. The heathen deity was represented wearing a radiant crown, holding in one hand an arrow, and in the other a brazier containing fire. This stupendous statue was overthrown by an earthquake about eighty years after its erection; and when the Saracens took Rhodes in 667, they loaded one hundred camels with the bronze that remained, and the rest was sold afterwards to a Jewish merchant for a sum equivalent in our money to thirty-six thousand pounds. Mr. Newton, in his recent "Travels and Discoveries in the Levant," supposes that he found some relics of the brazen Colossus.

An edifice, called by the inhabitants of the Archipelago the

"Lamp of Diogenes," stood on the shores of the Ægean Sea. It was a tomb erected in memory of Diogenes, who had such a knowledge of the art of navigation that no ancient mariner would undertake a voyage without consulting him. At the angles of this building were columns, on which fires were placed for the service of vessels navigating those dangerous seas.

In the earliest annals of our own country we find but scanty notices of coast-lights. The ancient Britons never made long voyages, although the Druids are said to have been acquainted with the magnet and the compass. There is no doubt that "beacons" or "watch-fires" were extensively used by the Romans in Britain. The harbours were strongly fortified, especially at the entrance, where they had a pharos or watch-tower, with lights to direct the course of ships in the night-time. The lighthouse erected by the Romans at Boulogne, to guide the vessels which passed from Britain into Gaul, was still to be traced in 1643. It was an eight-sided tower, with twelve stages or floors, rising to the height of one hundred and twenty-five feet. The remains of the Roman pharos or lighthouse at Dover proves the great ability of that wonderful people in their constructions. These ruins consist of an eight-sided tower, thirty or forty feet high, and which was, probably, of a much greater height. The walls are at least ten feet thick. This lighthouse is said to have been erected during the governorship of Britain by Aulius Plautius and Ostorius Scapula, the latter of whom left our country in the year 53. There are other remains of Roman lighthouses in England, but this at Dover is the most perfect illustration of the kind we possess.

During the Saxon period individuals were appointed to erect beacons, for the purposes of navigation, as necessity required, and the expenses were defrayed by the country. Some description of lighthouse seems to have stood at Winchelsea, Yarmouth, and other places from a very early period. In 1261 Henry III. issued a precept, that every ship laden with merchandise going to those ports, for the two following years, should pay twopence for the maintenance of the lights, unless it was shown that the barons had been accustomed to maintain lights at their own cost.

Concerning beacons, Lord Coke says: "Before the reign of Edward III. they were but stacks of wood set on high places, which were fired when the coming of enemies was descried; but in his reign, pitch-boxes (as now they be), instead of these stacks, were set up."

It was not until the reign of Elizabeth that active measures were taken to secure some permanent means for the erection and management of lighthouses. In the eighth year of this Queen's sovereignty an Act was passed, enabling the corporation of the Trinity Board to preserve ancient sea-marks and "signs for the sea." During this reign, in 1584, the Tour de Corduan was founded—a lighthouse which, in point of architectural effect, is the noblest edifice in the world. It is situated on an extensive reef at the mouth of the Garonne, serving as a guide to the shipping of Bordeaux and the Languedoc Canal, and, indeed, of all that part of the Bay of Biscay. This building (which was not completed until 1610, under Henry IV. of France) is one hundred and ninety-seven feet in height, and consists of a pile of masonry forming successive galleries, surrounded by a conical tower, which terminates in the lantern. Round the base is a wall one hundred and thirty-four feet in diameter, in which the lighthouse-keepers' apartments are formed. This wall is an outwork of defence, and receives the chief shock of the waves. The tower itself contains a chapel and various apartments, and the ascent is by a spacious staircase. This lighthouse was the only stone erection of its character out at sea in Europe, before the Eddystone Lighthouse was completed.

In the reign of Charles I. there are a few notices of lighthouses, which will serve to give some idea of the structures which were then raised for this important object. The first distinct intimation concerning a lighthouse on the North Forelands in Kent is in 1636, when that monarch granted a licence to continue and renew the buildings of the North and South Forelands. It seems that the lighthouse on the former height consisted merely of a small dwelling of timber, lath, and plaster, on the top of which a light was kept in a large glass lantern. This house, as might have been predicted, was burnt down in 1683, after which for some years a sort of beacon was used, but at the close of the same century a strong structure of flint was erected, on the top of which was an iron grate open to the air, in which a large fire of coals was kept blazing all night.

James II. granted the Trinity Board a fresh charter, which is now in force, and to this institution is entrusted the management and control of these invaluable "sentinels of the seas." The annual revenues of the corporation are very considerable, being derived from a toll varying between half a farthing and one penny per ton on shipping, which in return receives benefit from the lights, beacons, buoys, and ballast supplied by the board.

One of the greatest achievements of modern science in connexion with lighthouses is that effected by the famous engineer Smeaton on the dangerous Eddystone rocks, about fourteen miles distance from Plymouth, which are so exposed to the heavy swells from the Bay of Biscay and the Atlantic that the waves beat upon them at times with fearful violence. In 1696, notwithstanding the many difficulties which seemed to interfere with the erection of a lighthouse on rocks so situated, Henry Winstanley succeeded in accomplishing (for a time) the desired object. This gentleman was remarkable for his mechanical ingenuity; his house at Littlebury was full of curious objects manufactured by his own hand. On kicking an old slipper, placed as it were by accident on the floor of a room, a figure would start up representing a ghost. On sitting down in a particular chair, a couple of arms would immediately enfold the frightened intruder with such force that the assistance of an attendant was required to set him free. When sitting down in a certain arbour in the grounds by the side of a canal, a stranger would find himself drawn into the middle of the stream on a movable raft, which remained there until drawn back to its place by an attendant. These and many other singular contrivances amused the public, and determined Winstanley to open an exhibition in his own name in London.

The lighthouse on the Eddystone rocks was commenced in 1696, and the first light appeared on the 14th November, 1698. Finding that the tower was greatly exposed during the storms of winter—

the waves covering the lantern at times, although at the height of sixty feet—Winstanley encompassed the building with a new work of four feet in thickness from the foundation, making all solid to the height of twenty feet; he also took down the upper part of the first building, and enlarging every part in its proportion, raised it forty feet higher than it was originally, and yet the sea in stormy weather rose one hundred feet above the vane, and at times covered half the side of the house and the lantern, as if they were under water. The building was so fantastically constructed (in appearance like a Chinese pagoda), and seemed so slight, that general opinion was against its security, but the architect himself was so firmly convinced of its stability that he frequently wished he might be there in the greatest storm that could happen. This desire was fatally gratified. In November, 1703, Winstanley went out to the rocks to superintend some repairs, and that very night a fearful tempest arose, which so increased the following day, that the lighthouse and all its inmates were swept in the foaming waters. Gay, in his "Trivia," alludes to this calamity:

> "Famed Eddystone's far-shooting ray,
> That led the sailor through the stormy way,
> Was from its rocky roots by billows torn,
> And the huge turret in the whirlwind borne."

Nearly three years elapsed after this sad event before another attempt was made to replace the lighthouse on the Eddystone rocks, when John Rudyard, a silk-mercer of London, and a man of remarkable mechanical abilities, was selected for the purpose. The building was commenced in 1706, and was lighted two years afterwards. It was during its construction that an incident occurred which is highly creditable to the justice of Louis XIV., then King of France. The two nations, England and France, were then at war, and a French privateer took the men who were working at the lighthouse and carried them away prisoners, expecting a reward for this achievement. The monarch, however, ordered the men to be released and the captors to be put in their places, declaring "that although he was at war with England, he was not so with all mankind: the Eddystone lighthouse was so situated as to be of

## RUDYARD'S LIGHTHOUSE CONSUMED BY FIRE. 397

equal service to all nations." The Englishmen were conveyed back to their work, after receiving handsome presents.

Rudyard's lighthouse enjoyed an immunity from serious accidents for a space of thirty-eight years, when, at the close of 1744, a fearful storm occurred, in which the ship "Victory" was lost close to the building, which was considerably damaged in consequence, and an opening made into the store-room. In 1755 the catastophe occurred which destroyed the lighthouse. On the 2nd December in that year, the lighthouse-keeper then on watch, about two o'clock in the morning, went into the lantern to snuff the candles. He found the whole place in a smoke, and upon opening the door of the lantern into the balcony, a flame instantly burst from the inside of the cupola. He endeavoured to alarm his companions, but they being fast asleep were not able to come to his assistance so readily as the occasion required. He attempted to extinguish the flames with some water kept in a tub in the lantern, but the fire increasing, the poor fellow found himself unable to stop its progress. As he was looking upwards, a quantity of molten lead suddenly rushed like a torrent from the roof, and falling upon his head, face, and shoulders, burnt him fearfully. His companions, dismayed at the extent of the conflagration, descended to the rock, with little hope of being saved. It seems that at an early hour the flames were seen by some of the Cawsand fishermen ; and on intelligence being given, a fishing-boat, manned with a strong crew, was dispatched at once. The boat arrived about eight hours after the fire had broken out, during which time the three keepers of the lighthouse had not only been driven from all the rooms and the staircase, but to avoid the fall of the timber and red-hot bolts, they were found sitting in a hole or cave, on the east side of the rock, almost in a state of stupefaction. They were conveyed safely to Plymouth. Henry Hall, of Stonehouse, who had received such fearful injuries from the molten lead, had attained the age of ninety-four. On his death a solid piece of lead was found in his body, weighing upwards of seven ounces.

This fire occurred in 1753, and it was then determined that the lighthouse should be constructed of stone, and that no expense should be spared to render it the most perfect of its kind. The architect chosen was the famous John Smeaton, one of the most extraordinary men of the age. The first stone of the edifice was laid the 12th June, 1757, and the whole undertaking of constructing the lighthouse was accomplished within a space of little more than three years, without the loss of life or limb to those engaged in the perilous undertaking. It was an anxious time for Smeaton and those who were engaged with him. When the weather was tempestuous the lighthouse was inaccessible. One of the keepers, Henry Edwards, after a heavy storm had prevented any boat from approaching the rocks, sent a note to the manager of the works, stating "that the sea ran over the house in such a manner that for twelve days together they could not open the door of the lantern, nor any other. The house shook as if a man had been up in a great tree. The old men were almost frightened out of their lives, wishing they had never seen the place. The fear occasioned pains in the back, but rubbing them with oil of turpentine gave them relief." The lighthouse itself bore the storm admirably, and suffered nothing from it.

The present edifice is a circular tower sweeping up with a gentle curve from the base, and gradually diminishing to the top. The upper extremity is furnished with a kind of cornice, and is surmounted by a lantern, having a gallery around it with an iron balustrade. The tower is furnished with a door, and windows, and staircase. Round the upper store-room is the inscription: "Except the Lord build the house, they labour in vain that build it.—Psalm cxxvii." Over each side of the lantern are the words and date: "August 24th, 1759. Laus Deo."

On the completion of this structure only two light-keepers were stationed in charge, but an incident of a very extraordinary and distressing nature occurred which showed the necessity of an additional keeper. One of the two guardians of the lighthouse became ill and died; the dilemma in which this occurrence left the survivor was singularly painful. Apprehensive that if he threw the dead body of his companion into the sea—which was the only mode in his power of disposing of it—he might be charged with murder, he let the corpse lie, in hopes that the attending boat might be able to land, and relieve him from his distress. The body, however, became so putrid that it was not in his power to get rid of it without help, for it was nearly a month before the boat could effect a landing, owing to the severe weather. The assistance at length came, the corpse was thrown into the sea, but it was some time before the rooms in the lighthouse could be properly purified.

The greatest achievement in the erection of lighthouses since the days of Smeaton is that of the "Bell-Rock" tower in Scotland, built upon a dangerous sunken reef, about eleven miles from Arbroath, on the northern side of the entrance of the great estuary or arm of the sea called the Firth of Forth, and, as such, directly affecting the safety of all vessels entering the Firth of Tay. The "Inchcape," or Bell-Rock, had always been a perilous point to navigators, and in former times a bell was placed there by the Abbot of Aberbrothock, or Arbroath, which was put in movement by the waves. This was the only expedient that our ancestors could then devise. According to tradition, some pirates having carried off this bell, were, on a subsequent voyage, lost on the same rock. Southey's thrilling ballad of the "Inchcape Bell" is founded on this legend.

The building was commenced in 1807 (17th August), under the control of Mr. Robert Stephenson, the engineer to the Lighthouse Board, and whose plan—a tower of masonry, on the principle of the Eddystone Lighthouse—was adopted. From an account of these operations written by that eminent engineer, we learn how severe and perilous was the undertaking, the rock being only dry for a few hours at spring-tides, and affording but little time for laying the foundations of the building with the requisite security. This, however, under many difficulties, was effected, and the first stone of the lighthouse laid 10th July, 1808, at the depth of sixteen feet below high water at spring-tide. The whole of the masonry to the height of thirty feet was completed in 1810, the light being exhibited for the first time 1st February, 1811.

The most anxious period of Mr. Stephenson's personal superintendence of the erection of the lighthouse occurred in 1807, when the "Smeaton," a small vessel employed for the service of the workpeople, and moored to the rock, broke from her moorings and drifted away. Having both wind and tide against her, Stephenson, who was on the rock with his workmen, perceived with great anxiety that the vessel could not possibly return to the rock until it was covered by water, and the safety of the workmen and himself was thus imperilled. They were on a sunken rock in the middle of the ocean, which, in the progress of flood-tide, would be laid under water to the depth of at least twelve feet in a stormy sea. There were on that morning thirty-two persons at work on that rock, with only two boats which could contain only in fair weather twenty-four sitters, but to row to the floating light as a place of refuge, with so heavy a sea, eight men in each boat were as much as could with safety be attempted. In this manner only half the number of men on the rock could expect to get a chance of escape from a horrible death. Meanwhile the men were at work, little dreaming of the fearful position in which they were placed; but at length the water began to rise, and they became aware of their condition. At this critical moment Mr. Stephenson was standing on an elevated part of the rock, whence he endeavoured to trace the position of the "Smeaton." The melancholy solemnity of the group around him made a deep impression on his mind. He was considering various means of saving them, and the only chance seemed to be that they should embark in the two boats when the water rose high, and take their chance of being picked up. He was about to address the men, when a large boat was seen through the haze, making towards the rock. This at once rejoiced every heart. It proved to be the boat of James Spink, the Bell-Rock pilot. He had come from Arbroath with letters. Spink had for some time seen the "Smeaton," and had even supposed, from the state of the weather, that all the workmen from the rock were on board, until he approached more closely, and then observed people upon the rock. Not supposing, however, that the assistance of his boat was necessary, he anchored on the lee-side of the rock and began to fish, waiting, as usual, until the letters were sent for, as his boat was too large and unwieldy to approach the rock when there was any roughness or run of the sea at the entrance of the landing-creeks. Upon this fortunate change of circumstances, sixteen of the workmen were sent in two trips in one of the boats, with instructions for Spink to proceed with them to the temporary floating light. This being accomplished, the remaining sixteen followed in the two boats belonging to the service of the rock. Every one felt the most perfect happiness at leaving the Bell-Rock that morning, though a very hard and even dangerous passage to the floating light still awaited them, as the winds had increased by this time to a hard gale, accompanied with a considerable swell of sea. The boats left the rock about nine o'clock, but did not reach the vessel until twelve. Every one was completely drenched in water, and after much baling of water and severe work at the oars, the three boats reached the floating light.

There can be no doubt that the opportune arrival of James Spink and his boat on this critical occasion was the means of preventing a fearful loss of life at the rock; and it is pleasing to add that the worthy pilot, then in his seventieth year, received a small pension for his services.

On the completion of the lighthouse, the keepers were at first alarmed on seeing the waves beat in stormy weather most furiously against the building. The sea rose to a height exceeding one hundred feet above the surface of the rock, and the vibration of the building was very great.

On the 14th of November, 1812, at high water in the evening, a tremendous sea struck the lighthouse; the locks upon the doors were heard to rattle, and the whole building was shaken. The lighthouse-keepers sprang up into the balcony, thinking that some vessel had struck upon the rock. The tower, however, stood firm, and has ever since sustained its character for solidity.

Another celebrated stone lighthouse on the Scottish coast is that placed on the "Skerryvore" rocks, which lie about twelve miles off the Isle of Tyree, in Argyllshire. These rocks were for a long period the terror of mariners, and numerous shipwrecks had occurred in their vicinity. Owing to the great difficulty of landing upon these rocks, which are worn smooth by the continual beating of the Atlantic waves, it was not until 1834 that the idea of erecting a lighthouse was seriously entertained. In such a situation as that of Skerryvore everything had to be provided beforehand, and transported from a distance. The design for the building was made by Mr. Alan Stephenson, son of the celebrated architect of the Bell-Rock Lighthouse, and was an adaptation of Smeaton's Eddystone tower. Many were the vicissitudes and privations experienced in this undertaking, but Providence blessed the result, and this stately and noble building remains a boon to seamen, the signal of trust and confidence to the sea-bound mariner.

Other important lighthouses of stone might be mentioned, such as the "Bishop Rock," the "Needles," the "Smalls," &c. Iron lighthouses have of late been erected, and appear to be admirably suited to the purpose, and comparatively inexpensive. The "Northfleet" is built of this material, and is in open skeleton-work. Iron lighthouses have been adopted in several of the British colonies.

With regard to the height of lighthouses, from one hundred and fifty to two hundred feet is generally considered the best elevation for the height of a light above the water, but this must of course depend upon the locality. The greatest height on the coast of England is that of Lundy Island, five hundred and forty feet above the sea. In Scotland, Barrahead Light is six hundred and eighty feet high. In Ireland, the Skelligs are three hundred and seventy-two feet high.

*Bells*, as a warning to mariners, have been and are still generally employed at lighthouses as one of the best modes of signalling in times of fogs. I have already alluded to the Inchcape Bell, and to Mr. Stephenson's lighthouse on that dangerous rock. The machinery which causes the reflectors to revolve every half-minute is made to ring two large bells, each weighing about twelve hundred-weight, to warn the seaman of his danger when too near this rock.

In some lighthouses *guns* are fired during fogs: at those in Nova Scotia, *horns* are sounded during fogs, and these are heard at a distance of three miles. In the South-Stack Lighthouse, near Holyhead, built on the middle of an island under a cliff, and connected with the mainland by a bridge, tamed *sea-birds* are employed as signals. The gulls perch on the walls of the lighthouse, and utter cries that warn the sailor. This lighthouse has a bell and a gun, but the natural signal has been judged so superior that the cannon has been removed some distance from the rock for fear lest the noise should startle the birds. In this island the young gulls run about among the white rabbits, with whom they live on the most intimate terms.

*Gongs* are used in several lighthouses, and are found of great use.

Professor Holmes invented a *steam trumpet*, the sound of which is heard at a considerable distance. The instrument can be tuned at will, and thus produces different notes. A small quantity of steam suffices.

In Scotland *whistles* are placed in the lanterns of the lighthouses, and these communicate by tubes with the rooms below, in order to summon assistance if required, and thus avoid the necessity of the keeper in charge leaving his post until relieved.

In the absence of any authority respecting the material with which the earliest lighthouses were illuminated, we may naturally conclude that wood furnished the means, with any other substance which would give intensity to the flame, or contribute to its duration.

Among the Greeks the beacon consisted of an iron or brazen frame, wherein were three or four bars which stood upon a circular base of the same metal. They were bound with a hoop, and thus made capable of containing combustible matter. This was placed upon a high pole, and hung sloping, seaward, over the battlements of a tower or from the stern of a ship.

In our own country, lighthouses from an early period appear to have been illuminated by coal or wood fires contained in pans. At the close of the seventeeth century an iron grate on the top of the North Foreland Lighthouse, in Kent, contained a coal fire open to the air; and later, in 1732, the top of the tower was covered with a sort of lantern with large sash windows, and the light of the fire was kept up by bellows, which were moved during the night by attendants. The last coal-light—that of St. Bee's in

Cumberland—was only extinguished in 1822. To coal fires succeeded tallow candles, and these were fastened in wooden rods, as they are sometimes seen arranged before booths in fairs. These were in use for forty years at the Eddystone Lighthouse after it was completed by Smeaton.

The use of oil does not seem to date back beyond 1730: lamps with twisted cotton wicks were used, but these were always attended with smoke and a bad smell. The first decided improvement was made by M. Argand, a native of Geneva, who, in 1784, invented a lamp with a circular wick. The flame thus became a hollow cylinder, with a current of air ascending through the inside, so that the burning surface was doubled. To make these lamps more effective for lighthouses, and to prevent the rays of light from escaping on all sides, a reflector was added by M. Lenoir. This threw the light forward in parallel rays towards such points of the horizon as would be useful to mariners; but M. Augustin Fresnel was the first to introduce lenticular action into lighthouse illumination by the adoption of the annular or built lens. Along with Arago, he investigated the action exercised by polarized rays of light on each other, and the practical application of his theory to the improvement of the lighthouse system was of immense value, and quite abolished the old method of illuminating the "sea sentinels."

Among the later adaptations for this object are the introduction of gas, but this is attended by the uncertainty and other objections connected with its manufacture and use in remote and inaccessible places. It is, however, of great convenience and use in harbour lights.

The attention of scientific men, as far as lighthouses are concerned, is now almost confined to the discovery of the best modes of producing the light. That in ordinary use leaves little to be desired when the weather is tolerably clear; since a first-class oil light, at the height on which it is usually elevated, is visible from the masthead when the vessel comes above the horizon of the lighthouse. It is in hazy weather that a more intense light becomes desirable. There is the "Drummond" light, which consists in substituting for the Argand burner a small ball of lime ignited by the combustion of oxygen and hydrogen; but the difficulty of obtaining a continuous combustion has hitherto prevented the adoption of this means of illumination in lighthouses. The "electric" light, discovered by the late Professor Faraday, has undergone careful trials by the Government authorities. It possesses an advantage from its not being a mere spark of very small size, as compared with an oil lamp of the same power; for this enables much smaller optical apparatus to be used, occasioning not only a saving of cost, but a saving of light—the loss of light being less when the glass is thinner. The electro-magnetic light at the South Foreland, in Kent, has been seen thirty minutes after losing sight of the lower lights—that is, at the rate of a steamer's progress—a distance of about seven miles. There seem to be, however, impediments which render the electric light impracticable on rock stations, such as the Eddystone and the Bell-Rock Lighthouses.

To these notices of the structures raised for the guidance and security of mariners, I will now add some observations on the *animated* sentinels of the seas: those men to whose care these all-important buildings are entrusted. Life in a lighthouse would seem to us a terrible hardship. Perhaps one of the worst of criminals, who might be indifferent to most kinds of penal punishment, would be terrified if he were condemned to pass the remainder of his life on a solitary rock amidst the wild ocean. It would appear, indeed, difficult to reconcile the mind to a service so lonely and peculiar, not unfrequently attended at some places with risks and privations, and requiring an amount of vigilance and responsibility not very tempting to most men in search of employment. Yet it appears that these situations are frequently sought after, and by persons who have been engaged in far different occupations. Some of these applicants have been carpenters, blacksmiths, domestic servants, butchers, bricklayers, painters, bakers, coopers, tailors, &c. Among these individuals there are doubtless some whose taste for solitude may have induced them to forsake their occupations among the busy haunts of society, and others, perhaps, to whom the novelty of the employment might offer some attraction; but it is a singular circumstance, that almost all who have adopted a lighthouse for their home seem to have been satisfied with their choice, and some even have boasted that they would not change their solitary lot for any other. One of the keepers of the Casket Rocks Lighthouse, in the Channel, whose life is ordinarily spent on those bleak rocks far out at sea, after a temporary absence on shore, returned, declaring "he had no wish to enter the great world again."

The long service of many of these solitary watchers shows how readily the mind adapts itself to strange circumstances. Several of these worthy men have been born in the service; instances are recorded in the "Returns" of the Trinity Board, of thirty, forty, and fifty years' service. Another subject of remark is the large families of several of the keepers: ten, twelve, and fourteen children being stated in the "Returns" as the number of some of the families in lighthouses. In all the English and Scotch lighthouses the men are as comfortably lodged as circumstances will permit. They are provided with books, a great boon to men who pass so much of their time in solitude. In France the keepers are allowed to have an arm-chair, but in Great Britain this luxury is forbidden. In Denmark, where the lighthouse may be on land, the men have a piece of ground granted to them large enough to maintain a couple of cows.

Many lighthouse-keepers employ their leisure time in various pursuits. Their chief duty is to keep the apparatus for the lights in the most clean and polished condition. The Trinity Board Commissioners require particular care in these respects. During one of their visits to the Youghal Lighthouse, they had occasion to remark the unusual brilliancy of the brass-work, when it appeared that the keeper had been butler in a gentleman's family, and had turned his experience in cleaning plate to the advantage of the lighthouse. Where the situation of the building permits, the keepers add to the stock of provisions supplied them from the shore by fishing and the cultivation of a small garden; but this latter luxury is enjoyed but by few, as the rocks on which lighthouses are placed are bleak and barren, and in many cases are entirely destitute of verdure. Most of the men are good carpenters; one, mentioned in the "Returns," was the owner of a turning-lathe, which he had taught himself to use with great dexterity; another practised photography.

Thus far I have given a somewhat pleasing picture of life in a lighthouse; but I must not omit to tell you that these courageous sentinels of the seas are often exposed to severe hardships and perils. The storms, which are sometimes continuous for days, lash the waves of the ocean into fury round the lighthouses, and prevent any communication with shore, by which much distress for want of provisions is occasioned.

In the South Rock Lighthouse, in the Irish seas, the waves at high water cover the rock, and at high tide rises up the tower to the height of eighteen feet. The spray goes over the building, which, in heavy weather, shakes to the foundation. The Longship Lighthouse is built on the top of a conical rock opposite the Land's End, in Cornwall. In severe weather the waves break above the lantern, which is seventy-nine feet above high-water mark. There is a cavern under this lighthouse, at the end of a long slip in the rock, and during a heavy sea the noise produced by the escape of the pent-up air from the cavern is so great that the keepers can hardly sleep. It is said that one man, newly appointed, was so terrified by the noise that his hair turned white. The great rock on which the Caskets Lighthouse is erected, in the Channel, is thirty feet above the level of the sea. The force of the elements is sometimes severely tried on these isolated structures. In the storms of winter the wind howls furiously around them, and the sea, provoked by its violence, and receiving the additional impulse of the tidal current, dashes enormous volumes of water over the rock, striking and often damaging the lights. In 1823 a fearful storm entirely destroyed them. A small plot of ground is cultivated with a few vegetables on the Casket Rocks; but the whole of the earth employed for this purpose was brought from the island of Alderney.

In many lighthouses there is a great want of ventilation, the lanterns being very hot and close. The eyes of the keepers occasionally suffer from the glare. The want of fresh vegetables sometimes induced a tendency to scurvy, for which lime-juice and other remedies are now provided.

In the reports connected with lighthouses, published by the Trinity Board, instances of insanity among the keepers are mentioned; also loss of memory in others, and inability to perform duty in consequence of injuries received. One poor fellow, James Clarke, aged thirty-two, is stated to be in the receipt of a pension, in consequence of mental imbecility occasioned by fright and wounds received at a fire in a lighthouse, when his wife and five children were suffocated. One day, in 1862, two black flags were seen hoisted on the top of the Longship Lighthouse. It was a distress signal. Of the three men who inhabited the tower the one on duty at the time stabbed himself in a fit of insanity. His companions had endeavoured to staunch the blood. The sea was so rough and the landing so dangerous that it was some time before the wounded man could receive proper attention, and he died just after being conveyed on shore.

The present lighthouse on the Bishop's Rock, at Scilly, which occupies the site of a building destroyed in 1850 during a violent storm, is so difficult of access that the men in charge on coming from shore never approach it without their life-belts. They have to leap out of the boat on to a rock as smooth as marble, and if the foot slips, or the hand fails to grasp the angles of the rock, the man is hurled into the sea. This lighthouse was struck, in 1860, by a water-spout, which carried away its bell, hung one hundred feet above the ordinary high-water level.

> " The startled waves leap over it; the storm
>  Smites it with all the scourges of the rain;
> And steadily against its solid form
>  Press the great shoulders of the hurricane."

A few years ago, a lighthouse which stood on a point called the "Double Stanners," between Lytham and Blackpool, and which had given signs of insecurity, was noticed by the keepers, one night, to vibrate more than usual. The next morning they discovered that a portion of the front had fallen down, and that nearly all the foundation was undermined by the sea. They removed their furniture, but left the necessary implements to light the lamps. At nightfall the high tide surrounded them, and the wind blew with such violence that there was very little hope of the building holding out until morning; but still the light had never shone more brilliantly than on that night. The lighthouse was swept away next day; the keepers, however, had taken warning in time and escaped.

The most interesting associations connected with lighthouse-keepers centre in the family of the Darlings, of the Longstone Lighthouse. The name of Grace Darling is inseparably allied to it. The wonderful courage and humanity displayed by her on the occasion of the wreck of the "Forfarshire" steamer, in 1838, has often been related. The Farne Islands, where this event occurred, lie off the Northumbrian coast. They are a group of barren and desolate rocks, inhabited chiefly by sea-fowl, and their sides are in many parts exceedingly precipitous. Through the channels between the smaller Farne Islands the sea rushes with great impetuosity, and, doubtless, many a shipwreck of which there is no record has occurred there in former times, when there was no warning light to guide the seaman on his way through the deep. It was on one of the rocks I have mentioned that the "Forfarshire" struck, and was broken into two pieces; the after-part, containing the cabin and many passengers, being carried off by a rapid current, and the fore-part remaining on the rock, with the remainder of its living freight exposed to instant destruction. Soon after daybreak the wreck was seen from the Longstone Lighthouse, nearly a mile distant, by the Darlings. A mist hovered over the island, and though the wind had abated, the sea was raging fearfully, making any approach to the rugged pinnacles and sunken rocks which surround these islands a work of extreme peril. Even at a later period of the day, a reward of five pounds, offered by the steward of Bamborough Castle, could not induce a party of fishermen to venture from the mainland. To have braved the dangers of that terrible passage would have done the highest honour to the well-tried nerves of the stoutest of the male sex; but what shall be said of the errand of mercy being undertaken and accomplished through the strength of a female heart and arm? Through the dim mist, with the aid of a glass, the figures of the sufferers were seen clinging to the wreck. Darling, it is said, shrunk from the attempt to succour them, considering the case hopeless; but at his daughter's solicitation the boat was launched, with the assistance of Mrs. Darling, the father and daughter entering it, and each taking an oar.

In estimating the danger which the heroic adventurers risked, there is one circumstance which should be remembered. Had it not been ebb-tide the boat could not have passed between the islands, and they knew that the tide would be flowing on their return, when their united strength would be utterly insufficient to row the boat back to the lighthouse island; so that without the assistance of the survivors on their return, they themselves would have been compelled to remain on the rock, beside the wreck, until the tide again ebbed. It must have been to the Darlings but a forlorn hope; but their courage rose with the emergency—God's blessing accompanied them—and their efforts were crowned with success. The whole of the survivors of the wreck, nine in number, were received in the little bark, and conveyed in safety to the lighthouse. Here, owing to the violent seas which continued to prevail, they were obliged to remain two days, during which time they received every kindness and comfort that the Darlings could give. The subsequent events of Grace Darling's life are soon told. The noble deed she had done may be said to have wafted her name all over the world. The lonely Longstone Lighthouse became speedily the centre of attraction to sympathizing thousands, including many of the wealthy and great, who testified in several instances, by substantial tokens, the feelings with which they regarded the young heroine. A public subscription soon amounting to seven hundred pounds was raised for her, but with a modesty and good sense allied to her other noble qualities, she continued to reside at the lighthouse with her father and mother, finding in her limited sphere of domestic duty on that sea-girt isle, a more honourable and a more rational enjoyment than she could have derived in the crowded haunts of the mainland. Grace Darling did not live long in the enjoyment of the honours that had been showered upon her, dying of consumption the 25th of October, 1842, at the age of twenty-seven, and four years after the occurrence which has rendered her name so famous.

I have confined my remarks to lighthouses, but I must not omit to mention the *Floating Lights*, which also render invaluable services as sea sentinels. Many of them are placed in very exposed positions, but seldom go adrift, and I believe there is no instance on record where the crew have abandoned their perilous stations in stormy weather. When the vessels appropriated to this purpose have been driven from their moorings—and the rarity of such an occurrence has made it remarkable—the vessels have always been replaced in a very short time. None have ever been wrecked, and it does not appear that the lights, so indispensable to the safety of passing ships, have ever been accidentally extinguished. The Trinity House vessels are painted red; in Ireland they are black with a white streak. These two colours seem to contrast best with the colour of the sea. They are all distinguished by balls hoisted at the mastheads of the vessels, and by other signals. In foggy weather gongs are used as a warning to ships.

A considerable number of birds are caught at lighthouses:

"The sea-bird wheeling round them with the din
Of wind, and wings, and solitary cries,
Blinded and maddened with the light within,
Dashes itself against the glare, and dies."

At the "Smalls" woodcocks have been caught in September, as also larks, starlings, and blackbirds. The keeper once secured a young seal by descending quietly while the animal was sleeping on the rock, and placing a bag in front of him, into which the seal went on being stirred up. At Roche Point Lighthouse, Queenstown, on one occasion a duck got into the lantern through the cowl, and fluttering around, broke all the chimneys and extinguished the lights.

At Calais Lighthouse, the lantern is surrounded by a wire net, and its use is practically seen as a museum of stuffed birds, all of which have been caught or killed themselves at the light. The collection contains many rare small birds, a bittern, some large cormorants, and a swan. The latter flew against the lantern while the keeper of the lighthouse was engaged in cleaning the glass. The bird broke the panes, and injured the lens so much that one hundred and sixty pounds were expended in repairing it. The man said that the force with which the swan struck the glass was so great, that he might have been killed if he had not been seated at his work. The crash above his head was awful.

In concluding these brief notices of lighthouses, I trust you will often think of the lonely watchers to whose care they are entrusted with feelings of the deepest interest, for the lives of many brave men, and the security of valuable vessels, depend upon their vigilance and unceasing attention.

> " See! on the stormy brow of night
> A star! a hope! a bursting light!
> At its sudden gleam despair has fled—
> 'T is the light, the hallow'd light of the Head!
> We are safe! we are safe! there is help at hand!
> Glad voices that hail us from the strand.
> We are safe! we are safe! there is help at hand!
> GOD BLESS THE LIGHTS OF OUR NATIVE LAND!"

# INDEX.

## A.

Adventures with the walrus, 108
Affection of the Polar bear to its young, 115
,, walrus ,, 109
,, whales ,, 67, 68
Albatross, the, 244
"Almirante," treasures recovered from the wreck of the, 362
American accounts of the sea-serpent, 256
,, Submarine Company, 361
Ammonite, the, 201
Anecdotes connected with the whale fishery, 80
,, of tame seals, 53
,, of a Dutch whaling crew, 68
,, ,, seaman, 81
Anemones, beauty of sea, 188
,, their power of reproducing organs, 190
Angel-shark, the, 101
Angler, the, or fishing-frog, 332
Animalculæ in a drop of water, 122
Animal life in the ocean, minute, 119
Animated sentinels of the seas, 409
Anning, Mary, discovery of fossils by, 249
Apollo, colossal statue of, at Rhodes, 392
Apparatus for sea-soundings, 131
Apparitions at sea, 241
Archer-fish, the, 345
Archipelago, the Indian, 17
Artic and Antarctic circles, 26
,, explorers, courage of, 23
,, ,, descriptions of icebergs by, 31
,, regions, dryness of the air in the, 45
,, ,, horrors of the, 30
,, ,, modern expeditions to the, 24
,, ,, summer and sunrise in the, 44
Argand lamps in lighthouses, 404
Argonaut, difference between the, and the nautilus, 198

Atlantic Ocean, the, 12
,, ,, highway of commerce, 12
,, ,, origin of the name, 12
,, ,, submarine cable in the, 12
Atmospheric influences on the ocean, 208
Attack on a vessel by a whale, 80
,, on the whale, 75
Auk, the great, 373
,, razor-bill, 374
Aurora borealis, the, 210
Australia, 17

## B.

Baiting the shark, 94
Balboa, discovery of the Pacific by, 13
Banner-fish, the, 346
Battles between the walrus and the Polar bear, 110
Barnacle, superstitions respecting the, 245
Basse, the, or sea-perch, 343
Beacons, 394
Bearded or great seals, 50
Bears, Polar, 107, 113, 114, 116
Beautiful fishes, 337
Beauty of coral beds, 133
,, sea-anemones, 188
,, ,, worms, 126
Bell, the diving, 352
,, Rock lighthouse, 399
Bells, superstitions of seamen regarding, 241
Birds, booby, 388
,, caught at lighthouses, 411
,, frigate, 387
,, preying on molluscs, 305
,, sea, 363
,, tropical sea, 386
Black-backed gull, the great, 368
,, headed ,, 367
Bladder, the sea, 199

Blenny, or butterfly-fish, the, 346
Blessing the waters of the Neva, 240
Blubber of whales, its use, 60
Blue sharks, 101
Boar-fish, the, 342
Bore, the, 226
Boundaries of the Indian Ocean, 19
Bream, the sea, 341
Brill, the, 294
British Museum, fossil marine animals in the, 248
Brookes's apparatus for sea soundings, 131
Buckland's description of the ichthyosaurus, 249

### C.

Cable, submarine, in the Atlantic, 12
Cachalot whale, the, 62
Candle-fishes, how caught, 275
Capture of whales, a great, 65
Carnivorous fishes, 320
Carrageen moss, 161
Caul, superstitions respecting a child's, 242
Causes of whirlpools, 7
Caviare, how prepared, 280
Ceylon moss, 161
Changing colours of the dolphin, 338
„ „ icebergs, 32
Chœtodon, beauty of the, 183, 341
Chimæra, the, or rabbit-fish, 349
China seas, submarine beauty of the, 182
Chinese, birds trained to fish by the, 270
„ pearl fisheries, 152
Cingalese „ divers, 149
Clure, Captain Mc, discovery of the North-West Passage by, 25
„ perilous journey of, 22
Coal-fish, the, 293
Cod fishery, the, 291
Cold, human endurance of, 21
Coldness of the ice regions, reason of the, 27
Colossus of Rhodes, 392
Colours, beautiful, of sea-weeds, 158
„ „ shells, 151
„ of the ocean, 11
Columbus and the Gulf-weed, 155
Composition of shells, 173
„ water, 4
Conger, the great sea, 281
Conybeare's description of the plesiosaurus, 249
Cook, Captain, adventure with a walrus, 108
„ voyages of, 17
Coral beds, beauty of, 133
„ builders, wonders of the, 136
„ formerly supposed a marine plant, 134
„ polyps described, 135
„ reefs, perils of the, 138
„ „ shipwreck on, 138
„ superstitions regarding, 145
Corduan, the Tour de, lighthouse, 394
Cormorant, the, 375
„ „ fishing by, 143
Crabs, how taken, 296
„ hermit, 297
Crows guides to seamen, 243

Cruise among the whales, 70
Currents of the ocean, 5
„ effects of, 7
„ tidal influence on, 9
Cuttle-fish, the, 204
„ mode of taking, 206
Cuvier, wonderful anatomical knowledge of, 251
Cyclones, 225

### D.

Dangers of whalers from the ice, 84
„ from icebergs, 34
Darling, heroic conduct of Grace, 408
Day, disastrous fate of John, 359
Dead bodies at sea ominous to sailors, 246
"Dædalus," sea-serpent seen by the crew of the, 256
Deductor whale, the, 64
Deep, monsters of the, 248
Depth of the ocean, 10
Derivation of "fossil," 248
„ "gurnard," 323
Description of the ichthyosaurus, 249
„ sponges, 167
„ submarine scenery, 185
Devil, the sea, 320
Dexterity of the New Zealand fishermen, 78
Difference between the argonaut and true nautilus, 198
Different species of seals, 49
Discovery of the North-West Passage, 25
„ „ Pacific Ocean, 13
„ „ relics of Sir John Franklin, 24
Diver-birds, the, 372
Diving apparatus, 357
„ bell, the, 352
„ „ employed to recover sunken treasures, 353
„ „ at the Polytechnic Institution, 358
„ „ Smeaton's application of, to building uses, 358
Diving-dress, the, 359
Dog-fish, the, 101, 287
Dolphins attack the flying-fish, 339
„ changing colours of, 338
„ supposed to foretell storms, 245
Domestication of the walrus, 111
Dory, the John, 341
Dover, the Roman lighthouse at, 393
Dragons, sea, 248
"Dreadnought" ship attacked by a sword-fish, 336
Droll ceremonies at sea, 73
Dugong, the, 264
Dulse sea-weed, the, 161

### E.

Eagle, the great sea, 381
Earliest notices of lighthouses, 390
„ voyages in the Indian Ocean, 19
„ „ Pacific „ 17
Earthquakes at sea, 227

## INDEX

Edda, traditions of the sea-serpent in the, 257
Eddystone rocks, Smeaton's lighthouse on the, 395
Eel, the electric, 318
Eels, fishing for sand, 282
Effect of currents, 7
Electric fishes, 316
   ,, illumination of lighthouses, 405
   ,, light, fishing by the, 270
Enemies of the oyster, 304
Equipment of whaling-ships, 72
Escape from an iceberg, 35
   ,, of a whaling crew, 82
Esquimaux attack on whales, 61
   ,, capture of seals by the, 47
   ,, clever workpeople, 46
   ,, kayaks, or skin boats, 47
   ,, preparations for fishing, 46
   ,, ,, of blubber, 46
   ,, women's boats of the, 61
Etelis, the ruby-coloured, 184
Experiments on sponges by Ellis and Grant, 165
Extraordinary strength of sharks' teeth, 95

F.

Fight between a whale and a grampus, 66
Fishermen, superstitions of, 233
   ,, "good luck" among, 246
Fishes, air-bladder of, 312
   ,, banner, 346
   ,, beautiful, 339
   ,, blenny, 346
   ,, boar, 342
   ,, bodies of, 312
   ,, brain of, 315
   ,, bream, sea, 341
   ,, brill, 294
   ,, candle, 275
   ,, carnivorous, 320
   ,, chœtodon, 183, 345
   ,, chimæra, 349
   ,, circulation of blood in, 312
   ,, coal, 293
   ,, cross-bow, 182
   ,, cuttle, 204
   ,, Dory, John, 341.
   ,, eggs of, 315
   ,, electric, 316
   ,, etelis, 184
   ,, eyes of, 313
   ,, fins of, 311
   ,, flying, 326
   ,, ,, attacked by dolphins, 339
   ,, form of, 311
   ,, fox-shark, 341
   ,, frog, 332
   ,, gilt-heads, 341
   ,, goby, 326, 346
   ,, goldsinny, 348
   ,, goramy, 326
   ,, gurnards, 323, 326
   ,, jelly, 121
   ,, king, or opah, 342
   ,, ling, 293

Fishes, lumpsucker, 320
   ,, maigre, 329
   ,, mesoprion, 344
   ,, mullet, red, 342
   ,, musical, 328
   ,, odds and ends about, 310
   ,, onion-shaped, 346
   ,, parrot, 347
   ,, perch, sea, 342
   ,, pilot, 103
   ,, pipe-mouthed, 348
   ,, plectropoma, 344
   ,, pogonia, 329
   ,, porpoise, 276
   ,, respiration of, 312
   ,, riband-shaped, 346
   ,, rock, 348
   ,, ruminating, 348
   ,, scabbard, 346
   ,, scales of, 313
   ,, scaly-finned, 345
   ,, sea-devil, 330
   ,, ,, horse, 348
   ,, ,, owl snail, 320
   ,, ,, scorpion, 324
   ,, seranus, lettered, 344
   ,, ,, spiny, 344
   ,, smell of, 312
   ,, snail slime, 198
   ,, stinging, 318
   ,, sucking, 320
   ,, tail of, 311
   ,, taste of, 313
   ,, teeth of, 313
   ,, torpedo, 317
   ,, trumpet, 348
   ,, trygon, 318
   ,, turbot, 294
   ,, uses of, 315
   ,, weever, the great, 318
   ,, wrasse, 347
Fisheries, cod, 290
   ,, pearl, 148
   ,, sardine, 290
   ,, sponge, 166
   ,, whale, 70
Fishing, birds trained for, 271
   ,, by electric light, 270
   ,, torchlight, 275
   ,, dexterity of the cormorant in, 373
   ,, for gars, 277
   ,, sand-eels, 282
   ,, sturgeon, 279
   ,, hawk, or osprey, 383
   ,, mode of, in various countries, 268
   ,, of the South Sea Islanders, 272
   ,, tackle, 273
Floating lights at sea, 411
   ,, navigators of the ocean, 194
   ,, wing-shells, 203
Fog, red, at sea, 229
Food of seals, 52
   ,, whales, 59
Fossil, derivation of the term, 243
   ,, nautili, 200
   ,, marine animals, 248
   ,, teeth of sharks, 89

416                                    *INDEX.*

Fossil remains at Lyme Regis, 249
French lighthouses, 404
Frigate-birds, 387
Frozen Ocean, the, 20
   ,,      fantastic forms of icebergs in, 32
   ,,      fearful accident in, 27
   ,,      Franklin's death in, 24
   ,,      repelling features of, 20
   ,,  to death, 28
Fur seal, the, 50

### G.

Gann, John, the diver, 360
Gannet, the, 378
Gar, the, 277
Gardens, submarine, 188
Gilt-head, the, 341
Glaucus, the, 196
Goby, the, 346
Goldsinny, 348
"Good luck" of fishermen, 246
Goramy, the, 326
Grampus, pugnacity of the, 66
Greenland bear, the, 113
   ,,    icebergs formed in, 33
   ,,    shark, the, 102
Guillemots, the, 372
Gulf-Stream, the, 5
   ,,  weed, the, 156
Gulls, 365
   ,,  sea, an omen to sailors, 244
   ,,  black-headed, 367
   ,,  formerly a delicacy of the table, 368
   ,,  glaucous, 366
   ,,  herring, or silvery, 368
   ,,  Iceland, 367
   ,,  kittiwake, 368
   ,,  little, the, 367
   ,,  rapacity of, 366
   ,,  tricks played upon, 367
Gurnard, derivation of the name, 323
   ,,  flying, the, 326
   ,,  group of fishes, 323

### H.

Habits of seals, 52
Haddock, the, 293
Hakes, mode of taking, 287
Haloes, 213
Hammer-headed shark, the, 101
Harp-seal, the, 250
Height of waves, 9
Hermit-crab, the, 297
Herring fishery, the, 285
   ,,  or silvery gull, 368
   ,,  mode of curing the, 286
Hippocampus, or sea-horse, 348
Historical renown of sea-lampreys, 322
Hooks for shark-fishing, 97
Hooper, the, or wild swan, 381
Horrible fate of seamen from sharks, 99
Horrors of an Arctic winter, 30

Hull a whaling station, 71
   ,,  curious customs at, 71
Human endurance of cold, 21
Hurricanes, 225

### I.

Ice, accumulation of "packed," 43
   ,,  blink, 214
   ,,  dangers of whalers from the, 84
Icebergs, 30
   ,,  changing tints of, 30
   ,,  dangers arising from, 34
   ,,  described by navigators, 30
   ,,  escape from, 35
   ,,  fantastical shapes of, 30
   ,,  formed in Greenland, 33
   ,,  great height and length of, 33
   ,,  one of the wonders of the ocean, 30
   ,,  origin of, 33
   ,,  picnic on, 37
   ,,  provision of nature regarding, 38
   ,,  sublimity of, 35
   ,,  vessels destroyed by, 35
   ,,    ,,  mooring to, 36
Ice-field, Scoresby's deliverance from an, 39
Iceland gulls, 367
Icthyosaurus described, 249
Illumination of lighthouses, 403
Incident, fearful, in the frozen seas, 27
Indian Archipelago, the, 17
   ,,  Ocean, boundaries of, 19,
   ,,    ,,  earliest voyages on the, 19
Indiscriminate appetite of sharks, 90
Influence of ocean currents, 5
   ,,  winds, 9
Inhabitants of sea-weeds, 123
Instinct of the coral insects, 143
Isinglass, 310
Intervention of sea-saints, 234
Islands, floating, 255
   ,,  of the Pacific, 18
   ,,  pearl, the, 150
   ,,  volcanic, 227
Ives, St., pilchard fishery at, 283

### J.

Jelly-fish, medusa, or, 121
Jumping-Johnnies, 128

### K.

Kane, Dr., on human endurance of cold, 21
Kayaks, or skin boats of the Esquimaux, 47
Keepers, lighthouse, 405
Kelp, value of, 162
Kilda, St., sea-eagle destroyed at, 382
King-fish, the, 342
Kittiwake gull, the, 368
Kraken, the, 254

### L.

Lamprey, the, 322
Laver sea-weed, 161

# INDEX. 417

Lettered seranus, the, 344
Lighthouses, Bell-Rock, 399
,, birds caught at, 411
,, Bishop Rock, 408
,, Caskets, 407
,, Colossus of Rhodes, 392
,, earliest allusions to, 390
,, effects of storms on, 407
,, electric light in, 405
,, floating lights, 411
,, French, 404
,, Grace Darling and the "Longstone," 409
,, height of, 402
,, illumination of, 403
,, keepers of, 405
,, lamp of Diogenes, 392
,, Longship, 408
,, management of, 395
,, Pharos, the oldest of, 391
,, ,, Roman, at Dover, 393
,, Rudyard's Eddystone, 396
,, signals in, 402
,, Smeaton's Eddystone, 398
,, Skerryvore, 401
,, stone, 402
,, Tour de Corduan, 394
,, Winstanley's Eddystone, 395

## M.

Mackerel, the, 341
,, fishery, 283
Magellan's voyages, 16
Magnus, Olaus, on sea-monsters, 261
Magpies ominous, 244
Maigre-fishes, 329
Manatee or sea-cow, 264
Marbled seal, the, 53
Marine fossil animals, 248
,, prodigies, 253
,, sticklebacks, 324
Martyn on the colour of the ocean, 11
Medusa or jelly-fish, 121
Mediterranean Sea, the, 13
Merman seen off Norway, 263
Mermaids, exhibition of stuffed, 267
,, and mermen, 261
Mœsasaurus described, 251
Mesoprion, the one-spotted, 344
Milky sea, a, 11
Minute animal life in the ocean, 119
Miracles at sea, 232
Mirage, the, 208
Mode of curing pilchards, 289
,, fishing in various countries, 268
,, taking the sea-conger, 281
,, ,, crabs, 296
,, ,, cuttle-fish, 206
,, ,, gar-fish, 277
,, ,, haddocks, 293
,, ,, hakes, 287
,, ,, herrings, 285
,, ,, pilchards, 287
,, ,, prawns, 299
,, ,, shrimps, 299

Mode of taking sprats, 290
,, ,, tunnies, 278
,, ,, turbots, 294
,, ,, turtle, 295
,, ,, whitebait, 290
Modern expeditions to the Polar seas, 24
Molluscs, enemies of the, 305
Monarch of the ocean, the, 57
Monk seal, the, 55
Monsoons, 223
Monsters of the deep, 248
Monstrous skate, a, 332
Mullet, red, 342
Musical fish, 328
Mussel "farms," 300

## N.

Narwahl, the, 106
Nautili, fossil, 200
Nautilus, fables respecting the, 195
,, the pearly, 197
,, the, a wonderful builder, 190
Navigators, floating, of the ocean, 194
Nelson's encounter with a Polar bear, 116
"Neptune's Easy Shaving Shop," 73
Nereids, the, 127
Nettles, sea, 124
Nets: seine, trawl and drift, 269
,, used in earliest times, 268
Northern rorqual, the, 62
North-West Passage, 25

## O.

Ocean, Atlantic, the, 12
,, ,, divisions of the, 13
,, ,, origin of the name, 12
,, ,, submarine cable in the, 12
,, boundaries of the Indian, 19
,, earliest voyages in ,, 19
,, colour of the, 11
,, depth of the, 10
,, the, essential to man's existence, 3
,, facilities of intercourse by the, 3
,, floating navigators of the, 194
,, Frozen, the, 20
,, glaucus, a rower on the, 196
,, currents of the, 5
,, luminosity of the, 216
,, marine production of the, 3
,, minute animals of the, 119
,, monarch of the, 57
,, Pacific, the, 16
,, ,, discovery of the, 13
,, ,, early voyages on the, 17
,, ,, origin of the name, 16
,, phenomena of the, 208
,, pirate of the, 19
,, punishing a pirate of the, 93
,, profusion of life in the, 120
,, rock-builders of the, 132
,, saltness of the, 4
,, superstitions connected with the, 231
,, vegetation of the, 155
Odds and ends about fishes, 310

27

Oil, quantity of whale, 60
Old wives of the sea, 347
Oldest lighthouse, the, 391
Omens from birds, &c., 243
Omiak, or Esquimaux boat, 61
Onion-fish, the, 346
Opah, the, or king-fish, 342
Oriental pearls, 151
Origin of icebergs, 33
 ,, pearls, 151
 ,, tides, 8
Osprey, the, or fishing-hawk, 383
Otaries, seal, 55
Owen, Professor, on the sea-serpent, 257
Oyster-farming, 303
 ,, ememies of the, 304

P.

Pacific Ocean, discovery of the, 13
 ,, ,, early voyages in the, 17
 ,, ,, islands of the, 18
 ,, ,, Magellan's voyage to the, 16
 ,, ,, origin of the name, 16
Parhelia, or mock suns, 213
Parrot-fish, the, 347
Parry, Sir Edward, on arctic rigours, 22
Pearl Islands, the, 150
Pearls, Cingalese divers for, 147
 ,, fishing for, in China, 152
 ,, ,, in the Persian Gulf, 148
 ,, Oriental, 151
 ,, origin of, 151
 ,, preparation of, 151
Pearly nautilus, the, 197
Peculiarities of the hermit crab, 297
 ,, ,, pelican, 357
Perch family, the, 342
 ,, sea, 343
Perils of the coral reefs, 138
 ,, ,, whale fishery, 79
Perilous escape from water-spouts, 220
Peterhead a whaling station, 71
Periwinkle, the, 300
Petrels, 369
 ,, stormy, 243, 370
Phaeton, tropical sea-birds, 386
Phantom ship, the, 236
Pharos, the, 391
Phenomena of the ocean, 208
 ,, ,, tides, 9
Phoca vitulina, or sea-calf, 49
Phipps, William, 383
Physalis, its stinging properties, 319
Picnic on an iceberg, 37
Pilchards, curing of, 289
 ,, mode of taking, 287
Pilot-fish, the, 103
Pipe-mouthed fishes, 348
Pirate of the ocean, the, 89
Plectropoma, the beautiful, 344
Plesiosaurus described, 249
Poetry of the sea, 2
Polar bear, the, 107
 ,, ,, battle between the walrus and the, 110
 ,, ,, a, in a boat, 116

Polar bear in the Tower, 118
 ,, ,, Nelson's encounter with a, 117
Polyps, coral, 135
Polytechnic Institution, diving-bell at the, 358
Porpoise, the, formerly a royal dish, 277
 ,, ,, mistaken for the sea-serpent, 258
 ,, ,, white, fishing for the, 278
Portuguese man-of-war, the, 199
Prawns, 299
Preference of sharks for human food, 91
Preparations for seal-hunting, 46
 ,, whale fishing, 70
Proboscis, the, or elephant-seal, 54
Prodigies, marine, 253
Profusion of life in the ocean, 120
Provision of Nature regarding icebergs, 38
Power of sea-anemones to reproduce organs, 188
Punishing a shark, 93
Puffin, the, 374
Pugnacity of the squas, 369

R.

Rabbit-fish, the, 349
Rapacity of gulls, 366
Rats leaving ships, 242
Red mullet, the, 342
Remora, the, 321
Riband-fishes, 258
Risks attending cutting up whales, 88
Rock-builders of the ocean, 132
 ,, ,, instinct of the, 143
Rock-fish, the, 348
Rondelet's wonderful fishes, 254
"Royal George," wreck of the, 356
Rudyard's lighthouse on the Eddystone Rock, 397
Ruminating fishes, 348

S.

Saltness of the ocean, 4
Sand-eel fishing, 282
Sardine ,, 290
Sargassum or Gulf-weed, 156
Saw and sword-fishes, 67, 334
Scabbard-fishes, 246
Scallops, 304
Scaly-finned fishes, 345
Scoresby, anecdotes of, 81, 87
Scriptural allusion to the ocean, 2
Seals, 44
 ,, bear, 56
 ,, bearded, 50
 ,, blubber of, how prepared, 46
 ,, elephant, 54
 ,, Esquimaux hunting of, 47
 ,, food of, 52
 ,, formerly considered luxuries, 47
 ,, fur, 50
 ,, harp, 50
 ,, leopard, 55
 ,, lion, 56
 ,, marbled, 53

# INDEX. 419

Seals, monk, 55
" of the Southern seas, 54
" otaries, 55
" preparation for hunting, 46
" skins of, 46
" sometimes dangerous, 48
" taken on the ice, 48
" tame, 53
" various species of, 49
Sea-weeds, beautiful colours of, 158
" bladder, 159, 199
" dulse, 161
" fan, 159
" fern-leaf, 159
" inhabitants of, 123
" kelp, 162
" laver, 161
" net, 159
" peacock's tail, 159
" sea-silk, 159
" thongs, 159
" tangle, 161
" tree, 159
" uses of, 160
" value of, 157
" variety of, 160
" water-flannel, 159
" whip-lash, 159
Sentinels of the seas, the, 388
Sharks, angel, 101
" attack on boats, 98
" baiting, 94
" blue, 101
" charmers of, 148
" dog, 101
" fossil teeth of, 89
" Greenland, 102
" hammer-headed, 102
" hooks for, 97
" horrible death of seamen from, 99
" indiscriminate appetite of, 90
" preference for human food of, 91
" punishing, 93
" scavengers of the ocean, 104
" smooth, 101
" spinous, 101
" teeth of, 95
" vulnerable parts of, 92
" worship of, 96
Shells, beautiful colours of, 171
" clam, 173
" cockle, 178
" composition of, 173
" cowry, 178
" ear, 179
" floating wing, 203
" fountain, 175
" harp, 199
" helix, 173
" mother-of-pearl, 175
" murex or purple, 173
" pheasant, 180
" poached eggs, 179
" porcelain, 178
" razor, 180
" scallop, 177
" spindle, 179

Shells, strombus, 174
" structure of, 170
" top, 180
" trough, 180
" trumpet, 176
" use of, 174
" volute, 173
" weaver's shuttle, 179
" wentletrap, 180
Ships, fearful loss of whale-, 71
Shipwreck on a coral reef, 138
Shrimp, the trigger, 300
Shrimps, mode of taking, 299
Signals in lighthouses, 402
Skate, a monstrous, 332
Skimmers, the, 371
Snail-slime fishes, 198
Solan goose, the, 378
Soles, immense consumption of, 295
South Sea islanders, expert fishermen, 270
Sponges, 164
" description of, 167
" experiments of Ellis and Grant, 163
" mode of fishing for, 166
" where obtained, 166
Sprats, how caught, 290
Squas, the, 368
" pugnacity of, 367
Stellerus, the, 265
Stephenson's, Robert, lighthouse on the Bell-Rock, 399
" Allan, lighthouse on the Skerryvore, 401
Sticklebacks, marine, 324
Stinging-fish, 318
" powers of the physalis, 319
Stories about cuttle-fishes, 205
Sturgeon, the, a "royal" fish, 280
" fishery, 279
Sublimity of icebergs, 35
Submarine cable, Atlantic, 12
" Company, American, 361
" gardens, 188
" scenery, 181
" " brilliant colours of, 182
" " in the Red Sea, 191
" " of the tropics, 187
Sucking-fishes, 320
Suns, mock, 213
Superstitions connected with the ocean, 231
" apparitions, 241
" bells, 242
" birds and marine animals, 243
" blessing the waters, 248
" child's caul, a, 242
" connected with coral, 145
" days of the week, 241
" dead bodies at sea, 246
" "good luck," 246
" lightning at sea, 236
" of the Sardinian fishermen, 233
" phantom-ship, 236
" raising tempests, 238
" rats leaving ships, 242
" St. Elmo's lights, 237
" water-spouts, 236
Swan, the wild, 381

27—2

## T.

Tame seals, 53
Tangle sea-weeds, 161
Teleosaurus described, 251
Tempests, raising, 238
Tern, the, a good omen, 243
Terns, or sea-swallows, 369
Thor fishing for the sea-serpent, 259
Tides, origin of, 8
  ,, phenomena of the, 9
  ,, rip, 215
Tongues of whales, 60
Tornadoes, 222
Torpedo, 316
Tower, a Polar bear in the, 118
Trade-winds, the, 222
Traditions of floating islands, 255
"Trafalgar," escape of the whale-ship, 85
Treasures recovered from the ocean, 351
  ,, "Almirante," 360
  ,, "Lutine," 360
  ,, by William Phipps, 353
  ,, from the "Royal George," 356
Tree sea-weed, the, 159
Tremendous power of waves, 10
Tricks played upon gulls, 367
Trinity Board, the, 395
Tropic sea-birds, 386
Tunny fishery, the, 278
Turbot, the, 294
Turtle, how captured, 295

## U.

Unicorn, the sea, 111
Uses of the blubber of whales, 60
  ,, nets in early times, 268
  ,, sea-weeds, 160
  ,, shells, 174

## V.

Value of sea-weeds, 157
Variety and form of sea-weeds, 160
Varieties of coelacia, 58
Various colours of the ocean, 11

Vegetation of the ocean, 155
Vessels destroyed by icebergs, 35
  ,, mooring to ,, 36
Volcanic islands in the sea, 227
Voyages, early, in the Pacific, 17
  ,, of Captain Cook, 17
Vulnerable part of sharks, 92

## W.

Walrus, the, or sea-horse, 107
  ,, adventures with, 108
  ,, affection to the young, 108, 109
  ,, battles between the Polar bear and, 109, 110
  ,, domestication of, 111
Water, animalculæ in a drop of, 122
  ,, animal life in the deep, 129
  ,, composition of, 4
  ,, spouts, 219.
Waves, highest known, 9
  ,, tremendous force of, 10
Weever, the great, 319
Whirlpools, cause of, 7
Whitebait, 290
Whitstable diver, the, 361
Wind-waves, 9
Wing-shells, floating, 213
Winstanley's lighthouse on Eddystone Rock, 398
  ,, mechanical ability of, 395
Wonders of the coral builders, 136
Worms, sea, 125
  ,, wonderful beauty of, 126
Worship of sharks in Polynesia, 96
Wrasse, the, 347

## Y.

Yarmouth, herring fishery at, 285
  ,, mackerel ,, 285

## Z.

Zealand, New, gurnard, 232
Zealanders, New, dexterity in fishing, 78

www.ingramcontent.com/pod-product-compliance
Lightning Source LLC
Chambersburg PA
CBHW022135300426
44115CB00006B/189